Blue Morning
Volume 7
SuBLime Manga Edition

Story and Art by **Shoko Hidaka**

Translation—**Jocelyne Allen**
Touch-Up Art and Lettering—**Bianca Pistillo**
Cover and Graphic Design—**Shawn Carrico**
Editor—**Jennifer LeBlanc**

YUU–UTSU NA ASA
© SHOKO HIDAKA 2016
All rights reserved.
Original Japanese edition published by TOKUMA SHOTEN
PUBLISHING CO., LTD., Tokyo.
English version published WORLDWIDE by VIZ Media, LLC under
the license granted by TOKUMA SHOTEN PUBLISHING CO.,LTD.

COMICS

Printed in the U.S.A.

Published by SuBLime Manga
P.O. Box 77010
San Francisco, CA 94107

10 9 8 7 6 5 4 3 2 1
First printing, March 2018

www.SuBLimeManga.com

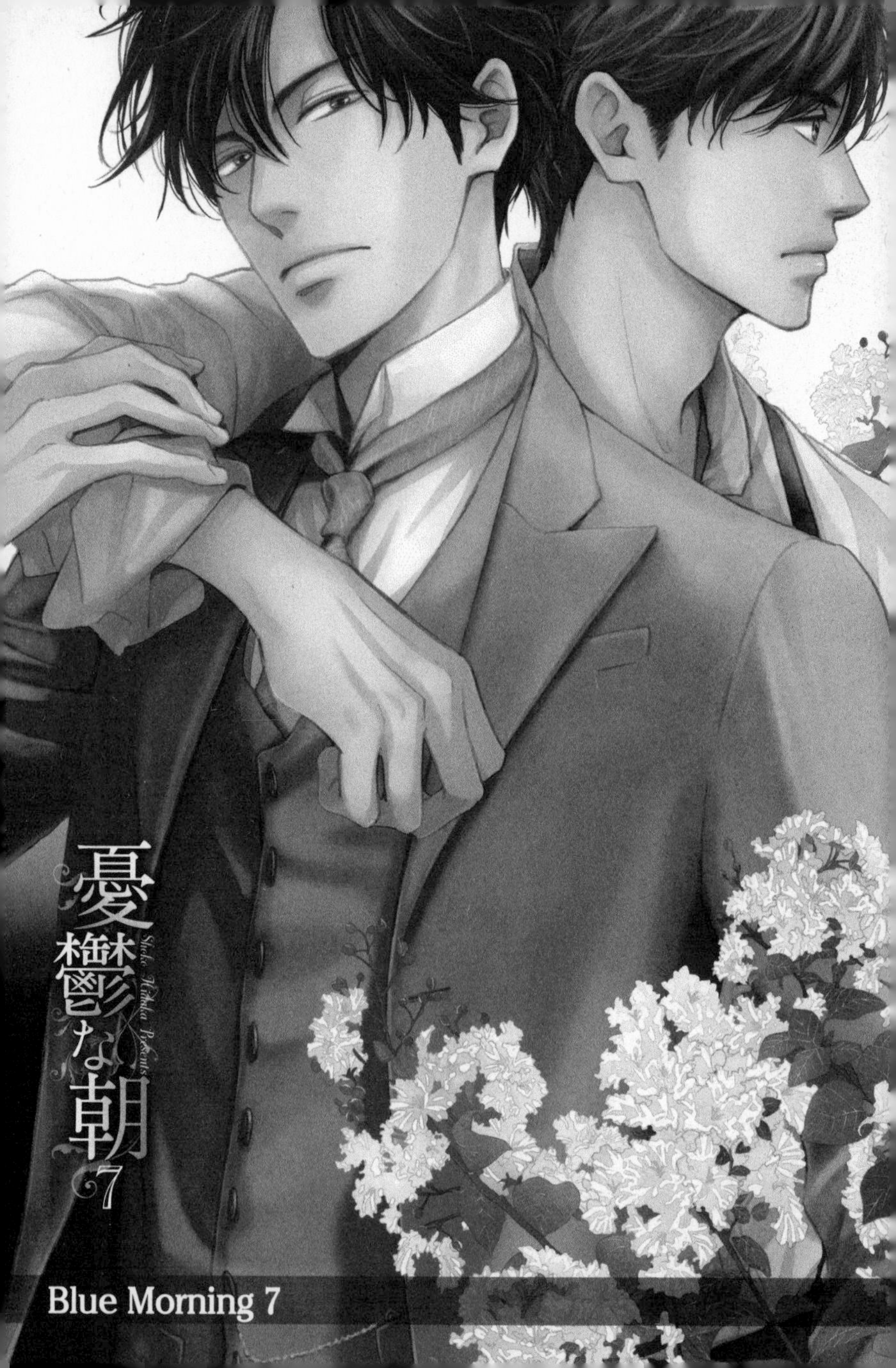
憂鬱な朝
Shoko Hidaka Presents
7
Blue Morning 7

Characters

Tomoyuki Katsuragi

This cool, capable butler uses even Akihito's feelings of love as long as it's for the sake of the Kuze house. He initially despised Akihito, but is now drawn to the younger man and the way he so firmly stands by his convictions. He left the Kuze house and is head clerk for the Ishizakis.

Akihito Kuze

The young head of the family, having succeeded the viscountcy at the tender age of ten. Straightforward and earnest but also very determined, he has adored his butler/tutor Katsuragi since childhood until they finally became lovers...

Takayuki Katsuragi

Tomoyuki Katsuragi's older brother, he's a banker and the head of the Katsuragi family. He despises Tomoyuki, but he acknowledges Akihito as the head of the family.

Soemon Ishizaki

Soichiro's father, he's a wealthy merchant who built a fortune in a generation. He truly understands Akihito's disinterest in status and class. Recognizing Katsuragi's talent, he selected him as head clerk.

Soichiro Ishizaki

Akihito's close friend, he has a big heart and appreciates that Akihito is not your typical noble. His relationship with Katsuragi is a negative one, but his guarded attitude softens once the older man becomes his tutor and he gets to know him.

Hiroyuki Katsuragi

The second son of the Katsuragi house, he's a talented advisor and offers support to his older brother Takayuki. A kind man, he also treats his younger brother Tomoyuki fairly.

Akinao Kuze

The former head of the Kuze family and Akihito's deceased father, he took in Katsuragi, who was not his legitimate child, to inherit his title and gave him a special education. A very proud man, he focused mainly on family status.

Rinzaburo Amamiya

The former Kuze houseboy, he is the current butler. He adores Katsuragi and was initially skeptical about Akihito, but he became Akihito's reliable right hand once he saw his young master's true nature.

Story

At ten years of age, Akihito becomes the young head of a viscountcy, and his butler and tutor, Katsuragi, takes over raising him and in a rather severe manner. Akihito's adoration of Katsuragi eventually changes to love, and he resolves to abandon his title for Katsuragi's sake. Learning of this decision, Katsuragi finally confesses his love for Akihito.

At Marquise Moriyama's evening party, Akihito comes face-to-face with the man Katsuragi had intended to make the next head of the family, his uncle Naotsugu—a meeting that makes him realize once more that he can't simply hand over the Kuze title. Katsuragi is furious at Akihito for moving ahead on his own on the matters of succession and his studying abroad, which Katsuragi only hears about secondhand. But Akihito embraces him fiercely, insisting that he will never let him go again!

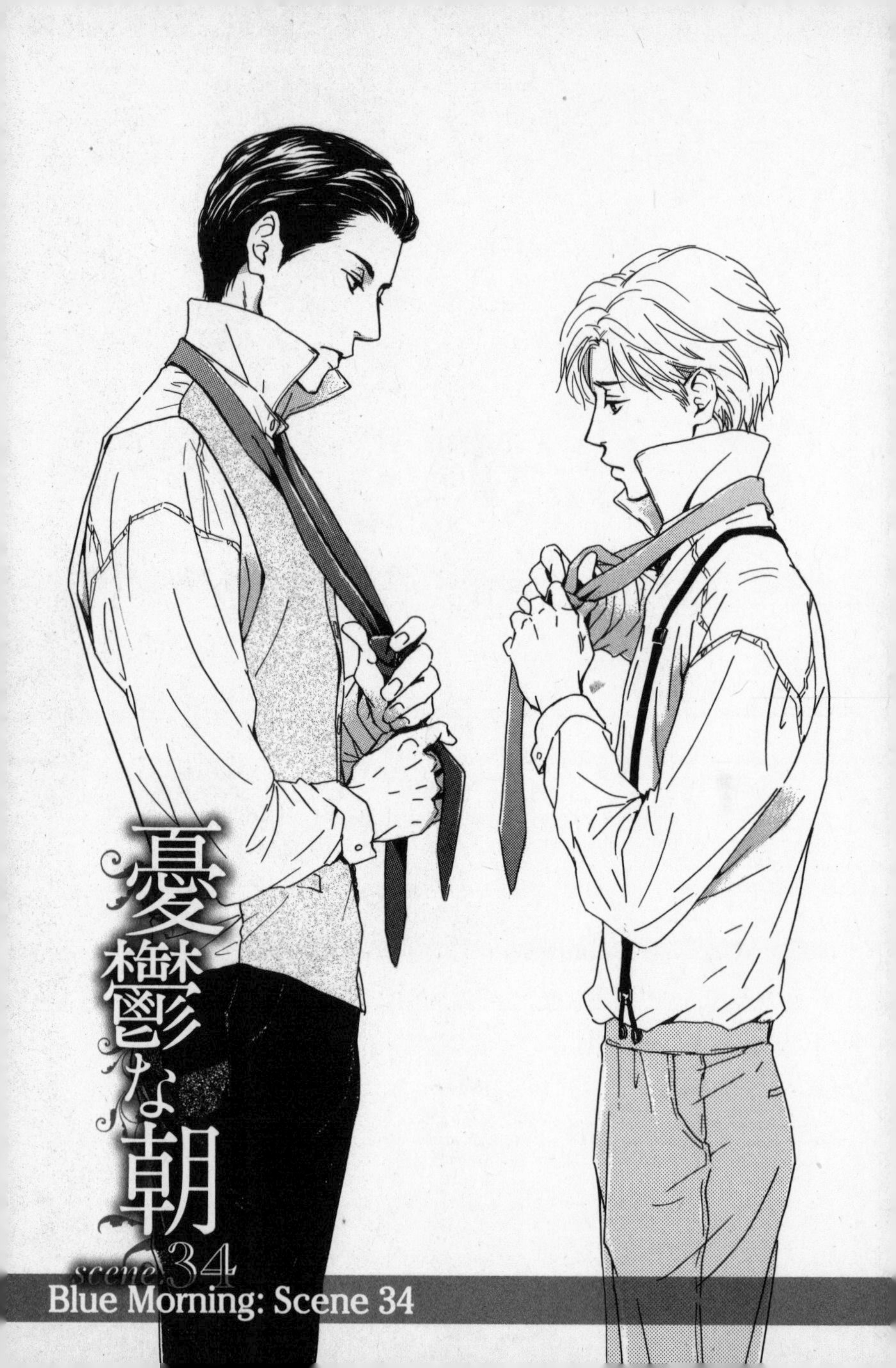

憂鬱な朝
scene.34
Blue Morning: Scene 34

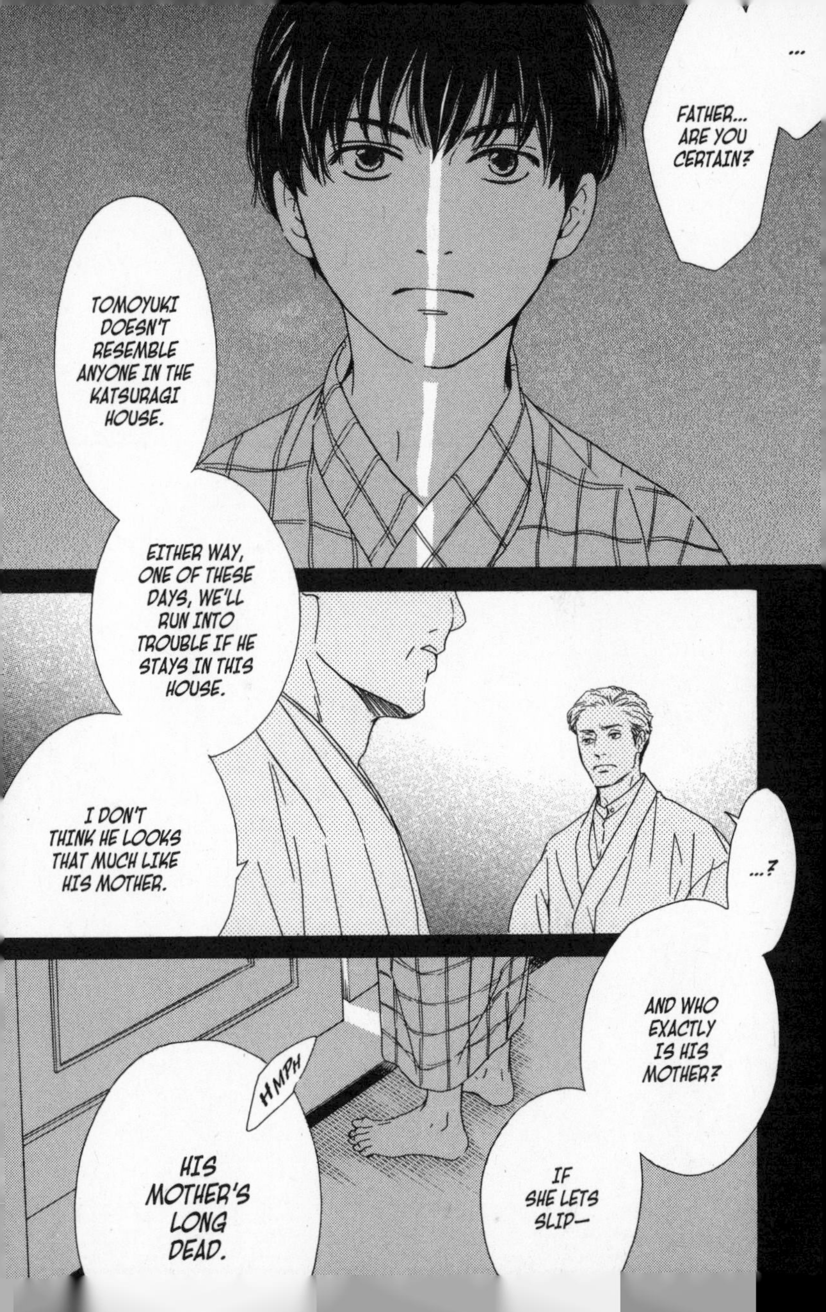
...
FATHER... ARE YOU CERTAIN?
TOMOYUKI DOESN'T RESEMBLE ANYONE IN THE KATSURAGI HOUSE.
EITHER WAY, ONE OF THESE DAYS, WE'LL RUN INTO TROUBLE IF HE STAYS IN THIS HOUSE.
...?
I DON'T THINK HE LOOKS THAT MUCH LIKE HIS MOTHER.
AND WHO EXACTLY IS HIS MOTHER?
IF SHE LETS SLIP—
HMPH
HIS MOTHER'S LONG DEAD.

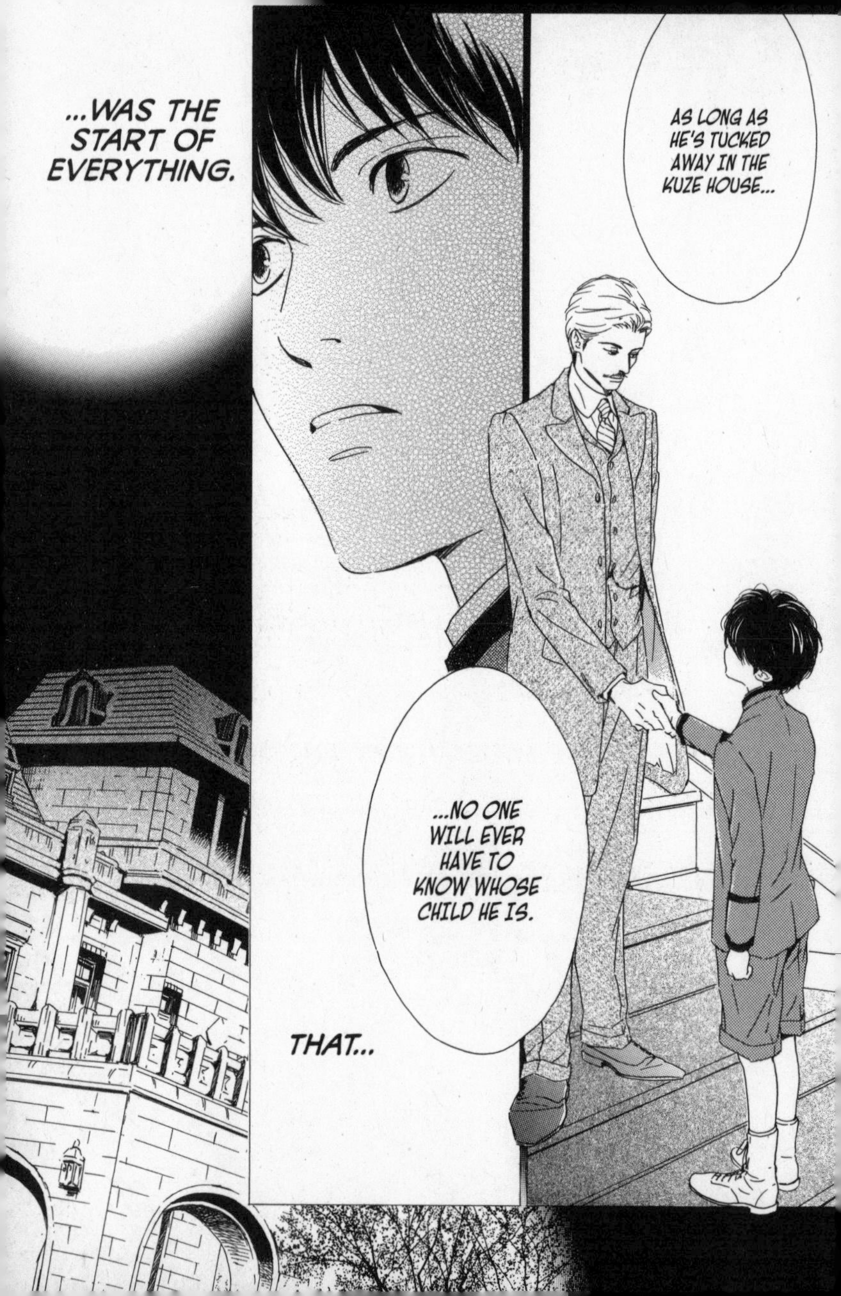
AS LONG AS HE'S TUCKED AWAY IN THE KUZE HOUSE...
...NO ONE WILL EVER HAVE TO KNOW WHOSE CHILD HE IS.
THAT...
...WAS THE START OF EVERYTHING.

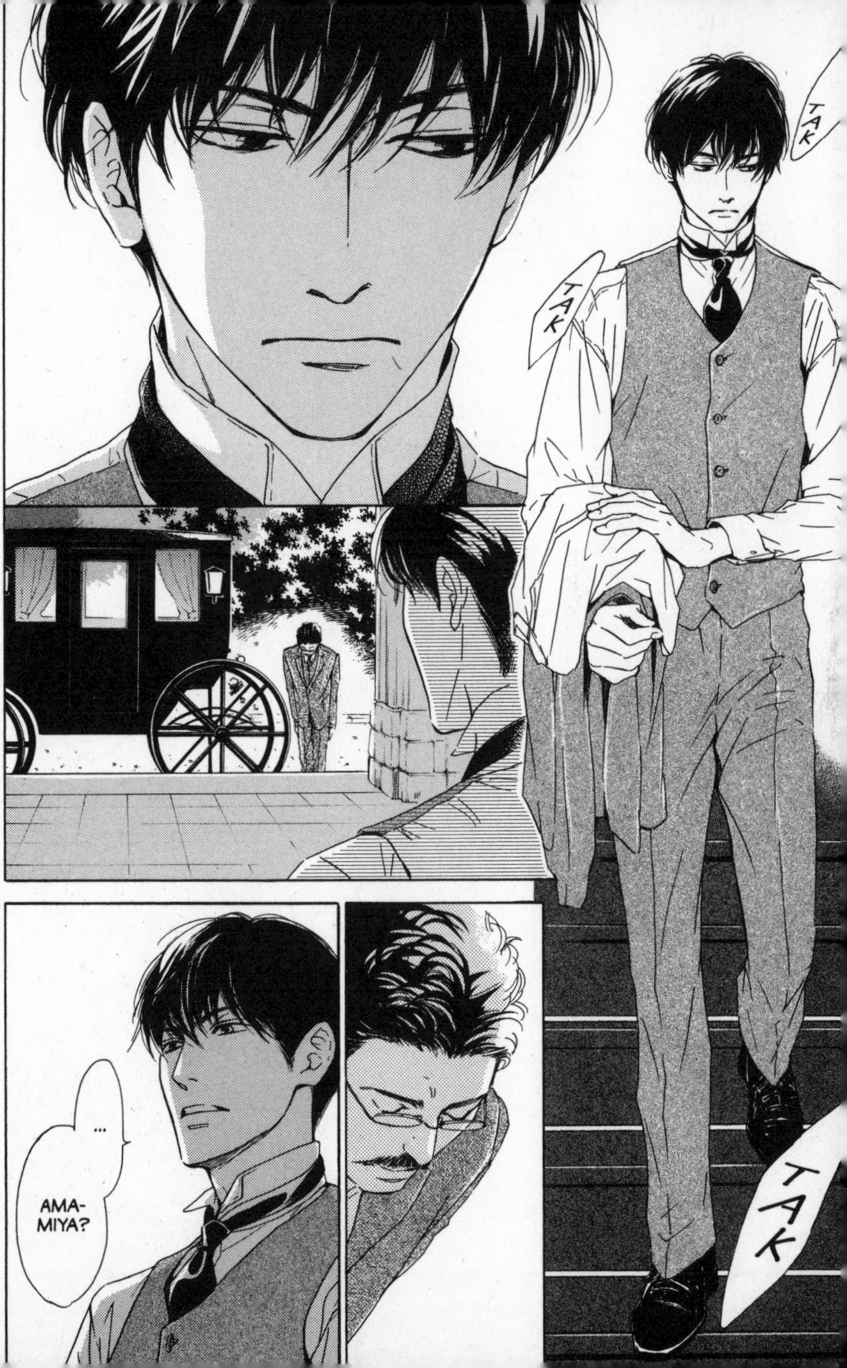
TAK
TAK
TAK
...
AMA-MIYA?

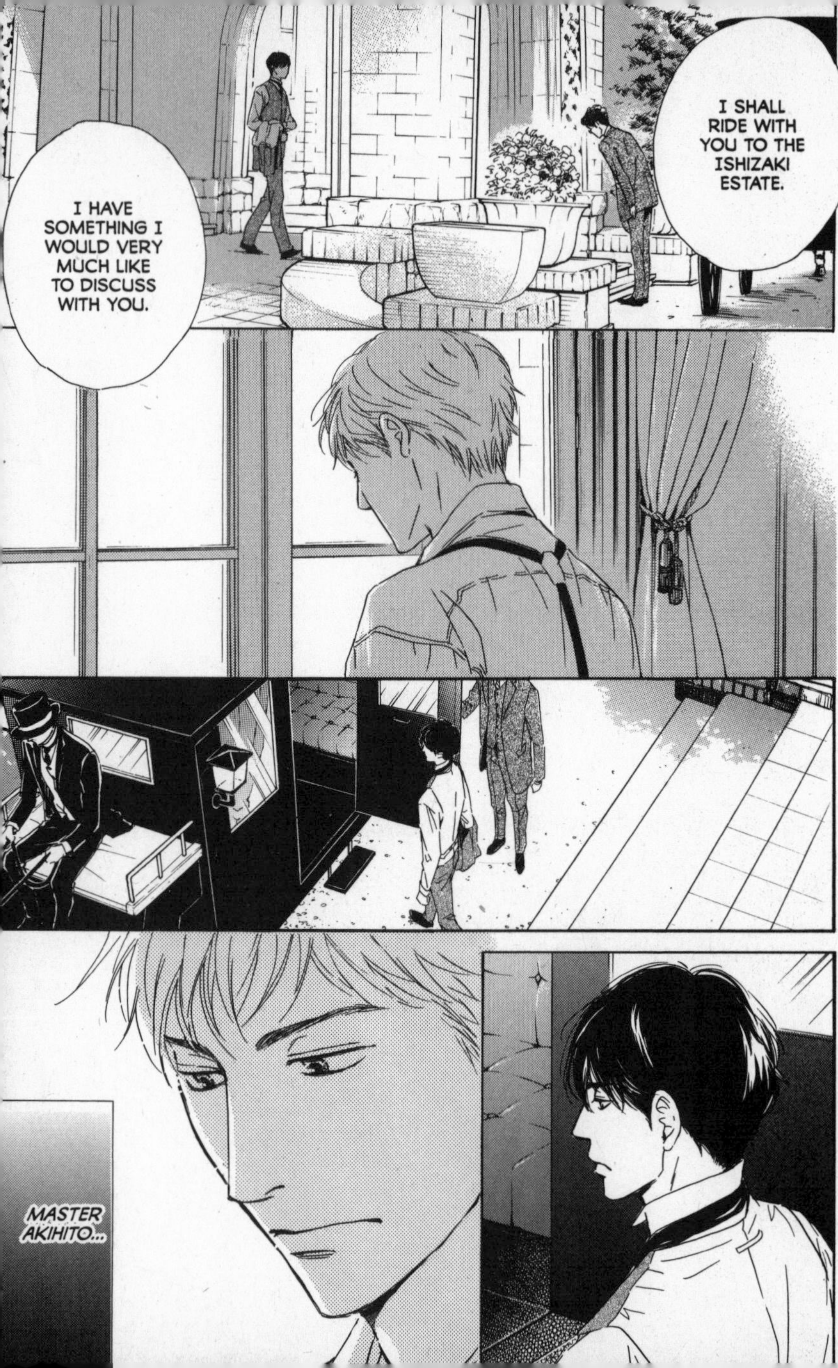
I SHALL RIDE WITH YOU TO THE ISHIZAKI ESTATE.
I HAVE SOMETHING I WOULD VERY MUCH LIKE TO DISCUSS WITH YOU.
MASTER AKIHITO...

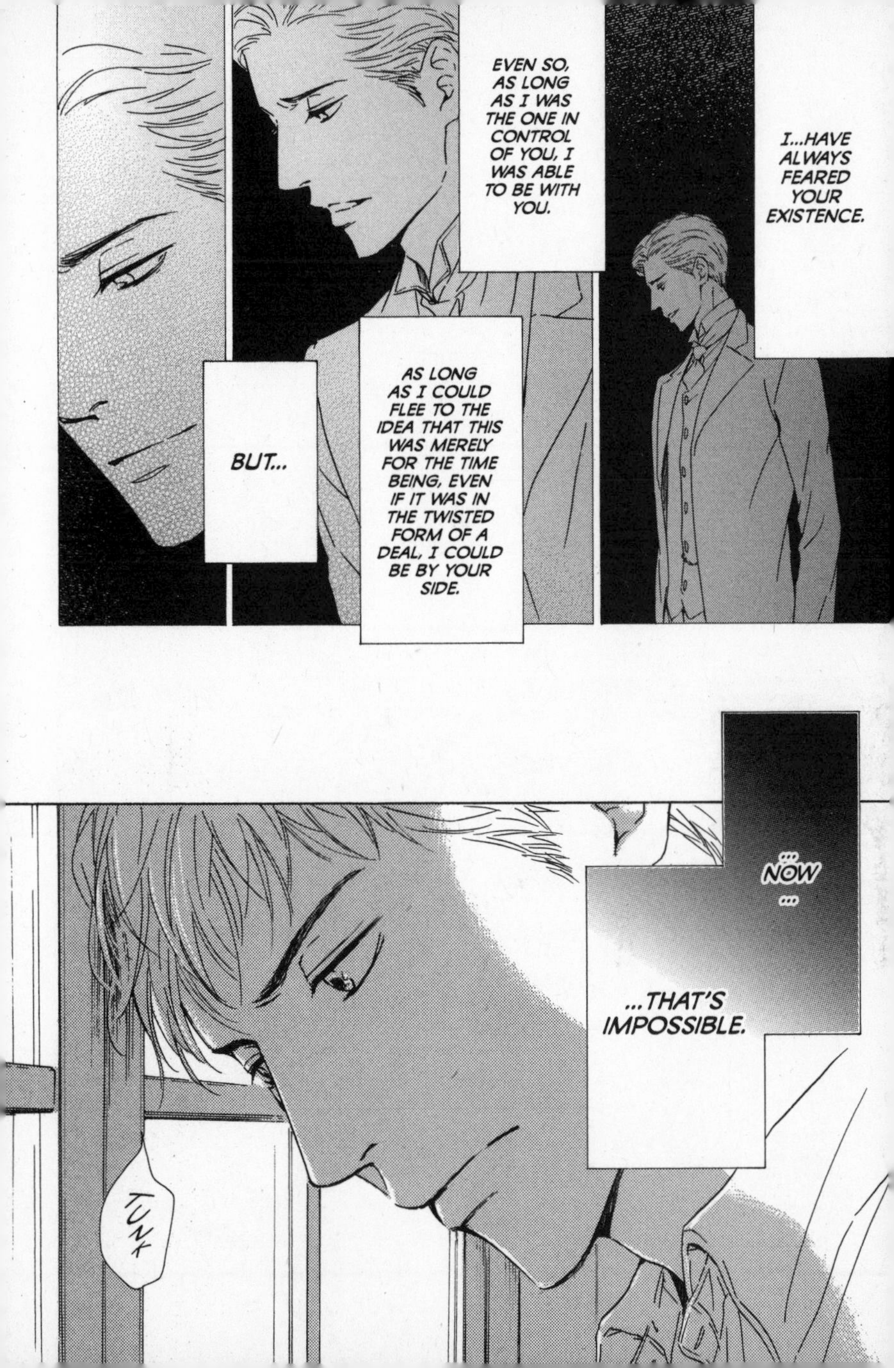
I...HAVE ALWAYS FEARED YOUR EXISTENCE.
EVEN SO, AS LONG AS I WAS THE ONE IN CONTROL OF YOU, I WAS ABLE TO BE WITH YOU.
AS LONG AS I COULD FLEE TO THE IDEA THAT THIS WAS MERELY FOR THE TIME BEING, EVEN IF IT WAS IN THE TWISTED FORM OF A DEAL, I COULD BE BY YOUR SIDE.
BUT...
...NOW...
...THAT'S IMPOSSIBLE.
TUNK

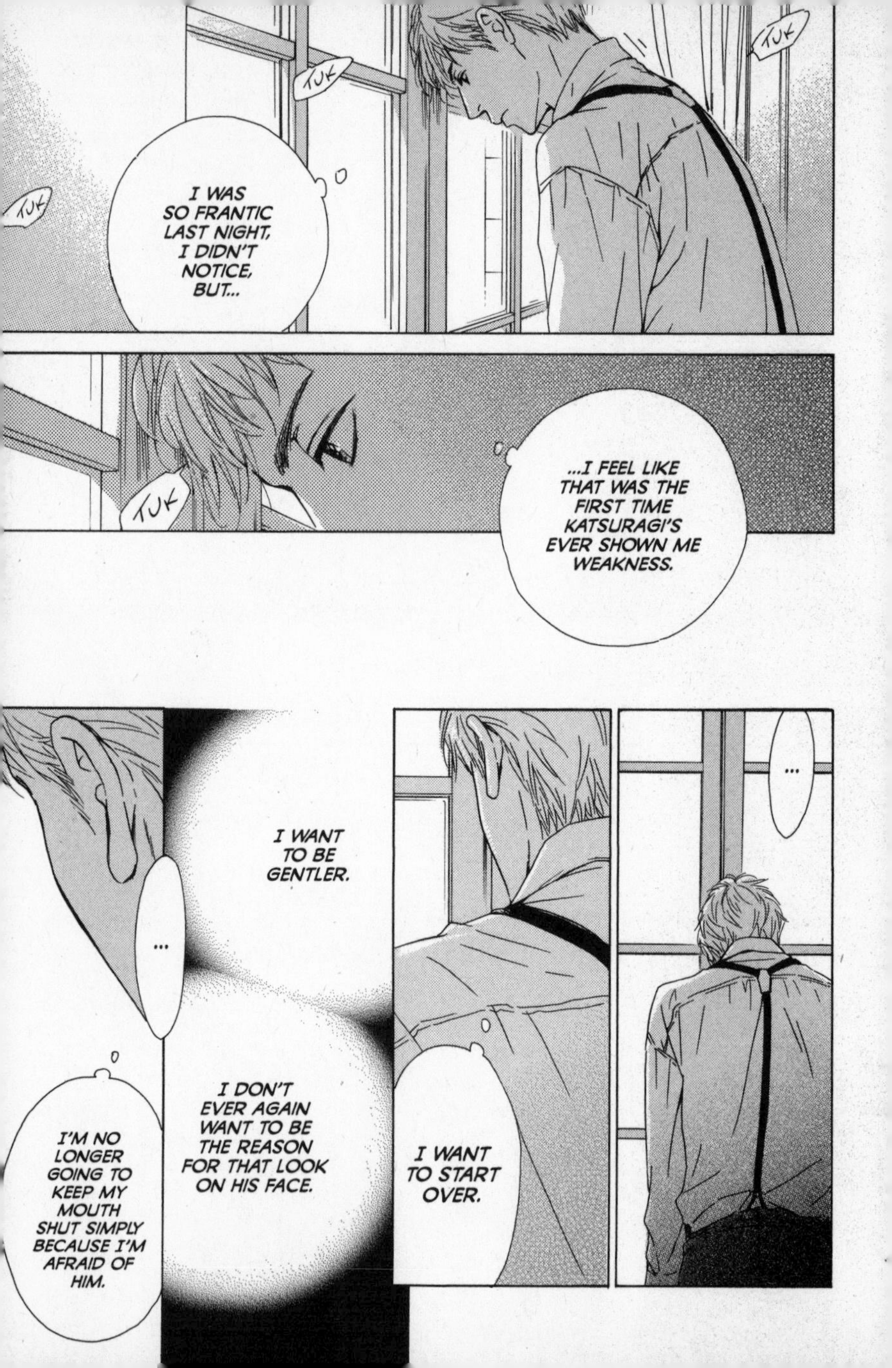
TUK
TUK
I WAS SO FRANTIC LAST NIGHT, I DIDN'T NOTICE, BUT...
TUK
...I FEEL LIKE THAT WAS THE FIRST TIME KATSURAGI'S EVER SHOWN ME WEAKNESS.
TUK
...
I WANT TO START OVER.
I WANT TO BE GENTLER.
...
I DON'T EVER AGAIN WANT TO BE THE REASON FOR THAT LOOK ON HIS FACE.
I'M NO LONGER GOING TO KEEP MY MOUTH SHUT SIMPLY BECAUSE I'M AFRAID OF HIM.

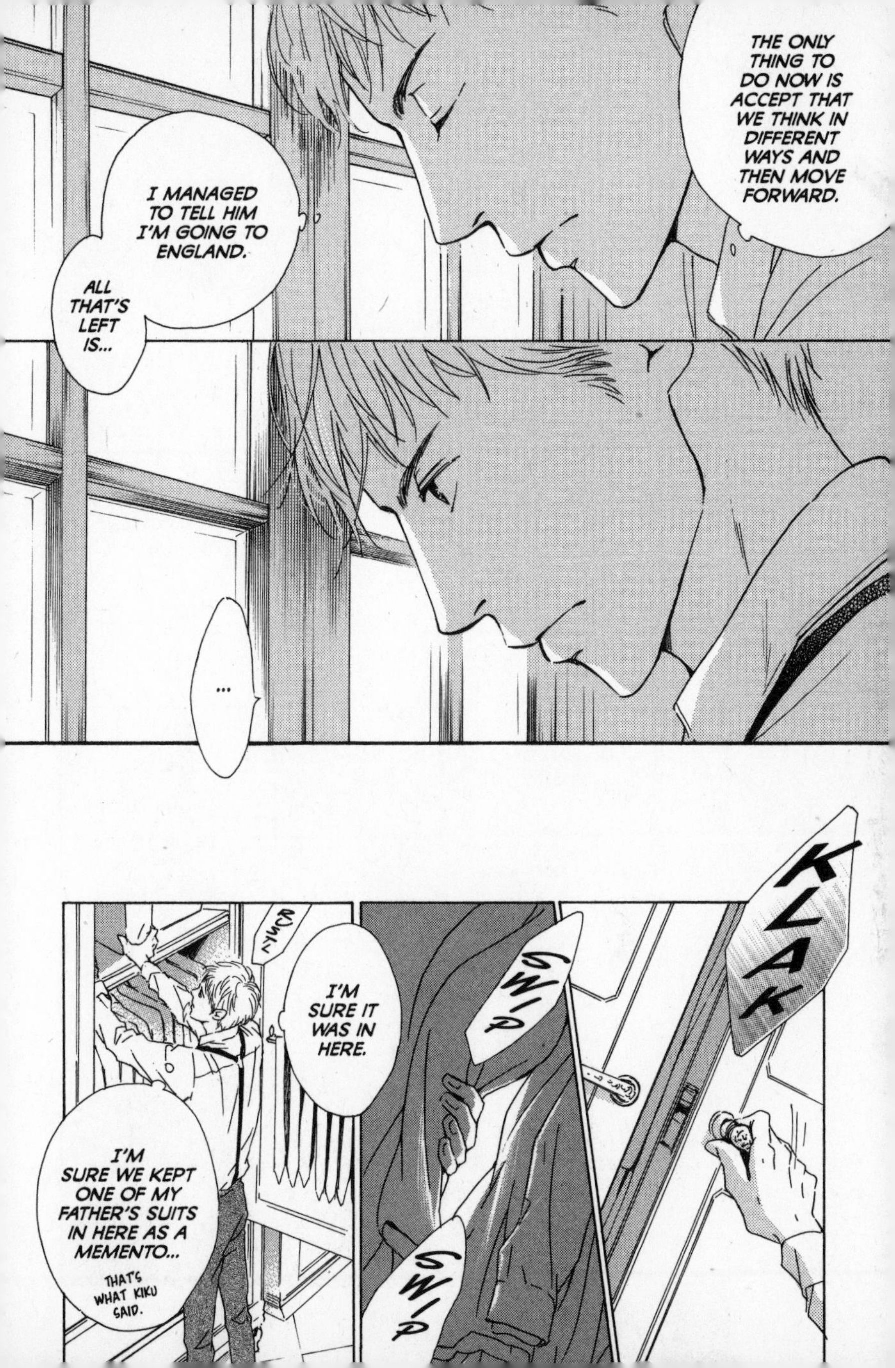
THE ONLY THING TO DO NOW IS ACCEPT THAT WE THINK IN DIFFERENT WAYS AND THEN MOVE FORWARD.
I MANAGED TO TELL HIM I'M GOING TO ENGLAND.
ALL THAT'S LEFT IS...
...
KLAK
SWIP
I'M SURE IT WAS IN HERE.
SWIP
I'M SURE WE KEPT ONE OF MY FATHER'S SUITS IN HERE AS A MEMENTO...
THAT'S WHAT KIKU SAID.

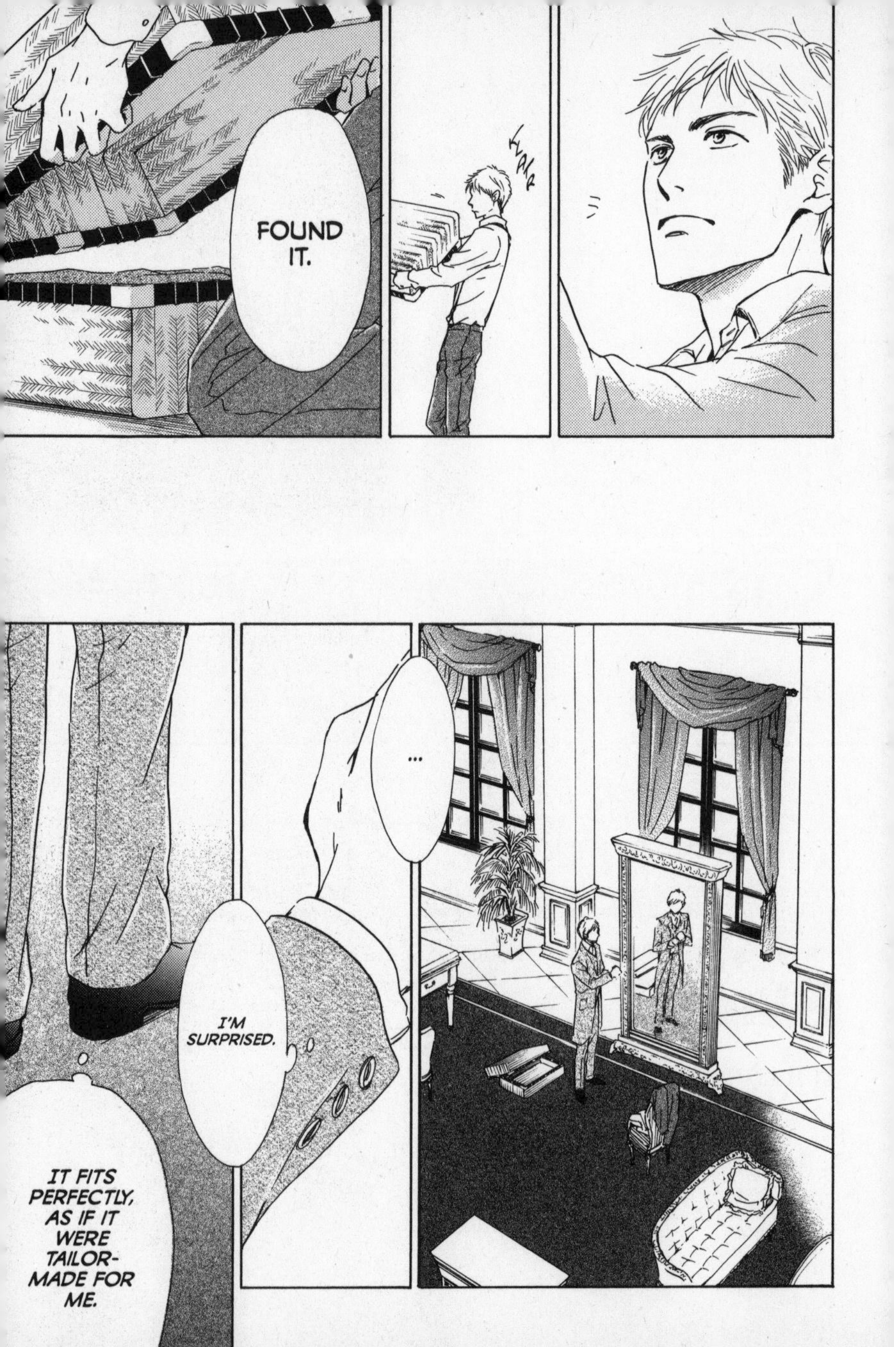
FOUND IT.
...
I'M SURPRISED.
IT FITS PERFECTLY, AS IF IT WERE TAILOR-MADE FOR ME.

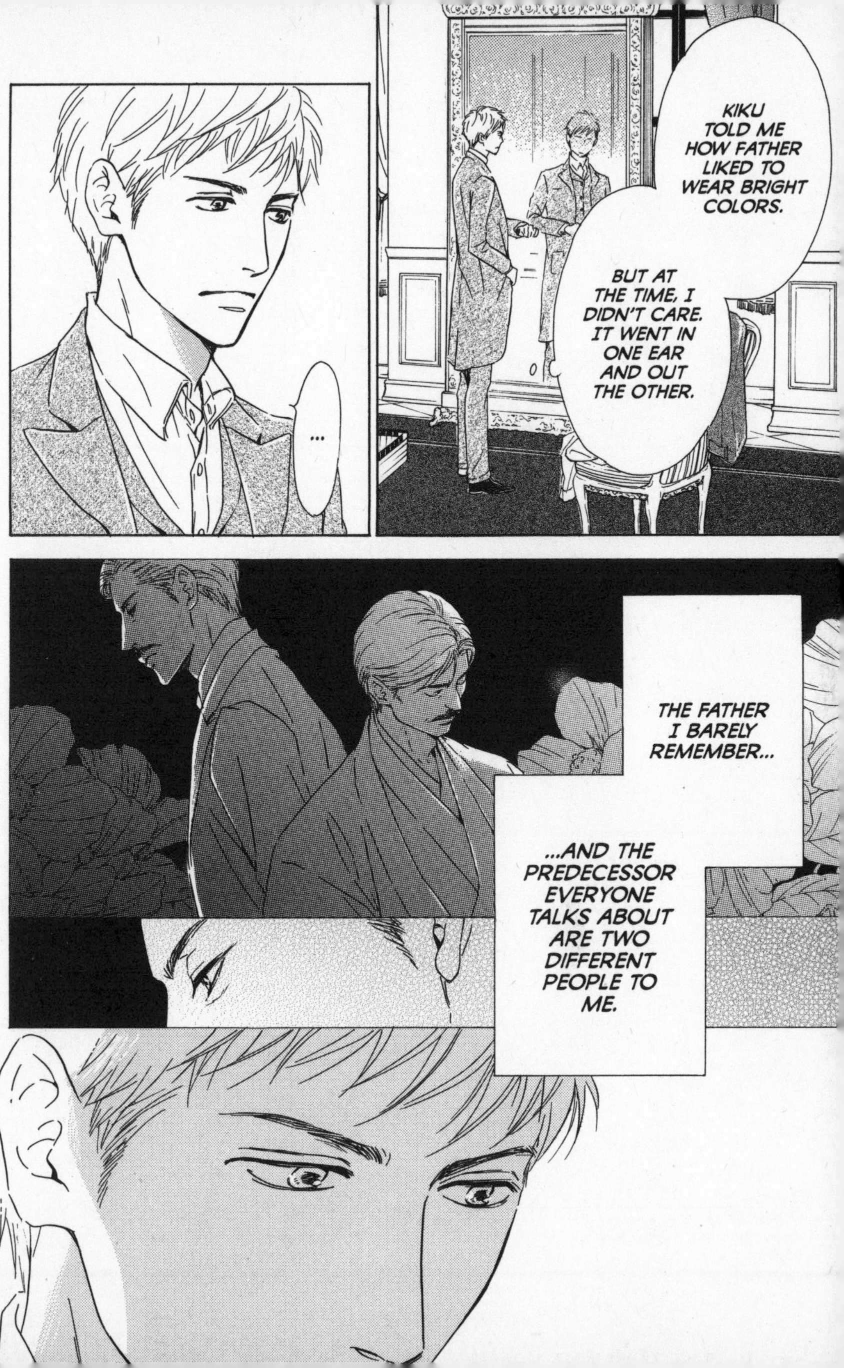
KIKU TOLD ME HOW FATHER LIKED TO WEAR BRIGHT COLORS.
BUT AT THE TIME, I DIDN'T CARE. IT WENT IN ONE EAR AND OUT THE OTHER.
...
THE FATHER I BARELY REMEMBER...
...AND THE PREDECESSOR EVERYONE TALKS ABOUT ARE TWO DIFFERENT PEOPLE TO ME.

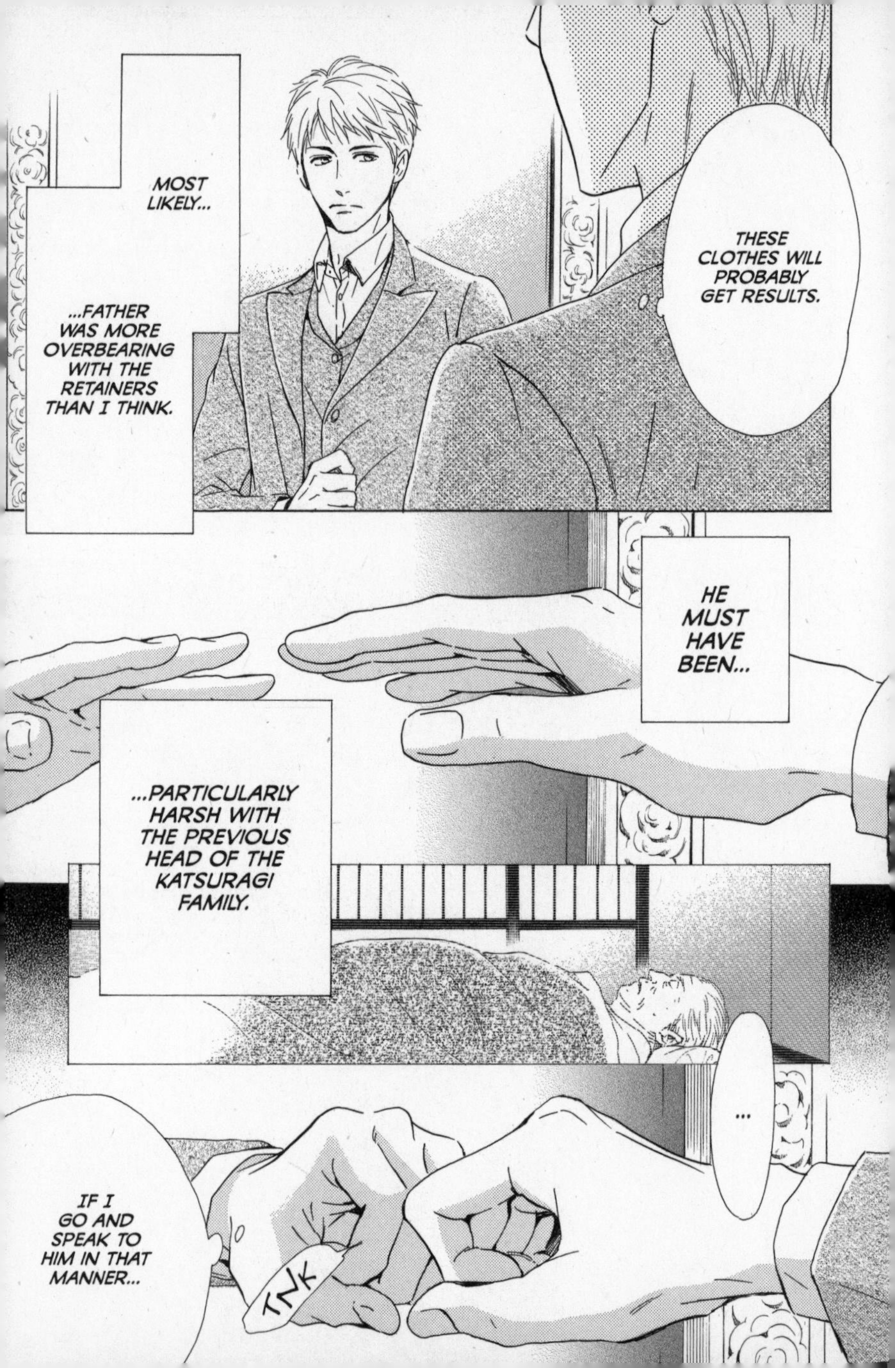
THESE CLOTHES WILL PROBABLY GET RESULTS.
MOST LIKELY...
...FATHER WAS MORE OVERBEARING WITH THE RETAINERS THAN I THINK.
HE MUST HAVE BEEN...
...PARTICULARLY HARSH WITH THE PREVIOUS HEAD OF THE KATSURAGI FAMILY.
...
IF I GO AND SPEAK TO HIM IN THAT MANNER...
TNK

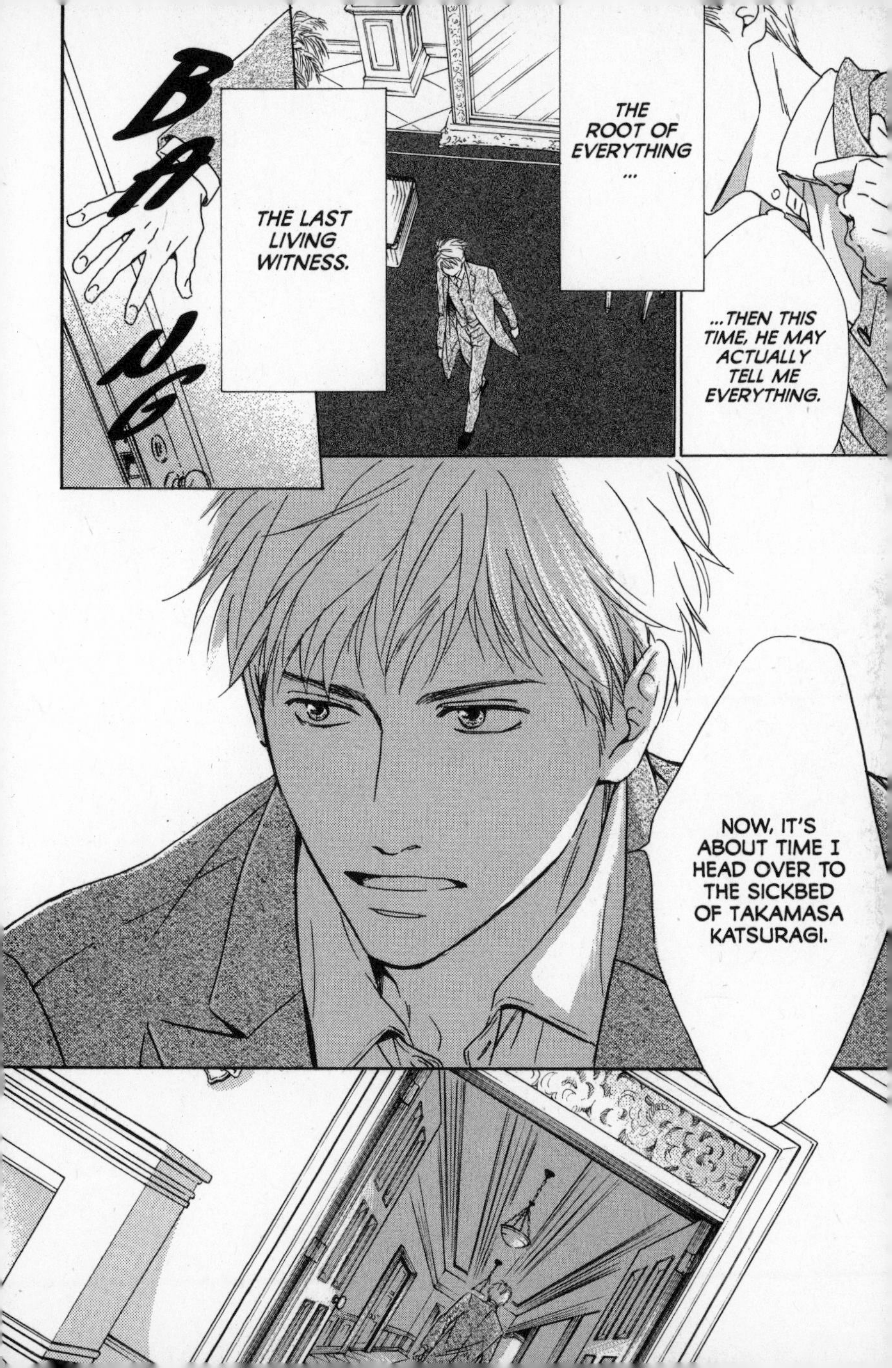
...THEN THIS TIME, HE MAY ACTUALLY TELL ME EVERYTHING.
THE ROOT OF EVERYTHING ...
THE LAST LIVING WITNESS.
BANG
NOW, IT'S ABOUT TIME I HEAD OVER TO THE SICKBED OF TAKAMASA KATSURAGI.

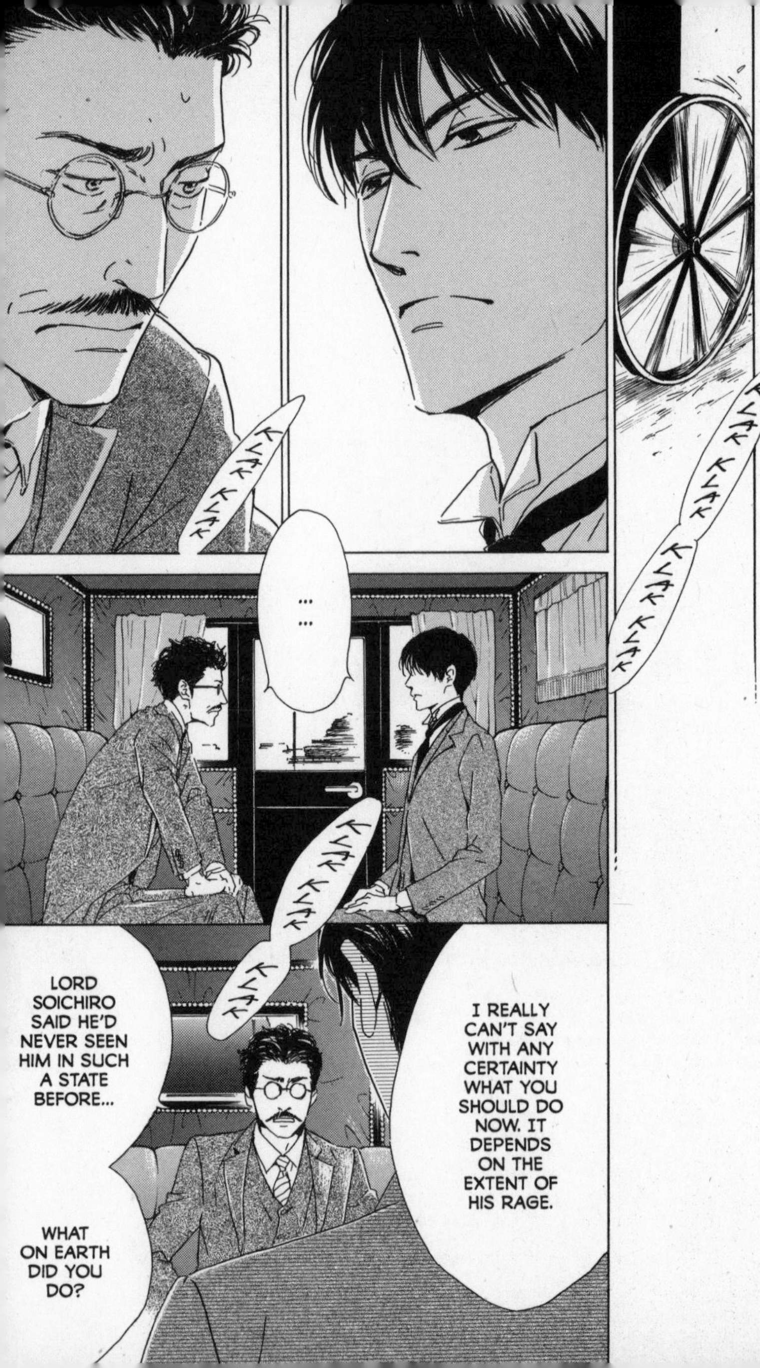
KLAK KLAK
KLAK KLAK KLAK
KLAK KLAK
...
...
KLAK KLAK KLAK
I REALLY CAN'T SAY WITH ANY CERTAINTY WHAT YOU SHOULD DO NOW. IT DEPENDS ON THE EXTENT OF HIS RAGE.
LORD SOICHIRO SAID HE'D NEVER SEEN HIM IN SUCH A STATE BEFORE...
WHAT ON EARTH DID YOU DO?

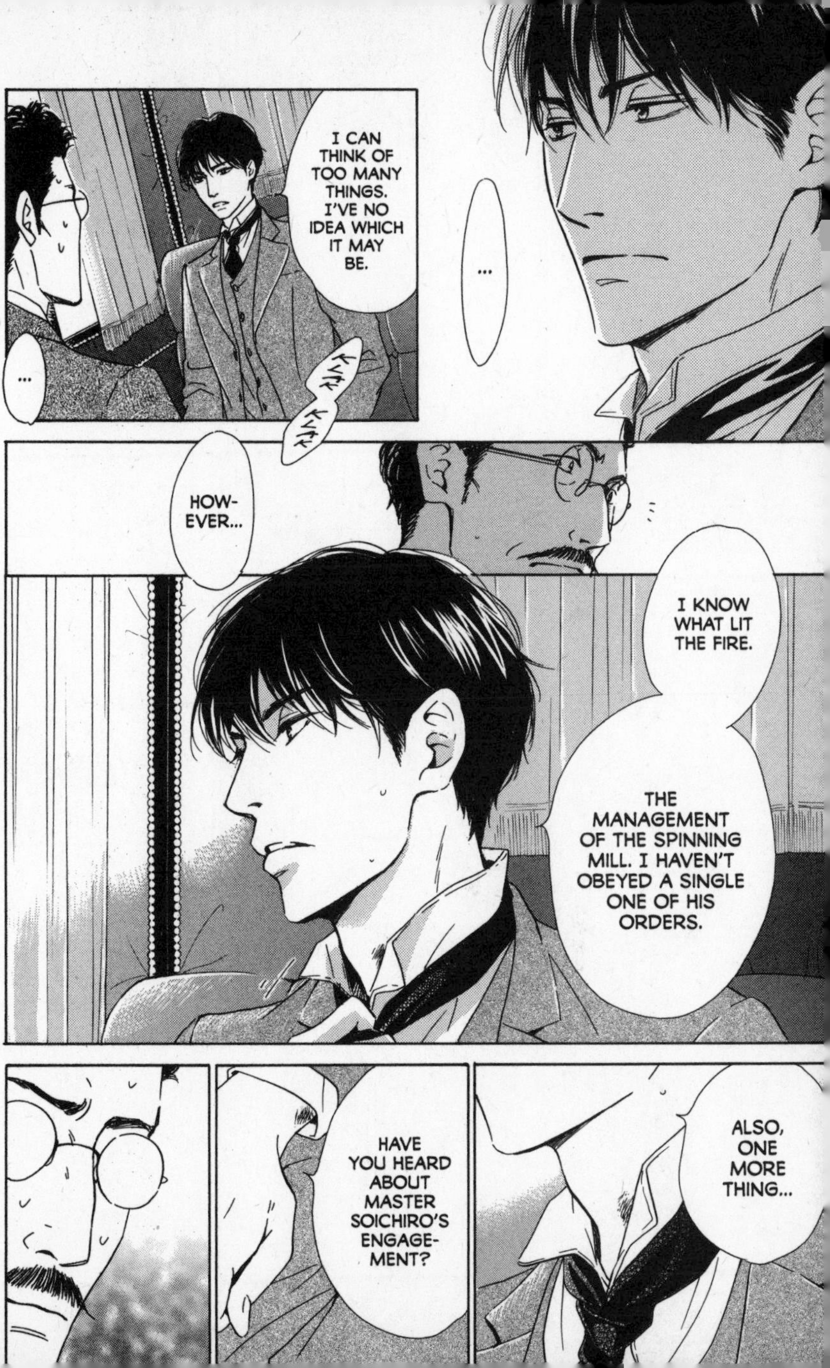
...
I CAN THINK OF TOO MANY THINGS. I'VE NO IDEA WHICH IT MAY BE.
...
HOW-EVER...
I KNOW WHAT LIT THE FIRE.
THE MANAGEMENT OF THE SPINNING MILL. I HAVEN'T OBEYED A SINGLE ONE OF HIS ORDERS.
ALSO, ONE MORE THING...
HAVE YOU HEARD ABOUT MASTER SOICHIRO'S ENGAGE-MENT?

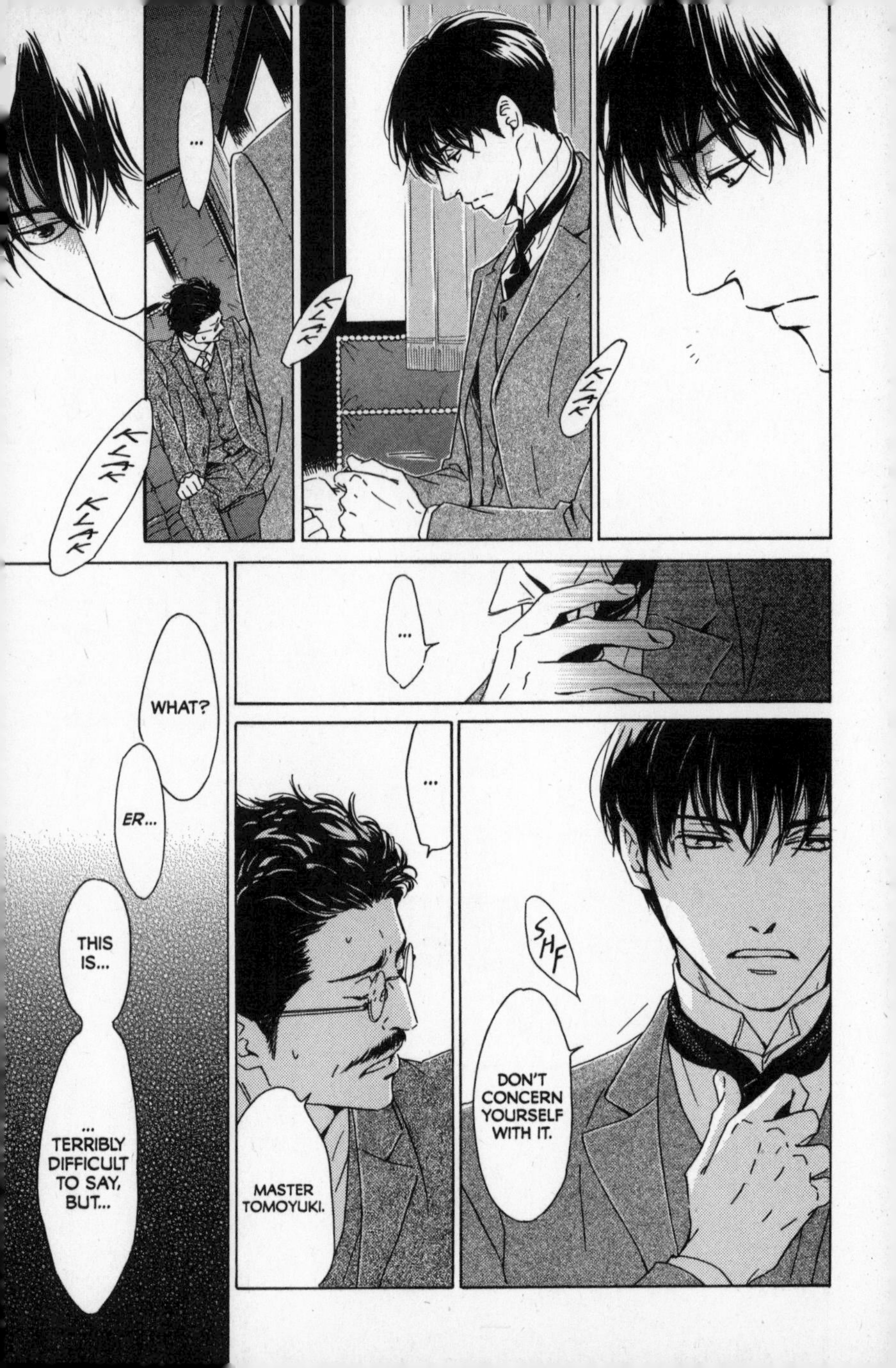
KLAK
KLAK
...
KLAK KLAK
...
SHF
DON'T CONCERN YOURSELF WITH IT.
...
MASTER TOMOYUKI.
WHAT?
ER...
THIS IS...
...TERRIBLY DIFFICULT TO SAY, BUT...

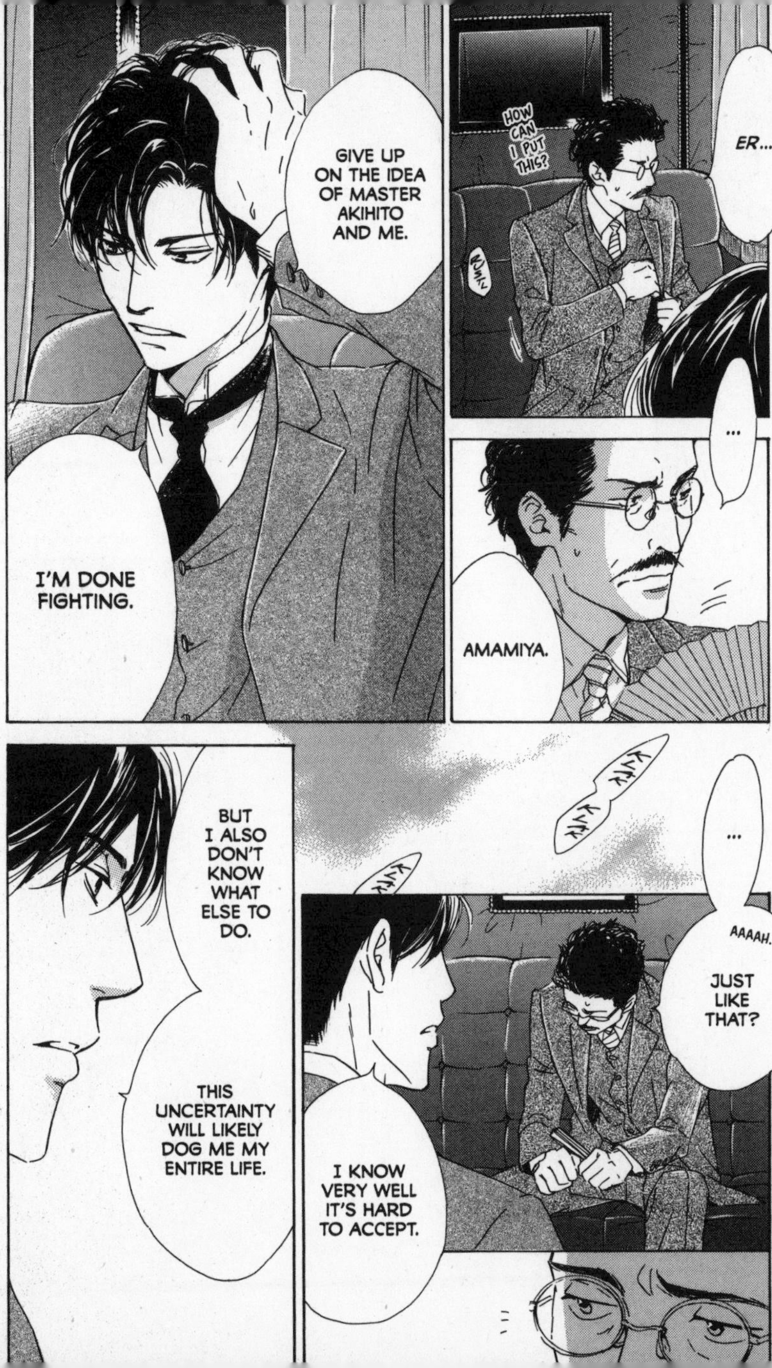
ER...
HOW CAN I PUT THIS?
...
AMAMIYA.
GIVE UP ON THE IDEA OF MASTER AKIHITO AND ME.
I'M DONE FIGHTING.
...
AAAAH.
JUST LIKE THAT?
I KNOW VERY WELL IT'S HARD TO ACCEPT.
BUT I ALSO DON'T KNOW WHAT ELSE TO DO.
THIS UNCERTAINTY WILL LIKELY DOG ME MY ENTIRE LIFE.

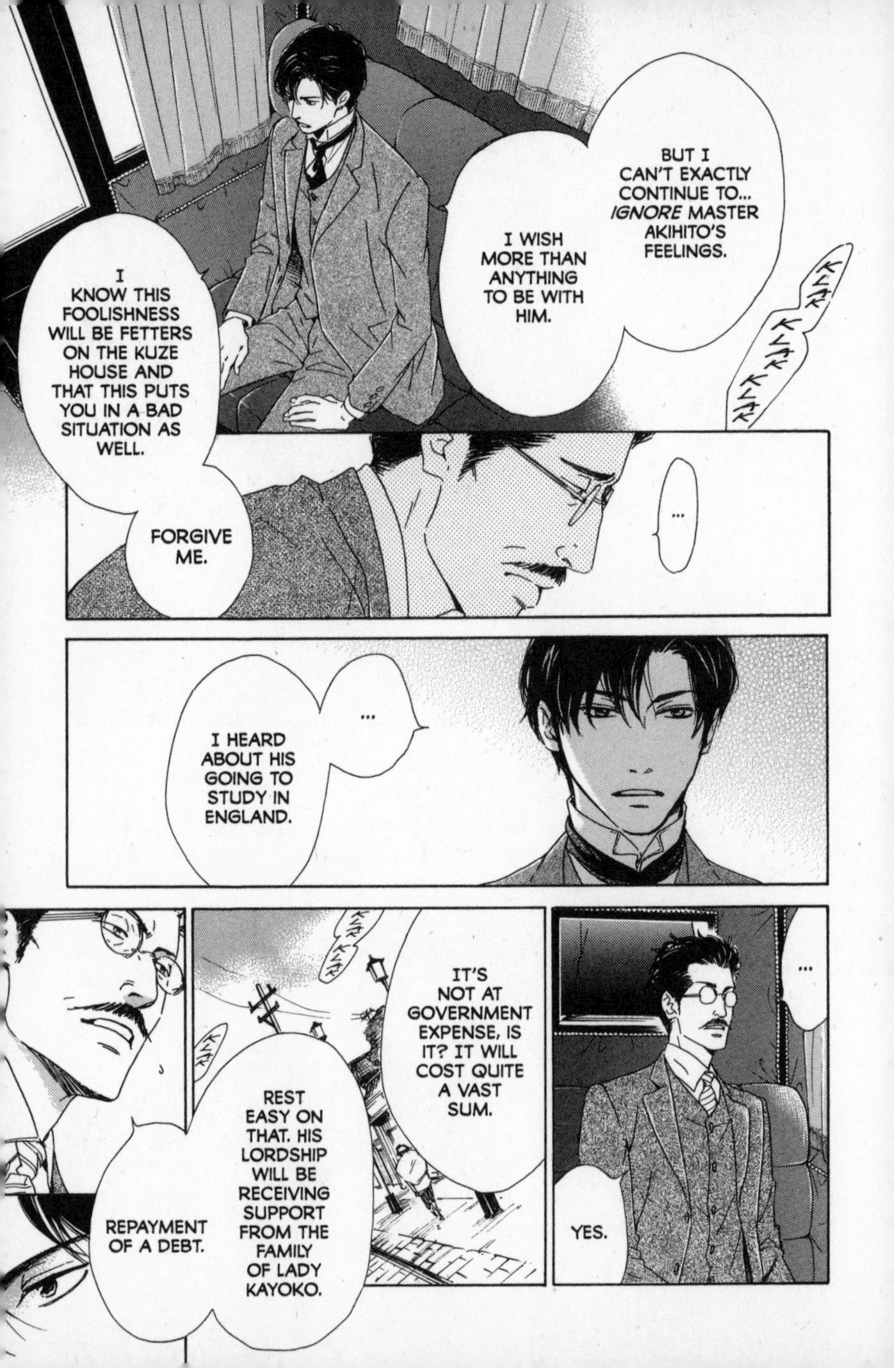
KLAK KLAK KLAK KLAK
BUT I CAN'T EXACTLY CONTINUE TO... *IGNORE* MASTER AKIHITO'S FEELINGS.
I WISH MORE THAN ANYTHING TO BE WITH HIM.
I KNOW THIS FOOLISHNESS WILL BE FETTERS ON THE KUZE HOUSE AND THAT THIS PUTS YOU IN A BAD SITUATION AS WELL.
...
FORGIVE ME.
...
I HEARD ABOUT HIS GOING TO STUDY IN ENGLAND.
...
YES.
IT'S NOT AT GOVERNMENT EXPENSE, IS IT? IT WILL COST QUITE A VAST SUM.
KLAK KLAK
KLAK
REST EASY ON THAT. HIS LORDSHIP WILL BE RECEIVING SUPPORT FROM THE FAMILY OF LADY KAYOKO.
REPAYMENT OF A DEBT.

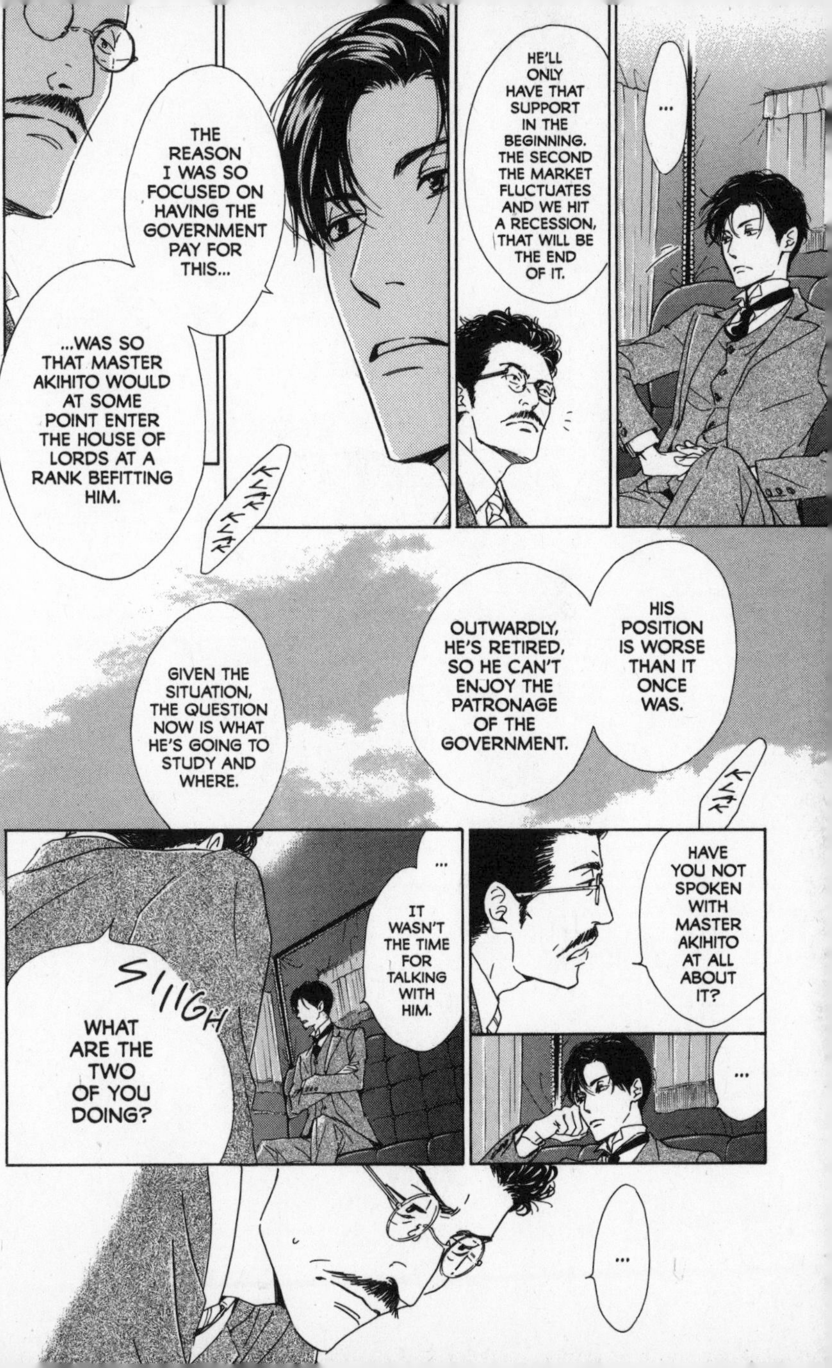
...
HE'LL ONLY HAVE THAT SUPPORT IN THE BEGINNING. THE SECOND THE MARKET FLUCTUATES AND WE HIT A RECESSION, THAT WILL BE THE END OF IT.
THE REASON I WAS SO FOCUSED ON HAVING THE GOVERNMENT PAY FOR THIS...
...WAS SO THAT MASTER AKIHITO WOULD AT SOME POINT ENTER THE HOUSE OF LORDS AT A RANK BEFITTING HIM.
HIS POSITION IS WORSE THAN IT ONCE WAS.
OUTWARDLY, HE'S RETIRED, SO HE CAN'T ENJOY THE PATRONAGE OF THE GOVERNMENT.
GIVEN THE SITUATION, THE QUESTION NOW IS WHAT HE'S GOING TO STUDY AND WHERE.
HAVE YOU NOT SPOKEN WITH MASTER AKIHITO AT ALL ABOUT IT?
...
...
IT WASN'T THE TIME FOR TALKING WITH HIM.
SIIIGH
WHAT ARE THE TWO OF YOU DOING?
...

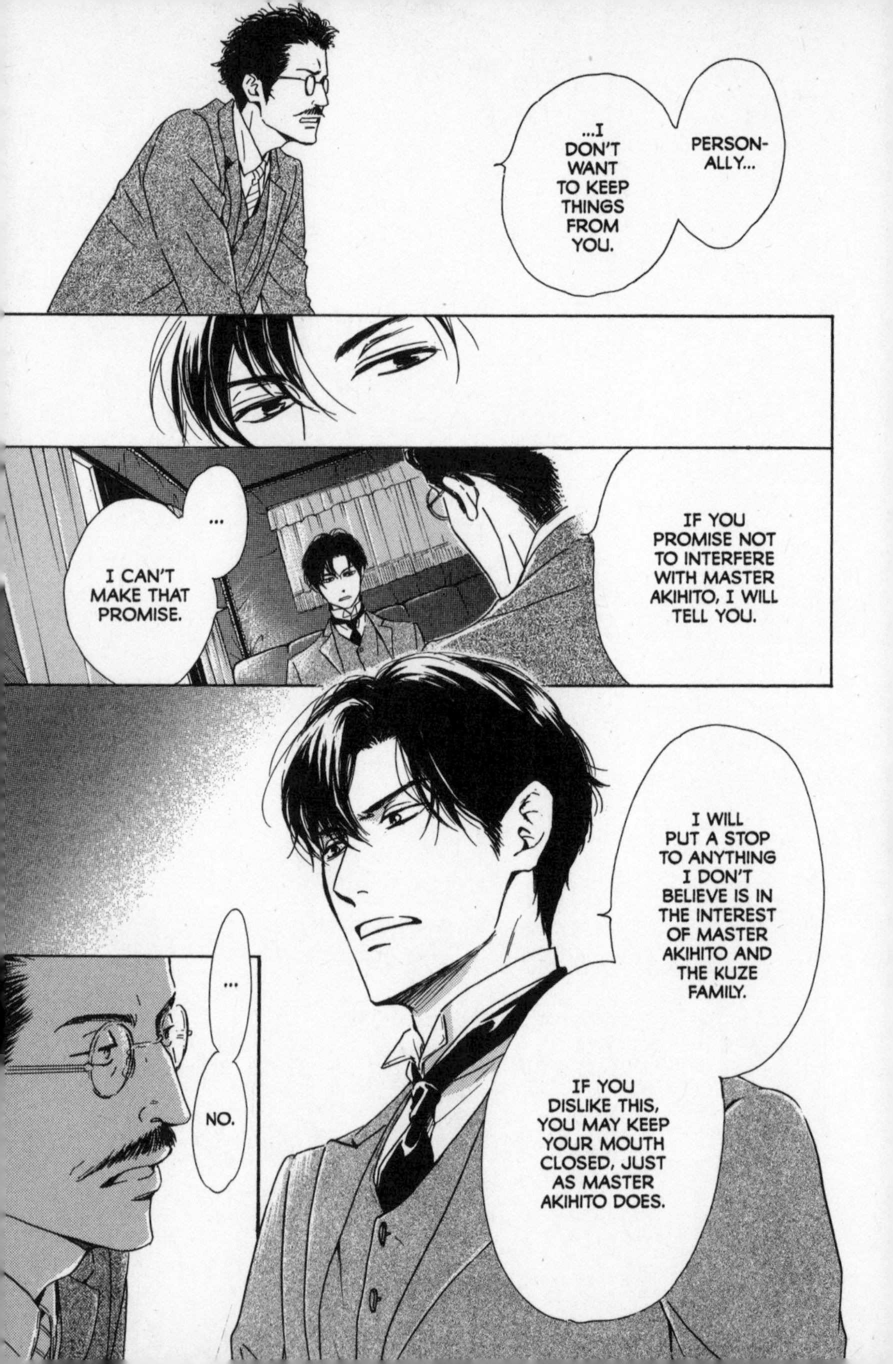
PERSON-ALLY...
...I DON'T WANT TO KEEP THINGS FROM YOU.
IF YOU PROMISE NOT TO INTERFERE WITH MASTER AKIHITO, I WILL TELL YOU.
...
I CAN'T MAKE THAT PROMISE.
I WILL PUT A STOP TO ANYTHING I DON'T BELIEVE IS IN THE INTEREST OF MASTER AKIHITO AND THE KUZE FAMILY.
IF YOU DISLIKE THIS, YOU MAY KEEP YOUR MOUTH CLOSED, JUST AS MASTER AKIHITO DOES.
...
NO.

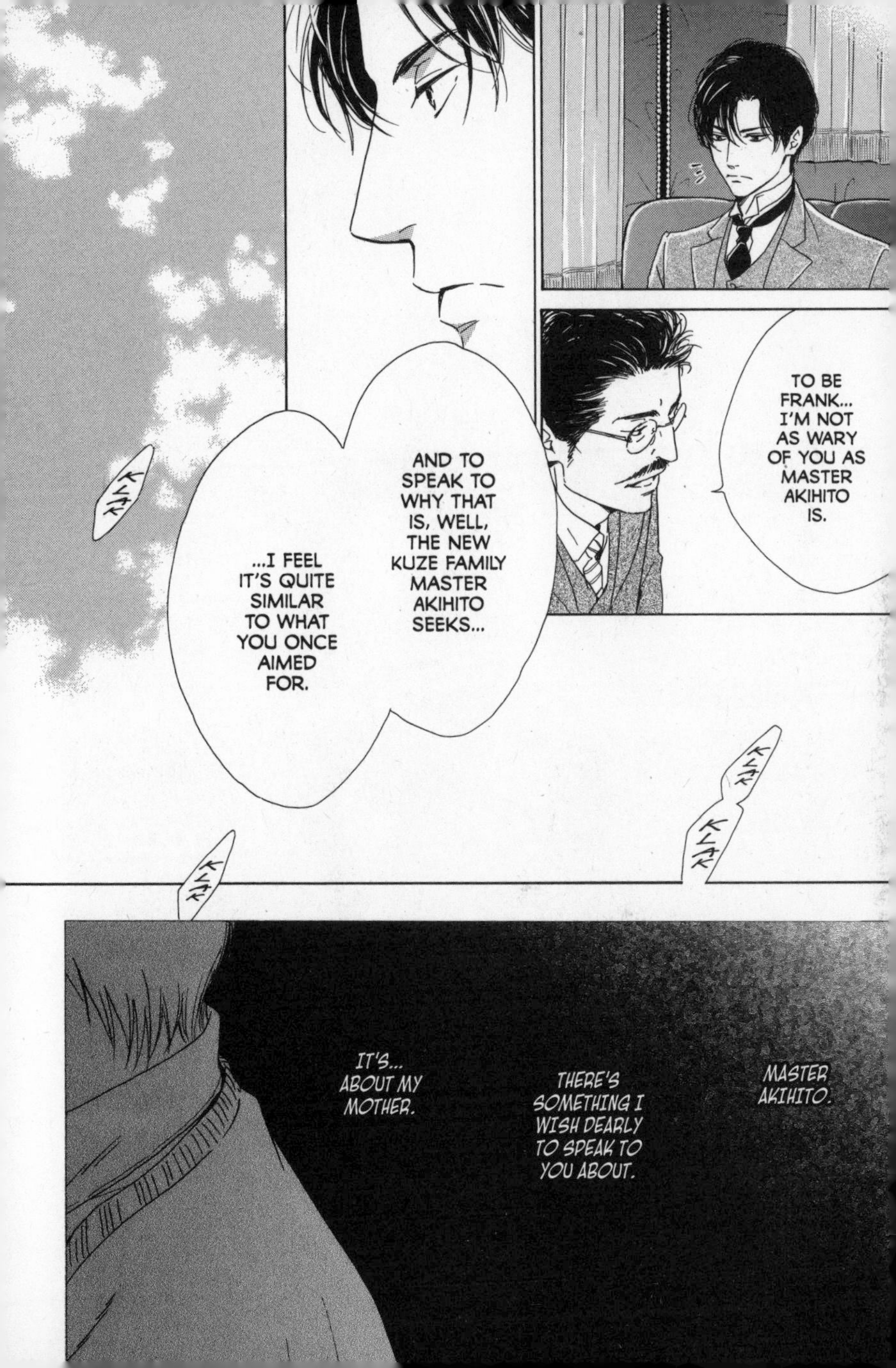
TO BE FRANK... I'M NOT AS WARY OF YOU AS MASTER AKIHITO IS.
AND TO SPEAK TO WHY THAT IS, WELL, THE NEW KUZE FAMILY MASTER AKIHITO SEEKS...
...I FEEL IT'S QUITE SIMILAR TO WHAT YOU ONCE AIMED FOR.
KLAK
KLAK
KLAK
KLAK
MASTER AKIHITO.
THERE'S SOMETHING I WISH DEARLY TO SPEAK TO YOU ABOUT.
IT'S... ABOUT MY MOTHER.

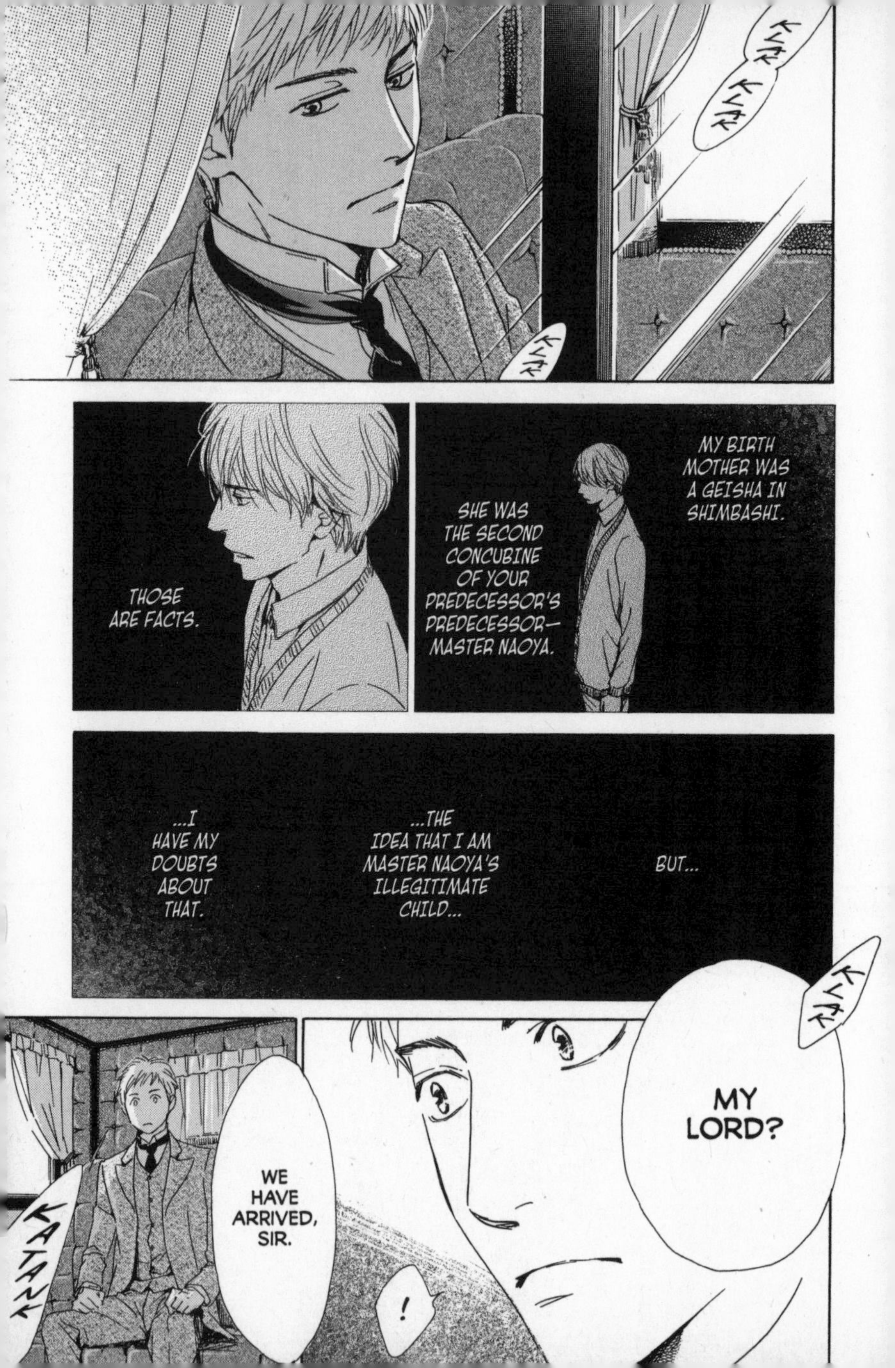
KLAK KLAK
KLAK
MY BIRTH MOTHER WAS A GEISHA IN SHIMBASHI.
SHE WAS THE SECOND CONCUBINE OF YOUR PREDECESSOR'S PREDECESSOR— MASTER NAOYA.
THOSE ARE FACTS.
BUT...
...THE IDEA THAT I AM MASTER NAOYA'S ILLEGITIMATE CHILD...
...I HAVE MY DOUBTS ABOUT THAT.
KLAK
MY LORD?
!
WE HAVE ARRIVED, SIR.
KATANK

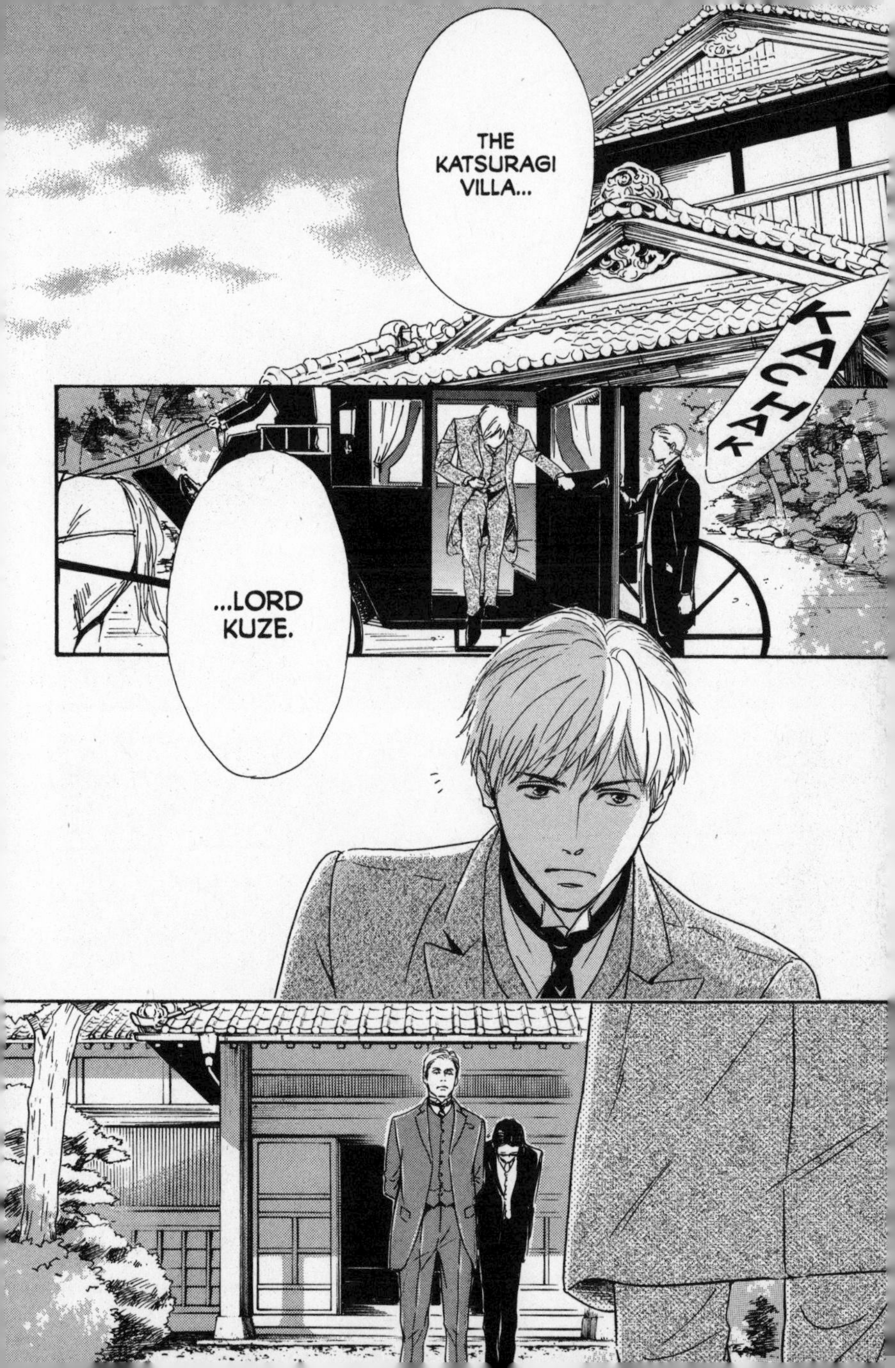
THE KATSURAGI VILLA...
KACHAK
...LORD KUZE.

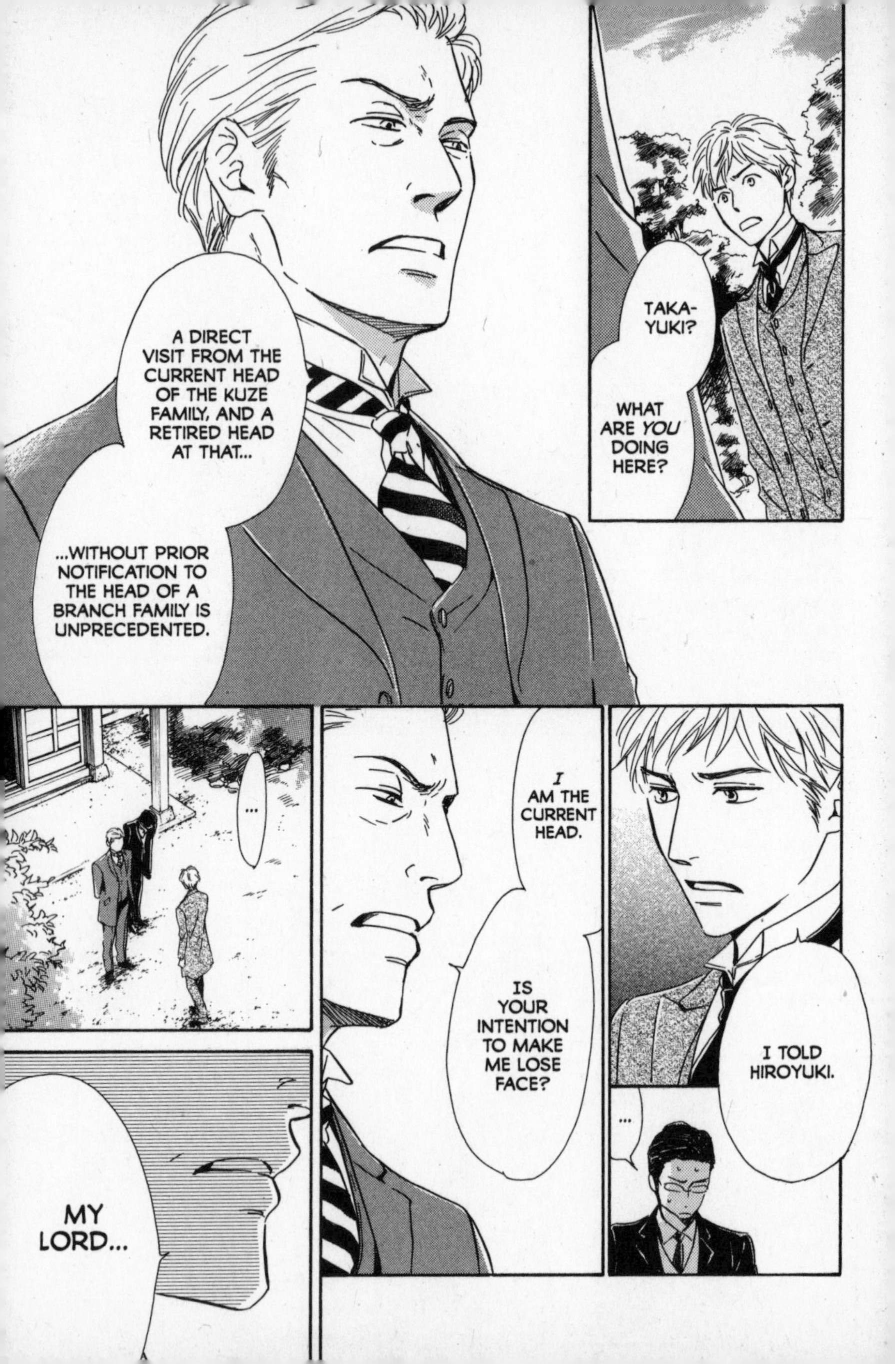
TAKA-YUKI?
WHAT ARE *YOU* DOING HERE?
A DIRECT VISIT FROM THE CURRENT HEAD OF THE KUZE FAMILY, AND A RETIRED HEAD AT THAT...
...WITHOUT PRIOR NOTIFICATION TO THE HEAD OF A BRANCH FAMILY IS UNPRECEDENTED.
I TOLD HIROYUKI.
...
I AM THE CURRENT HEAD.
IS YOUR INTENTION TO MAKE ME LOSE FACE?
...
MY LORD...

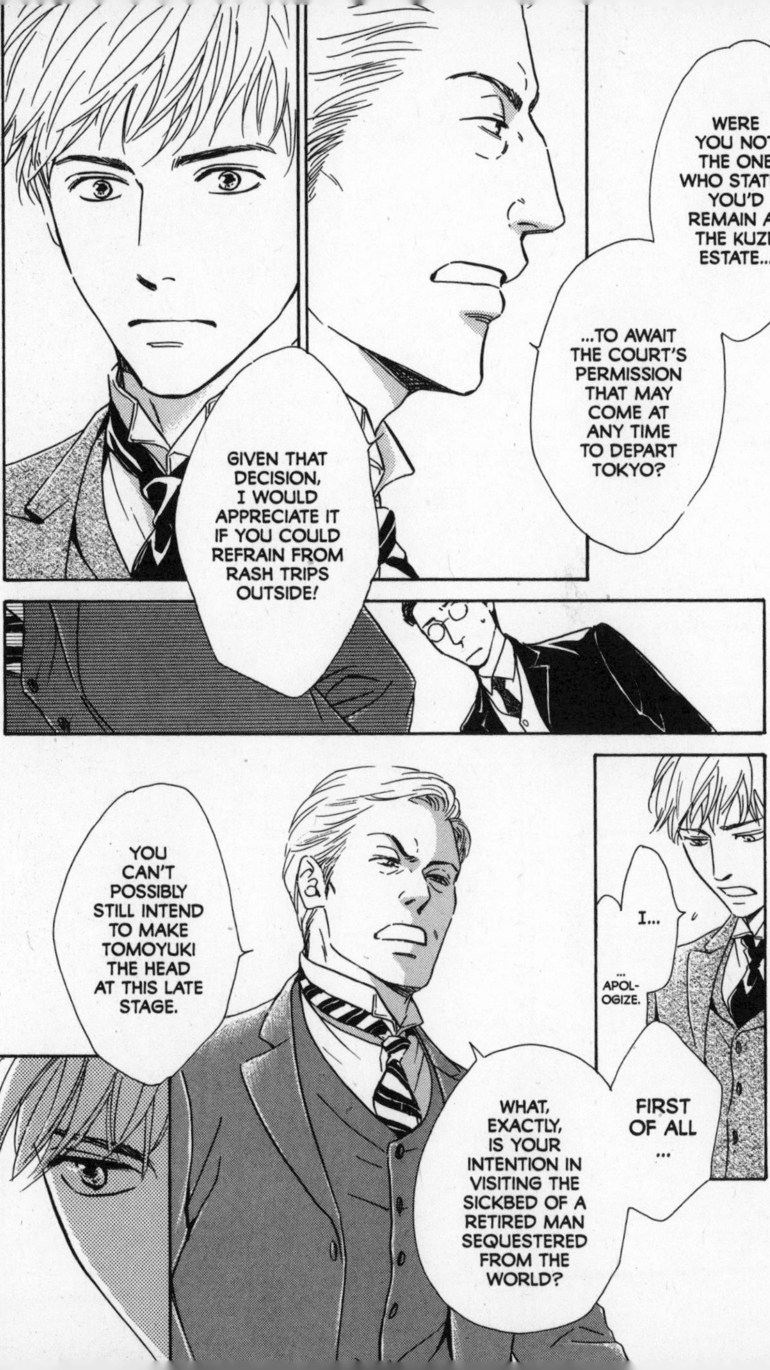
WERE YOU NOT THE ONE WHO STATED YOU'D REMAIN AT THE KUZE ESTATE...
...TO AWAIT THE COURT'S PERMISSION THAT MAY COME AT ANY TIME TO DEPART TOKYO?
GIVEN THAT DECISION, I WOULD APPRECIATE IT IF YOU COULD REFRAIN FROM RASH TRIPS OUTSIDE!
I...
...APOLOGIZE.
FIRST OF ALL...
WHAT, EXACTLY, IS YOUR INTENTION IN VISITING THE SICKBED OF A RETIRED MAN SEQUESTERED FROM THE WORLD?
YOU CAN'T POSSIBLY STILL INTEND TO MAKE TOMOYUKI THE HEAD AT THIS LATE STAGE.

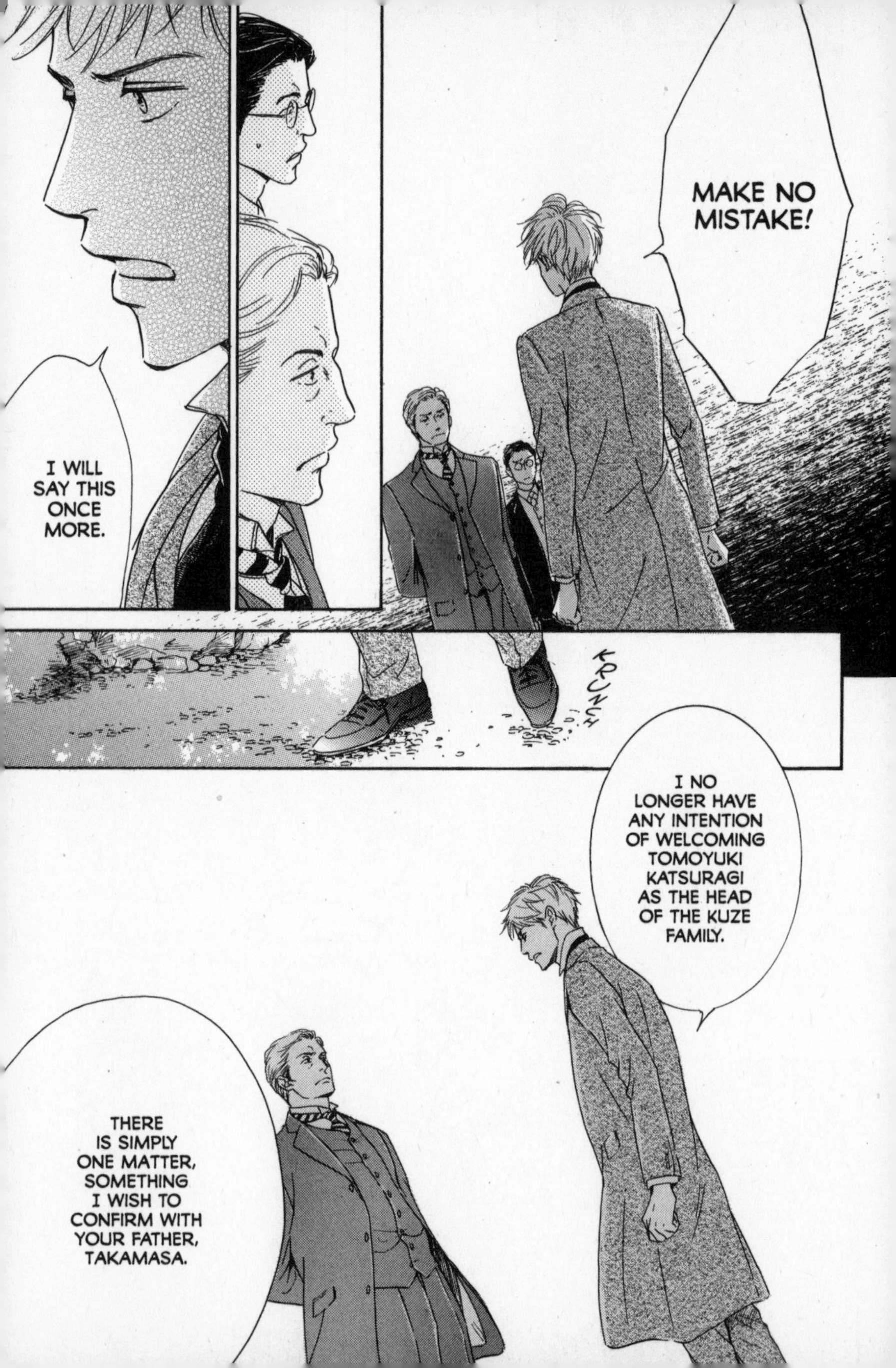
MAKE NO MISTAKE!
I WILL SAY THIS ONCE MORE.
KRUNCH
I NO LONGER HAVE ANY INTENTION OF WELCOMING TOMOYUKI KATSURAGI AS THE HEAD OF THE KUZE FAMILY.
THERE IS SIMPLY ONE MATTER, SOMETHING I WISH TO CONFIRM WITH YOUR FATHER, TAKAMASA.

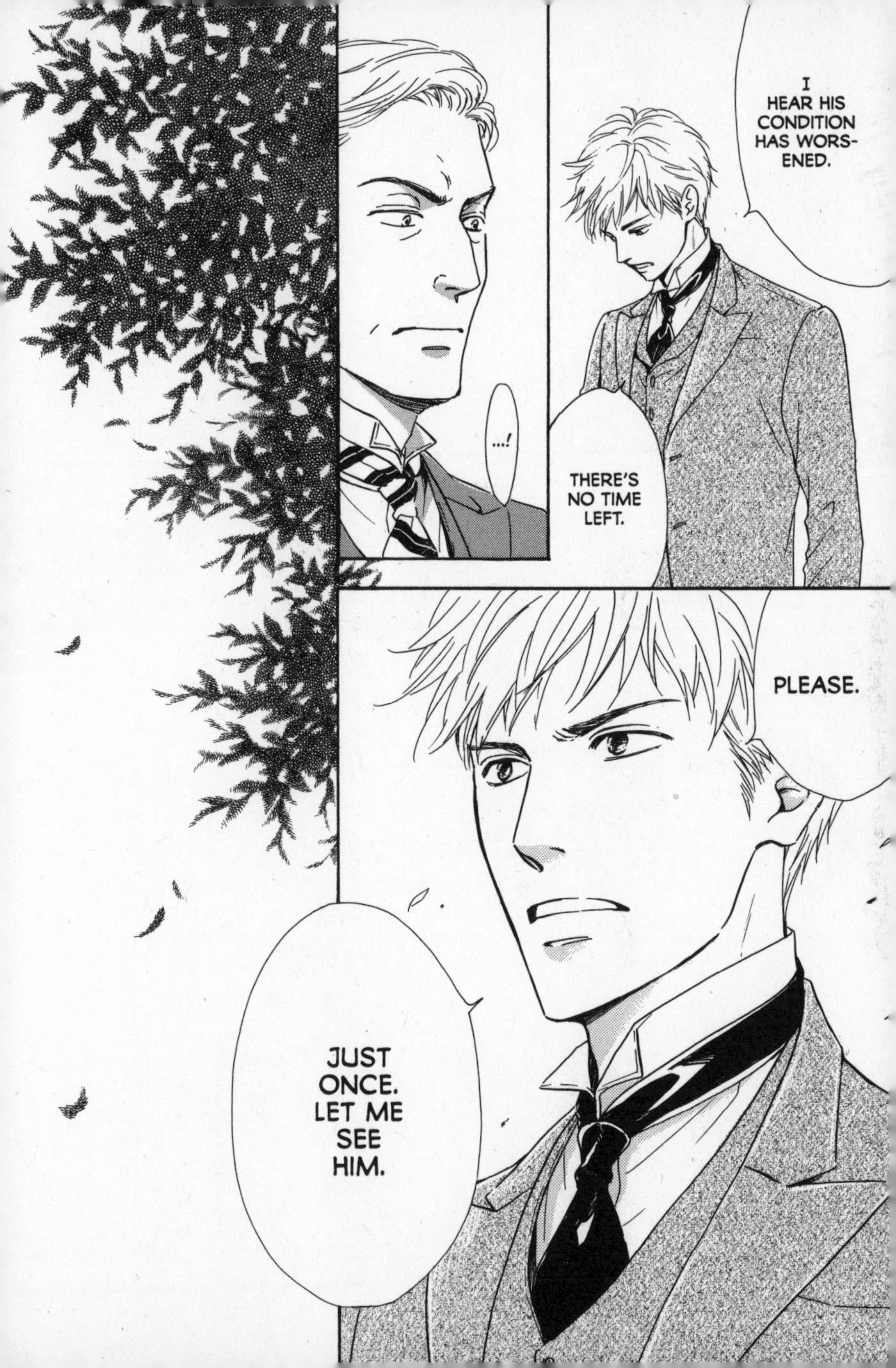
I HEAR HIS CONDITION HAS WORSENED.
THERE'S NO TIME LEFT.
...!
PLEASE.
JUST ONCE. LET ME SEE HIM.

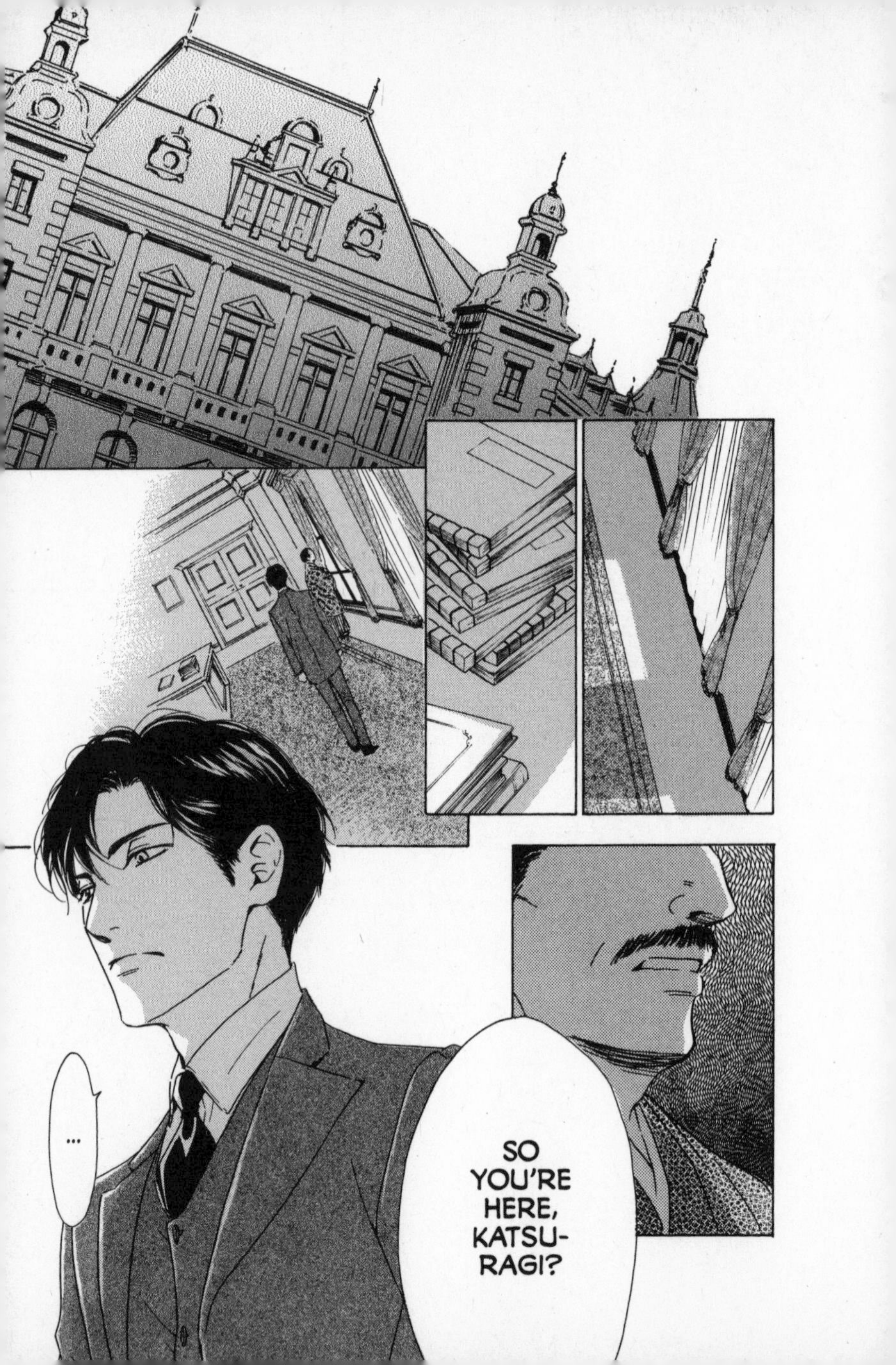
SO YOU'RE HERE, KATSURAGI?
...

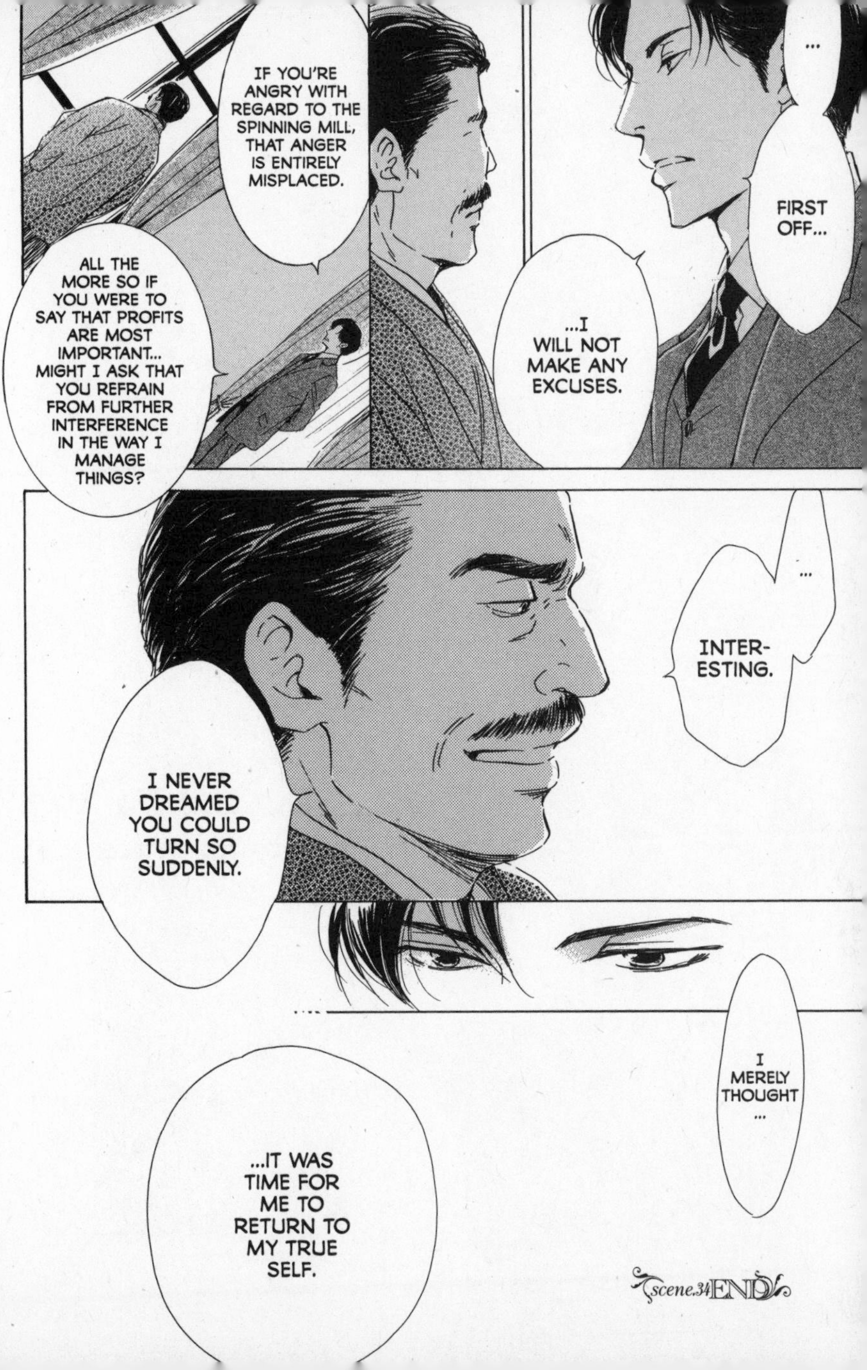
...
FIRST OFF...
...I WILL NOT MAKE ANY EXCUSES.
IF YOU'RE ANGRY WITH REGARD TO THE SPINNING MILL, THAT ANGER IS ENTIRELY MISPLACED.
ALL THE MORE SO IF YOU WERE TO SAY THAT PROFITS ARE MOST IMPORTANT... MIGHT I ASK THAT YOU REFRAIN FROM FURTHER INTERFERENCE IN THE WAY I MANAGE THINGS?
...
INTER-ESTING.
I NEVER DREAMED YOU COULD TURN SO SUDDENLY.
....
I MERELY THOUGHT...
...IT WAS TIME FOR ME TO RETURN TO MY TRUE SELF.
scene.34 END

憂鬱な朝

Blue Morning

憂鬱な朝

Blue Morning

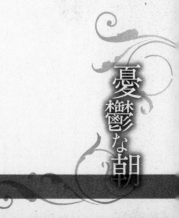

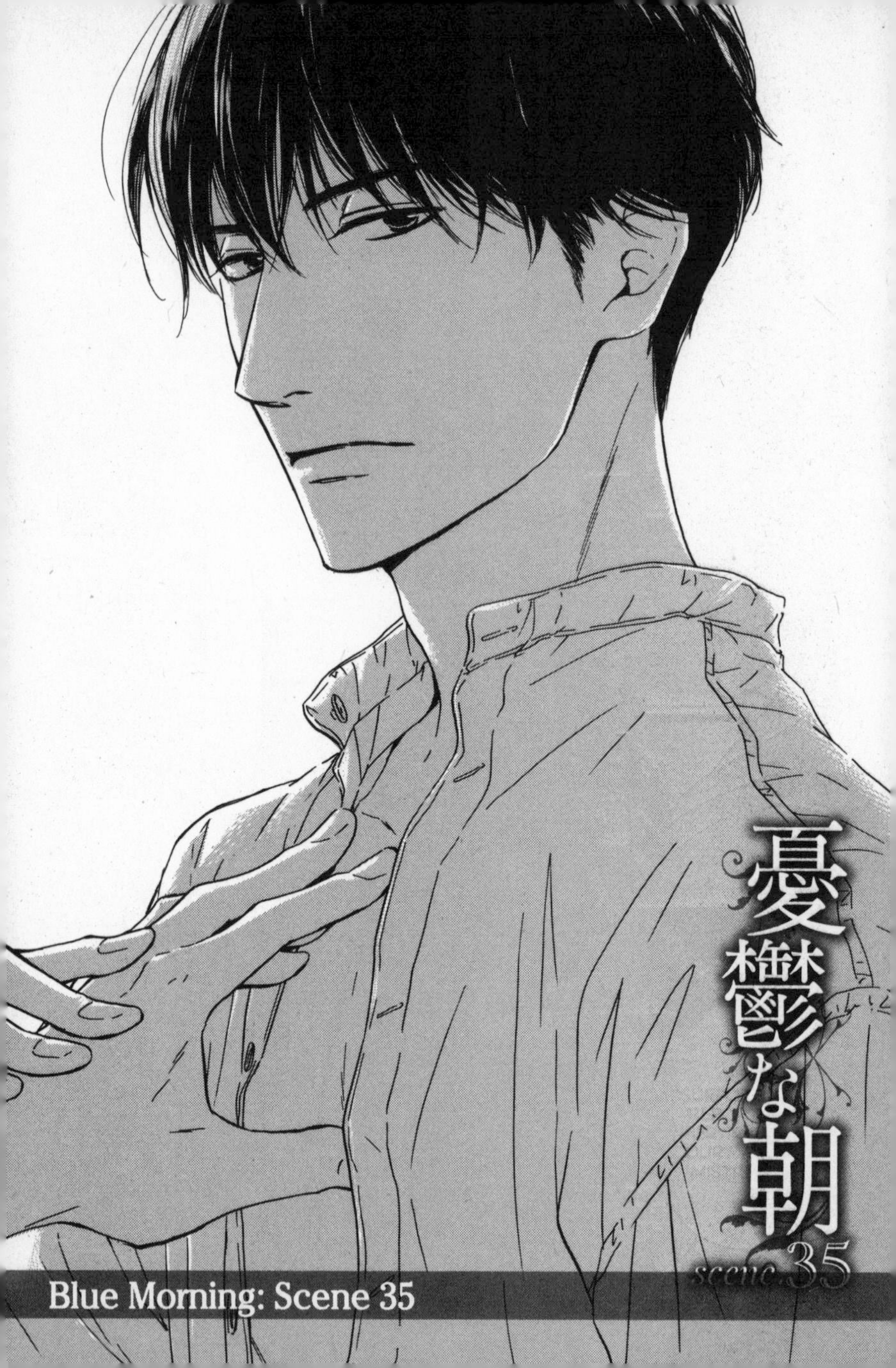
憂鬱な朝
scene 35
Blue Morning: Scene 35

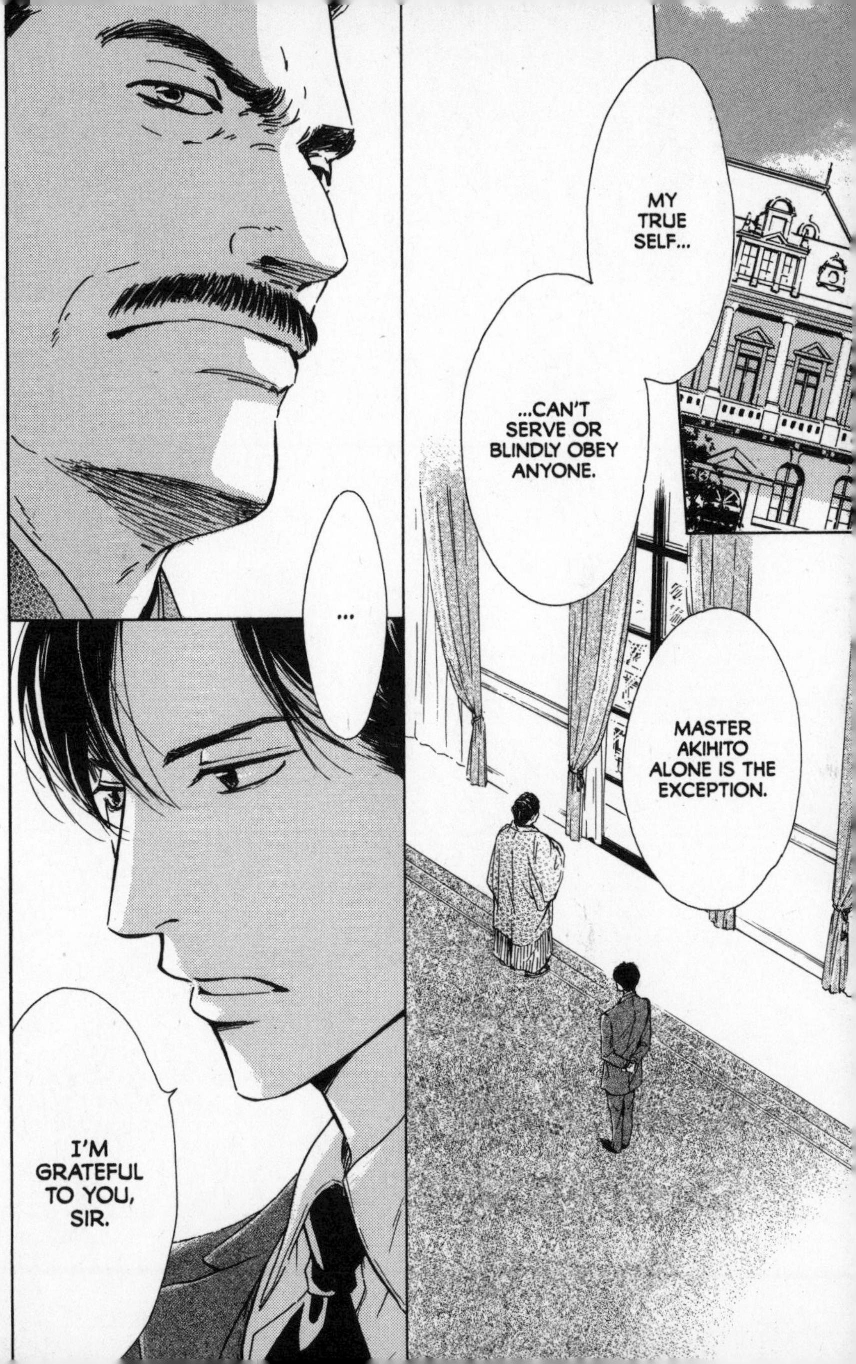
MY TRUE SELF...
...CAN'T SERVE OR BLINDLY OBEY ANYONE.
MASTER AKIHITO ALONE IS THE EXCEPTION.
...
I'M GRATEFUL TO YOU, SIR.

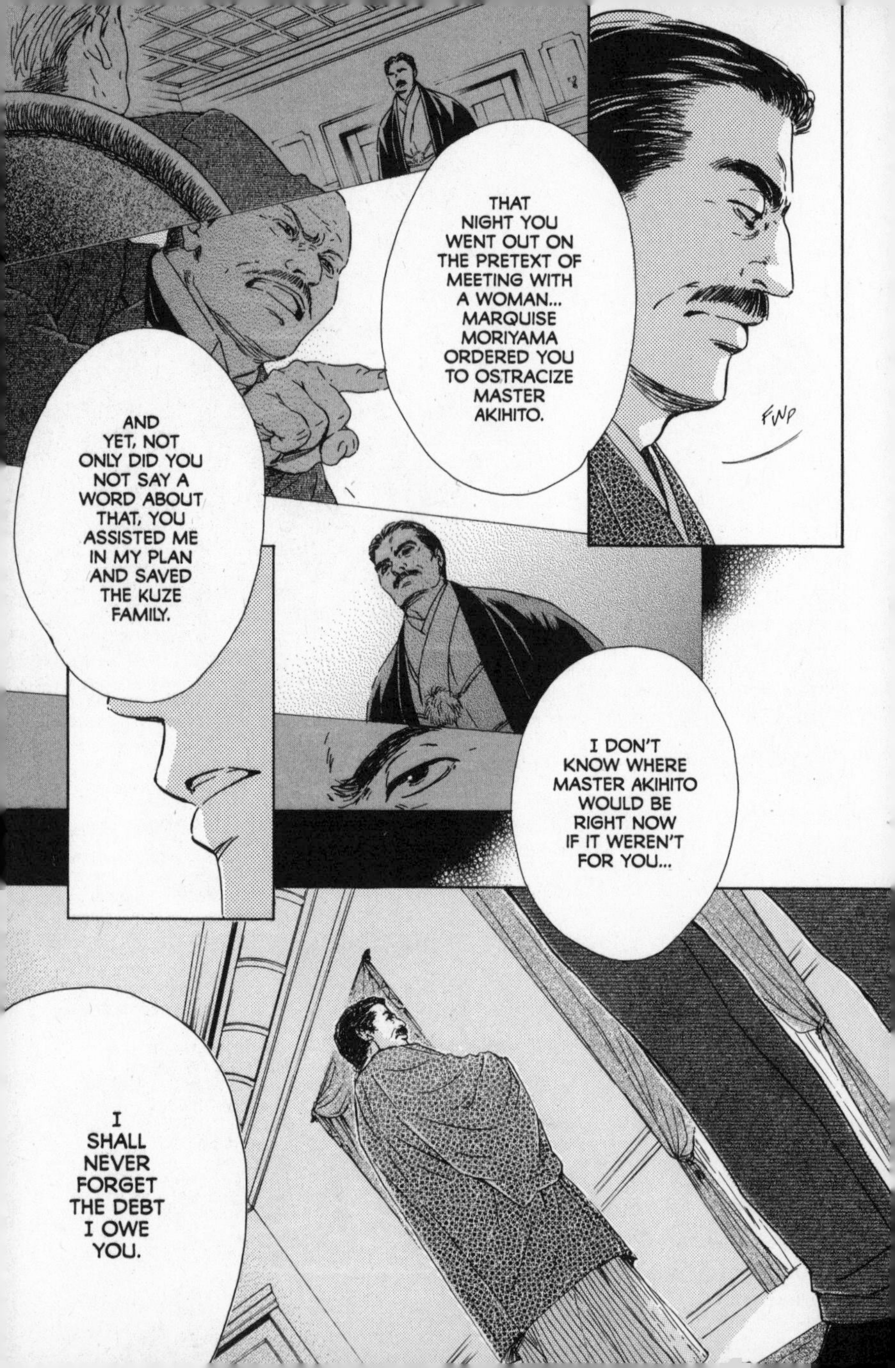
THAT NIGHT YOU WENT OUT ON THE PRETEXT OF MEETING WITH A WOMAN... MARQUISE MORIYAMA ORDERED YOU TO OSTRACIZE MASTER AKIHITO.
FWP
AND YET, NOT ONLY DID YOU NOT SAY A WORD ABOUT THAT, YOU ASSISTED ME IN MY PLAN AND SAVED THE KUZE FAMILY.
I DON'T KNOW WHERE MASTER AKIHITO WOULD BE RIGHT NOW IF IT WEREN'T FOR YOU...
I SHALL NEVER FORGET THE DEBT I OWE YOU.

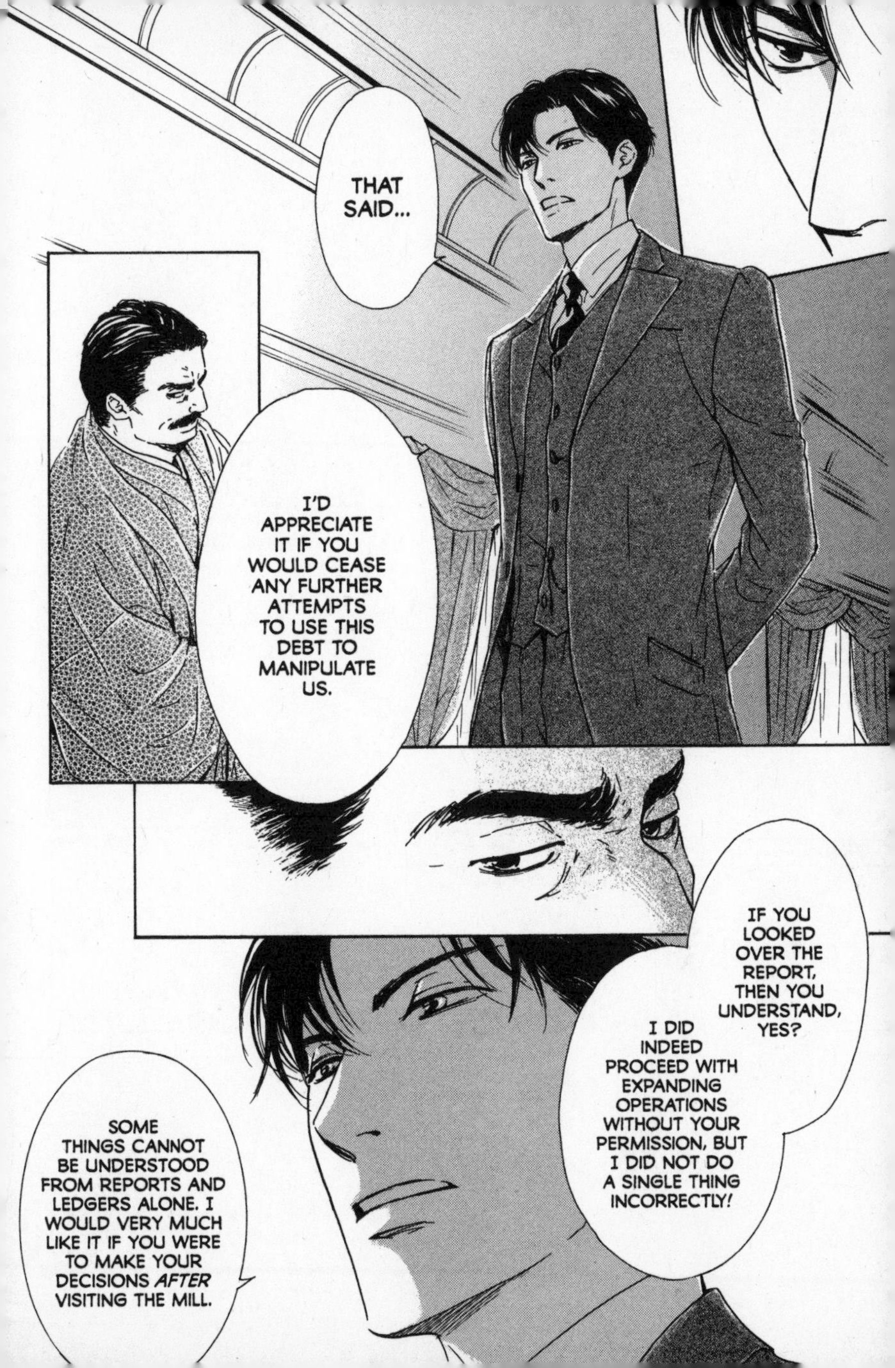
THAT SAID...
I'D APPRECIATE IT IF YOU WOULD CEASE ANY FURTHER ATTEMPTS TO USE THIS DEBT TO MANIPULATE US.
IF YOU LOOKED OVER THE REPORT, THEN YOU UNDERSTAND, YES?
I DID INDEED PROCEED WITH EXPANDING OPERATIONS WITHOUT YOUR PERMISSION, BUT I DID NOT DO A SINGLE THING INCORRECTLY!
SOME THINGS CANNOT BE UNDERSTOOD FROM REPORTS AND LEDGERS ALONE. I WOULD VERY MUCH LIKE IT IF YOU WERE TO MAKE YOUR DECISIONS *AFTER* VISITING THE MILL.

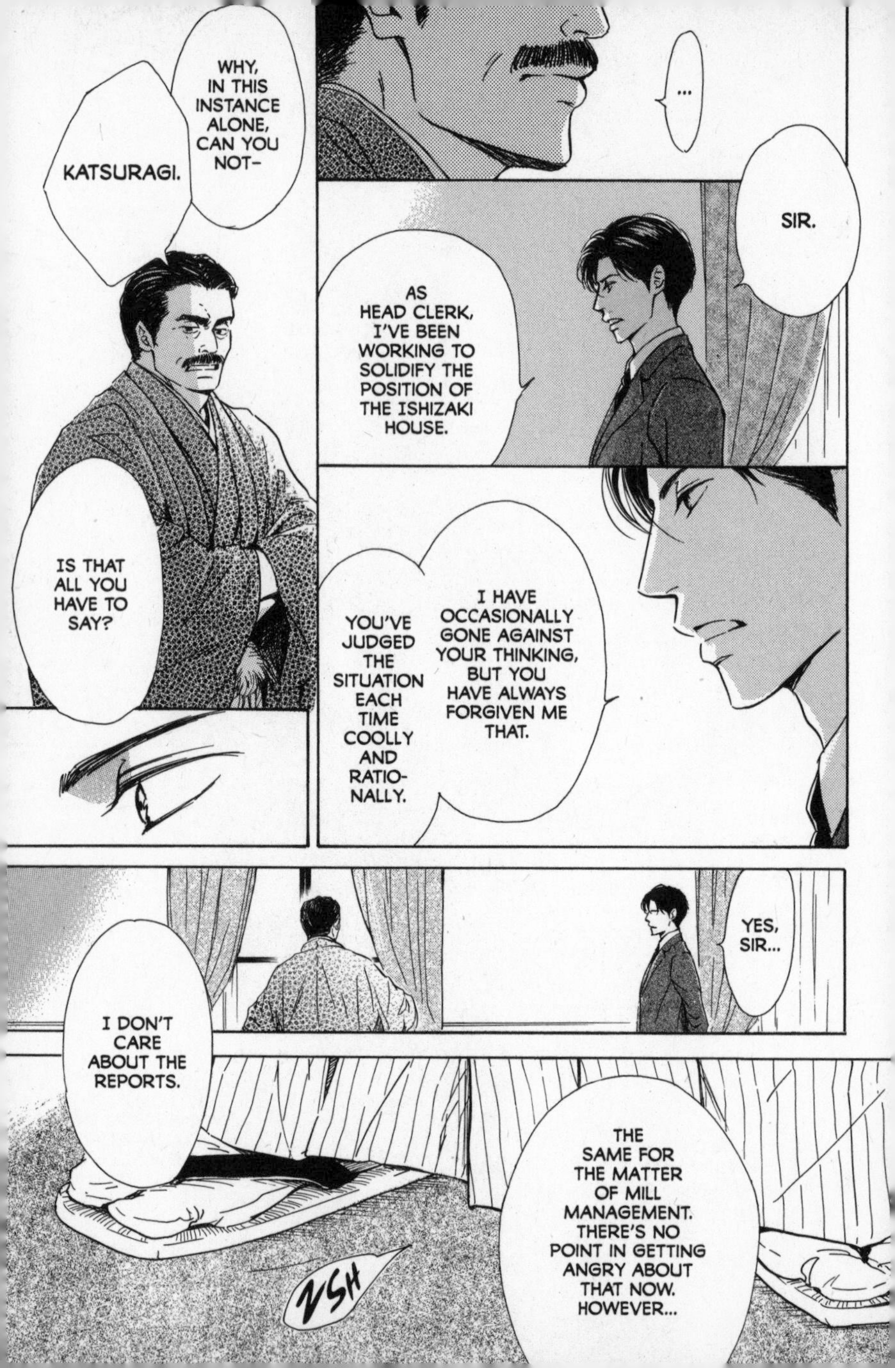
...
SIR.
AS HEAD CLERK, I'VE BEEN WORKING TO SOLIDIFY THE POSITION OF THE ISHIZAKI HOUSE.
I HAVE OCCASIONALLY GONE AGAINST YOUR THINKING, BUT YOU HAVE ALWAYS FORGIVEN ME THAT.
YOU'VE JUDGED THE SITUATION EACH TIME COOLLY AND RATIO-NALLY.
KATSURAGI.
WHY, IN THIS INSTANCE ALONE, CAN YOU NOT-
IS THAT ALL YOU HAVE TO SAY?
YES, SIR...
I DON'T CARE ABOUT THE REPORTS.
THE SAME FOR THE MATTER OF MILL MANAGEMENT. THERE'S NO POINT IN GETTING ANGRY ABOUT THAT NOW. HOWEVER...
ZSH

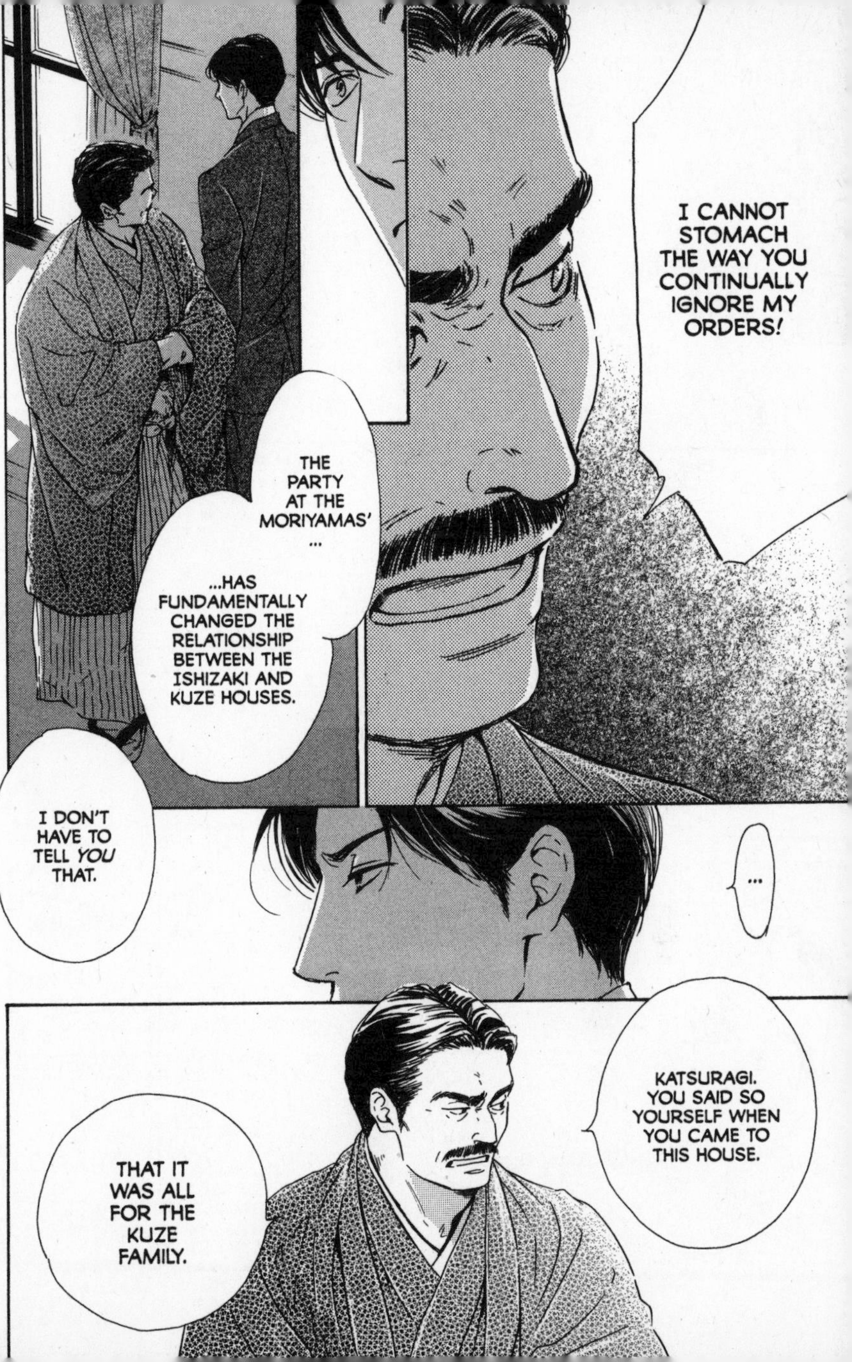
I CANNOT STOMACH THE WAY YOU CONTINUALLY IGNORE MY ORDERS!
THE PARTY AT THE MORIYAMAS'...
...HAS FUNDAMENTALLY CHANGED THE RELATIONSHIP BETWEEN THE ISHIZAKI AND KUZE HOUSES.
I DON'T HAVE TO TELL *YOU* THAT.
...
KATSURAGI. YOU SAID SO YOURSELF WHEN YOU CAME TO THIS HOUSE.
THAT IT WAS ALL FOR THE KUZE FAMILY.

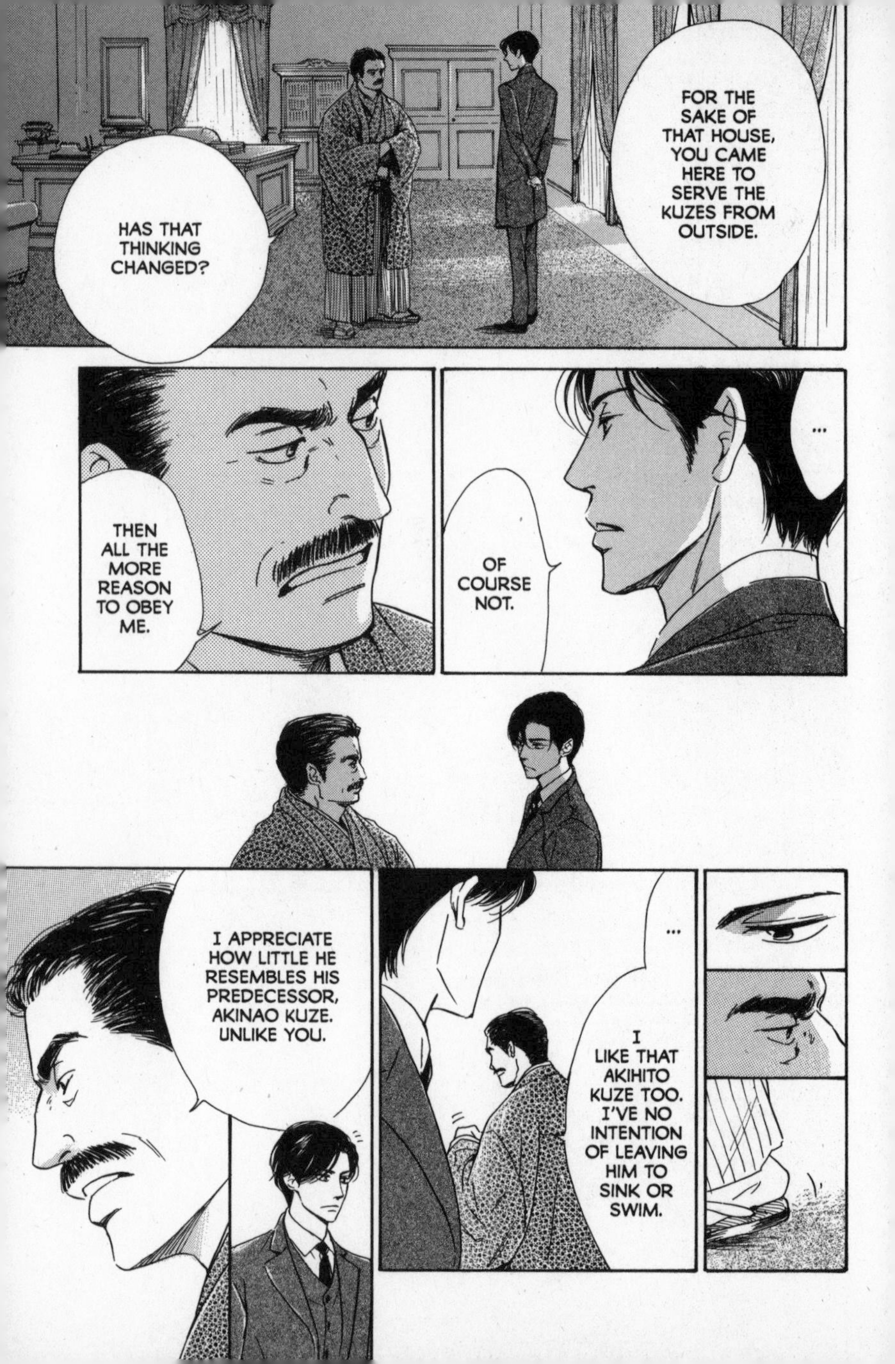
FOR THE SAKE OF THAT HOUSE, YOU CAME HERE TO SERVE THE KUZES FROM OUTSIDE.
HAS THAT THINKING CHANGED?
...
OF COURSE NOT.
THEN ALL THE MORE REASON TO OBEY ME.
...
I LIKE THAT AKIHITO KUZE TOO. I'VE NO INTENTION OF LEAVING HIM TO SINK OR SWIM.
I APPRECIATE HOW LITTLE HE RESEMBLES HIS PREDECESSOR, AKINAO KUZE. UNLIKE YOU.

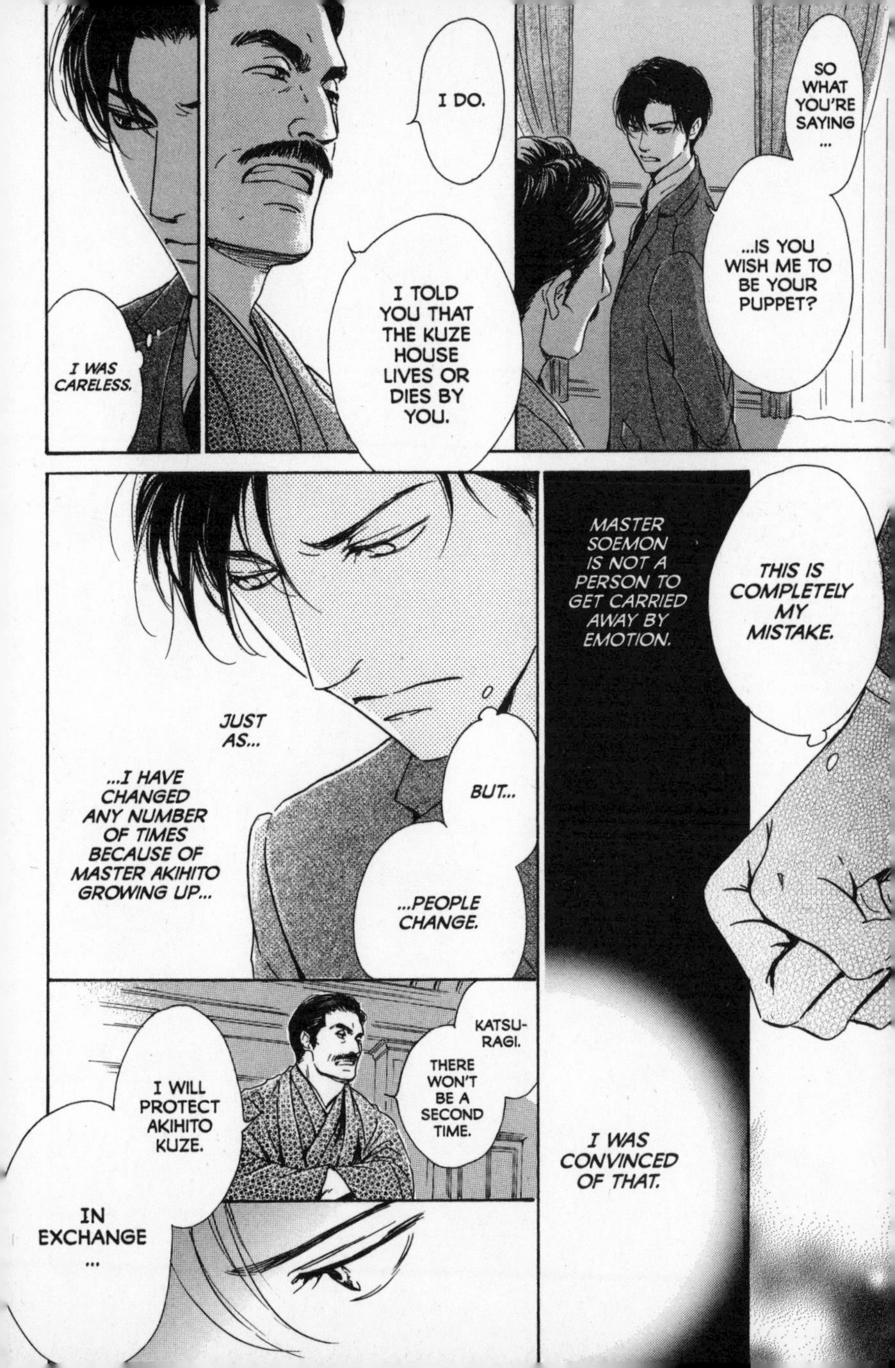

SO WHAT YOU'RE SAYING...
...IS YOU WISH ME TO BE YOUR PUPPET?
I DO.
I TOLD YOU THAT THE KUZE HOUSE LIVES OR DIES BY YOU.
I WAS CARELESS.
THIS IS COMPLETELY MY MISTAKE.
MASTER SOEMON IS NOT A PERSON TO GET CARRIED AWAY BY EMOTION.
I WAS CONVINCED OF THAT.
BUT...
...PEOPLE CHANGE.
JUST AS...
...I HAVE CHANGED ANY NUMBER OF TIMES BECAUSE OF MASTER AKIHITO GROWING UP...
KATSU-RAGI.
THERE WON'T BE A SECOND TIME.
I WILL PROTECT AKIHITO KUZE.
IN EXCHANGE...

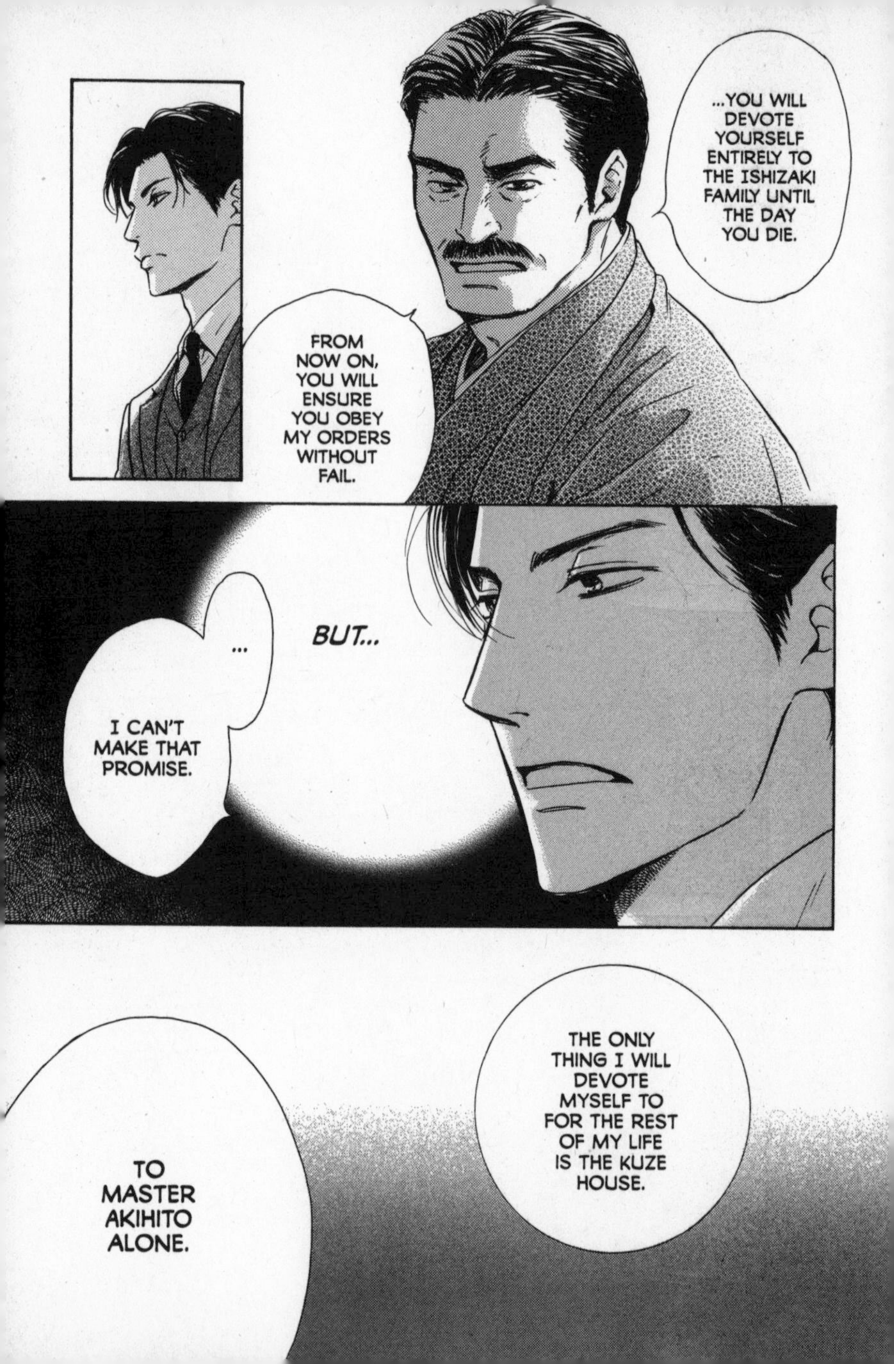
...YOU WILL DEVOTE YOURSELF ENTIRELY TO THE ISHIZAKI FAMILY UNTIL THE DAY YOU DIE.
FROM NOW ON, YOU WILL ENSURE YOU OBEY MY ORDERS WITHOUT FAIL.
BUT...
...
I CAN'T MAKE THAT PROMISE.
THE ONLY THING I WILL DEVOTE MYSELF TO FOR THE REST OF MY LIFE IS THE KUZE HOUSE.
TO MASTER AKIHITO ALONE.

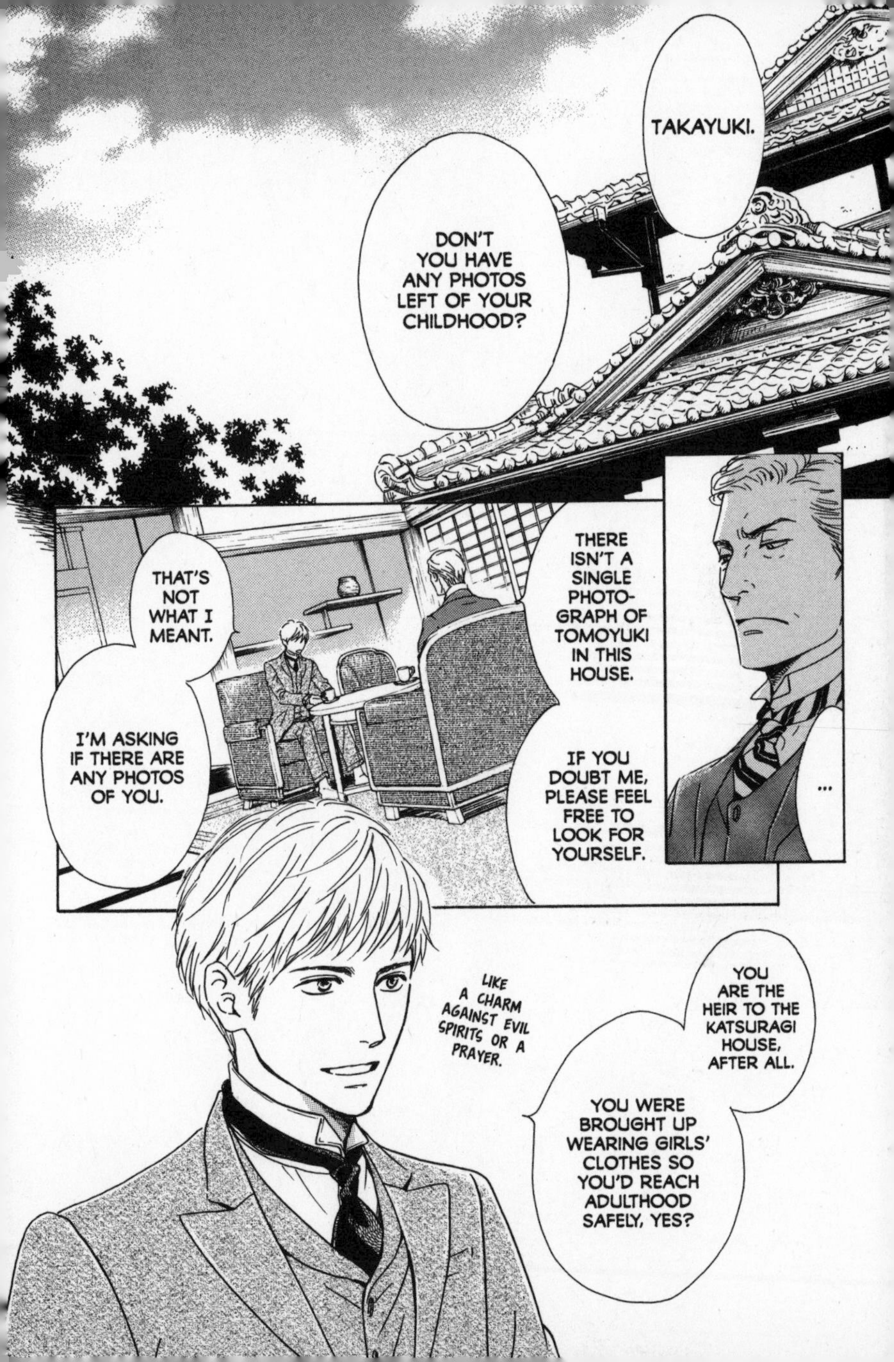
TAKAYUKI.
DON'T YOU HAVE ANY PHOTOS LEFT OF YOUR CHILDHOOD?
...
THERE ISN'T A SINGLE PHOTO-GRAPH OF TOMOYUKI IN THIS HOUSE.
IF YOU DOUBT ME, PLEASE FEEL FREE TO LOOK FOR YOURSELF.
THAT'S NOT WHAT I MEANT.
I'M ASKING IF THERE ARE ANY PHOTOS OF YOU.
YOU ARE THE HEIR TO THE KATSURAGI HOUSE, AFTER ALL.
YOU WERE BROUGHT UP WEARING GIRLS' CLOTHES SO YOU'D REACH ADULTHOOD SAFELY, YES?
LIKE A CHARM AGAINST EVIL SPIRITS OR A PRAYER.

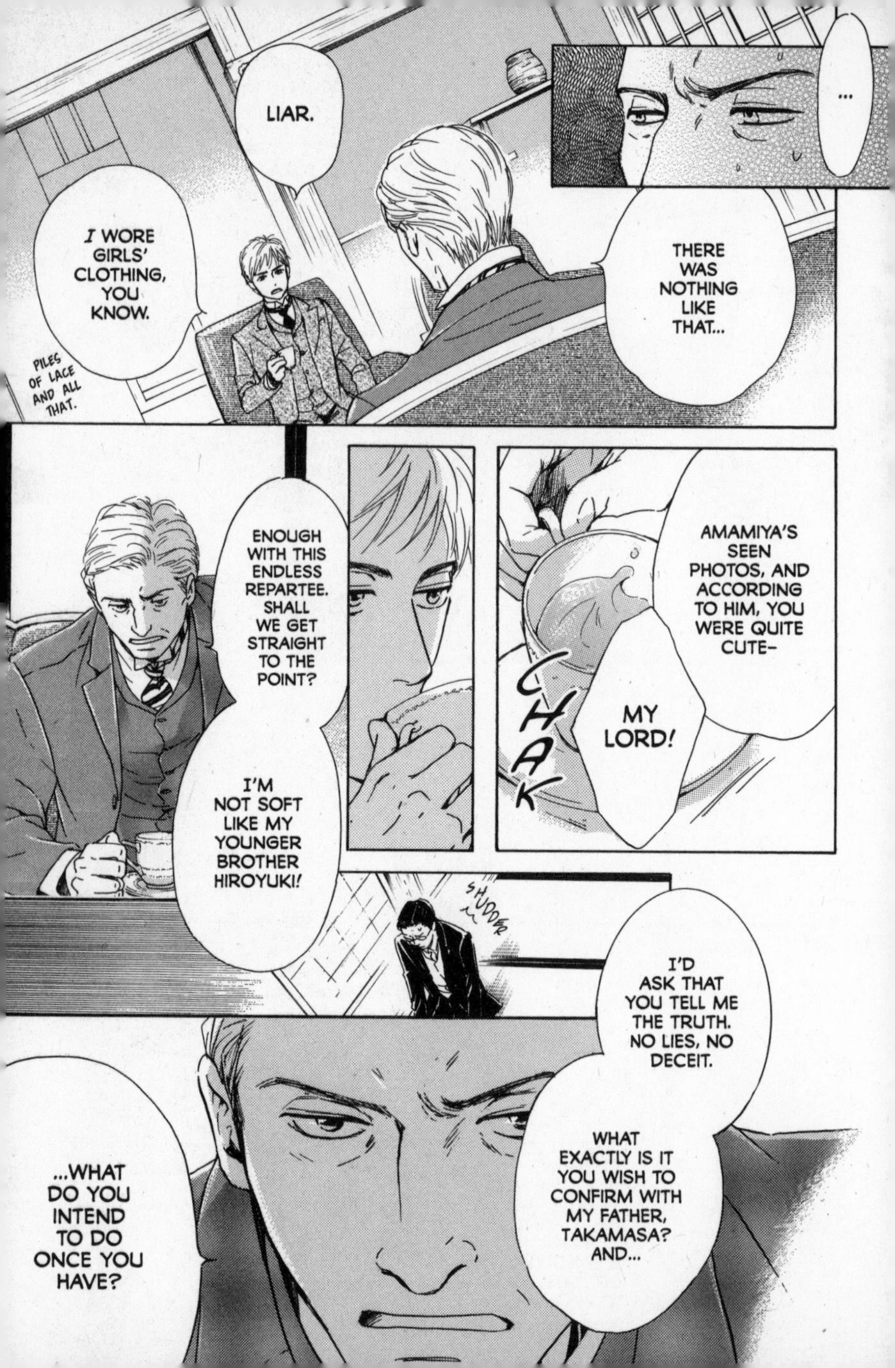
...
THERE WAS NOTHING LIKE THAT...
LIAR.
I WORE GIRLS' CLOTHING, YOU KNOW.
PILES OF LACE AND ALL THAT.
AMAMIYA'S SEEN PHOTOS, AND ACCORDING TO HIM, YOU WERE QUITE CUTE–
MY LORD!
CHAK
ENOUGH WITH THIS ENDLESS REPARTEE. SHALL WE GET STRAIGHT TO THE POINT?
I'M NOT SOFT LIKE MY YOUNGER BROTHER HIROYUKI!
SHUDDER
I'D ASK THAT YOU TELL ME THE TRUTH. NO LIES, NO DECEIT.
WHAT EXACTLY IS IT YOU WISH TO CONFIRM WITH MY FATHER, TAKAMASA? AND...
...WHAT DO YOU INTEND TO DO ONCE YOU HAVE?

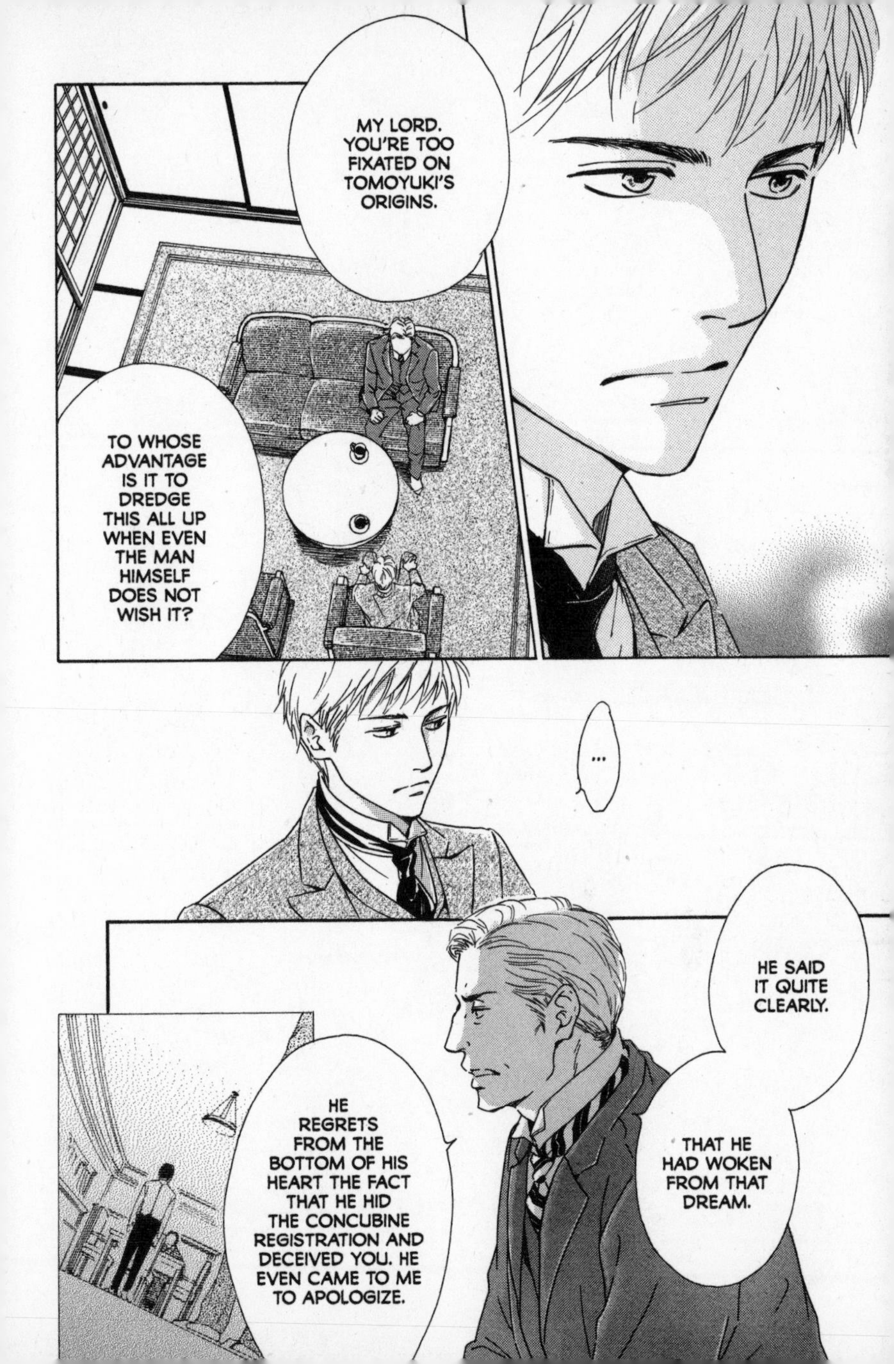
MY LORD. YOU'RE TOO FIXATED ON TOMOYUKI'S ORIGINS.
TO WHOSE ADVANTAGE IS IT TO DREDGE THIS ALL UP WHEN EVEN THE MAN HIMSELF DOES NOT WISH IT?
...
HE SAID IT QUITE CLEARLY.
THAT HE HAD WOKEN FROM THAT DREAM.
HE REGRETS FROM THE BOTTOM OF HIS HEART THE FACT THAT HE HID THE CONCUBINE REGISTRATION AND DECEIVED YOU. HE EVEN CAME TO ME TO APOLOGIZE.

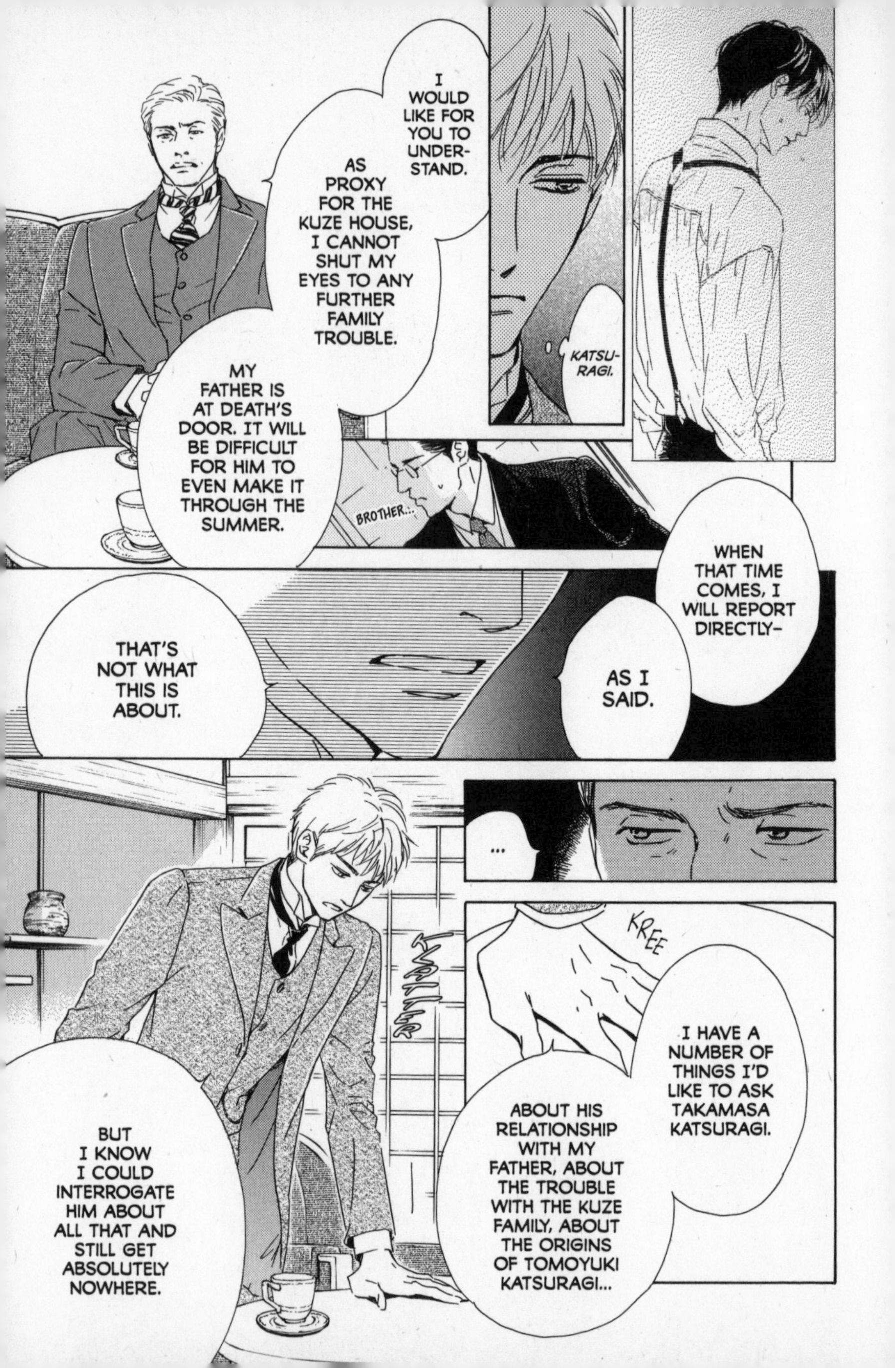
I WOULD LIKE FOR YOU TO UNDER-STAND.
KATSU-RAGI.
AS PROXY FOR THE KUZE HOUSE, I CANNOT SHUT MY EYES TO ANY FURTHER FAMILY TROUBLE.
MY FATHER IS AT DEATH'S DOOR. IT WILL BE DIFFICULT FOR HIM TO EVEN MAKE IT THROUGH THE SUMMER.
BROTHER...
WHEN THAT TIME COMES, I WILL REPORT DIRECTLY-
AS I SAID.
THAT'S NOT WHAT THIS IS ABOUT.
...
KREE
I HAVE A NUMBER OF THINGS I'D LIKE TO ASK TAKAMASA KATSURAGI.
ABOUT HIS RELATIONSHIP WITH MY FATHER, ABOUT THE TROUBLE WITH THE KUZE FAMILY, ABOUT THE ORIGINS OF TOMOYUKI KATSURAGI...
BUT I KNOW I COULD INTERROGATE HIM ABOUT ALL THAT AND STILL GET ABSOLUTELY NOWHERE.

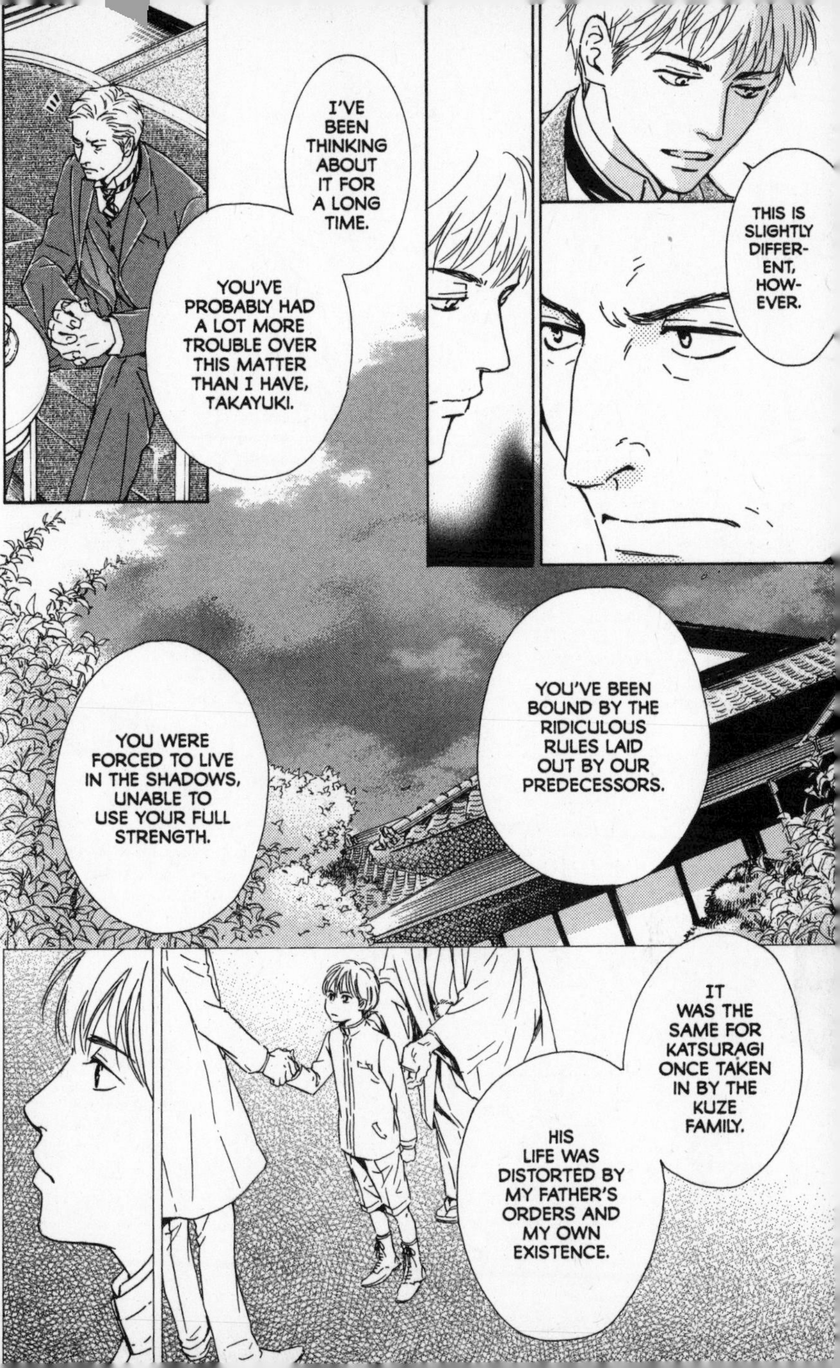
THIS IS SLIGHTLY DIFFERENT, HOWEVER.
I'VE BEEN THINKING ABOUT IT FOR A LONG TIME.
YOU'VE PROBABLY HAD A LOT MORE TROUBLE OVER THIS MATTER THAN I HAVE, TAKAYUKI.
YOU'VE BEEN BOUND BY THE RIDICULOUS RULES LAID OUT BY OUR PREDECESSORS.
YOU WERE FORCED TO LIVE IN THE SHADOWS, UNABLE TO USE YOUR FULL STRENGTH.
IT WAS THE SAME FOR KATSURAGI ONCE TAKEN IN BY THE KUZE FAMILY.
HIS LIFE WAS DISTORTED BY MY FATHER'S ORDERS AND MY OWN EXISTENCE.

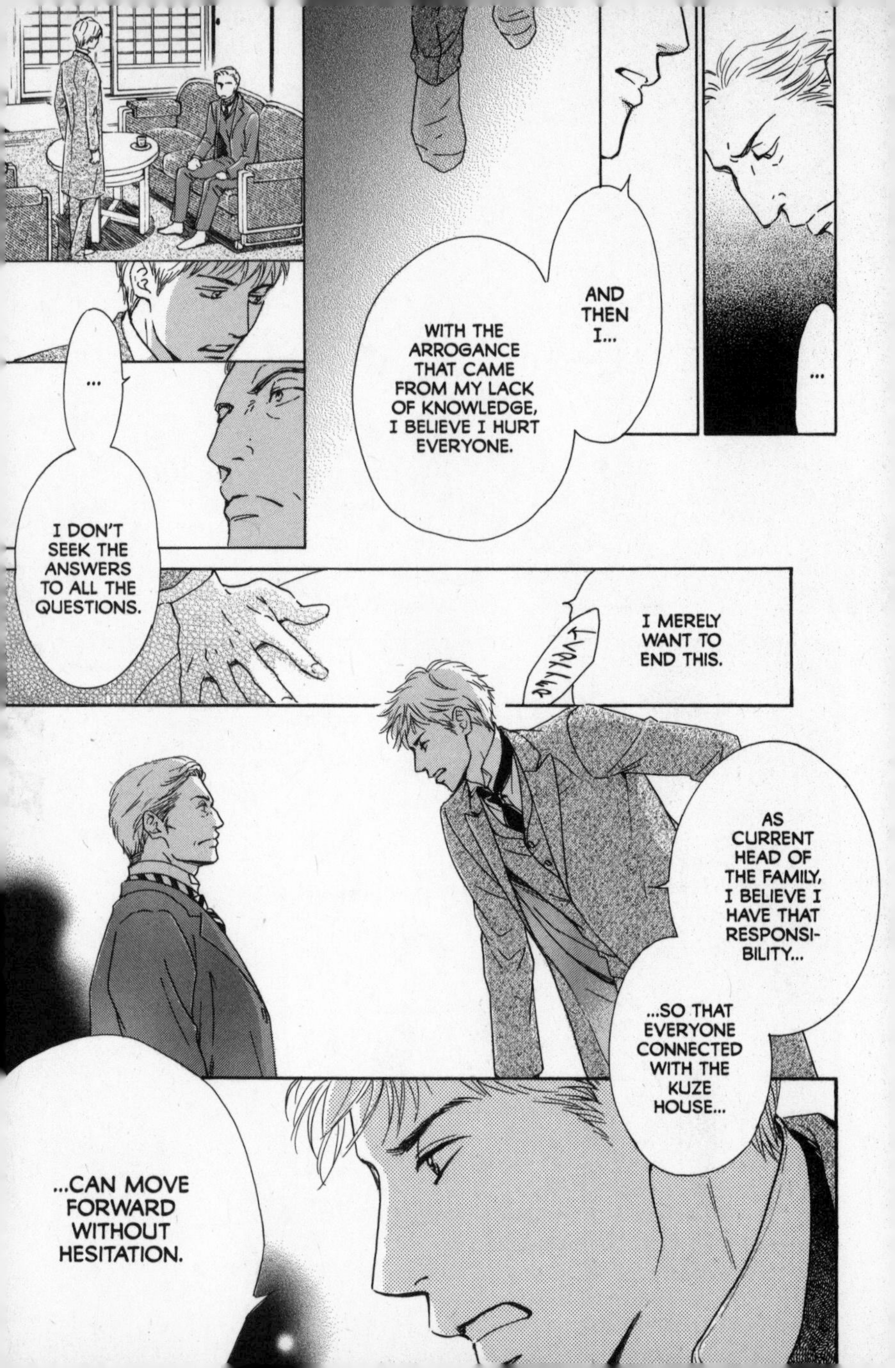
...
AND THEN I...
WITH THE ARROGANCE THAT CAME FROM MY LACK OF KNOWLEDGE, I BELIEVE I HURT EVERYONE.
...
I DON'T SEEK THE ANSWERS TO ALL THE QUESTIONS.
I MERELY WANT TO END THIS.
AS CURRENT HEAD OF THE FAMILY, I BELIEVE I HAVE THAT RESPONSI-BILITY...
...SO THAT EVERYONE CONNECTED WITH THE KUZE HOUSE...
...CAN MOVE FORWARD WITHOUT HESITATION.

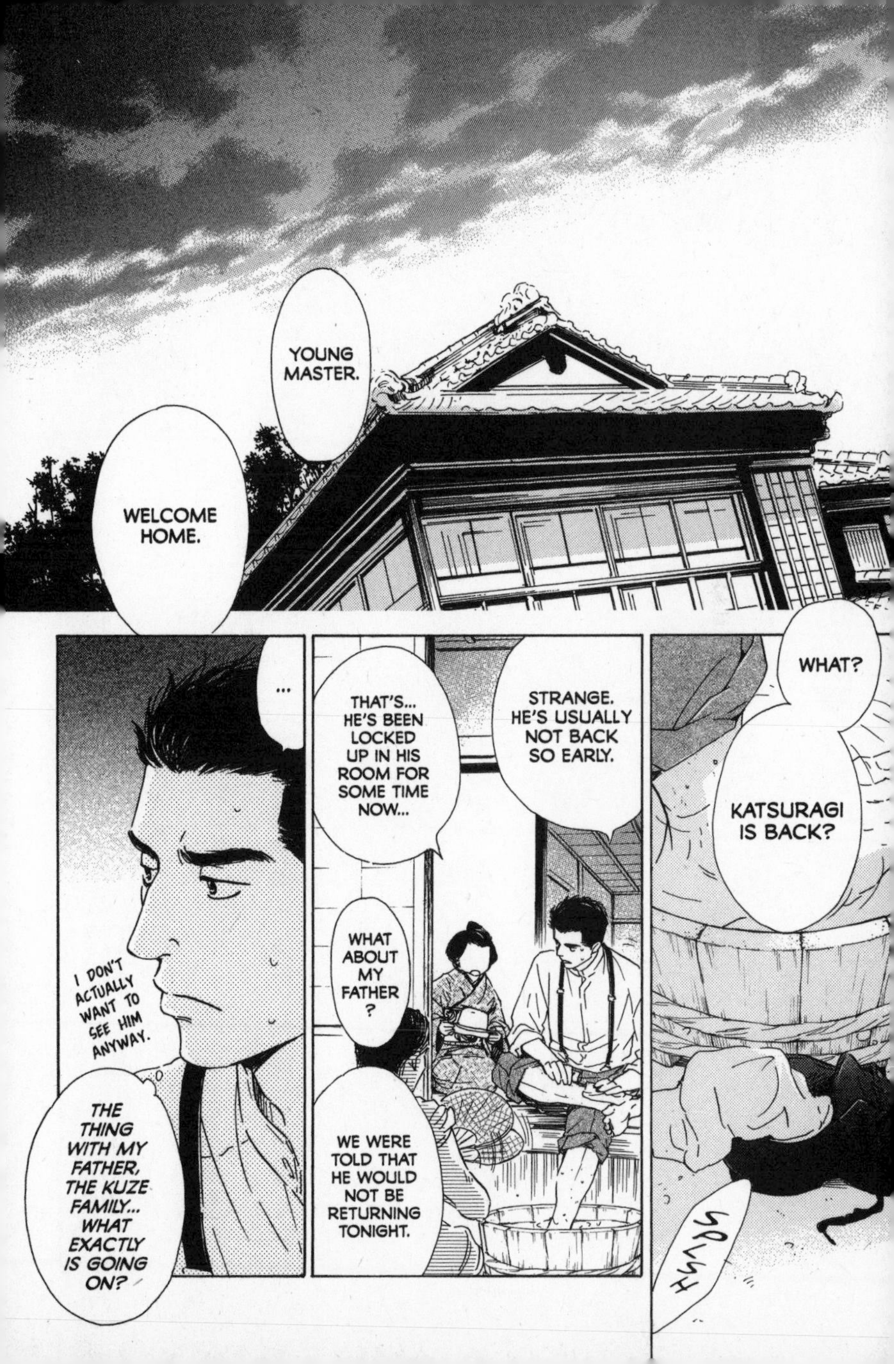
YOUNG MASTER.
WELCOME HOME.
WHAT?
KATSURAGI IS BACK?
SPLASH
STRANGE. HE'S USUALLY NOT BACK SO EARLY.
THAT'S... HE'S BEEN LOCKED UP IN HIS ROOM FOR SOME TIME NOW...
WHAT ABOUT MY FATHER?
WE WERE TOLD THAT HE WOULD NOT BE RETURNING TONIGHT.
...
I DON'T ACTUALLY WANT TO SEE HIM ANYWAY.
THE THING WITH MY FATHER, THE KUZE FAMILY... WHAT EXACTLY IS GOING ON?

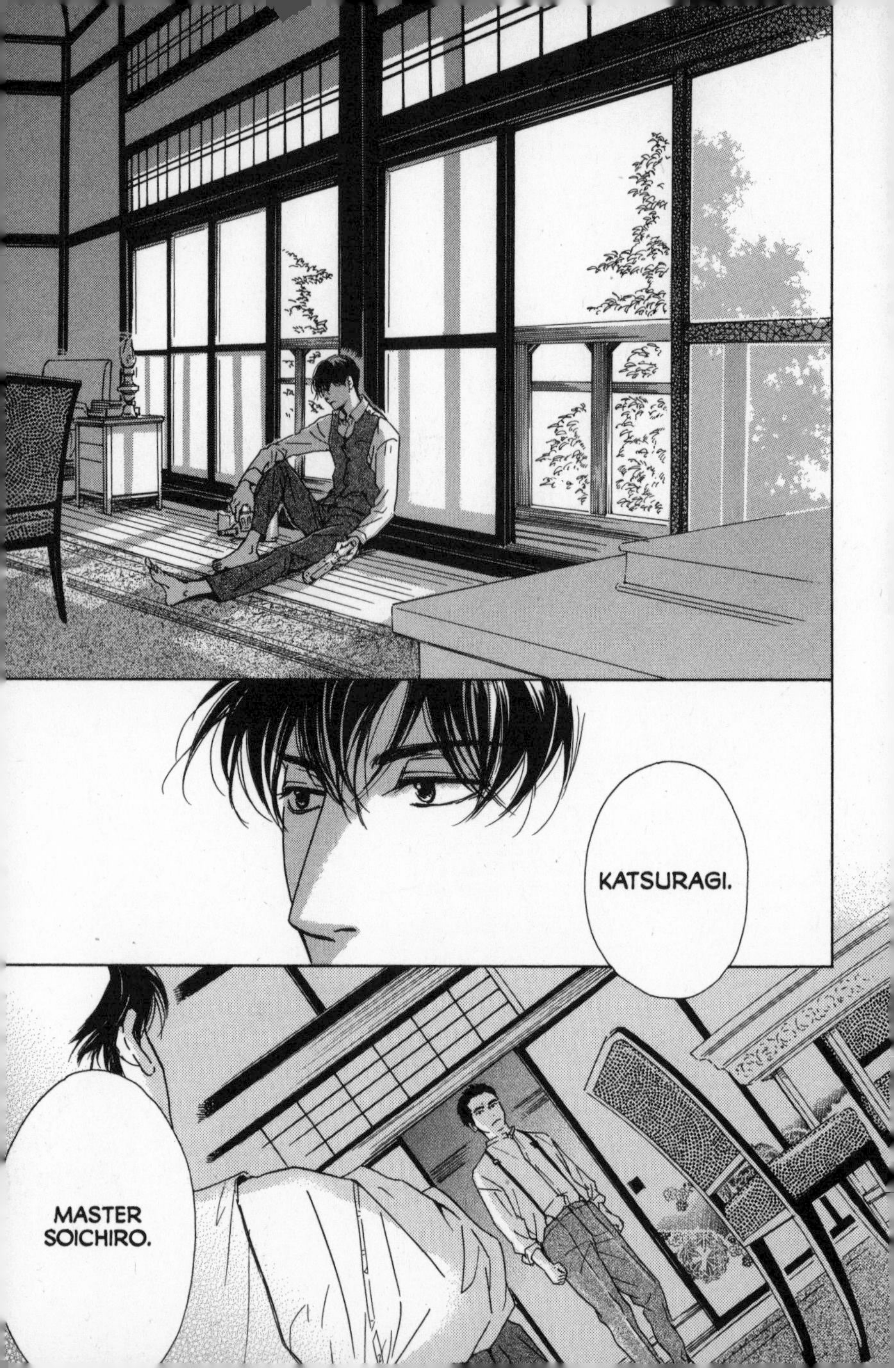
KATSURAGI.
MASTER SOICHIRO.

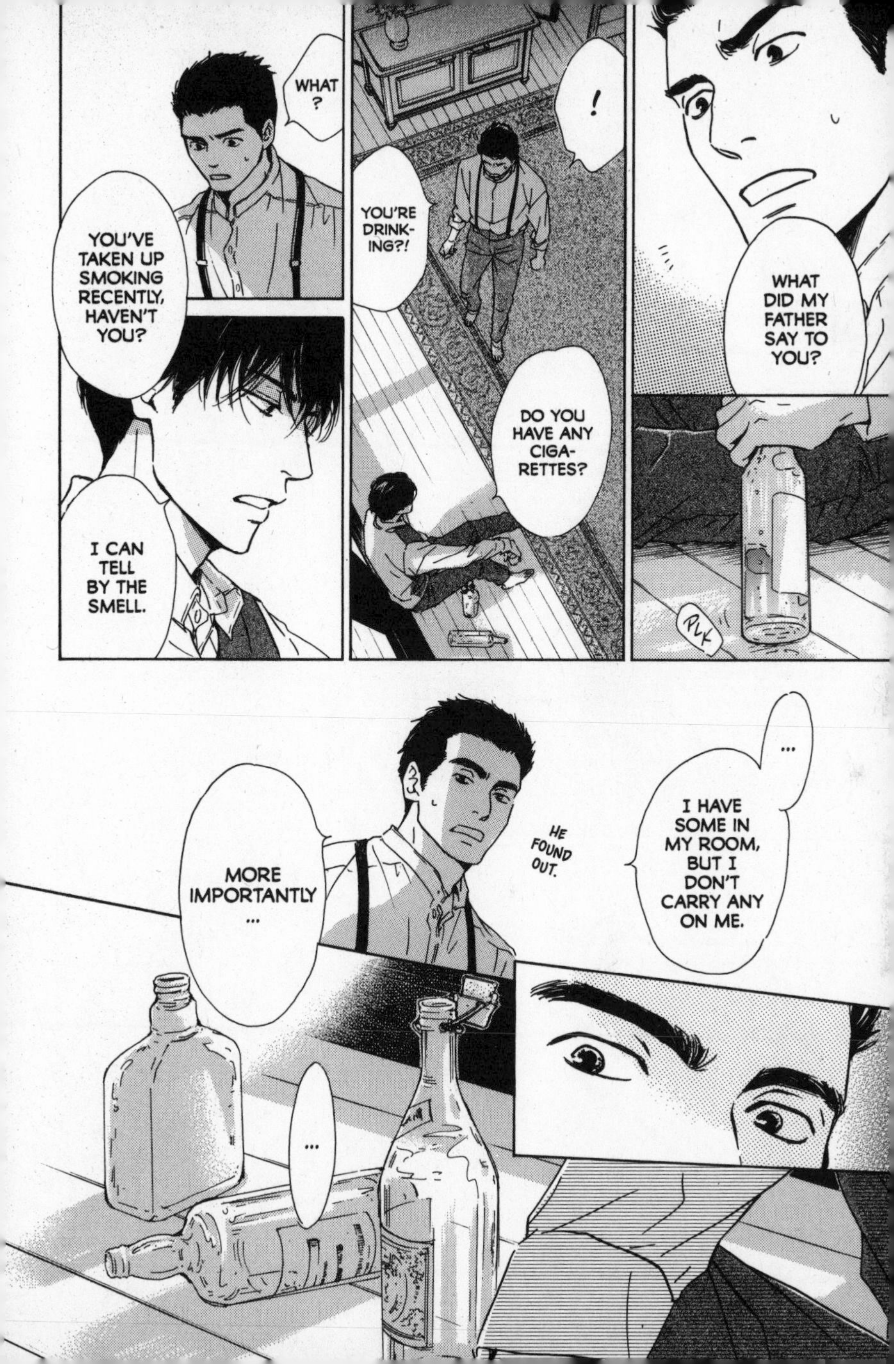
WHAT DID MY FATHER SAY TO YOU?
PLK
!
YOU'RE DRINKING?!
DO YOU HAVE ANY CIGARETTES?
WHAT ?
YOU'VE TAKEN UP SMOKING RECENTLY, HAVEN'T YOU?
I CAN TELL BY THE SMELL.
...
I HAVE SOME IN MY ROOM, BUT I DON'T CARRY ANY ON ME.
HE FOUND OUT.
MORE IMPORTANTLY ...
...

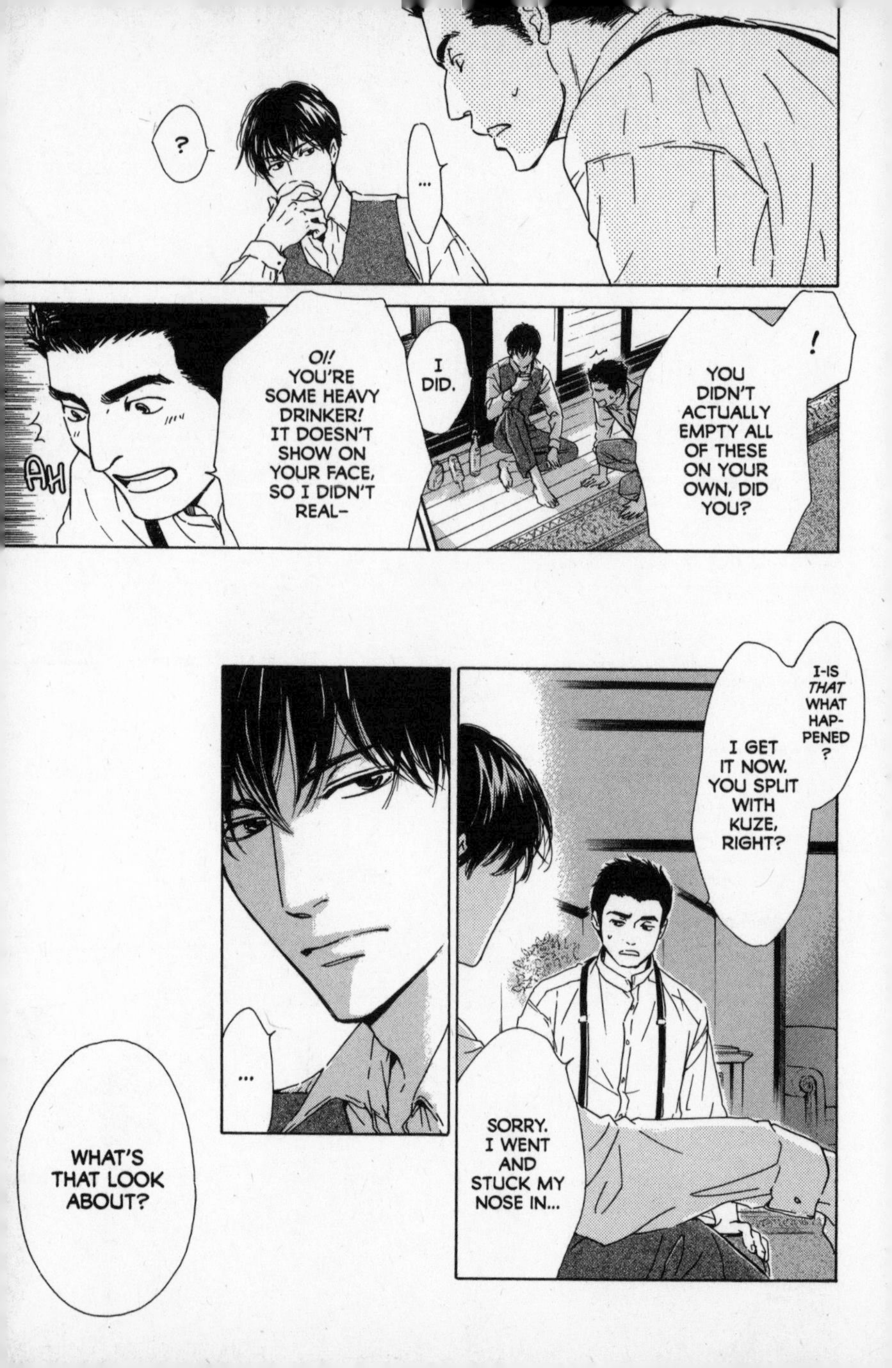
...
?
!
YOU DIDN'T ACTUALLY EMPTY ALL OF THESE ON YOUR OWN, DID YOU?
I DID.
OI! YOU'RE SOME HEAVY DRINKER! IT DOESN'T SHOW ON YOUR FACE, SO I DIDN'T REAL–
AH
I-IS *THAT* WHAT HAP-PENED?
I GET IT NOW. YOU SPLIT WITH KUZE, RIGHT?
SORRY. I WENT AND STUCK MY NOSE IN...
...
WHAT'S THAT LOOK ABOUT?

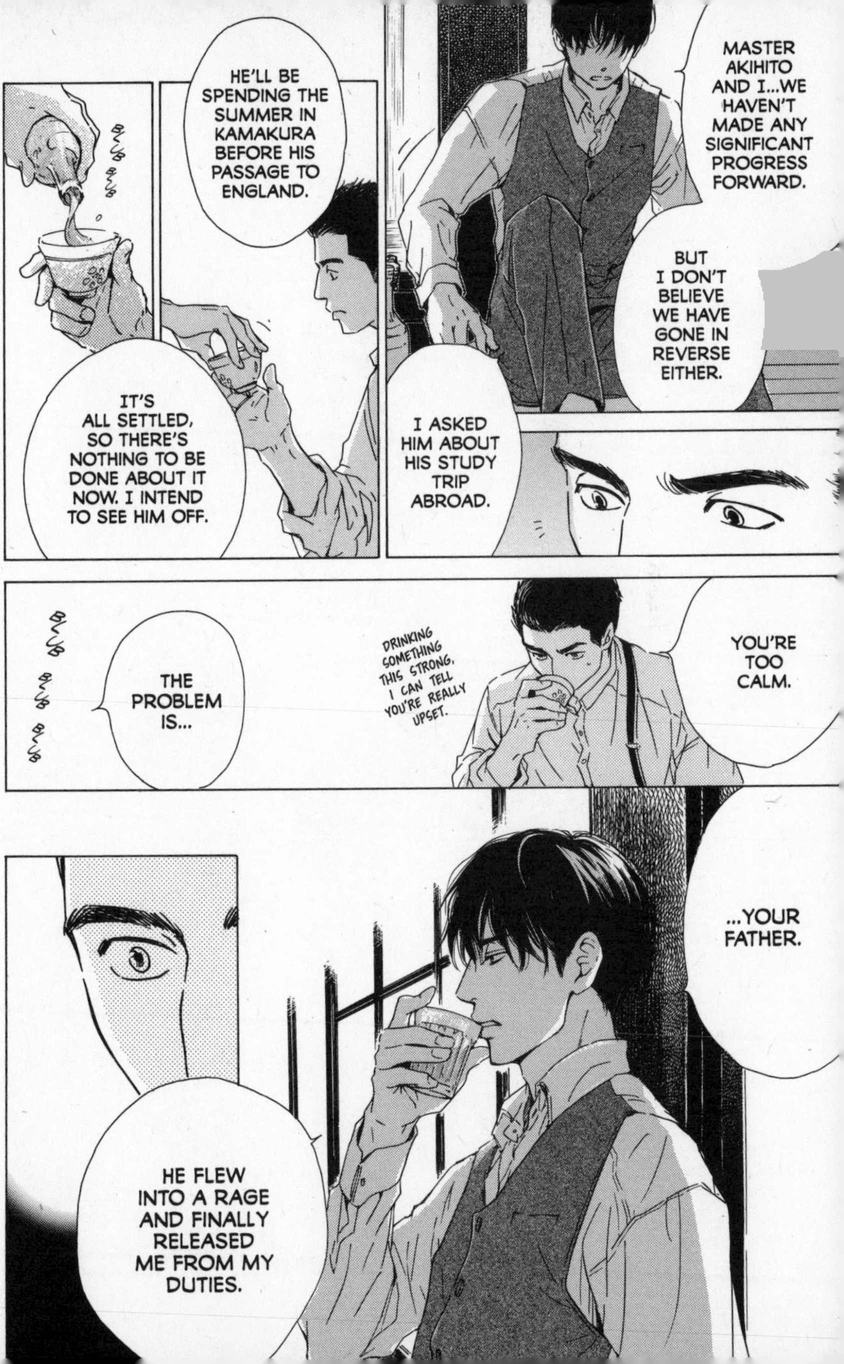
MASTER AKIHITO AND I...WE HAVEN'T MADE ANY SIGNIFICANT PROGRESS FORWARD.
BUT I DON'T BELIEVE WE HAVE GONE IN REVERSE EITHER.
I ASKED HIM ABOUT HIS STUDY TRIP ABROAD.
HE'LL BE SPENDING THE SUMMER IN KAMAKURA BEFORE HIS PASSAGE TO ENGLAND.
IT'S ALL SETTLED, SO THERE'S NOTHING TO BE DONE ABOUT IT NOW. I INTEND TO SEE HIM OFF.
YOU'RE TOO CALM.
DRINKING SOMETHING THIS STRONG, I CAN TELL YOU'RE REALLY UPSET.
THE PROBLEM IS...
...YOUR FATHER.
HE FLEW INTO A RAGE AND FINALLY RELEASED ME FROM MY DUTIES.

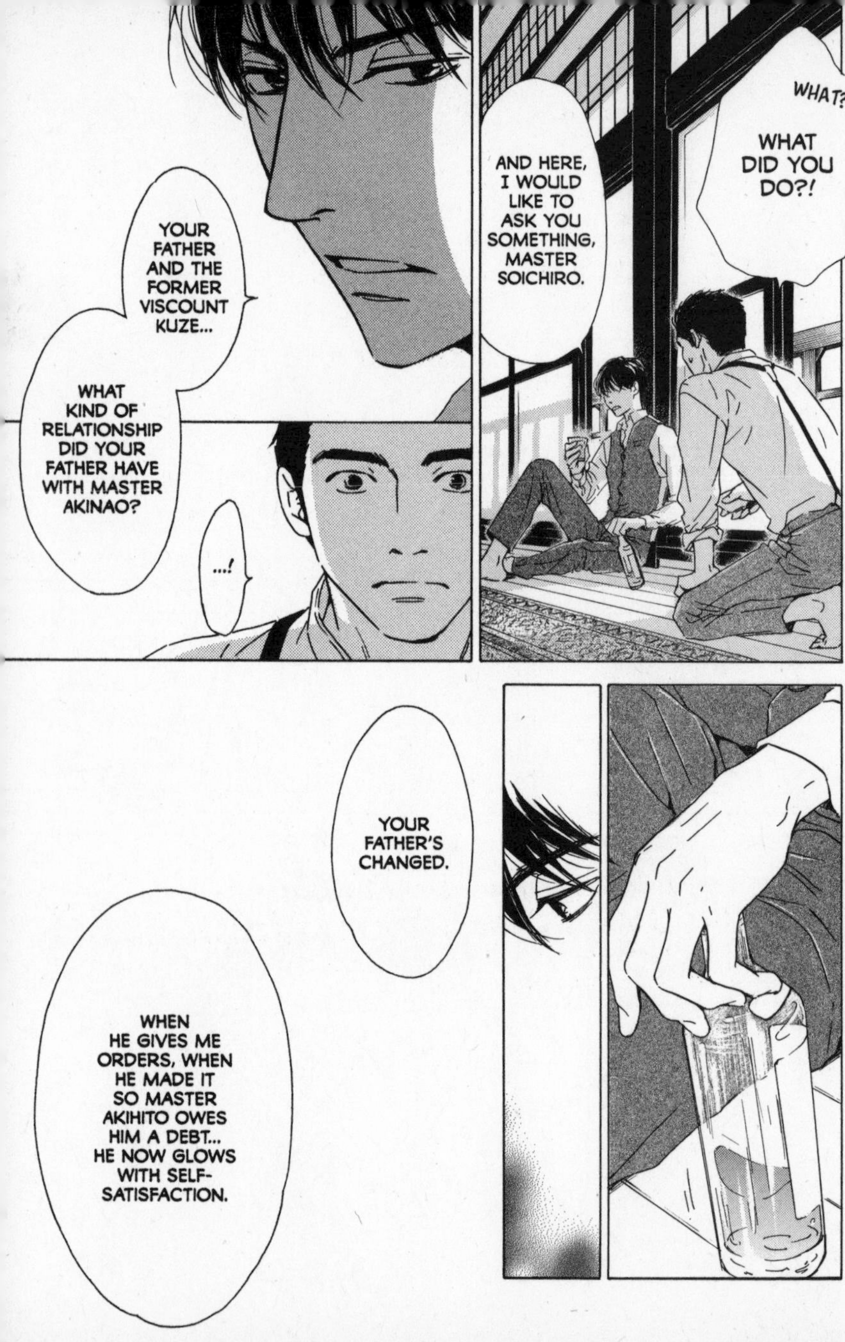
WHAT?!
WHAT DID YOU DO?!
AND HERE, I WOULD LIKE TO ASK YOU SOMETHING, MASTER SOICHIRO.
YOUR FATHER AND THE FORMER VISCOUNT KUZE...
WHAT KIND OF RELATIONSHIP DID YOUR FATHER HAVE WITH MASTER AKINAO?
...!
YOUR FATHER'S CHANGED.
WHEN HE GIVES ME ORDERS, WHEN HE MADE IT SO MASTER AKIHITO OWES HIM A DEBT... HE NOW GLOWS WITH SELF-SATISFACTION.

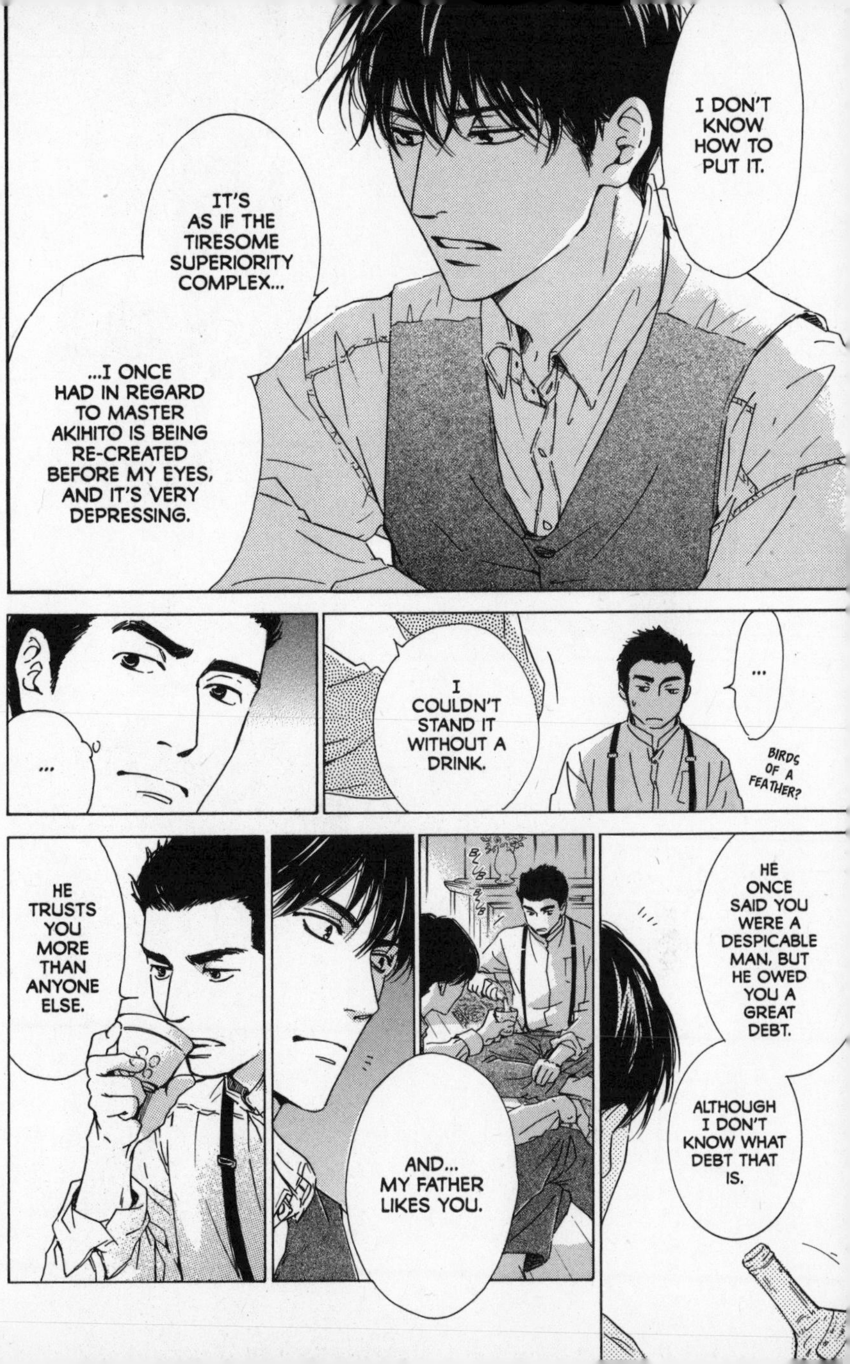
I DON'T KNOW HOW TO PUT IT.
IT'S AS IF THE TIRESOME SUPERIORITY COMPLEX...
...I ONCE HAD IN REGARD TO MASTER AKIHITO IS BEING RE-CREATED BEFORE MY EYES, AND IT'S VERY DEPRESSING.
...
I COULDN'T STAND IT WITHOUT A DRINK.
BIRDS OF A FEATHER?
...
HE ONCE SAID YOU WERE A DESPICABLE MAN, BUT HE OWED YOU A GREAT DEBT.
ALTHOUGH I DON'T KNOW WHAT DEBT THAT IS.
BLUB
BLUB
AND... MY FATHER LIKES YOU.
HE TRUSTS YOU MORE THAN ANYONE ELSE.

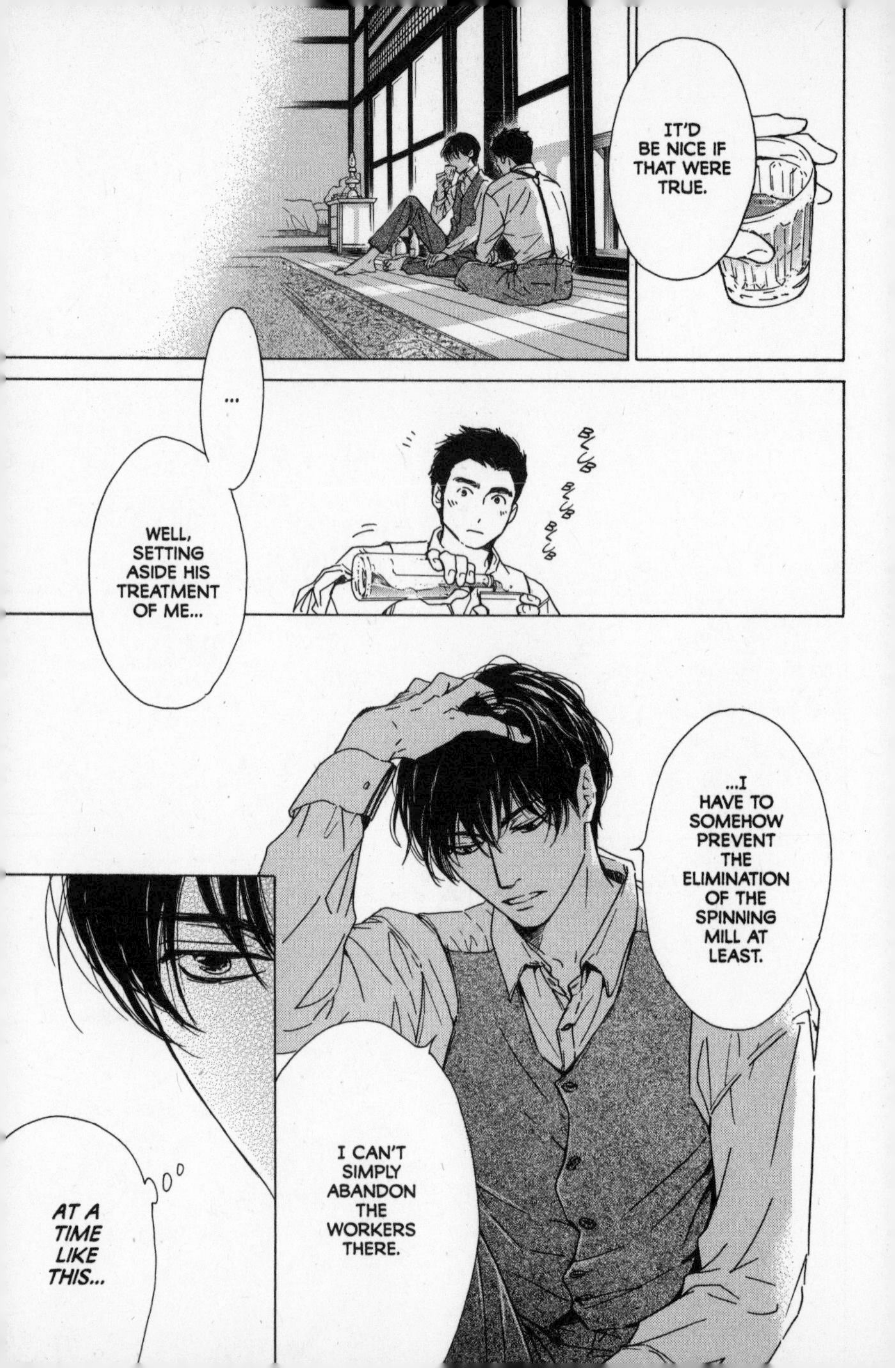
IT'D BE NICE IF THAT WERE TRUE.
BLUB
BLUB
BLUB
...
WELL, SETTING ASIDE HIS TREATMENT OF ME...
...I HAVE TO SOMEHOW PREVENT THE ELIMINATION OF THE SPINNING MILL AT LEAST.
I CAN'T SIMPLY ABANDON THE WORKERS THERE.
AT A TIME LIKE THIS...

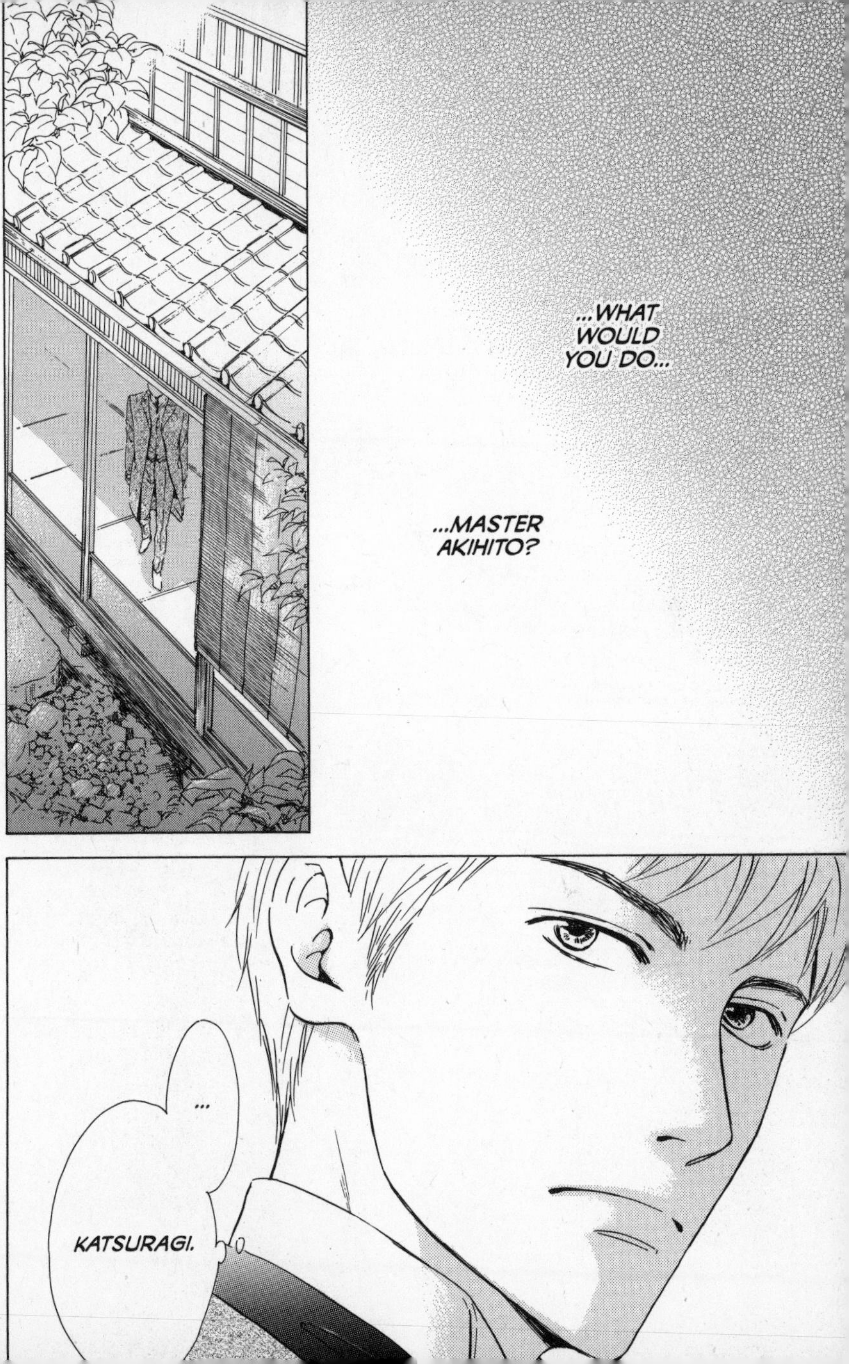
...WHAT WOULD YOU DO...
...MASTER AKIHITO?
...
KATSURAGI.

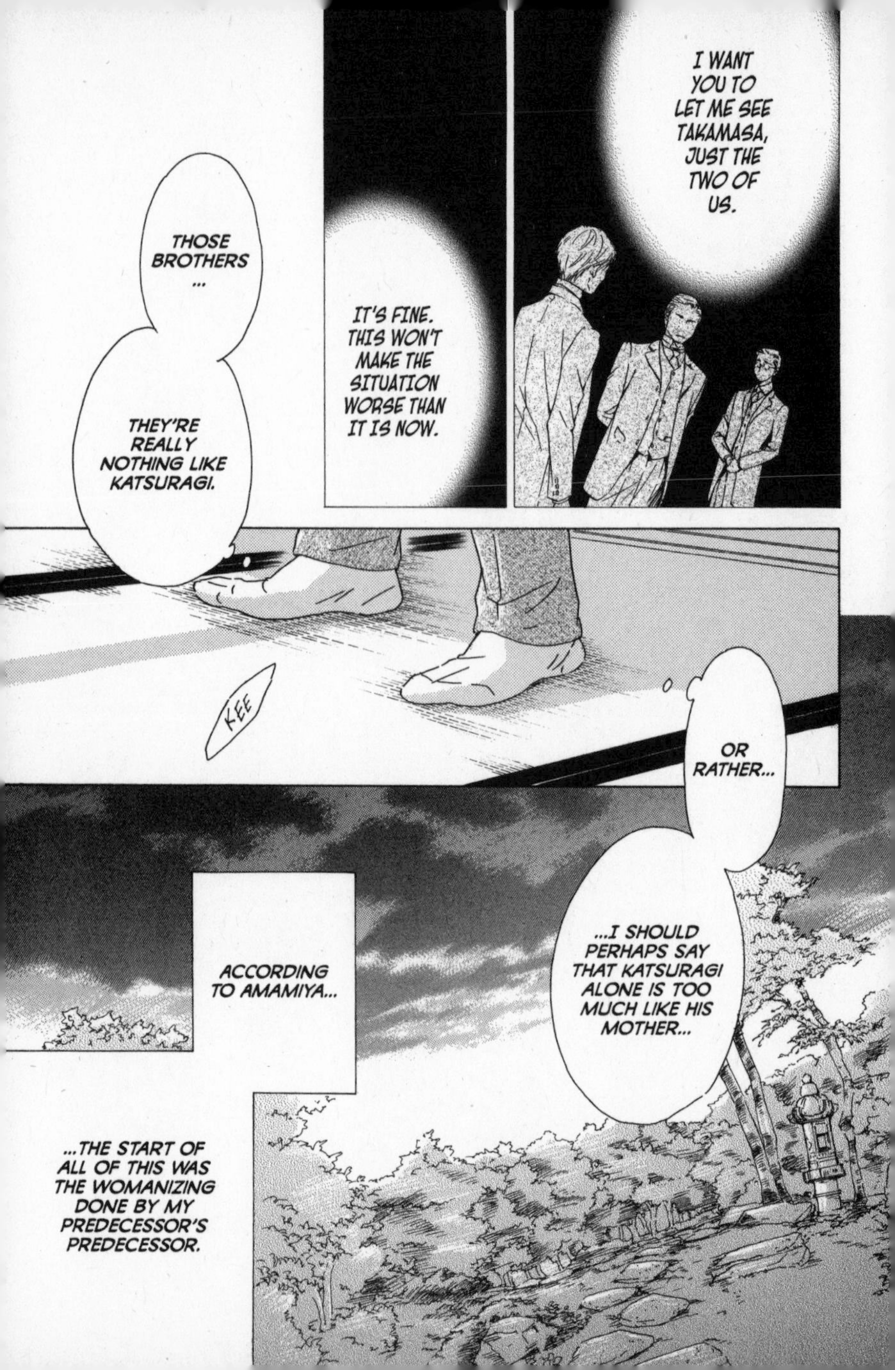
I WANT YOU TO LET ME SEE TAKAMASA, JUST THE TWO OF US.
IT'S FINE. THIS WON'T MAKE THE SITUATION WORSE THAN IT IS NOW.
THOSE BROTHERS ...
THEY'RE REALLY NOTHING LIKE KATSURAGI.
KEE
OR RATHER...
...I SHOULD PERHAPS SAY THAT KATSURAGI ALONE IS TOO MUCH LIKE HIS MOTHER...
ACCORDING TO AMAMIYA...
...THE START OF ALL OF THIS WAS THE WOMANIZING DONE BY MY PREDECESSOR'S PREDECESSOR.

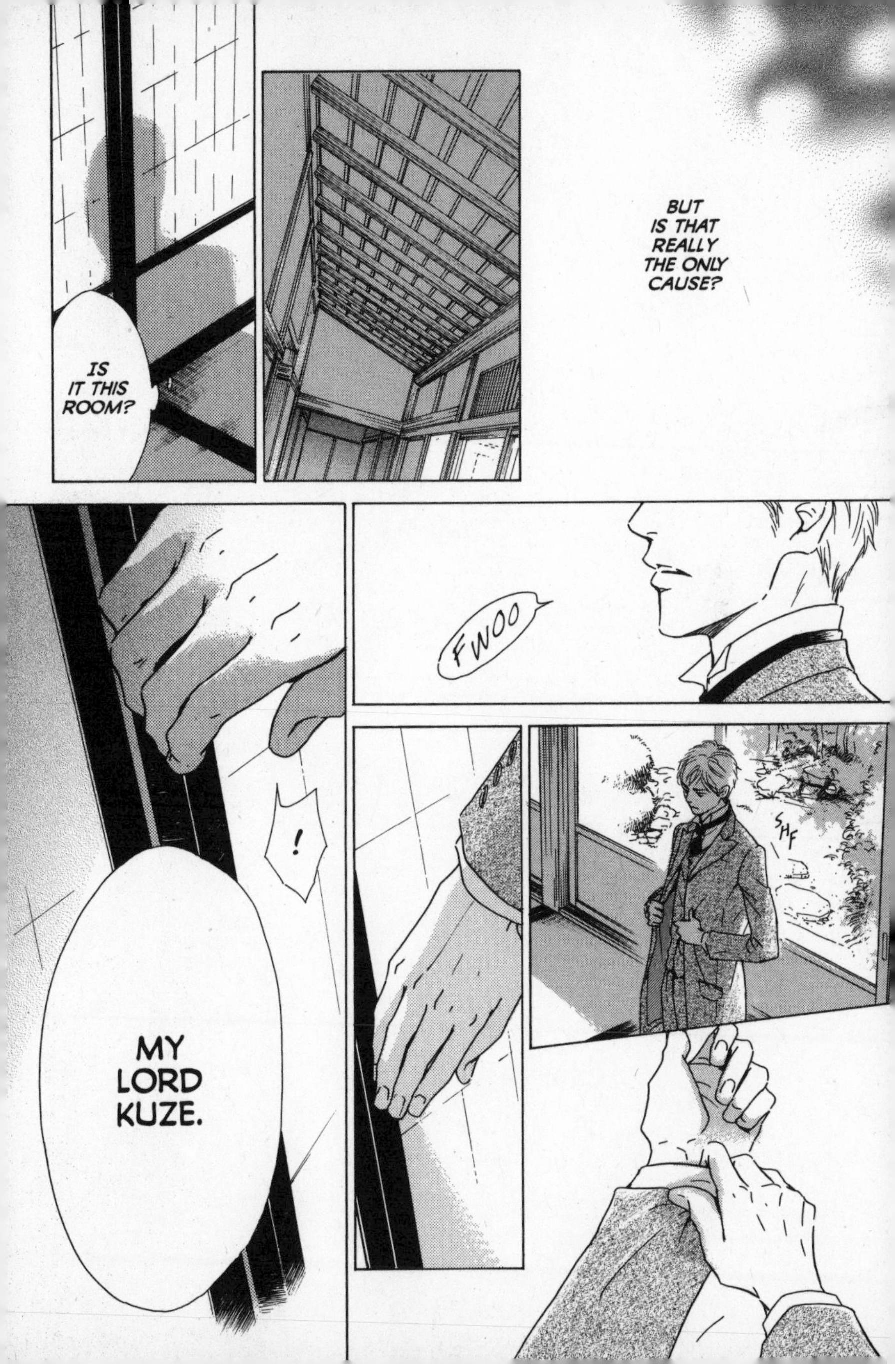
BUT IS THAT REALLY THE ONLY CAUSE?
IS IT THIS ROOM?
FWOO
SHF
!
MY LORD KUZE.

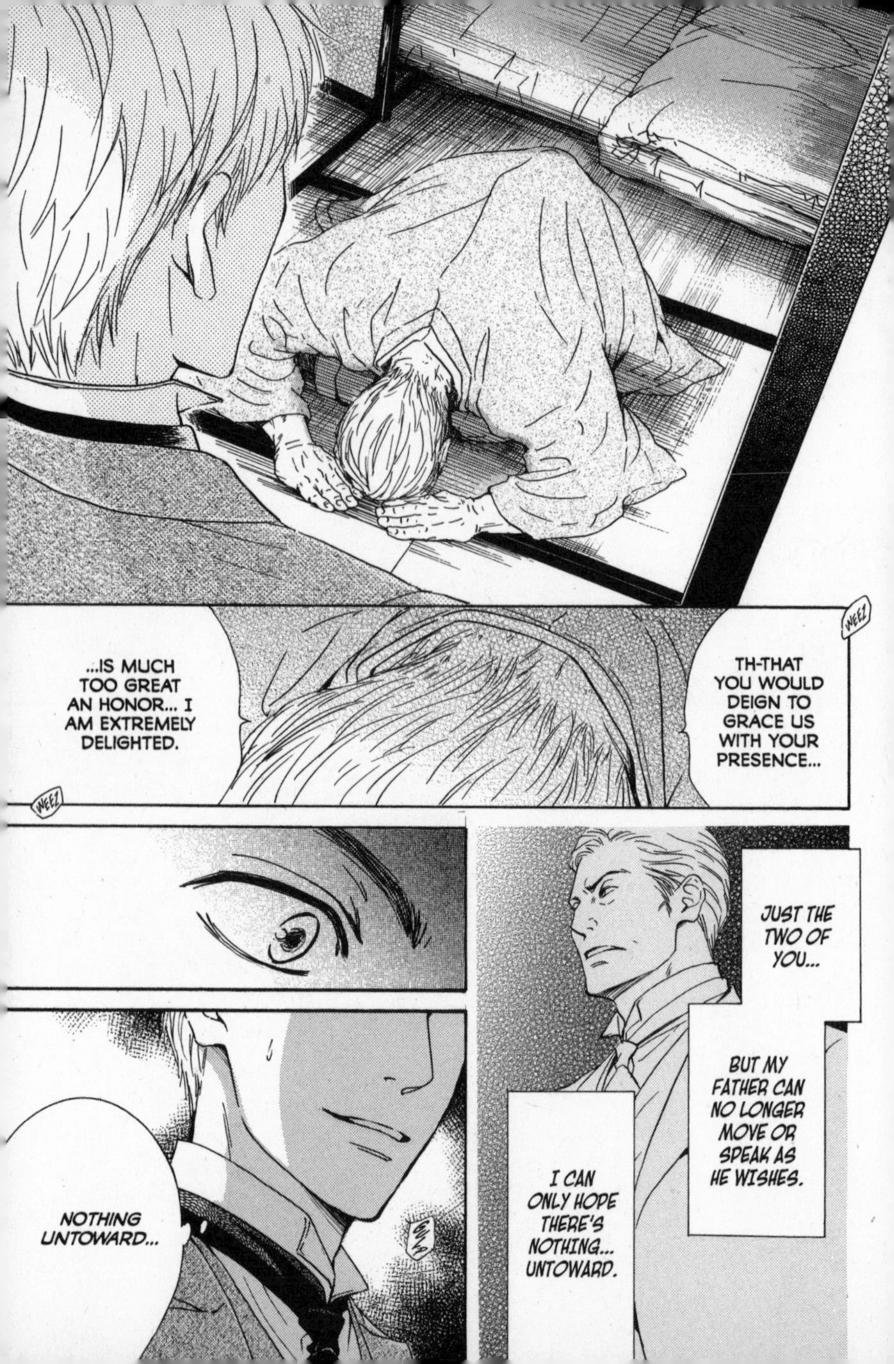
WEEZ
TH-THAT YOU WOULD DEIGN TO GRACE US WITH YOUR PRESENCE...
...IS MUCH TOO GREAT AN HONOR... I AM EXTREMELY DELIGHTED.
WEEZ
JUST THE TWO OF YOU...
BUT MY FATHER CAN NO LONGER MOVE OR SPEAK AS HE WISHES.
I CAN ONLY HOPE THERE'S NOTHING... UNTOWARD.
NOTHING UNTOWARD...

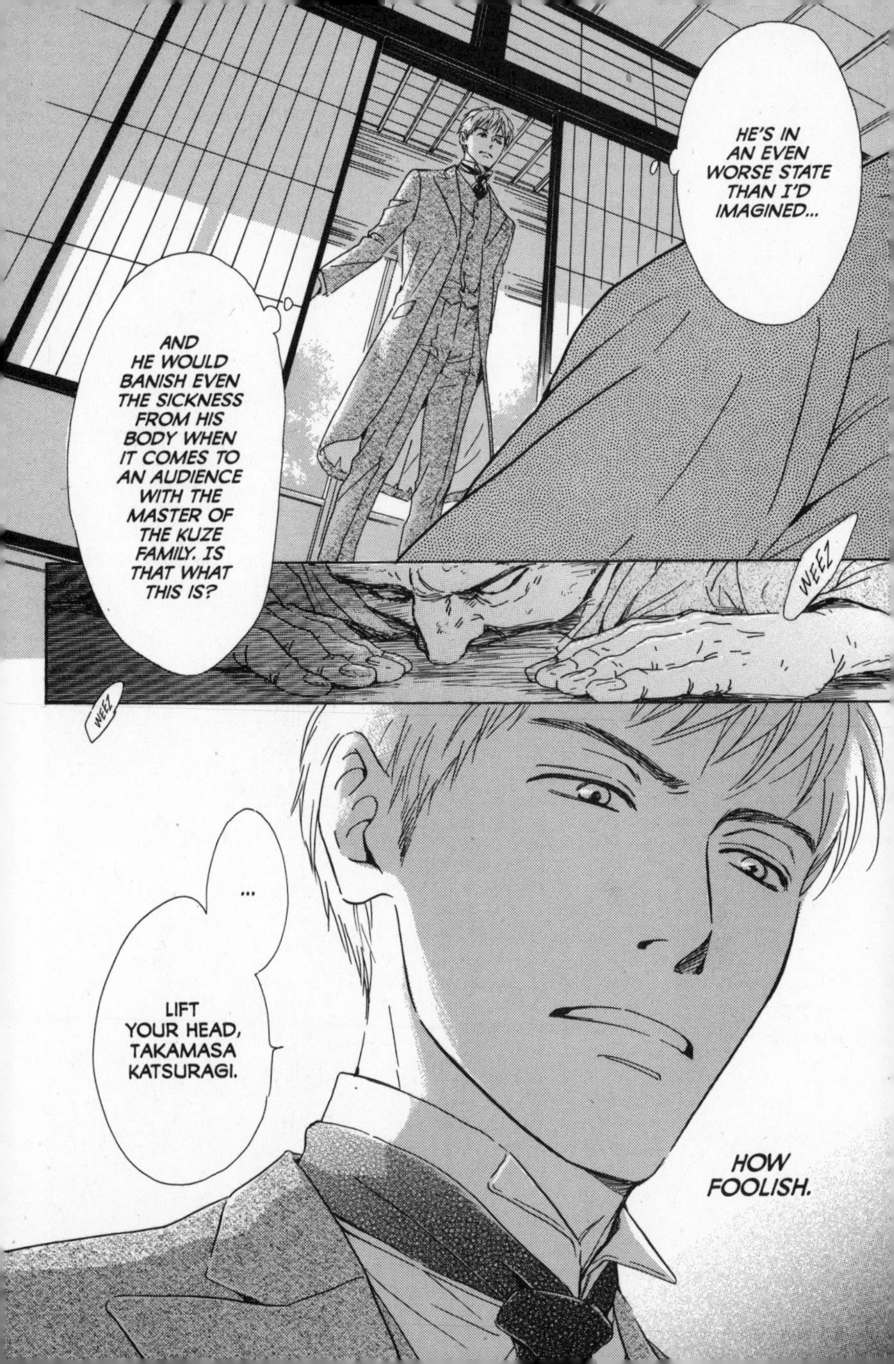
HE'S IN AN EVEN WORSE STATE THAN I'D IMAGINED...
AND HE WOULD BANISH EVEN THE SICKNESS FROM HIS BODY WHEN IT COMES TO AN AUDIENCE WITH THE MASTER OF THE KUZE FAMILY. IS THAT WHAT THIS IS?
WEEZ
WEEZ
...
LIFT YOUR HEAD, TAKAMASA KATSURAGI.
HOW FOOLISH.

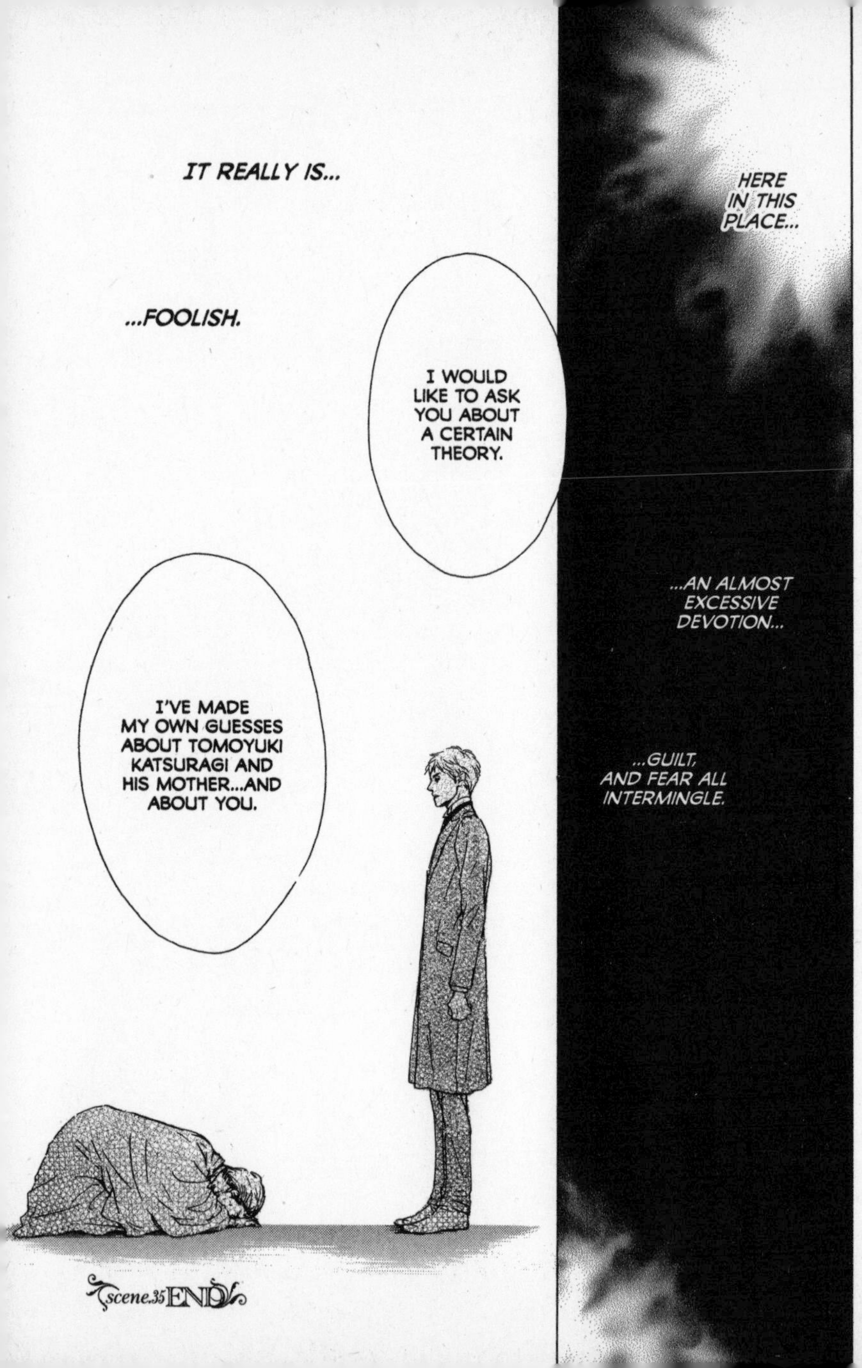
HERE IN THIS PLACE...
...AN ALMOST EXCESSIVE DEVOTION...
...GUILT, AND FEAR ALL INTERMINGLE.
IT REALLY IS...
...FOOLISH.
I WOULD LIKE TO ASK YOU ABOUT A CERTAIN THEORY.
I'VE MADE MY OWN GUESSES ABOUT TOMOYUKI KATSURAGI AND HIS MOTHER...AND ABOUT YOU.
scene.35 END

憂鬱な朝

Blue Morning

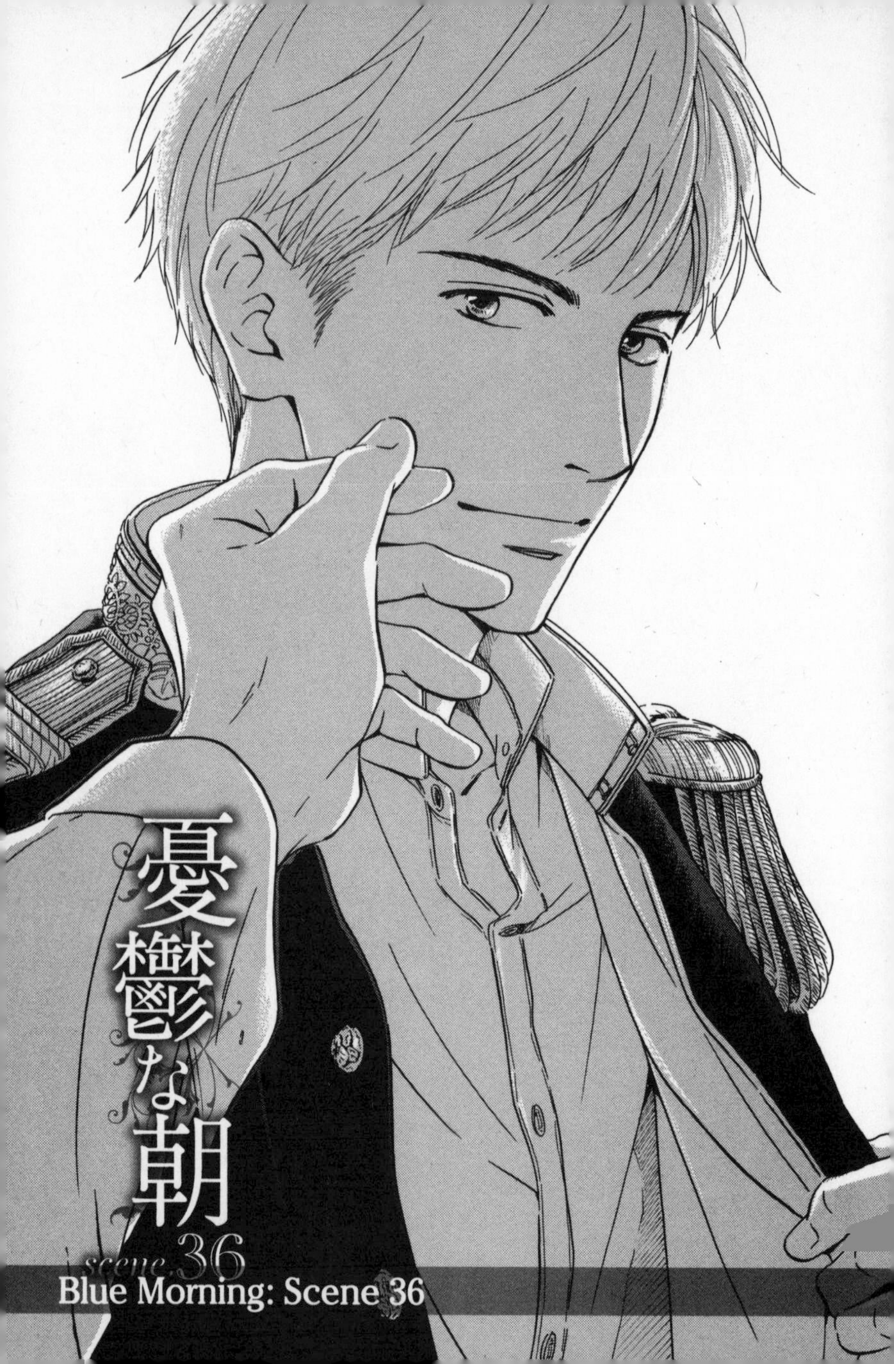
憂鬱な朝
scene.36
Blue Morning: Scene 36

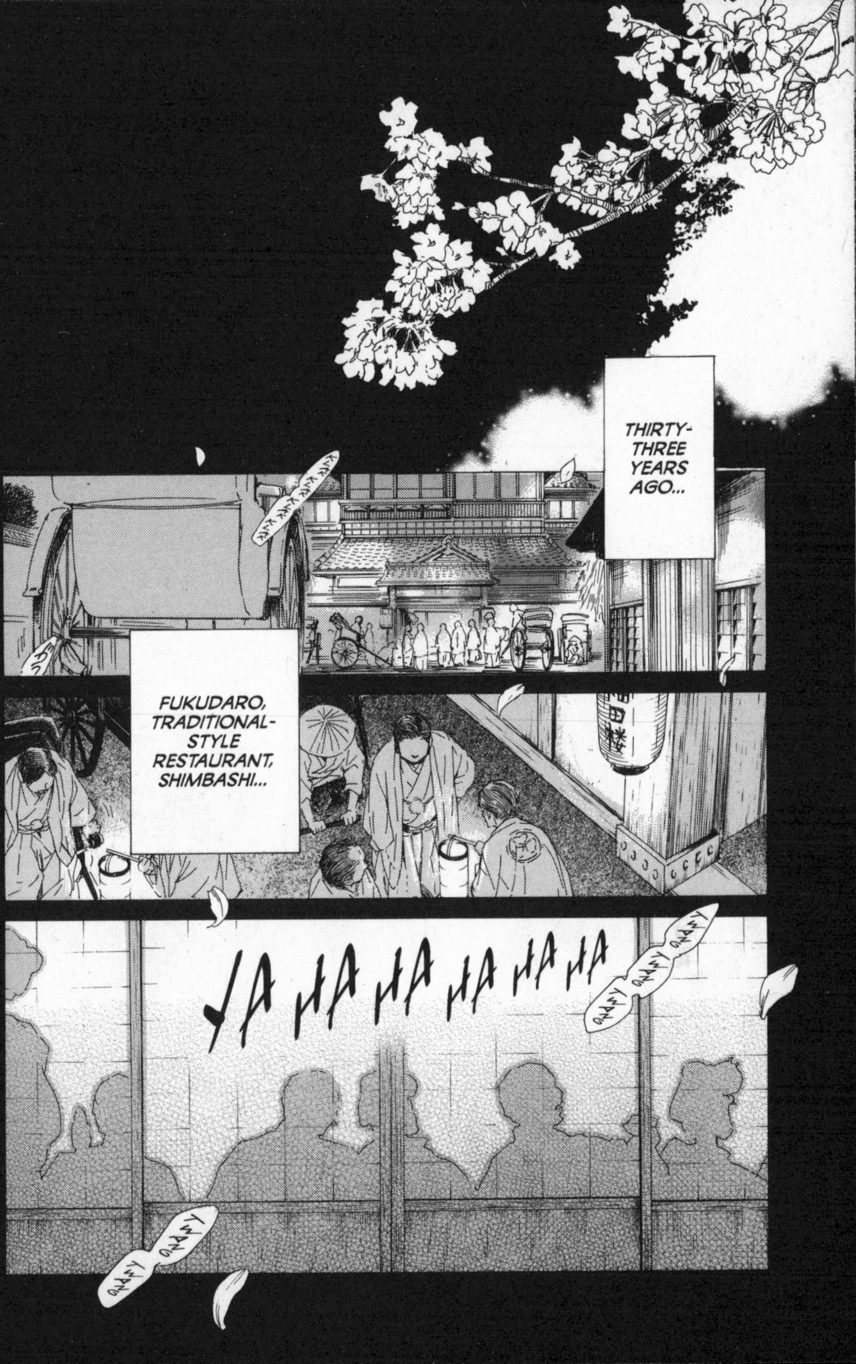
THIRTY-THREE YEARS AGO...
KURK KURK KURK KURK
FUKUDARO, TRADITIONAL-STYLE RESTAURANT, SHIMBASHI...
TWANG TWANG TWANG
YA HA HA HA HA HA
TWANG TWANG

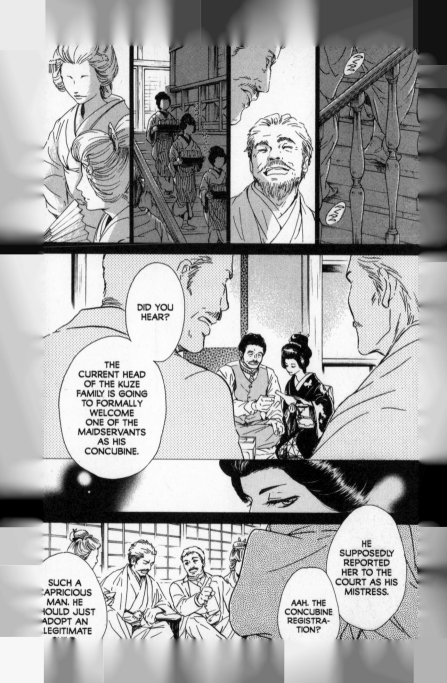

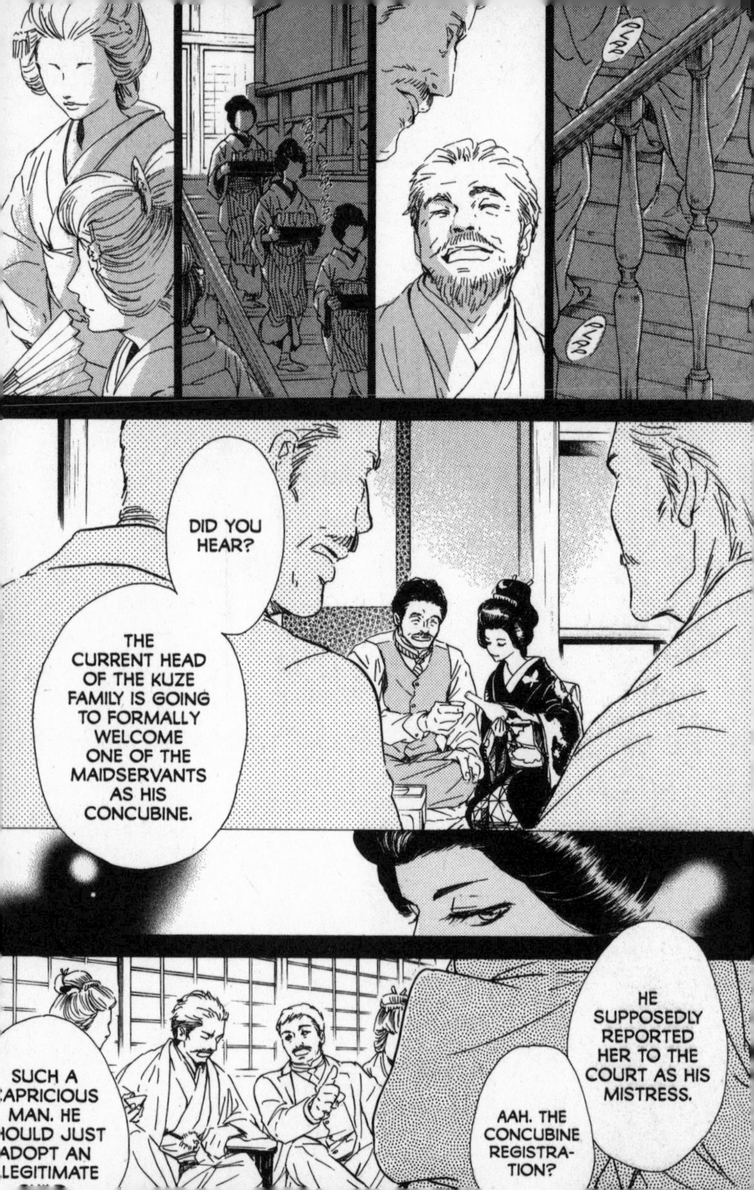
DID YOU HEAR?
THE CURRENT HEAD OF THE KUZE FAMILY IS GOING TO FORMALLY WELCOME ONE OF THE MAIDSERVANTS AS HIS CONCUBINE.
HE SUPPOSEDLY REPORTED HER TO THE COURT AS HIS MISTRESS.
AAH. THE CONCUBINE REGISTRA- TION?
SUCH A APRICIOUS MAN. HE HOULD JUST ADOPT AN LEGITIMATE

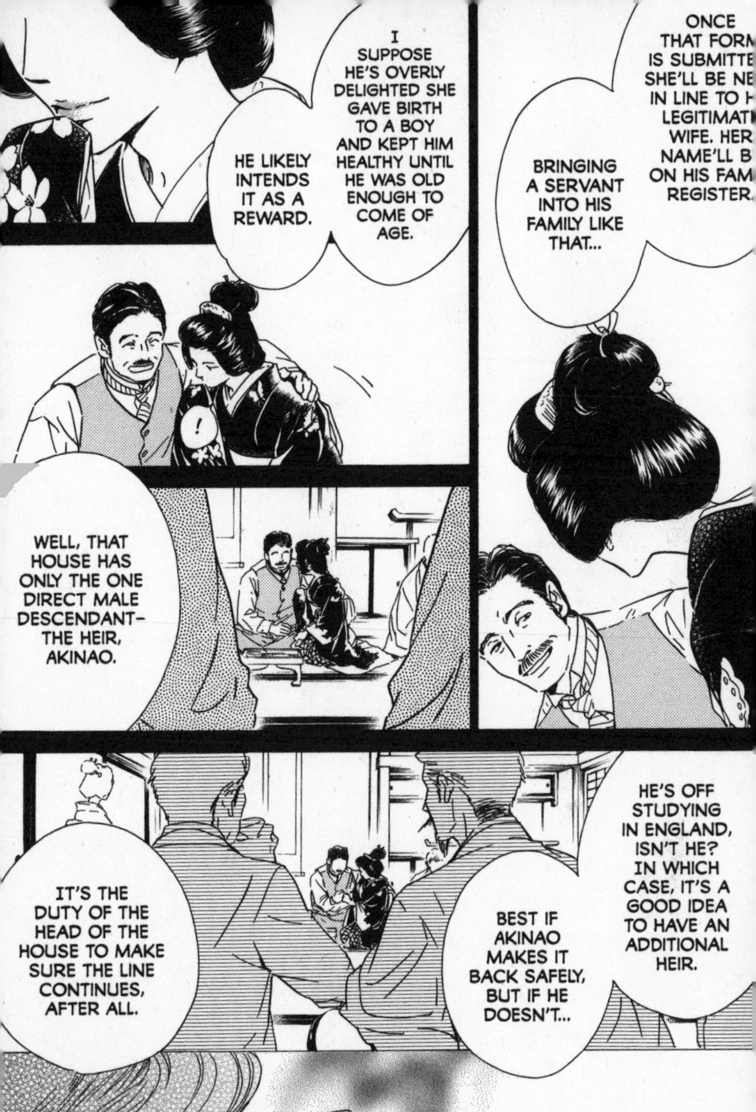
ONCE THAT FORM IS SUBMITTE SHE'LL BE NE IN LINE TO H LEGITIMAT WIFE. HER NAME'LL B ON HIS FAM REGISTER.
BRINGING A SERVANT INTO HIS FAMILY LIKE THAT...
I SUPPOSE HE'S OVERLY DELIGHTED SHE GAVE BIRTH TO A BOY AND KEPT HIM HEALTHY UNTIL HE WAS OLD ENOUGH TO COME OF AGE.
HE LIKELY INTENDS IT AS A REWARD.
!
WELL, THAT HOUSE HAS ONLY THE ONE DIRECT MALE DESCENDANT— THE HEIR, AKINAO.
HE'S OFF STUDYING IN ENGLAND, ISN'T HE? IN WHICH CASE, IT'S A GOOD IDEA TO HAVE AN ADDITIONAL HEIR.
BEST IF AKINAO MAKES IT BACK SAFELY, BUT IF HE DOESN'T...
IT'S THE DUTY OF THE HEAD OF THE HOUSE TO MAKE SURE THE LINE CONTINUES, AFTER ALL.

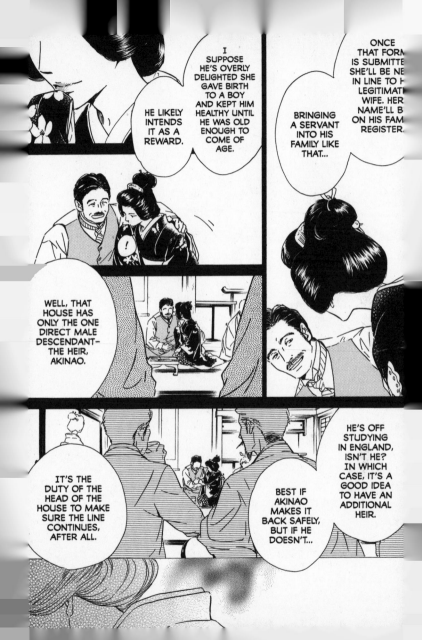

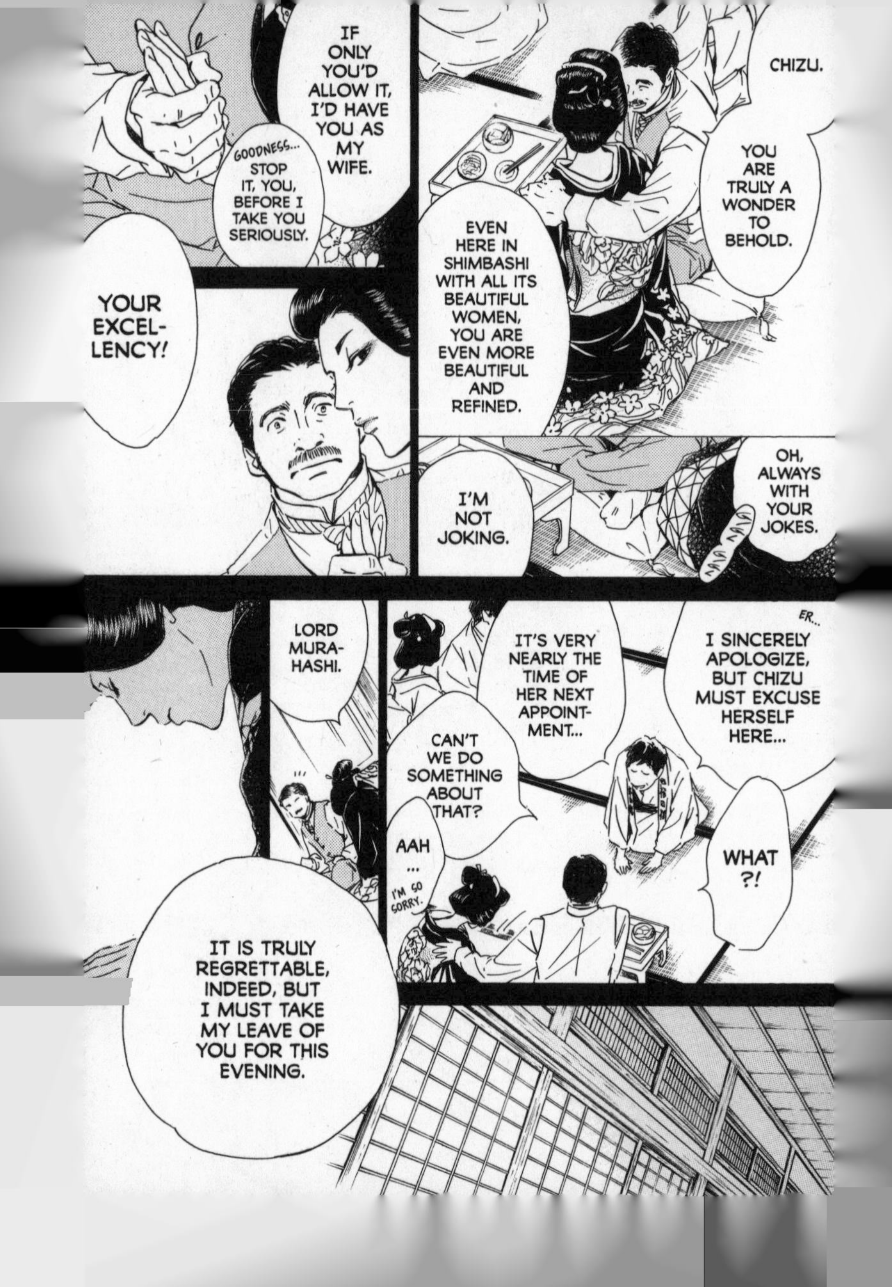
CHIZU.
YOU ARE TRULY A WONDER TO BEHOLD.
EVEN HERE IN SHIMBASHI WITH ALL ITS BEAUTIFUL WOMEN, YOU ARE EVEN MORE BEAUTIFUL AND REFINED.
OH, ALWAYS WITH YOUR JOKES.
I'M NOT JOKING.
IF ONLY YOU'D ALLOW IT, I'D HAVE YOU AS MY WIFE.
GOODNESS... STOP IT, YOU, BEFORE I TAKE YOU SERIOUSLY.
YOUR EXCEL-LENCY!
ER...
I SINCERELY APOLOGIZE, BUT CHIZU MUST EXCUSE HERSELF HERE...
IT'S VERY NEARLY THE TIME OF HER NEXT APPOINT-MENT...
WHAT?!
CAN'T WE DO SOMETHING ABOUT THAT?
AAH...
I'M SO SORRY.
LORD MURA-HASHI.
IT IS TRULY REGRETTABLE, INDEED, BUT I MUST TAKE MY LEAVE OF YOU FOR THIS EVENING.

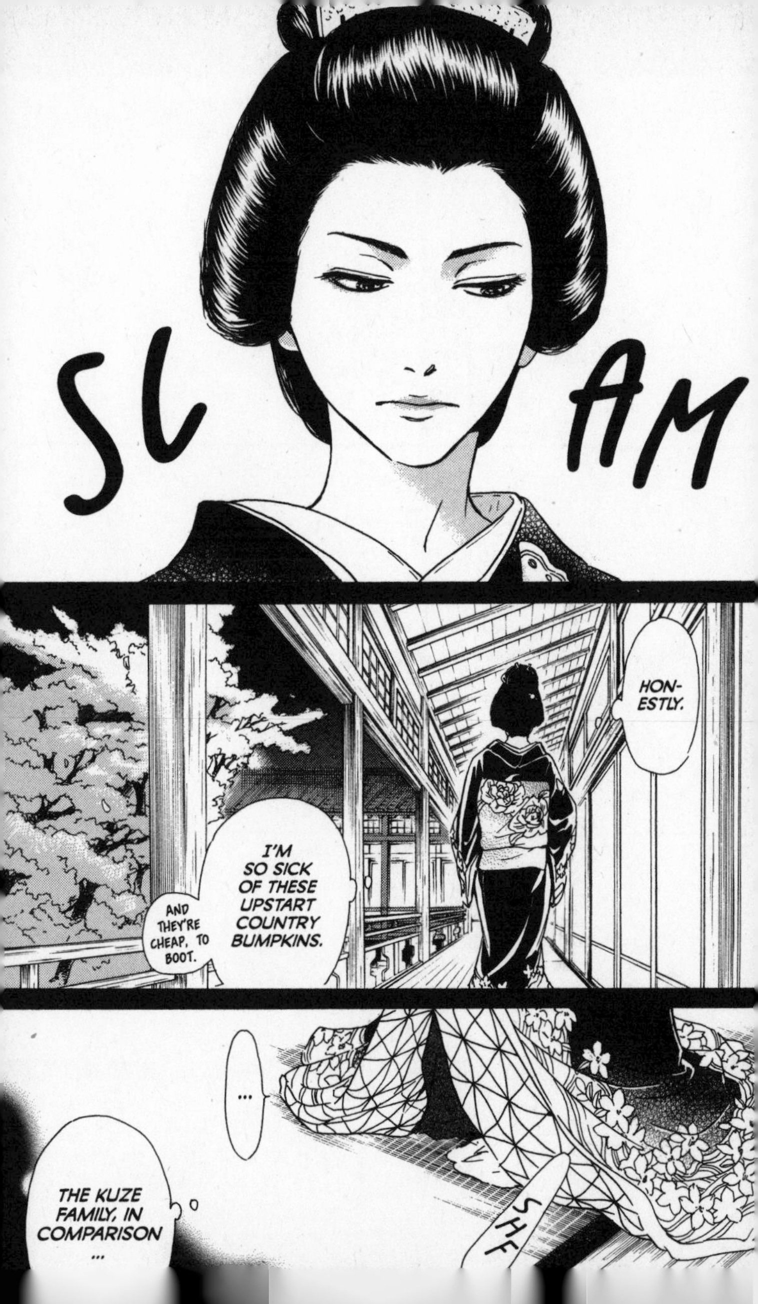
SLAM
HON-ESTLY.
I'M SO SICK OF THESE UPSTART COUNTRY BUMPKINS.
AND THEY'RE CHEAP, TO BOOT.
...
SHF
THE KUZE FAMILY, IN COMPARISON ...

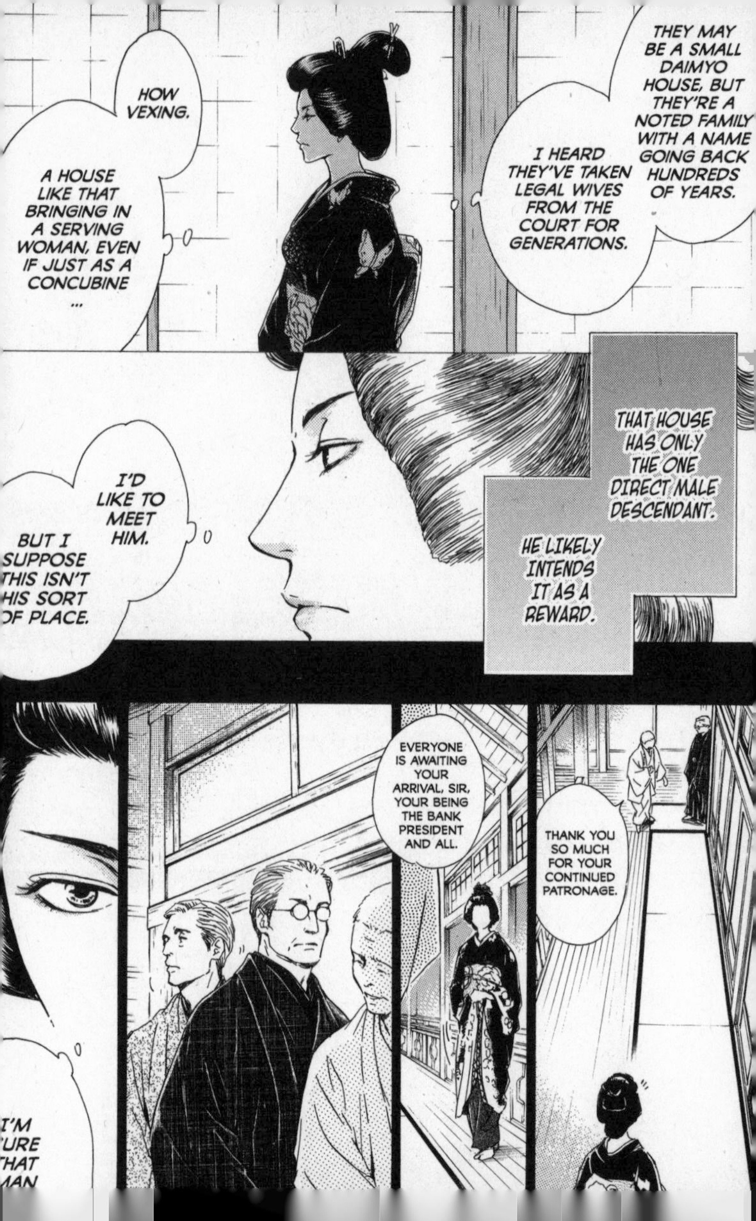
THEY MAY BE A SMALL DAIMYO HOUSE, BUT THEY'RE A NOTED FAMILY WITH A NAME GOING BACK HUNDREDS OF YEARS.
I HEARD THEY'VE TAKEN LEGAL WIVES FROM THE COURT FOR GENERATIONS.
HOW VEXING.
A HOUSE LIKE THAT BRINGING IN A SERVING WOMAN, EVEN IF JUST AS A CONCUBINE ...
THAT HOUSE HAS ONLY THE ONE DIRECT MALE DESCENDANT.
HE LIKELY INTENDS IT AS A REWARD.
I'D LIKE TO MEET HIM.
BUT I SUPPOSE THIS ISN'T HIS SORT OF PLACE.
THANK YOU SO MUCH FOR YOUR CONTINUED PATRONAGE.
EVERYONE IS AWAITING YOUR ARRIVAL, SIR, YOUR BEING THE BANK PRESIDENT AND ALL.
I'M URE THAT MAN

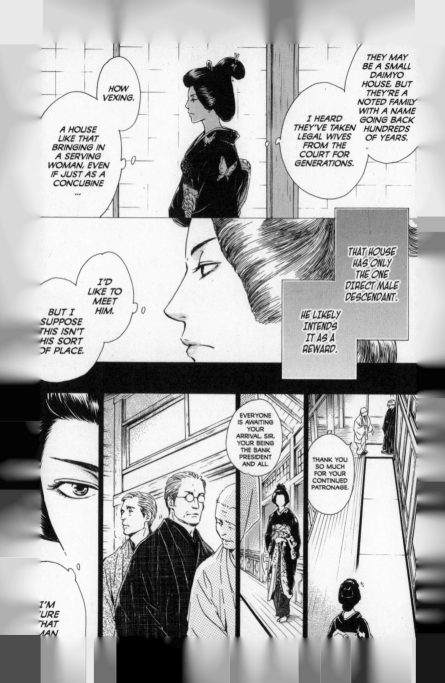

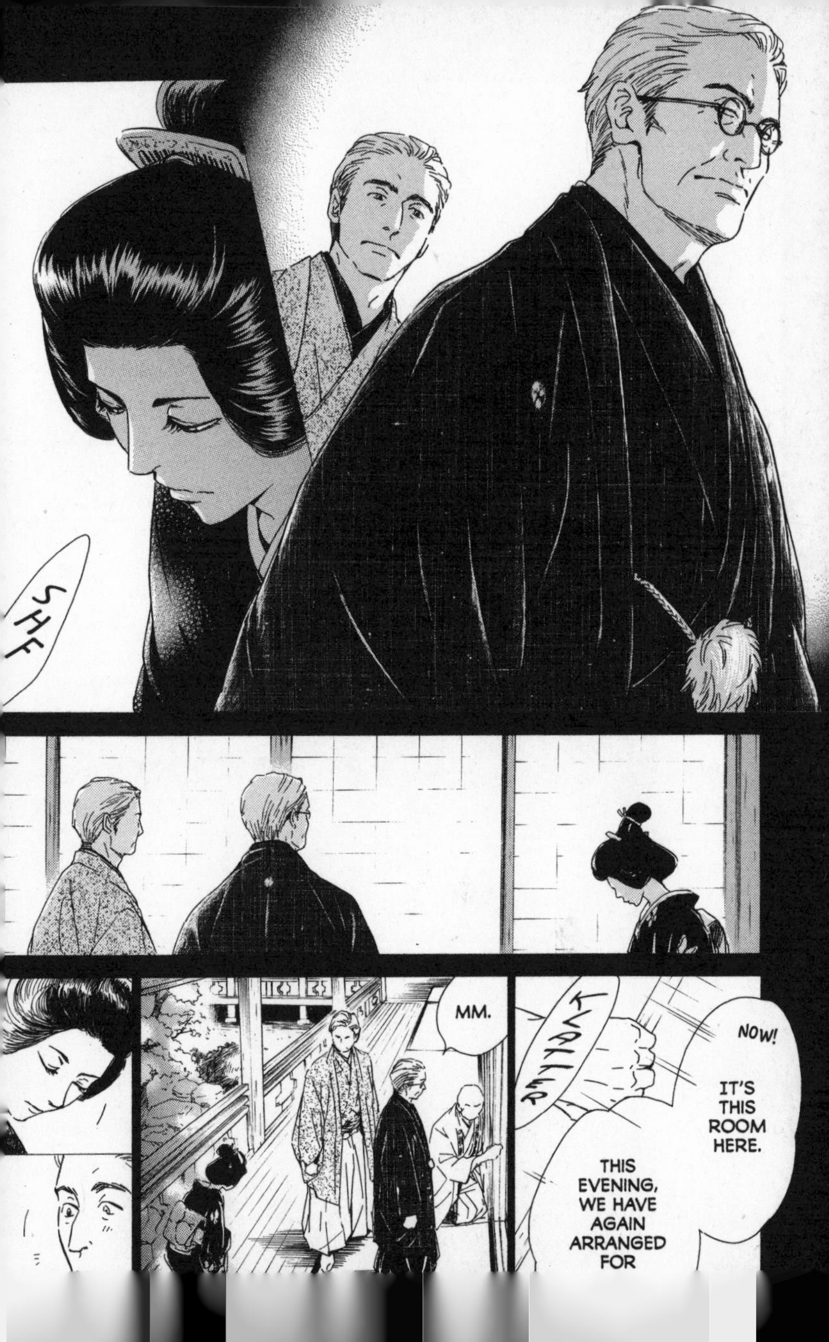
SHF
NOW!
IT'S THIS ROOM HERE.
THIS EVENING, WE HAVE AGAIN ARRANGED FOR
KRATTER
MM.

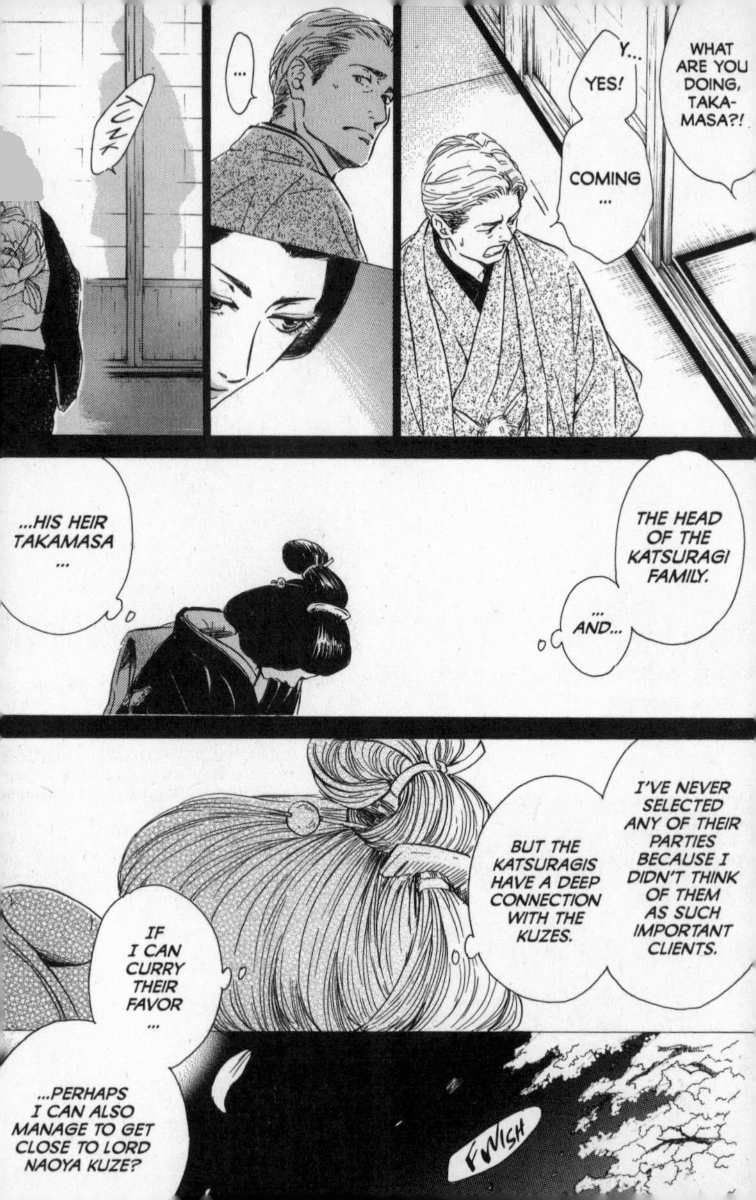
WHAT ARE YOU DOING, TAKA-MASA?!
Y... YES!
COMING ...
...
TUNK
THE HEAD OF THE KATSURAGI FAMILY.
... AND...
...HIS HEIR TAKAMASA ...
I'VE NEVER SELECTED ANY OF THEIR PARTIES BECAUSE I DIDN'T THINK OF THEM AS SUCH IMPORTANT CLIENTS.
BUT THE KATSURAGIS HAVE A DEEP CONNECTION WITH THE KUZES.
IF I CAN CURRY THEIR FAVOR ...
...PERHAPS I CAN ALSO MANAGE TO GET CLOSE TO LORD NAOYA KUZE?
FWISH

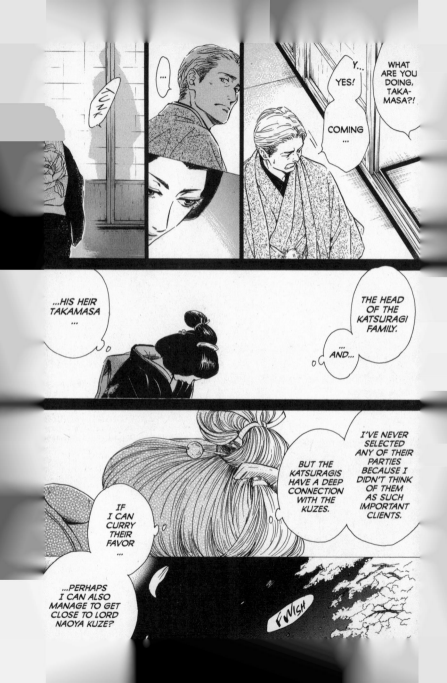

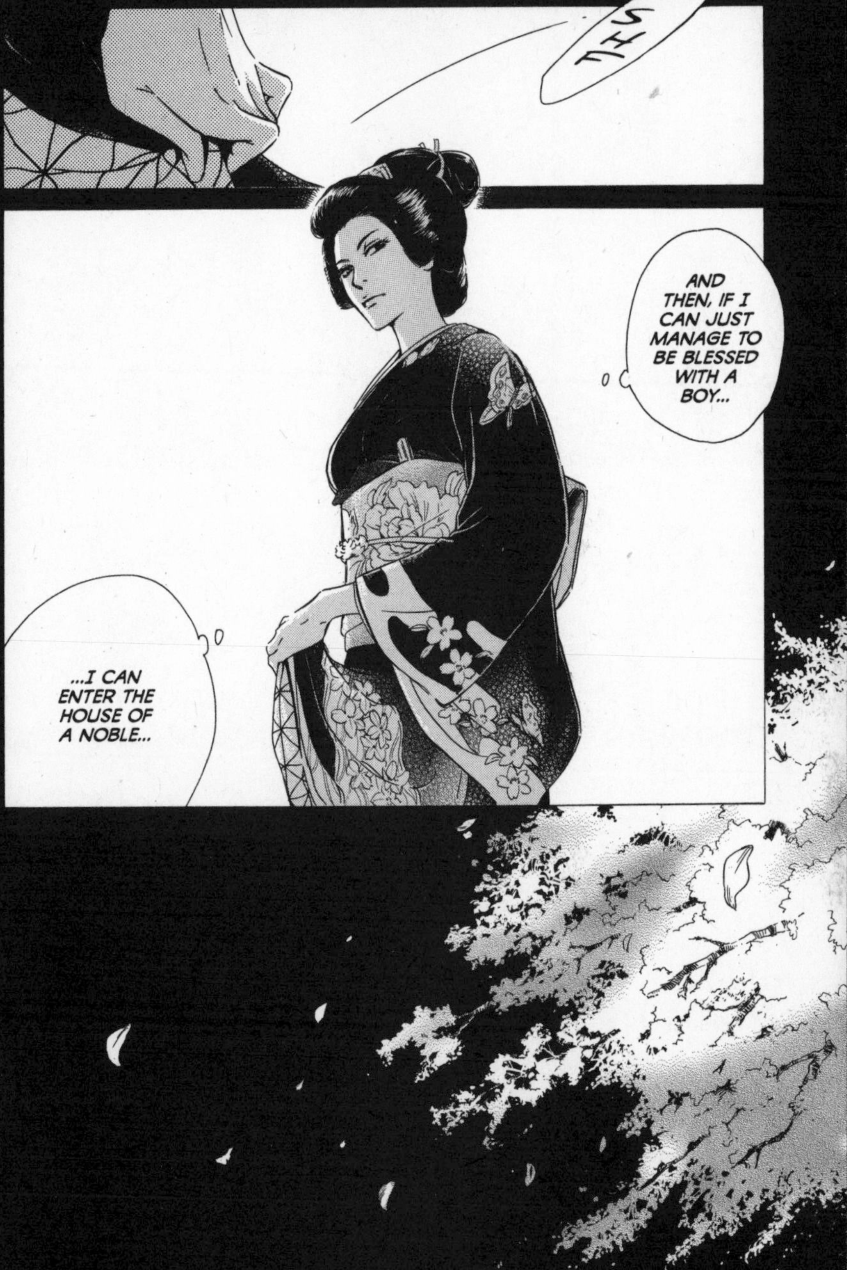
SHF
AND THEN, IF I CAN JUST MANAGE TO BE BLESSED WITH A BOY...
...I CAN ENTER THE HOUSE OF A NOBLE...

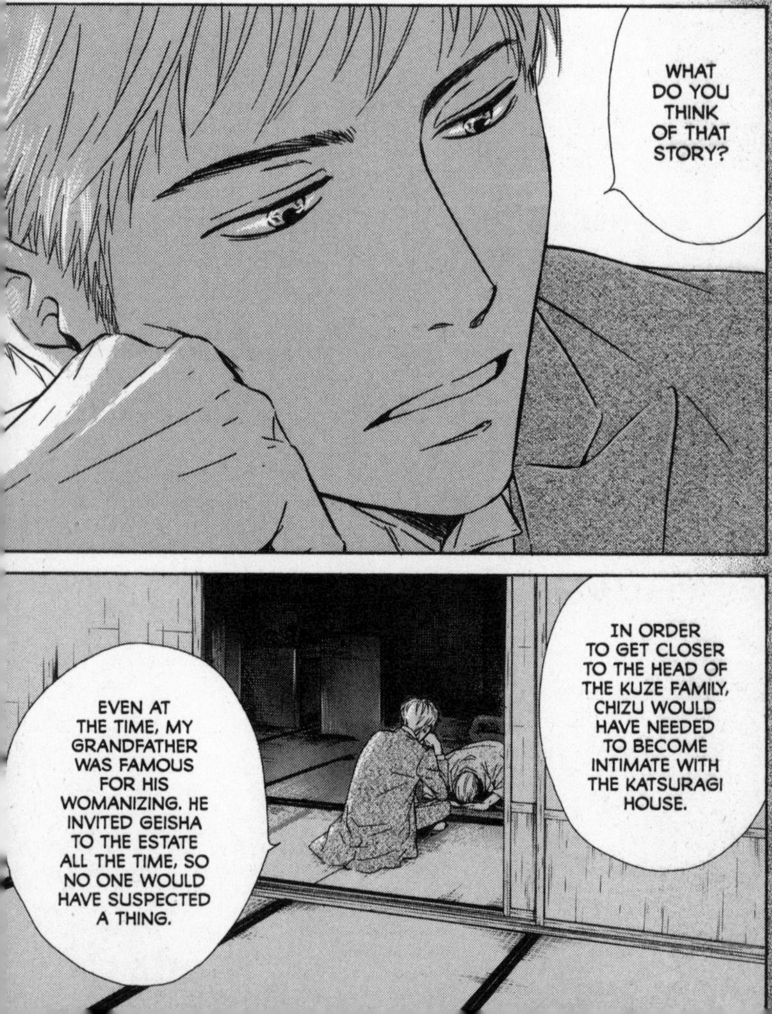
WHAT DO YOU THINK OF THAT STORY?
IN ORDER TO GET CLOSER TO THE HEAD OF THE KUZE FAMILY, CHIZU WOULD HAVE NEEDED TO BECOME INTIMATE WITH THE KATSURAGI HOUSE.
EVEN AT THE TIME, MY GRANDFATHER WAS FAMOUS FOR HIS WOMANIZING. HE INVITED GEISHA TO THE ESTATE ALL THE TIME, SO NO ONE WOULD HAVE SUSPECTED A THING.

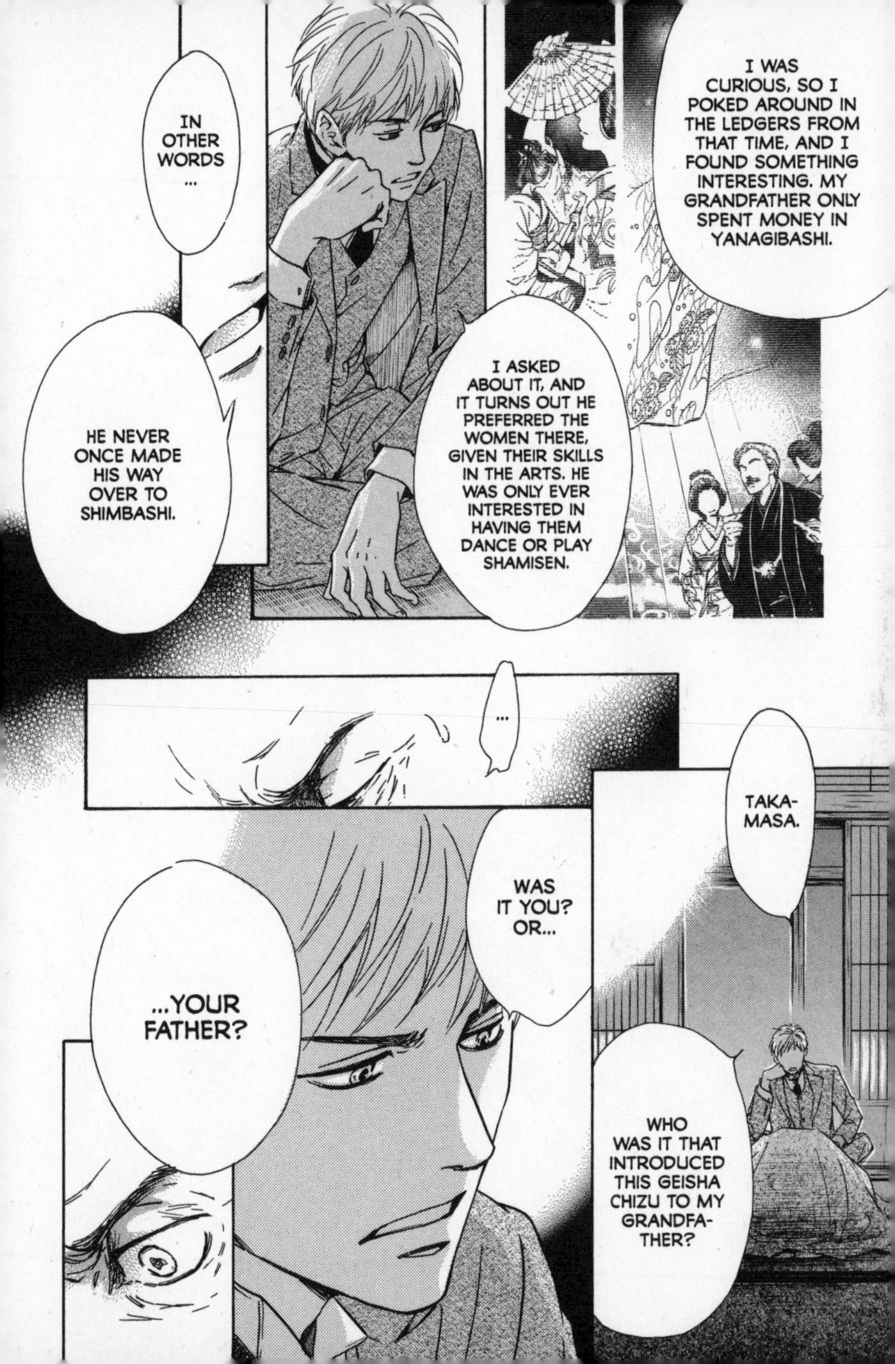
I WAS CURIOUS, SO I POKED AROUND IN THE LEDGERS FROM THAT TIME, AND I FOUND SOMETHING INTERESTING. MY GRANDFATHER ONLY SPENT MONEY IN YANAGIBASHI.
I ASKED ABOUT IT, AND IT TURNS OUT HE PREFERRED THE WOMEN THERE, GIVEN THEIR SKILLS IN THE ARTS. HE WAS ONLY EVER INTERESTED IN HAVING THEM DANCE OR PLAY SHAMISEN.
IN OTHER WORDS ...
HE NEVER ONCE MADE HIS WAY OVER TO SHIMBASHI.
...
TAKA-MASA.
WHO WAS IT THAT INTRODUCED THIS GEISHA CHIZU TO MY GRANDFA-THER?
WAS IT YOU? OR...
...YOUR FATHER?

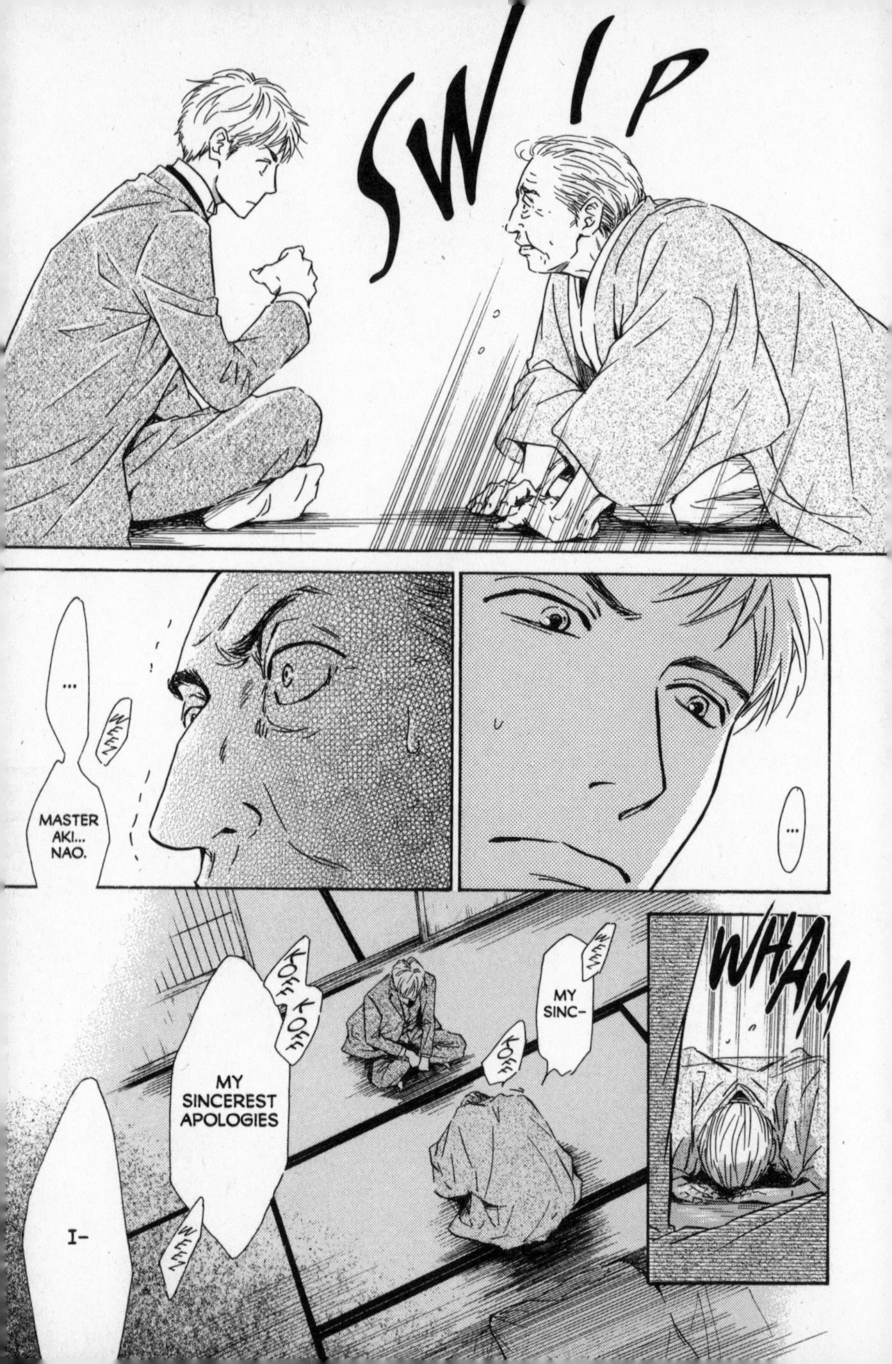
SWIP
...
...
WEEN
MASTER AKI... NAO.
WHAM
WEEN
MY SINC-
KOFF
KOFF KOFF
MY SINCEREST APOLOGIES
WEEN
I-

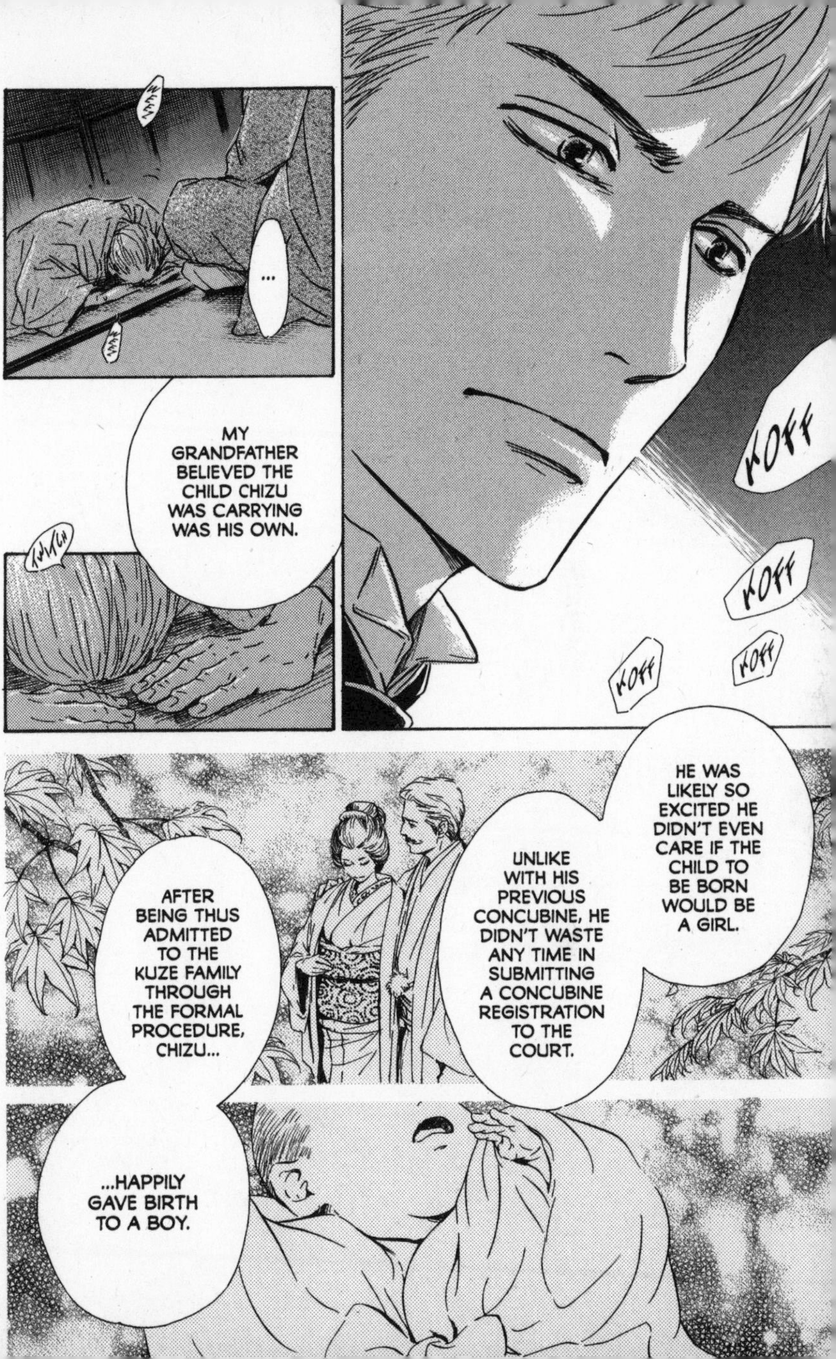
KOFF
KOFF
KOFF
KOFF
WEEP
...
MY GRANDFATHER BELIEVED THE CHILD CHIZU WAS CARRYING WAS HIS OWN.
TWITCH
HE WAS LIKELY SO EXCITED HE DIDN'T EVEN CARE IF THE CHILD TO BE BORN WOULD BE A GIRL.
UNLIKE WITH HIS PREVIOUS CONCUBINE, HE DIDN'T WASTE ANY TIME IN SUBMITTING A CONCUBINE REGISTRATION TO THE COURT.
AFTER BEING THUS ADMITTED TO THE KUZE FAMILY THROUGH THE FORMAL PROCEDURE, CHIZU...
...HAPPILY GAVE BIRTH TO A BOY.

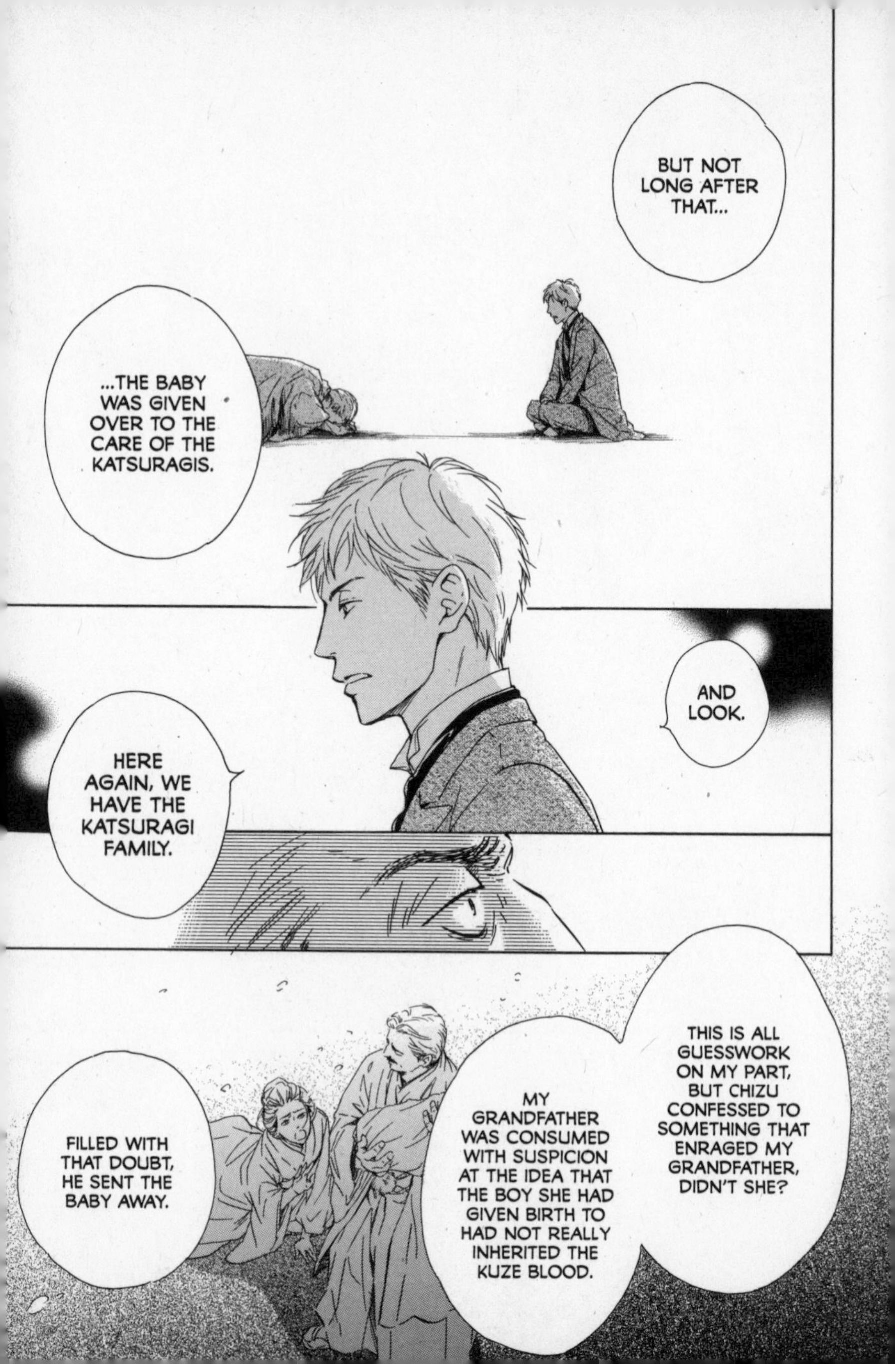
BUT NOT LONG AFTER THAT...
...THE BABY WAS GIVEN OVER TO THE CARE OF THE KATSURAGIS.
AND LOOK.
HERE AGAIN, WE HAVE THE KATSURAGI FAMILY.
THIS IS ALL GUESSWORK ON MY PART, BUT CHIZU CONFESSED TO SOMETHING THAT ENRAGED MY GRANDFATHER, DIDN'T SHE?
MY GRANDFATHER WAS CONSUMED WITH SUSPICION AT THE IDEA THAT THE BOY SHE HAD GIVEN BIRTH TO HAD NOT REALLY INHERITED THE KUZE BLOOD.
FILLED WITH THAT DOUBT, HE SENT THE BABY AWAY.

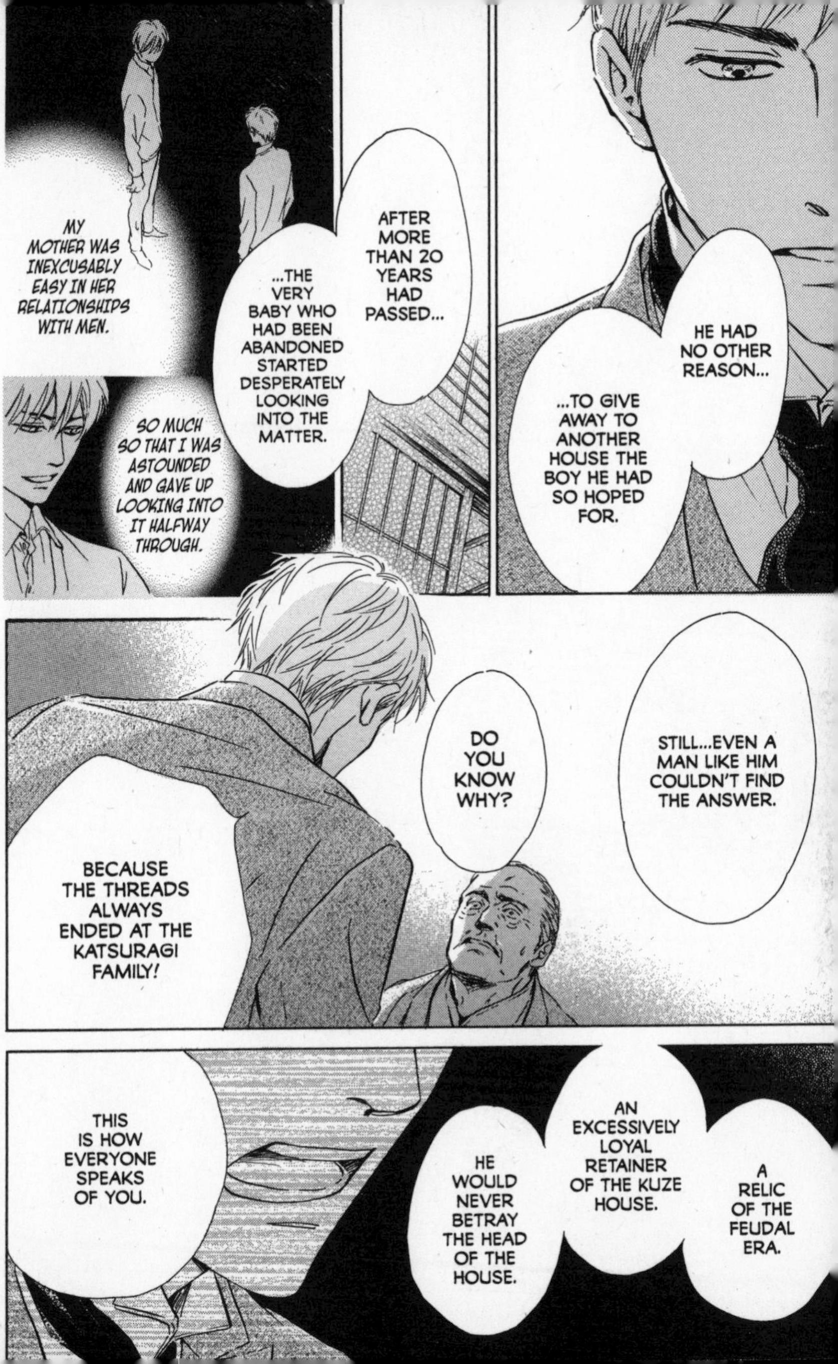

HE HAD NO OTHER REASON...
...TO GIVE AWAY TO ANOTHER HOUSE THE BOY HE HAD SO HOPED FOR.
AFTER MORE THAN 20 YEARS HAD PASSED...
...THE VERY BABY WHO HAD BEEN ABANDONED STARTED DESPERATELY LOOKING INTO THE MATTER.
MY MOTHER WAS INEXCUSABLY EASY IN HER RELATIONSHIPS WITH MEN.
SO MUCH SO THAT I WAS ASTOUNDED AND GAVE UP LOOKING INTO IT HALFWAY THROUGH.
STILL...EVEN A MAN LIKE HIM COULDN'T FIND THE ANSWER.
DO YOU KNOW WHY?
BECAUSE THE THREADS ALWAYS ENDED AT THE KATSURAGI FAMILY!
A RELIC OF THE FEUDAL ERA.
AN EXCESSIVELY LOYAL RETAINER OF THE KUZE HOUSE.
HE WOULD NEVER BETRAY THE HEAD OF THE HOUSE.
THIS IS HOW EVERYONE SPEAKS OF YOU.

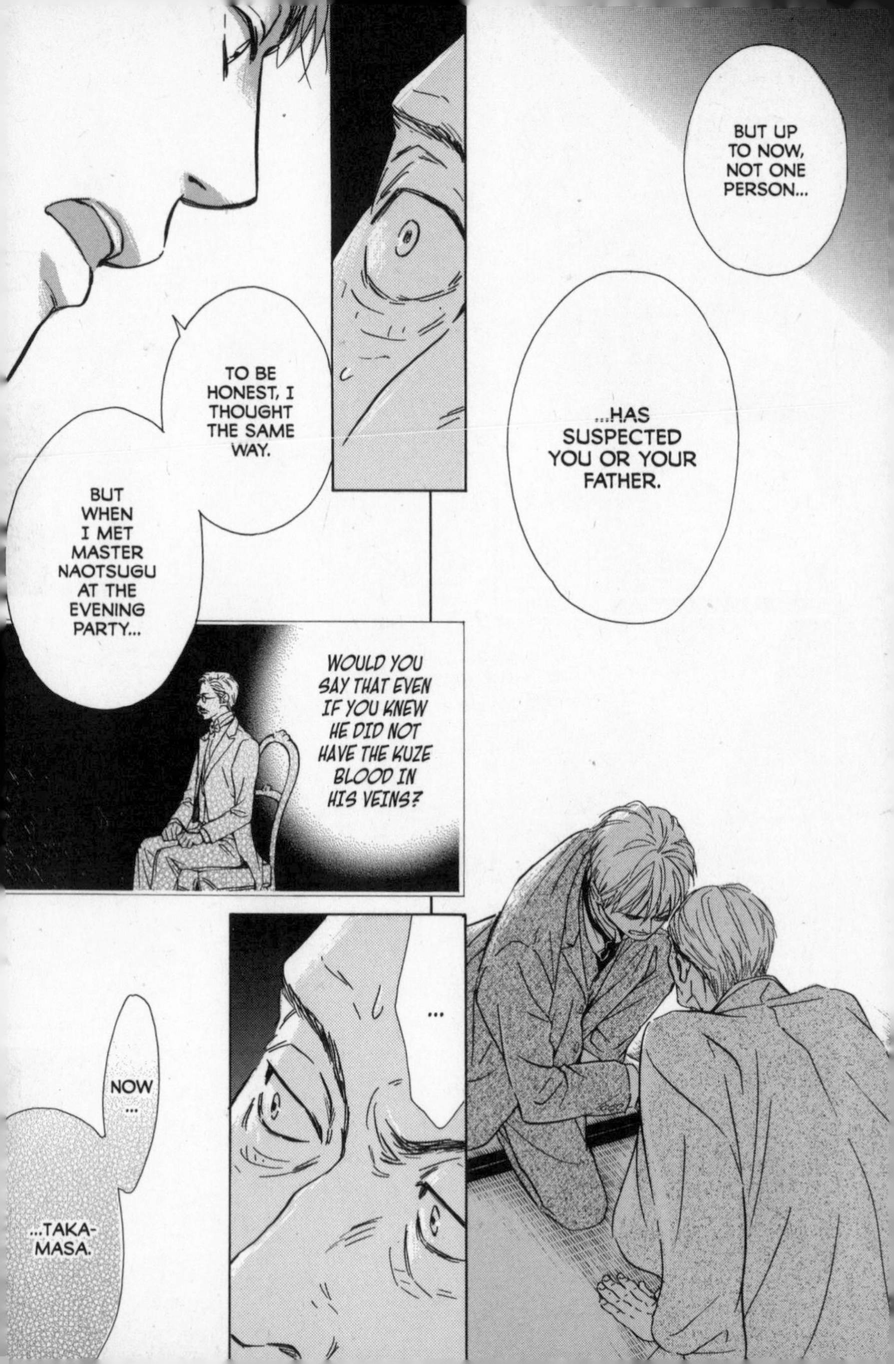

BUT UP TO NOW, NOT ONE PERSON...
...HAS SUSPECTED YOU OR YOUR FATHER.
TO BE HONEST, I THOUGHT THE SAME WAY.
BUT WHEN I MET MASTER NAOTSUGU AT THE EVENING PARTY...
WOULD YOU SAY THAT EVEN IF YOU KNEW HE DID NOT HAVE THE KUZE BLOOD IN HIS VEINS?
...
NOW...
...TAKA-MASA.

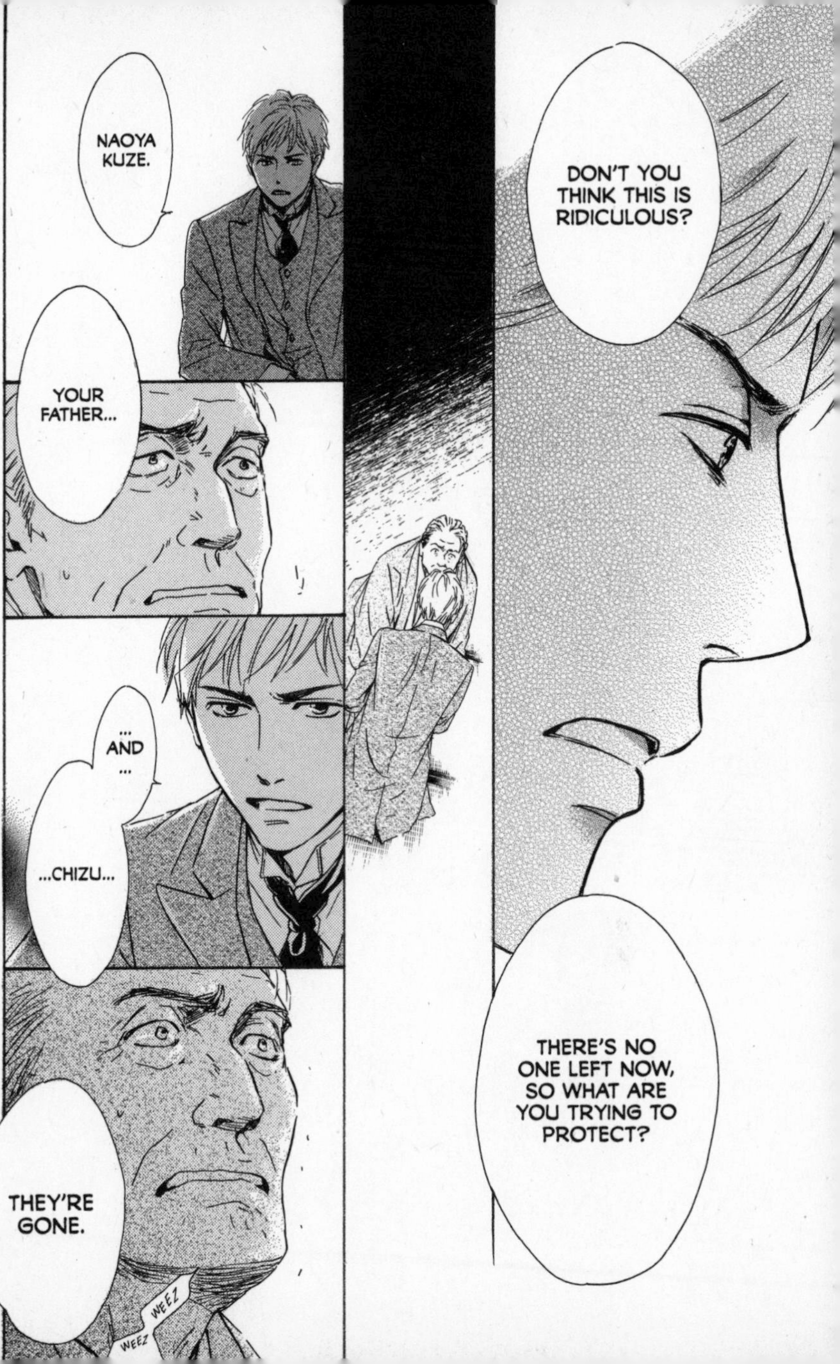
DON'T YOU THINK THIS IS RIDICULOUS?
THERE'S NO ONE LEFT NOW, SO WHAT ARE YOU TRYING TO PROTECT?
NAOYA KUZE.
YOUR FATHER...
... AND ...
...CHIZU...
THEY'RE GONE.
WEEZ
WEEZ

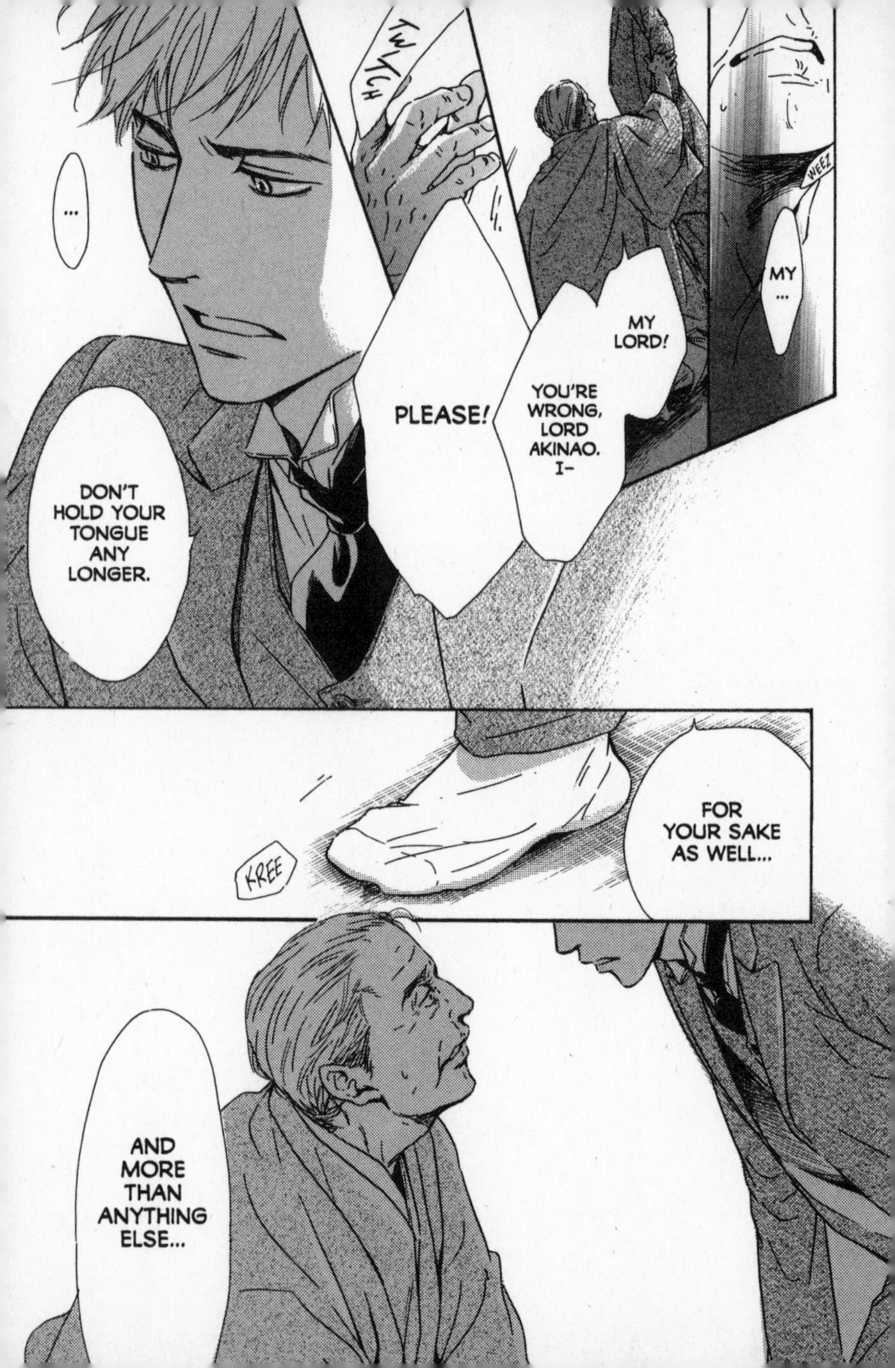
MY ...
WEEZ
MY LORD!
YOU'RE WRONG, LORD AKINAO. I-
PLEASE!
TWITCH
...
DON'T HOLD YOUR TONGUE ANY LONGER.
FOR YOUR SAKE AS WELL...
KREE
AND MORE THAN ANYTHING ELSE...

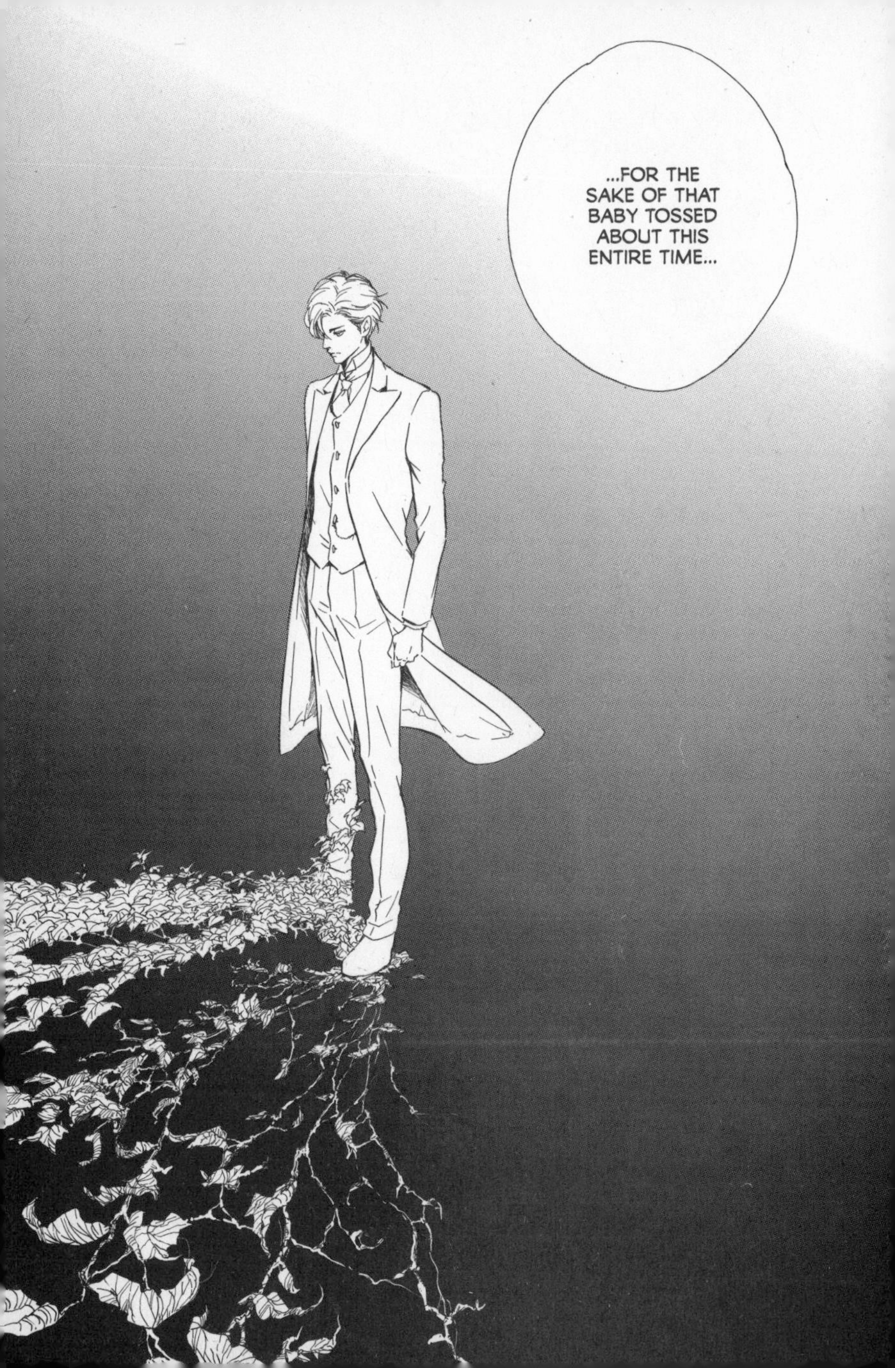
...FOR THE SAKE OF THAT BABY TOSSED ABOUT THIS ENTIRE TIME...

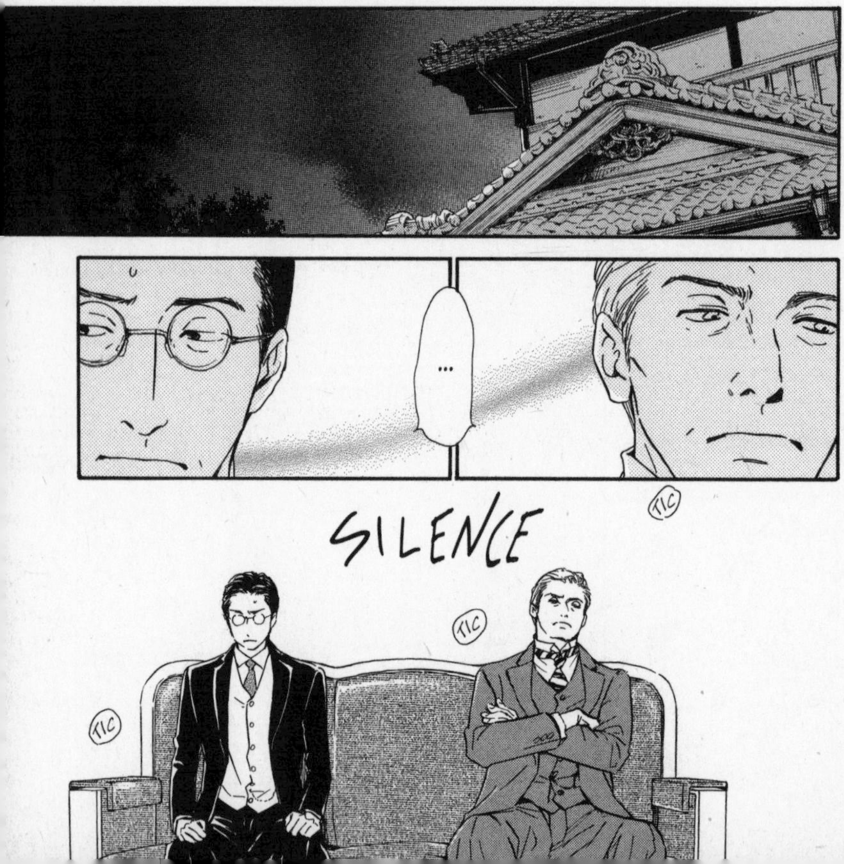
...
TIC
SILENCE
TIC
TIC

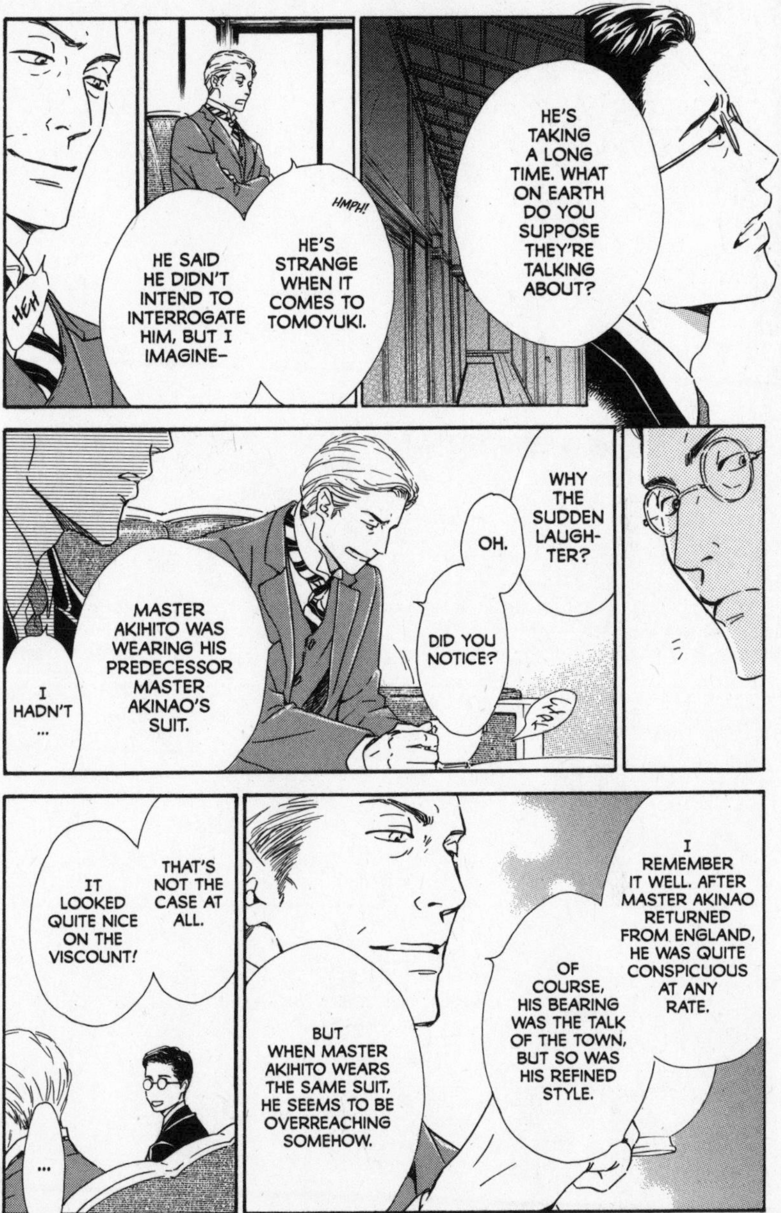
HE'S TAKING A LONG TIME. WHAT ON EARTH DO YOU SUPPOSE THEY'RE TALKING ABOUT?
HMPH!
HE'S STRANGE WHEN IT COMES TO TOMOYUKI.
HEH
HE SAID HE DIDN'T INTEND TO INTERROGATE HIM, BUT I IMAGINE–
WHY THE SUDDEN LAUGHTER?
OH.
DID YOU NOTICE?
MASTER AKIHITO WAS WEARING HIS PREDECESSOR MASTER AKINAO'S SUIT.
I HADN'T ...
I REMEMBER IT WELL. AFTER MASTER AKINAO RETURNED FROM ENGLAND, HE WAS QUITE CONSPICUOUS AT ANY RATE.
OF COURSE, HIS BEARING WAS THE TALK OF THE TOWN, BUT SO WAS HIS REFINED STYLE.
BUT WHEN MASTER AKIHITO WEARS THE SAME SUIT, HE SEEMS TO BE OVERREACHING SOMEHOW.
THAT'S NOT THE CASE AT ALL.
IT LOOKED QUITE NICE ON THE VISCOUNT!
...

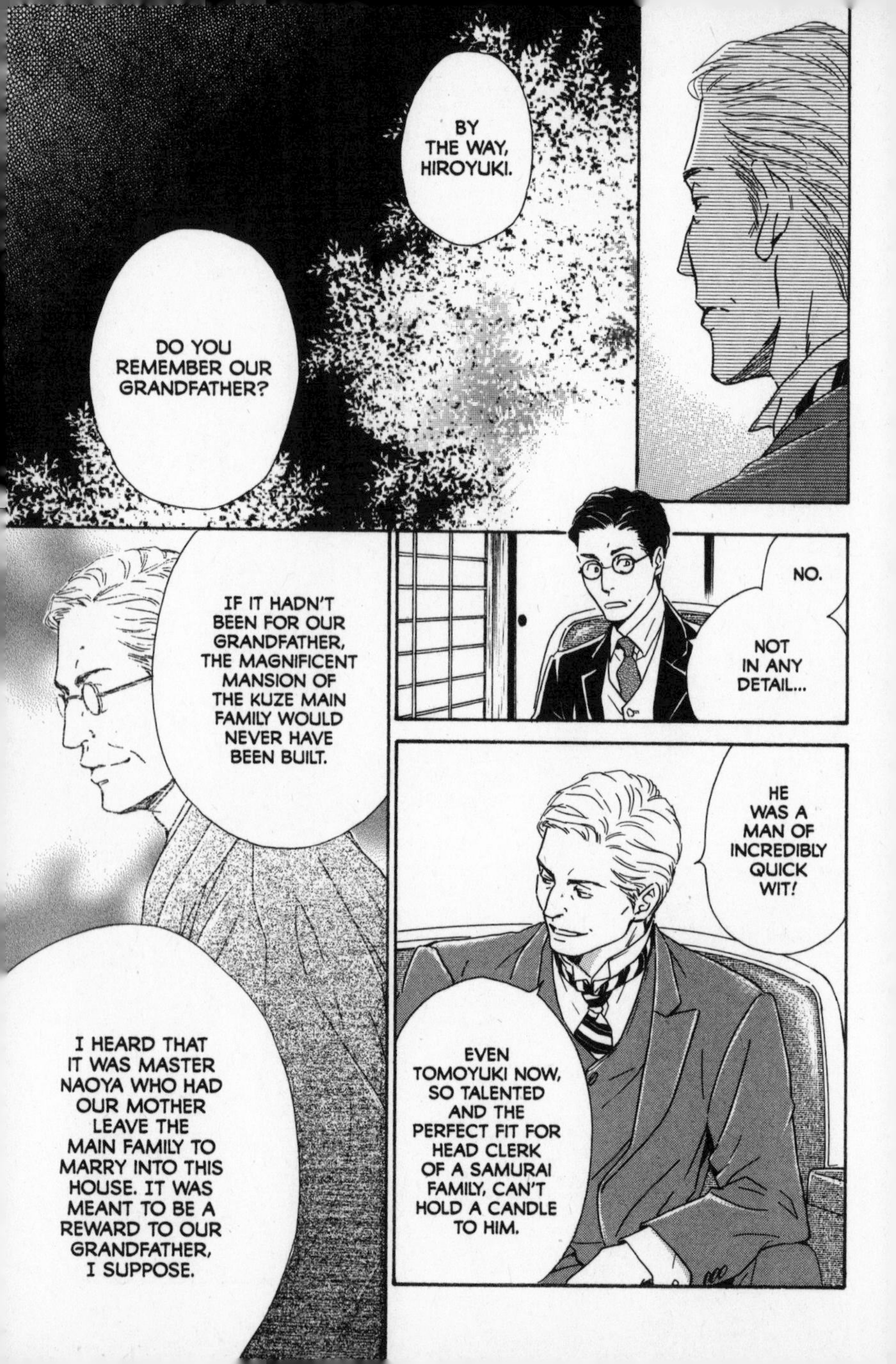
BY THE WAY, HIROYUKI.
DO YOU REMEMBER OUR GRANDFATHER?
NO.
NOT IN ANY DETAIL...
HE WAS A MAN OF INCREDIBLY QUICK WIT!
EVEN TOMOYUKI NOW, SO TALENTED AND THE PERFECT FIT FOR HEAD CLERK OF A SAMURAI FAMILY, CAN'T HOLD A CANDLE TO HIM.
IF IT HADN'T BEEN FOR OUR GRANDFATHER, THE MAGNIFICENT MANSION OF THE KUZE MAIN FAMILY WOULD NEVER HAVE BEEN BUILT.
I HEARD THAT IT WAS MASTER NAOYA WHO HAD OUR MOTHER LEAVE THE MAIN FAMILY TO MARRY INTO THIS HOUSE. IT WAS MEANT TO BE A REWARD TO OUR GRANDFATHER, I SUPPOSE.

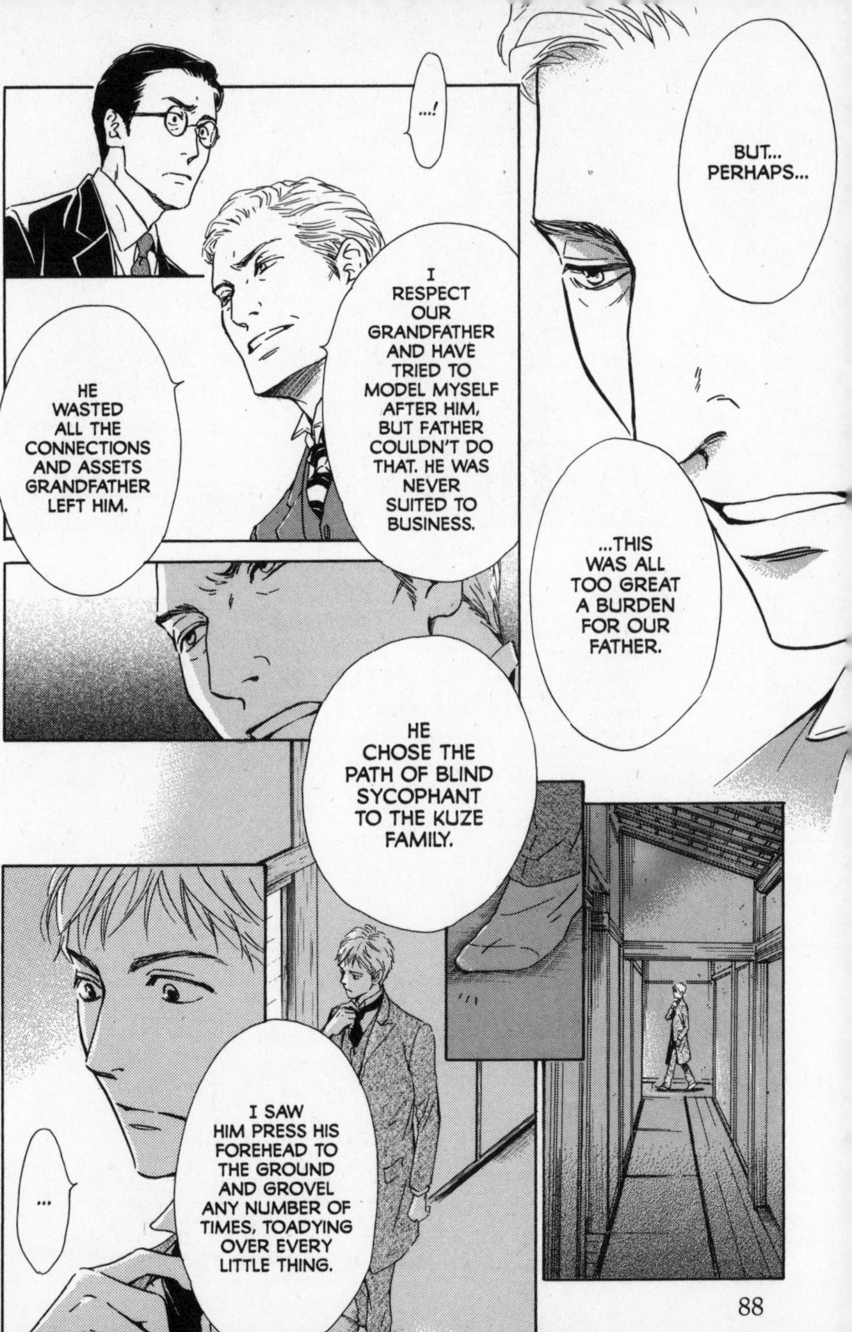
BUT... PERHAPS...
...THIS WAS ALL TOO GREAT A BURDEN FOR OUR FATHER.
...!
I RESPECT OUR GRANDFATHER AND HAVE TRIED TO MODEL MYSELF AFTER HIM, BUT FATHER COULDN'T DO THAT. HE WAS NEVER SUITED TO BUSINESS.
HE WASTED ALL THE CONNECTIONS AND ASSETS GRANDFATHER LEFT HIM.
HE CHOSE THE PATH OF BLIND SYCOPHANT TO THE KUZE FAMILY.
I SAW HIM PRESS HIS FOREHEAD TO THE GROUND AND GROVEL ANY NUMBER OF TIMES, TOADYING OVER EVERY LITTLE THING.
...

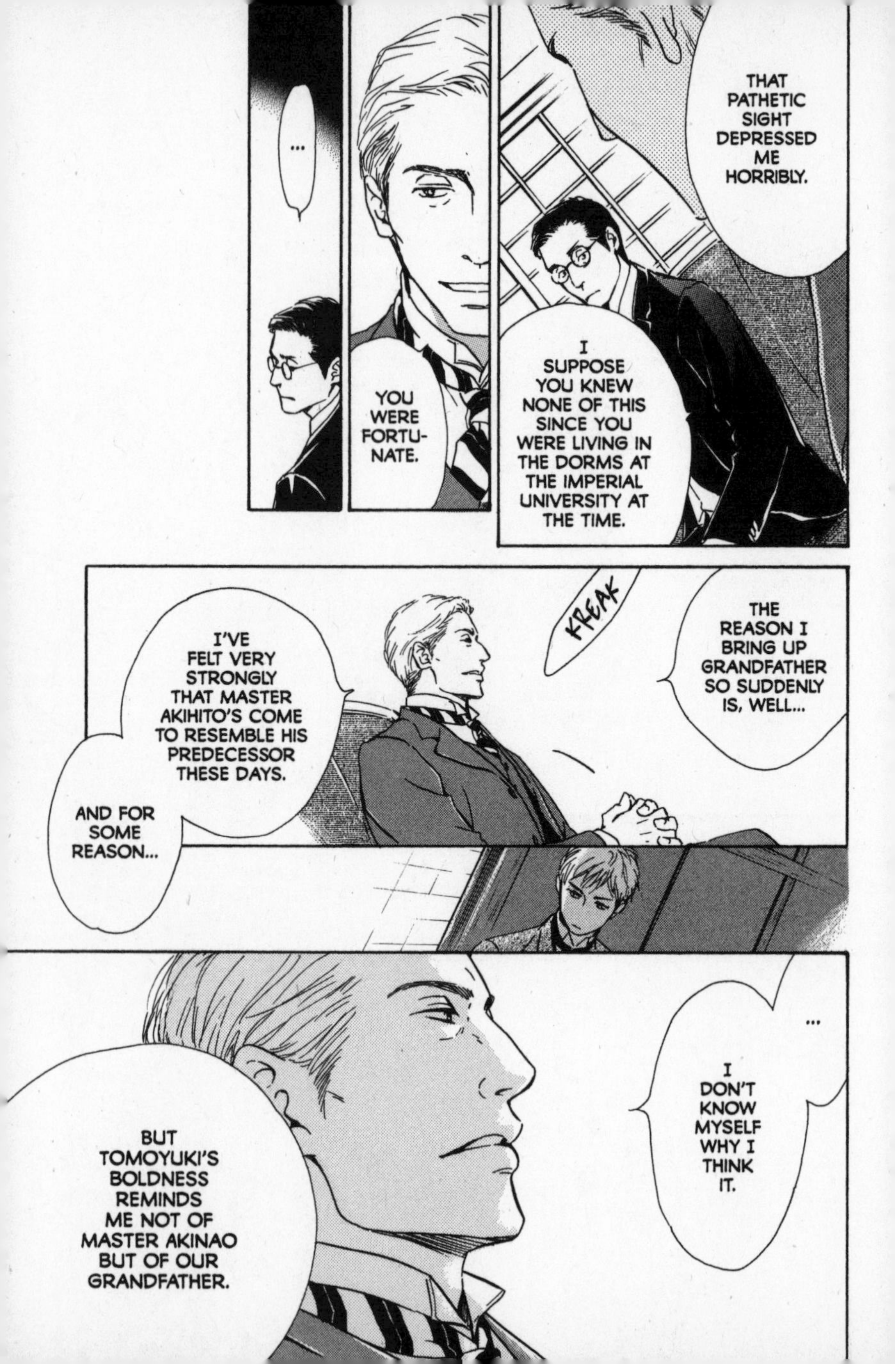
THAT PATHETIC SIGHT DEPRESSED ME HORRIBLY.
I SUPPOSE YOU KNEW NONE OF THIS SINCE YOU WERE LIVING IN THE DORMS AT THE IMPERIAL UNIVERSITY AT THE TIME.
YOU WERE FORTU-NATE.
...
THE REASON I BRING UP GRANDFATHER SO SUDDENLY IS, WELL...
KREAK
I'VE FELT VERY STRONGLY THAT MASTER AKIHITO'S COME TO RESEMBLE HIS PREDECESSOR THESE DAYS.
AND FOR SOME REASON...
...
I DON'T KNOW MYSELF WHY I THINK IT.
BUT TOMOYUKI'S BOLDNESS REMINDS ME NOT OF MASTER AKINAO BUT OF OUR GRANDFATHER.

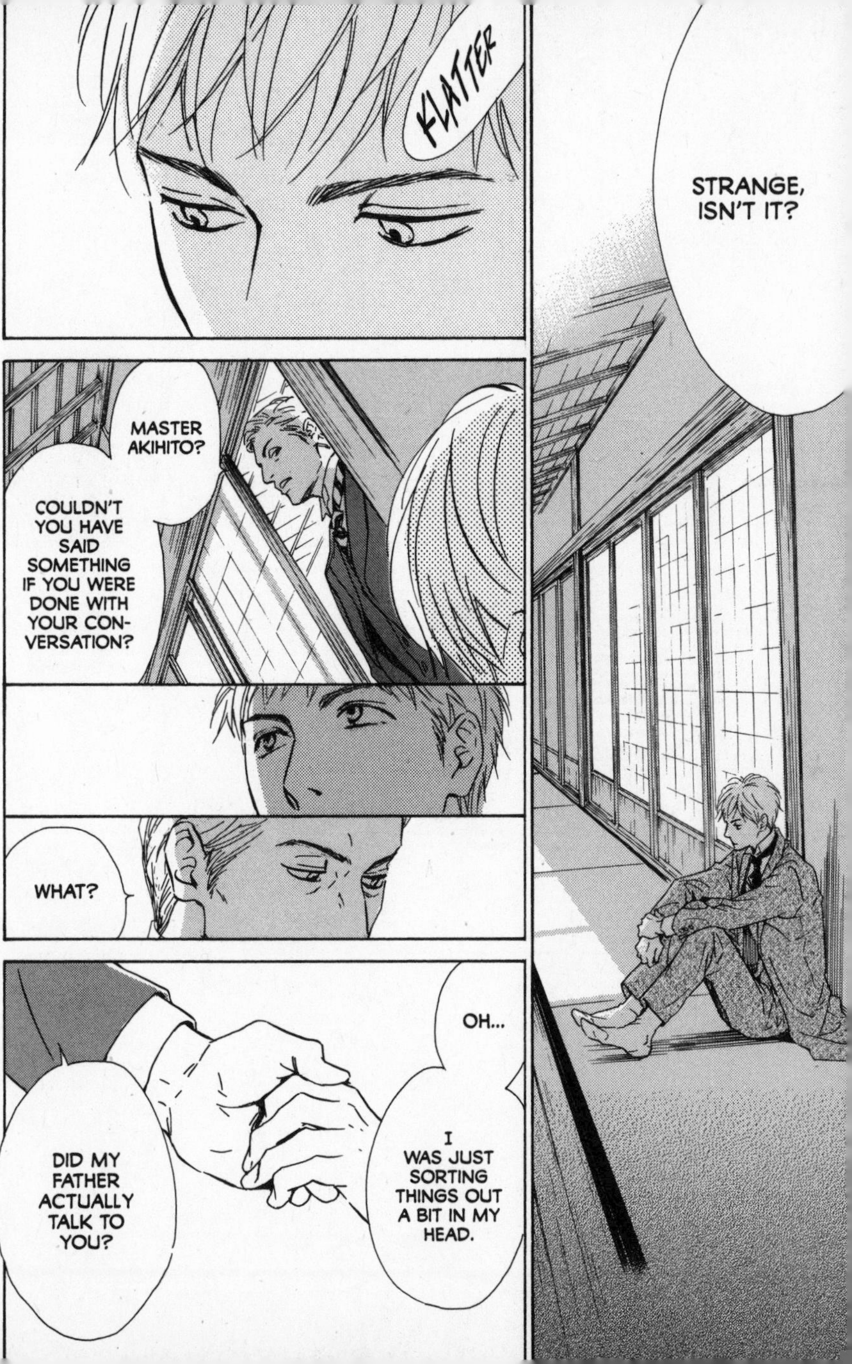
STRANGE, ISN'T IT?
KLATTER
MASTER AKIHITO?
COULDN'T YOU HAVE SAID SOMETHING IF YOU WERE DONE WITH YOUR CON-VERSATION?
WHAT?
OH...
I WAS JUST SORTING THINGS OUT A BIT IN MY HEAD.
DID MY FATHER ACTUALLY TALK TO YOU?

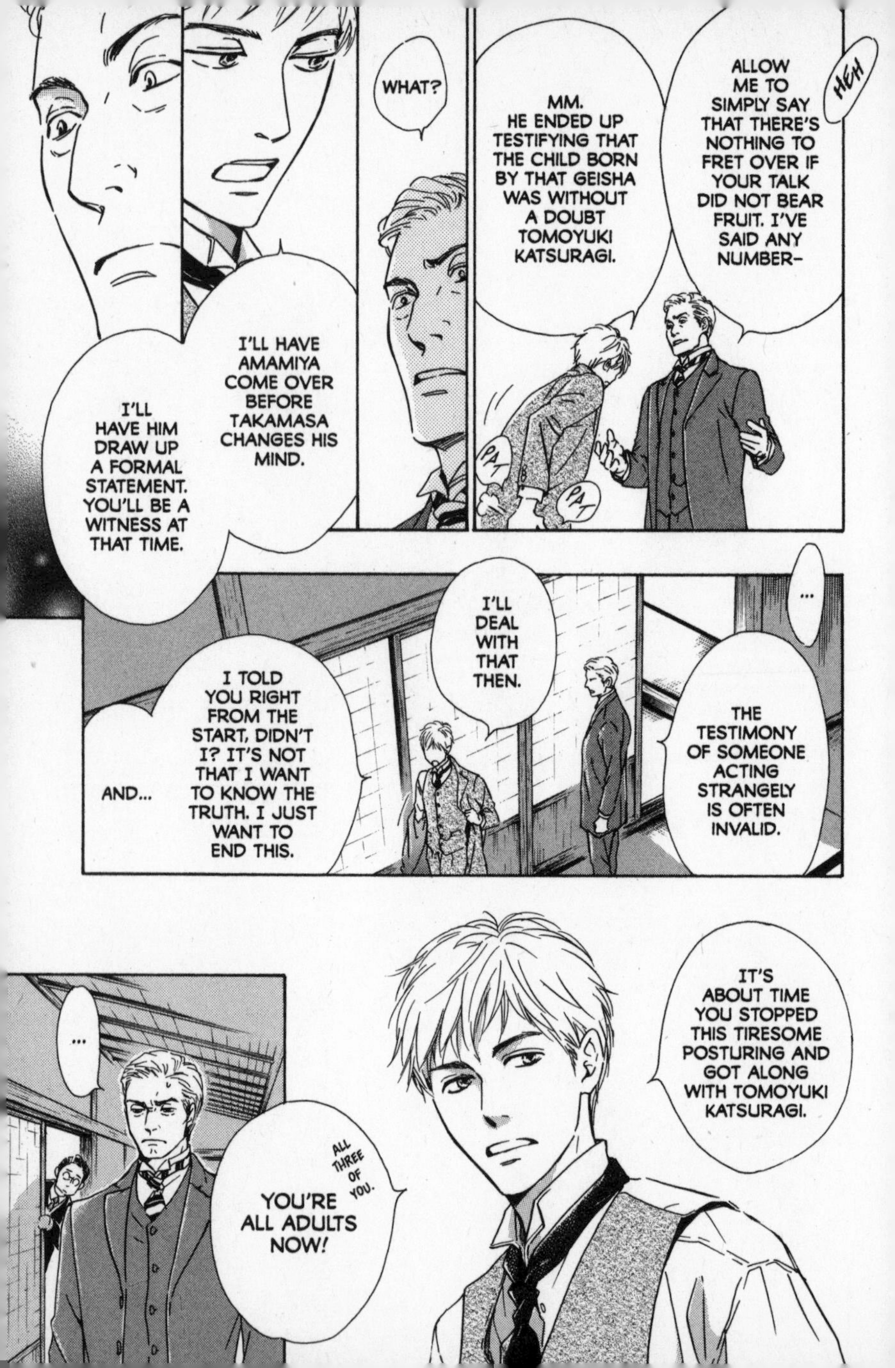
HEH
ALLOW ME TO SIMPLY SAY THAT THERE'S NOTHING TO FRET OVER IF YOUR TALK DID NOT BEAR FRUIT. I'VE SAID ANY NUMBER–
MM. HE ENDED UP TESTIFYING THAT THE CHILD BORN BY THAT GEISHA WAS WITHOUT A DOUBT TOMOYUKI KATSURAGI.
PAT
PAT
WHAT?
I'LL HAVE AMAMIYA COME OVER BEFORE TAKAMASA CHANGES HIS MIND.
I'LL HAVE HIM DRAW UP A FORMAL STATEMENT. YOU'LL BE A WITNESS AT THAT TIME.
...
THE TESTIMONY OF SOMEONE ACTING STRANGELY IS OFTEN INVALID.
I'LL DEAL WITH THAT THEN.
I TOLD YOU RIGHT FROM THE START, DIDN'T I? IT'S NOT THAT I WANT TO KNOW THE TRUTH. I JUST WANT TO END THIS.
AND...
IT'S ABOUT TIME YOU STOPPED THIS TIRESOME POSTURING AND GOT ALONG WITH TOMOYUKI KATSURAGI.
ALL THREE OF YOU.
YOU'RE ALL ADULTS NOW!
...

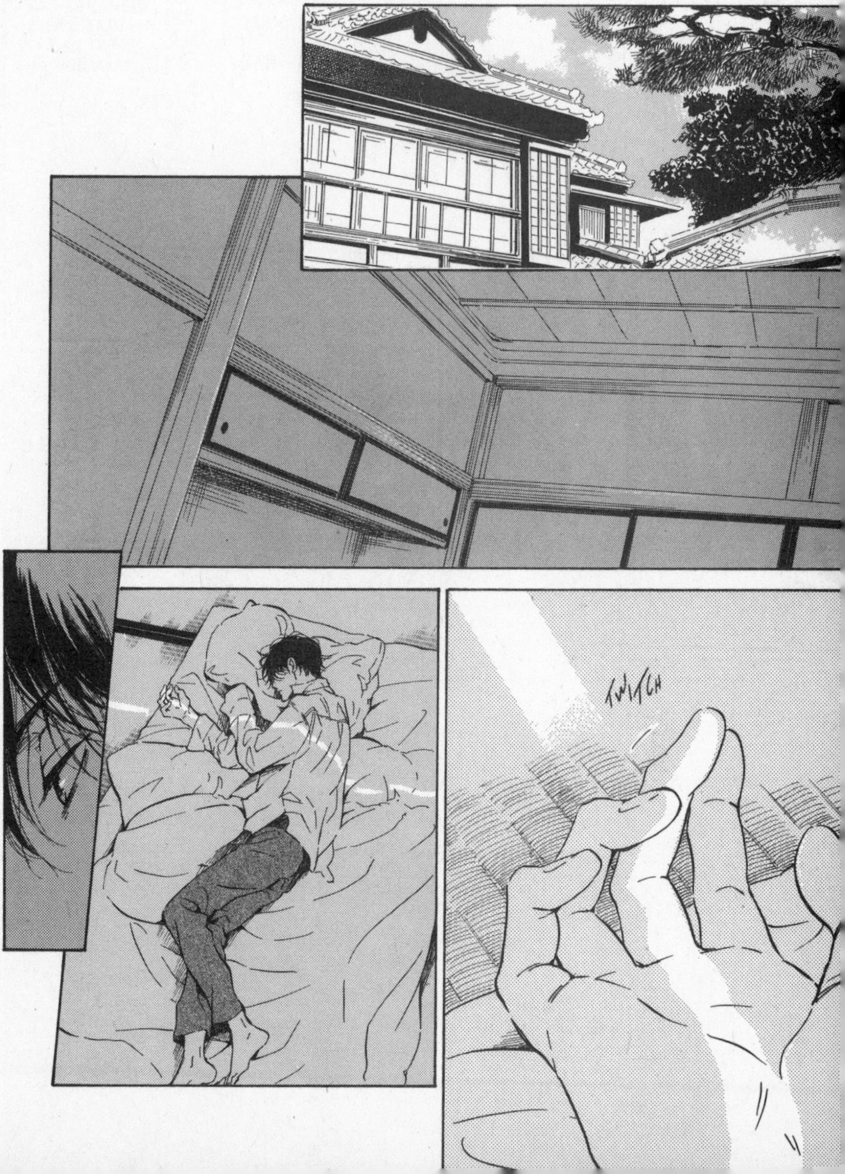
TWITCH

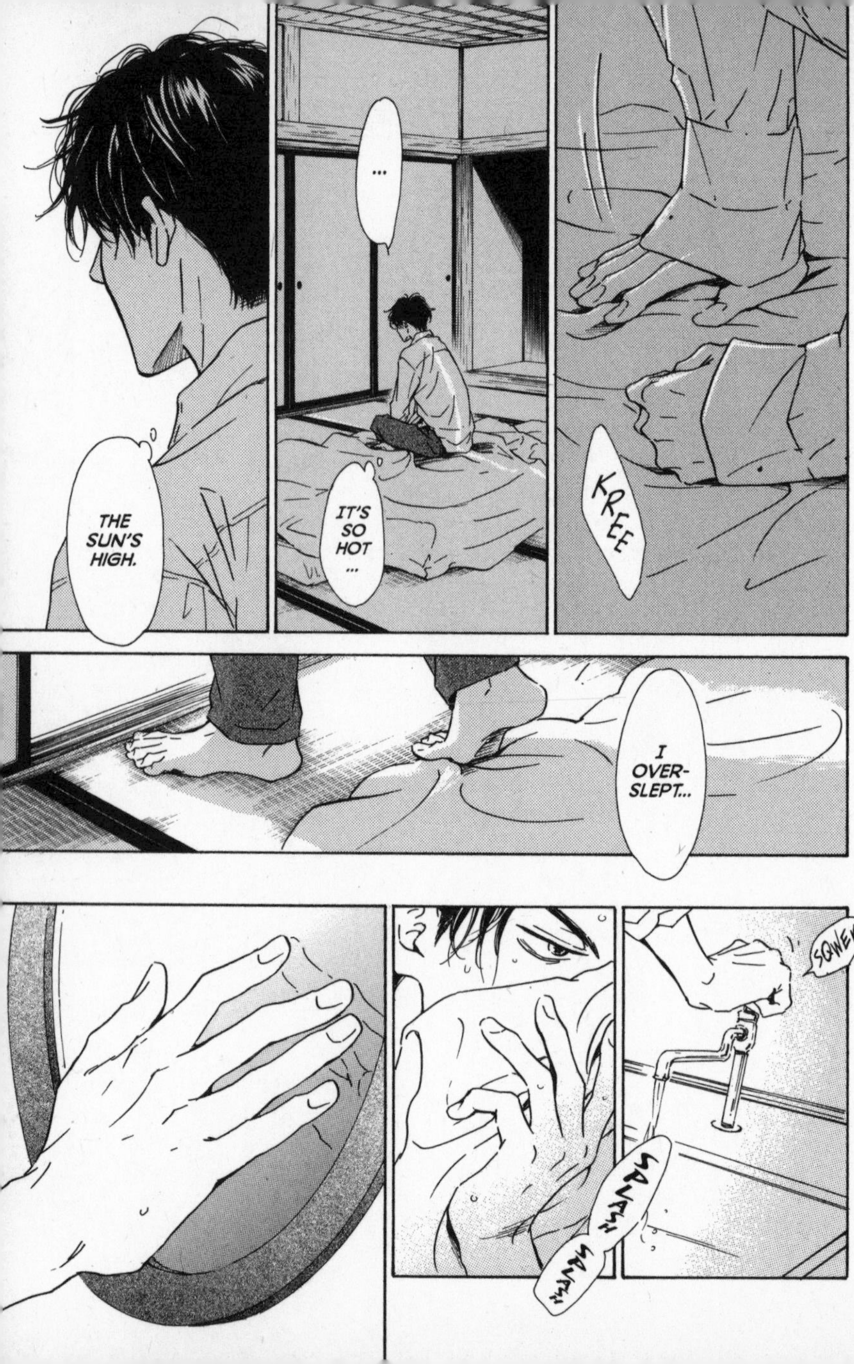

KREE
...
IT'S SO HOT ...
THE SUN'S HIGH.
I OVER-SLEPT...
SQWEK
SPLASH SPLASH

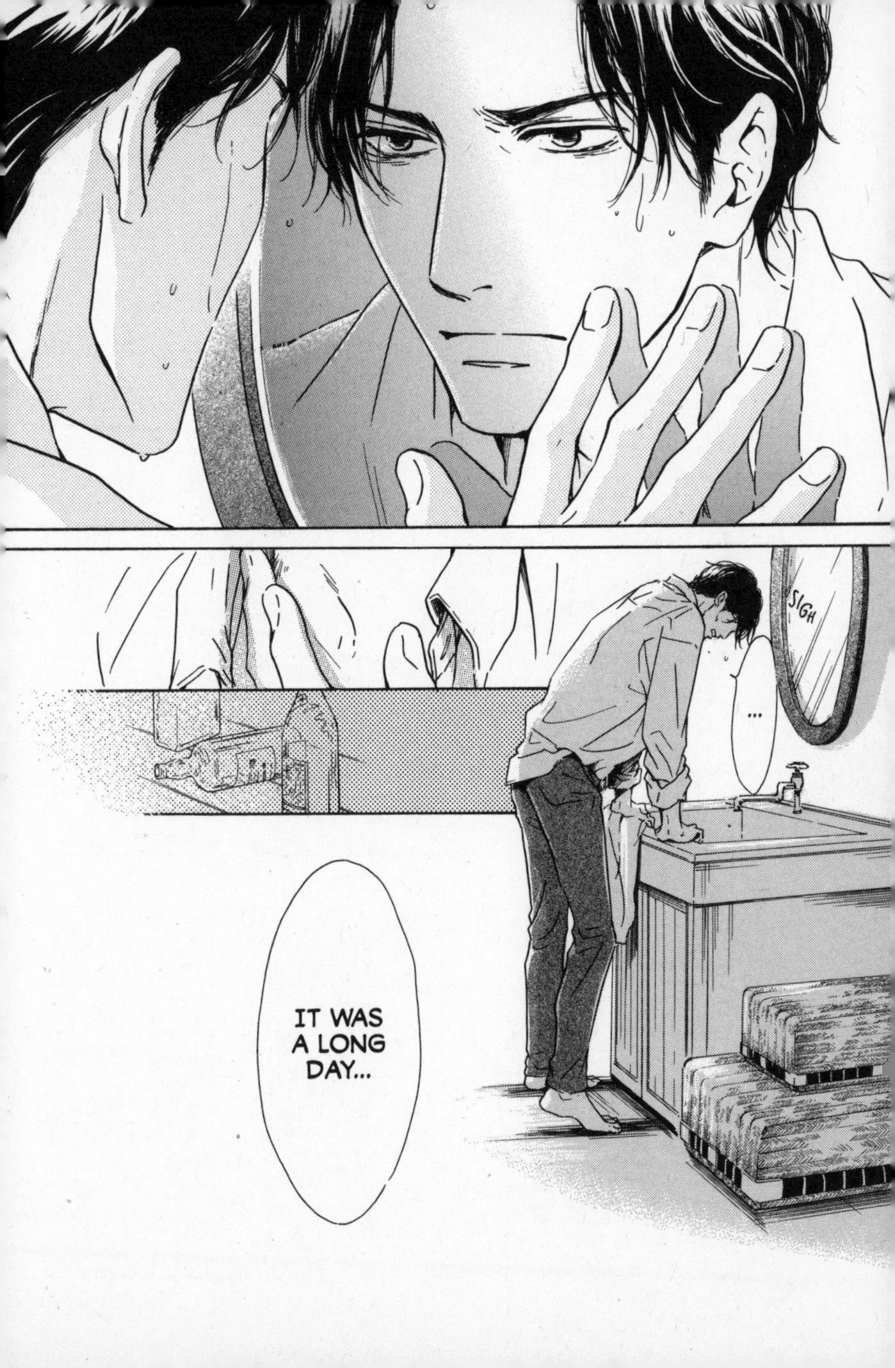
SIGH
...
IT WAS A LONG DAY...

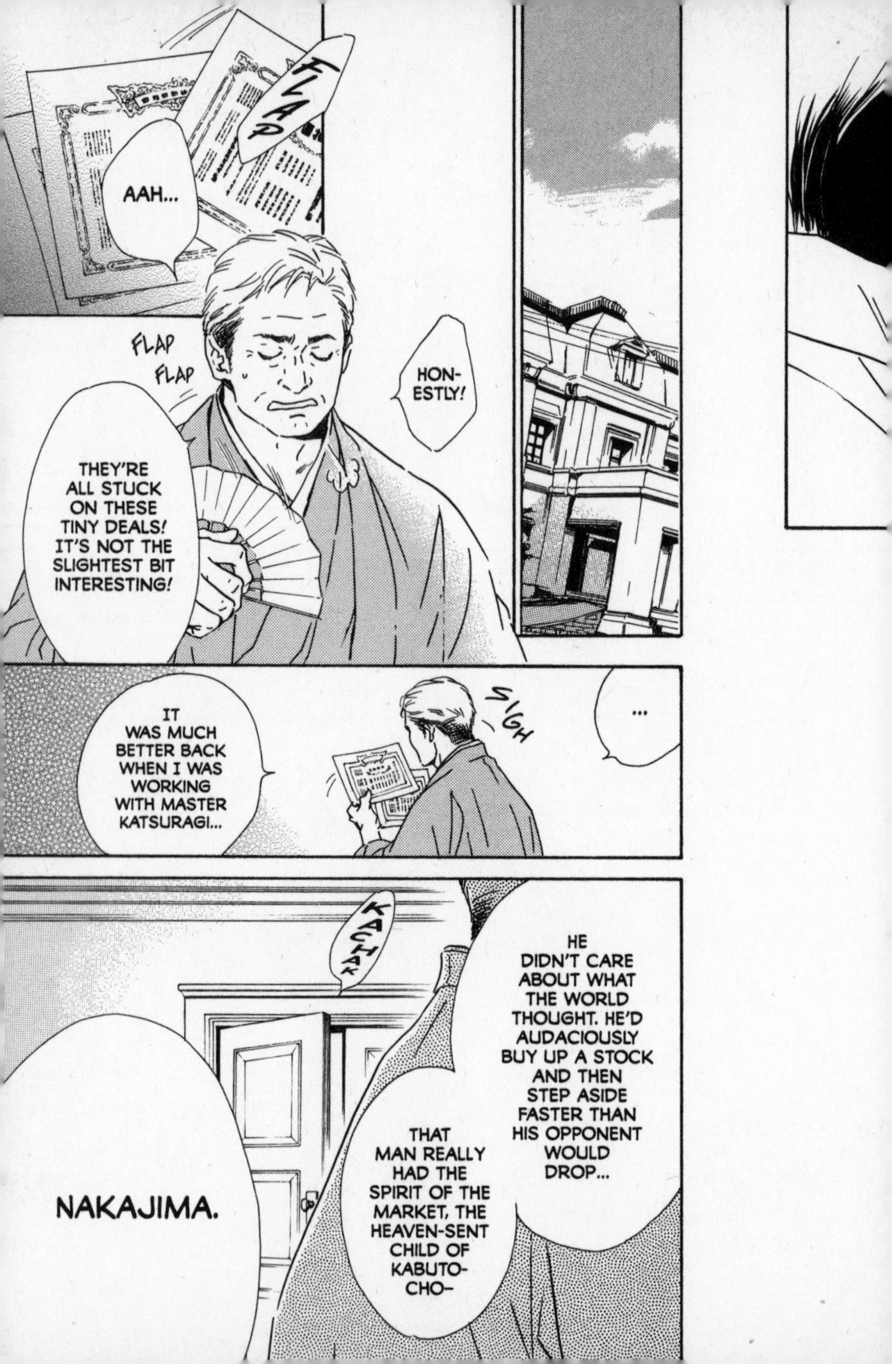
FLAP
AAH...
HON-ESTLY!
FLAP FLAP
THEY'RE ALL STUCK ON THESE TINY DEALS! IT'S NOT THE SLIGHTEST BIT INTERESTING!
...
SIGH
IT WAS MUCH BETTER BACK WHEN I WAS WORKING WITH MASTER KATSURAGI...
KACHAK
HE DIDN'T CARE ABOUT WHAT THE WORLD THOUGHT. HE'D AUDACIOUSLY BUY UP A STOCK AND THEN STEP ASIDE FASTER THAN HIS OPPONENT WOULD DROP...
THAT MAN REALLY HAD THE SPIRIT OF THE MARKET, THE HEAVEN-SENT CHILD OF KABUTO-CHO-
NAKAJIMA.

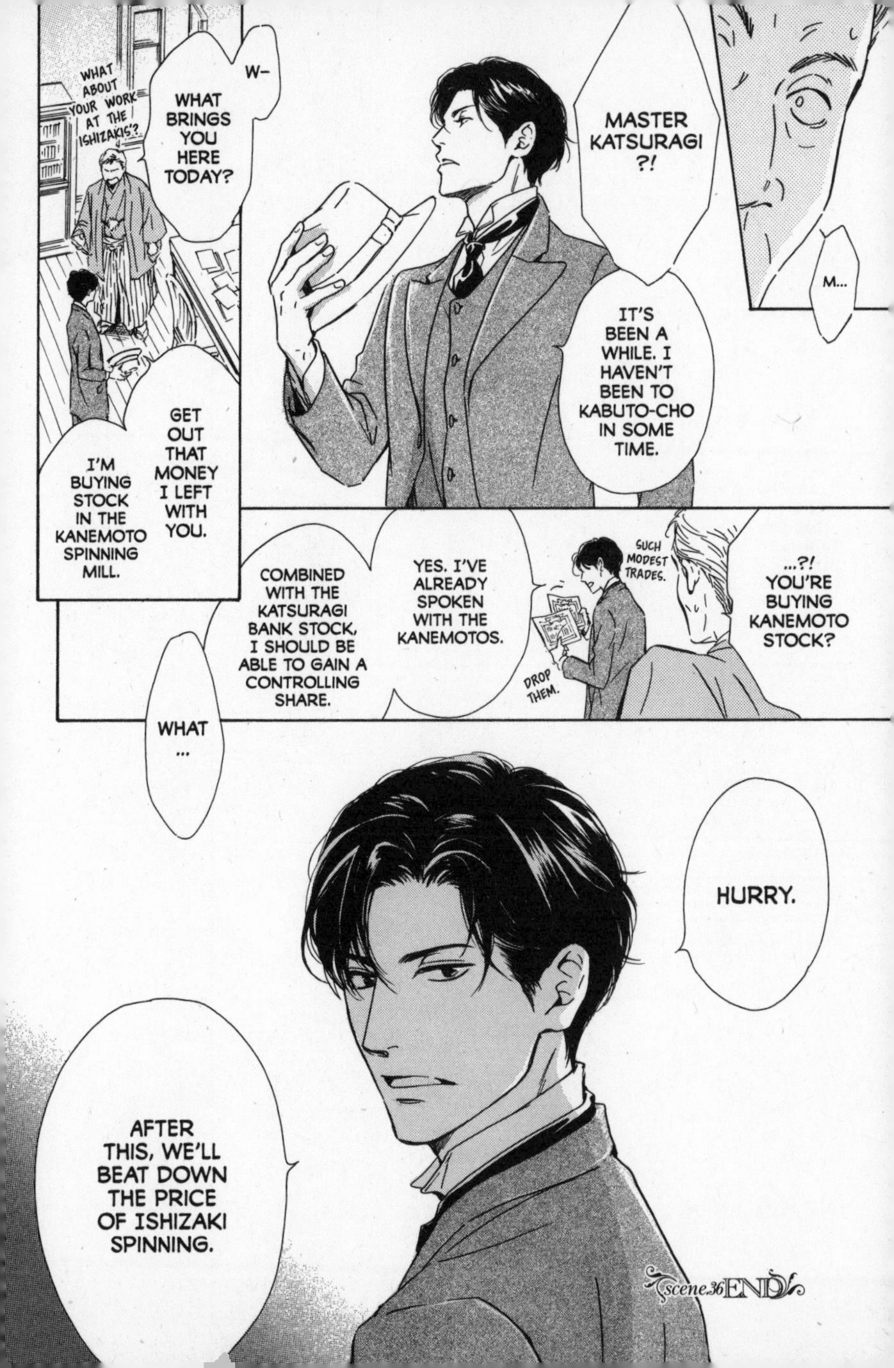
M...
MASTER KATSURAGI ?!
IT'S BEEN A WHILE. I HAVEN'T BEEN TO KABUTO-CHO IN SOME TIME.
W- WHAT BRINGS YOU HERE TODAY?
WHAT ABOUT YOUR WORK AT THE ISHIZAKIS'?
GET OUT THAT MONEY I LEFT WITH YOU.
I'M BUYING STOCK IN THE KANEMOTO SPINNING MILL.
...?! YOU'RE BUYING KANEMOTO STOCK?
SUCH MODEST TRADES.
DROP THEM.
YES. I'VE ALREADY SPOKEN WITH THE KANEMOTOS.
COMBINED WITH THE KATSURAGI BANK STOCK, I SHOULD BE ABLE TO GAIN A CONTROLLING SHARE.
WHAT ...
HURRY.
AFTER THIS, WE'LL BEAT DOWN THE PRICE OF ISHIZAKI SPINNING.
scene.36 END

憂鬱な朝

Blue Morning

憂鬱な朝

Blue Morning

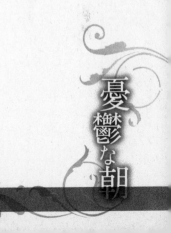

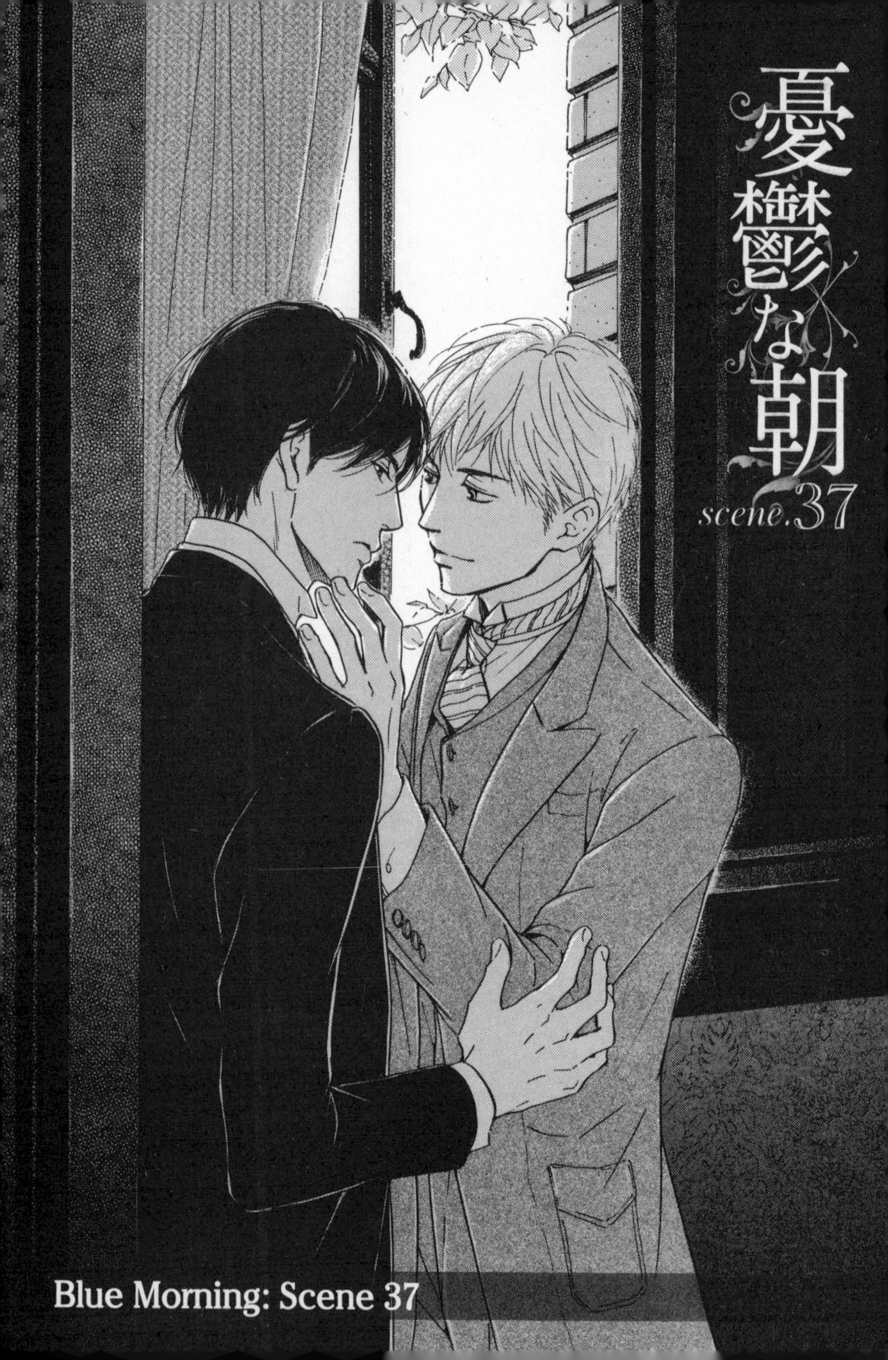
憂鬱な朝
scene.37
Blue Morning: Scene 37

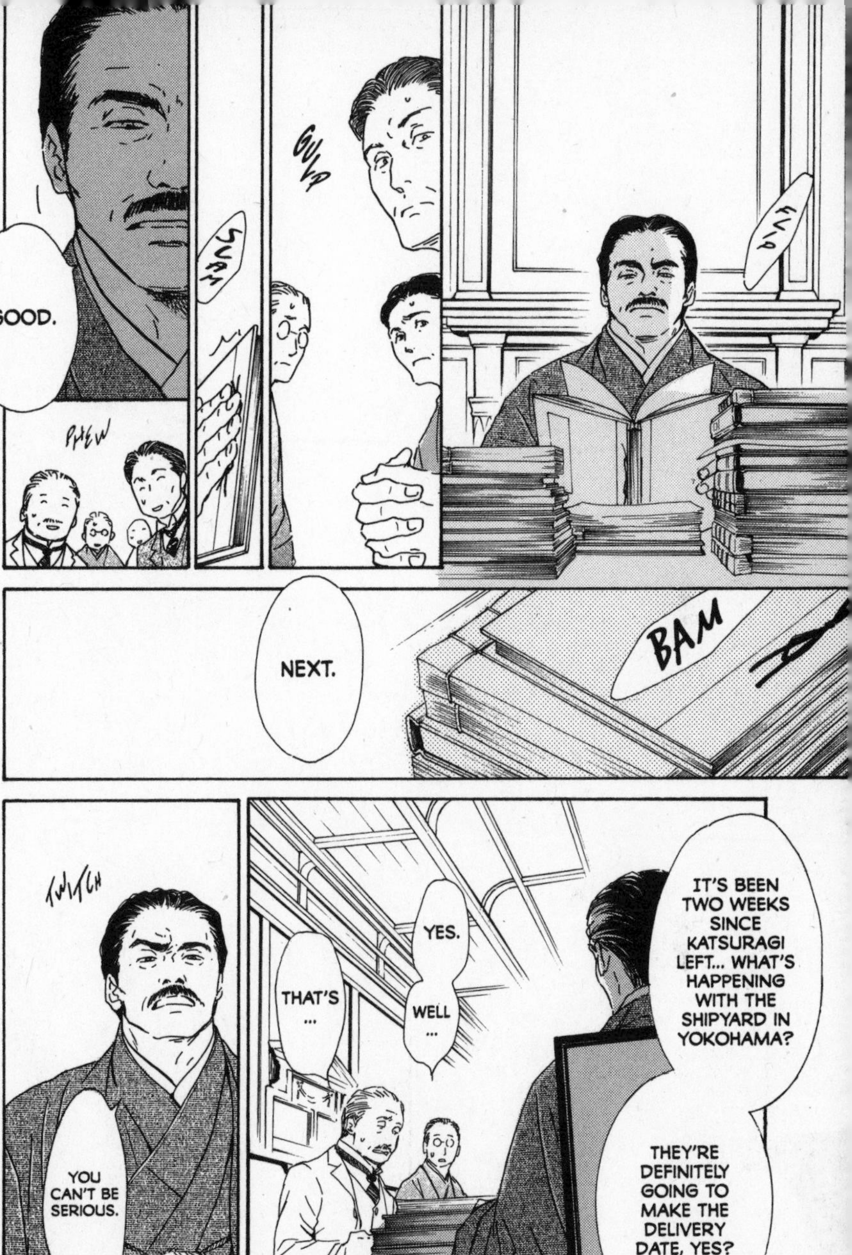
GULP
GOOD.
PHEW
BAM
NEXT.
IT'S BEEN TWO WEEKS SINCE KATSURAGI LEFT... WHAT'S HAPPENING WITH THE SHIPYARD IN YOKOHAMA?
THEY'RE DEFINITELY GOING TO MAKE THE DELIVERY DATE, YES?
YES.
WELL...
THAT'S...
TWITCH
YOU CAN'T BE SERIOUS.

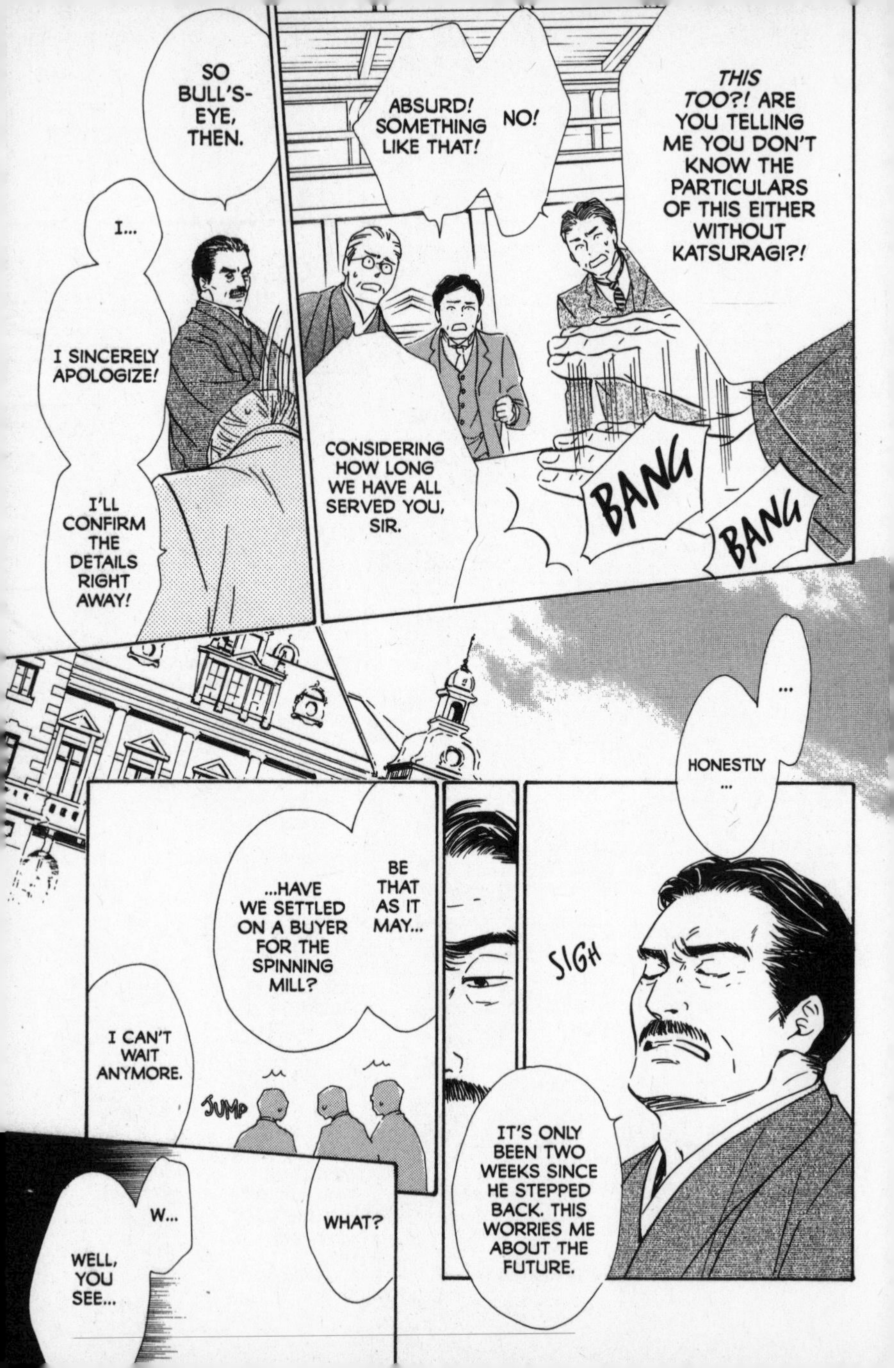
THIS TOO?! ARE YOU TELLING ME YOU DON'T KNOW THE PARTICULARS OF THIS EITHER WITHOUT KATSURAGI?!
NO!
ABSURD! SOMETHING LIKE THAT!
CONSIDERING HOW LONG WE HAVE ALL SERVED YOU, SIR.
BANG
BANG
SO BULL'S-EYE, THEN.
I...
I SINCERELY APOLOGIZE!
I'LL CONFIRM THE DETAILS RIGHT AWAY!
...
HONESTLY ...
SIGH
IT'S ONLY BEEN TWO WEEKS SINCE HE STEPPED BACK. THIS WORRIES ME ABOUT THE FUTURE.
BE THAT AS IT MAY...
...HAVE WE SETTLED ON A BUYER FOR THE SPINNING MILL?
I CAN'T WAIT ANYMORE.
JUMP
WHAT?
W...
WELL, YOU SEE...

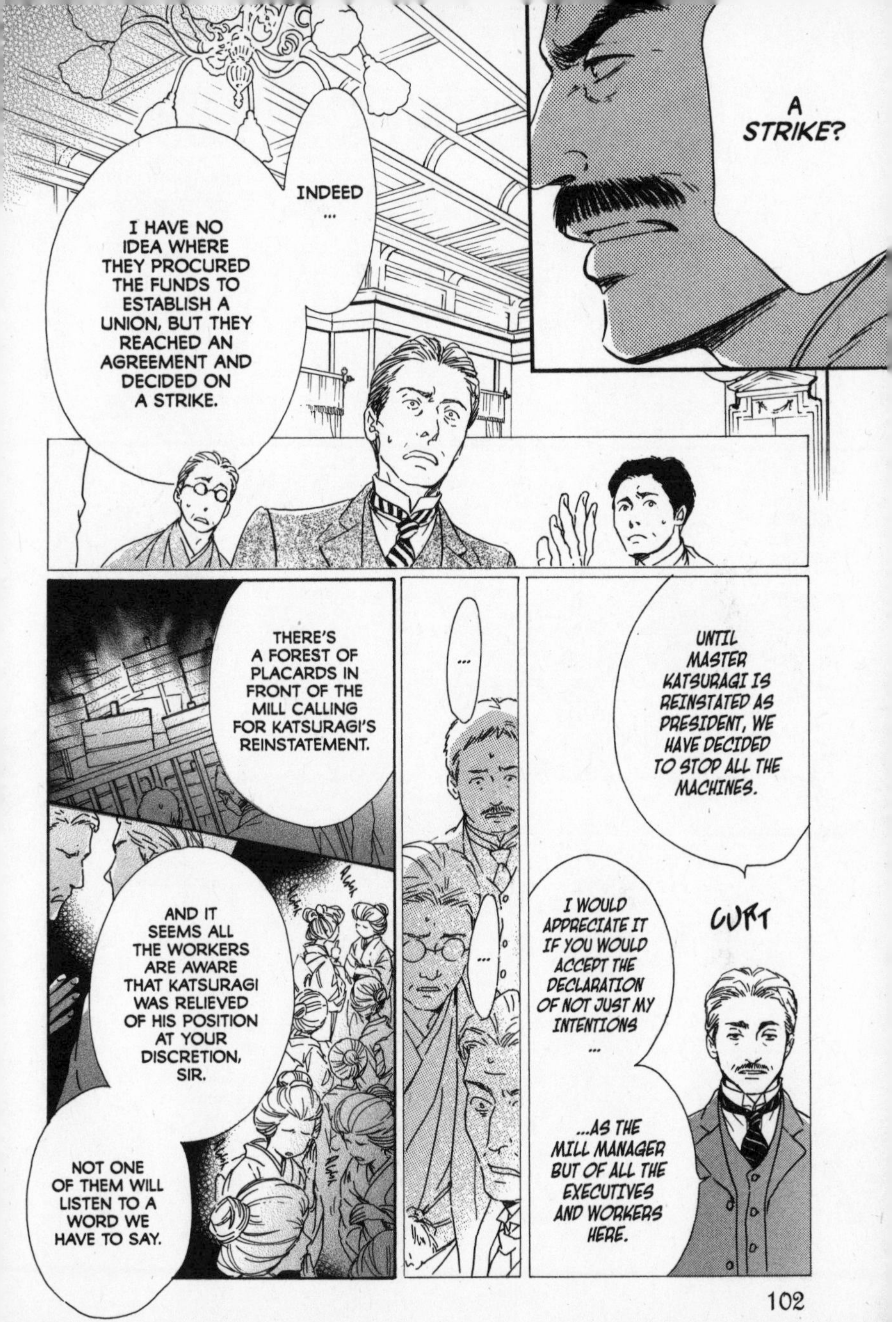
A STRIKE?
INDEED ...
I HAVE NO IDEA WHERE THEY PROCURED THE FUNDS TO ESTABLISH A UNION, BUT THEY REACHED AN AGREEMENT AND DECIDED ON A STRIKE.
UNTIL MASTER KATSURAGI IS REINSTATED AS PRESIDENT, WE HAVE DECIDED TO STOP ALL THE MACHINES.
CURT
I WOULD APPRECIATE IT IF YOU WOULD ACCEPT THE DECLARATION OF NOT JUST MY INTENTIONS ...
...AS THE MILL MANAGER BUT OF ALL THE EXECUTIVES AND WORKERS HERE.
...
...
THERE'S A FOREST OF PLACARDS IN FRONT OF THE MILL CALLING FOR KATSURAGI'S REINSTATEMENT.
AND IT SEEMS ALL THE WORKERS ARE AWARE THAT KATSURAGI WAS RELIEVED OF HIS POSITION AT YOUR DISCRETION, SIR.
NOT ONE OF THEM WILL LISTEN TO A WORD WE HAVE TO SAY.

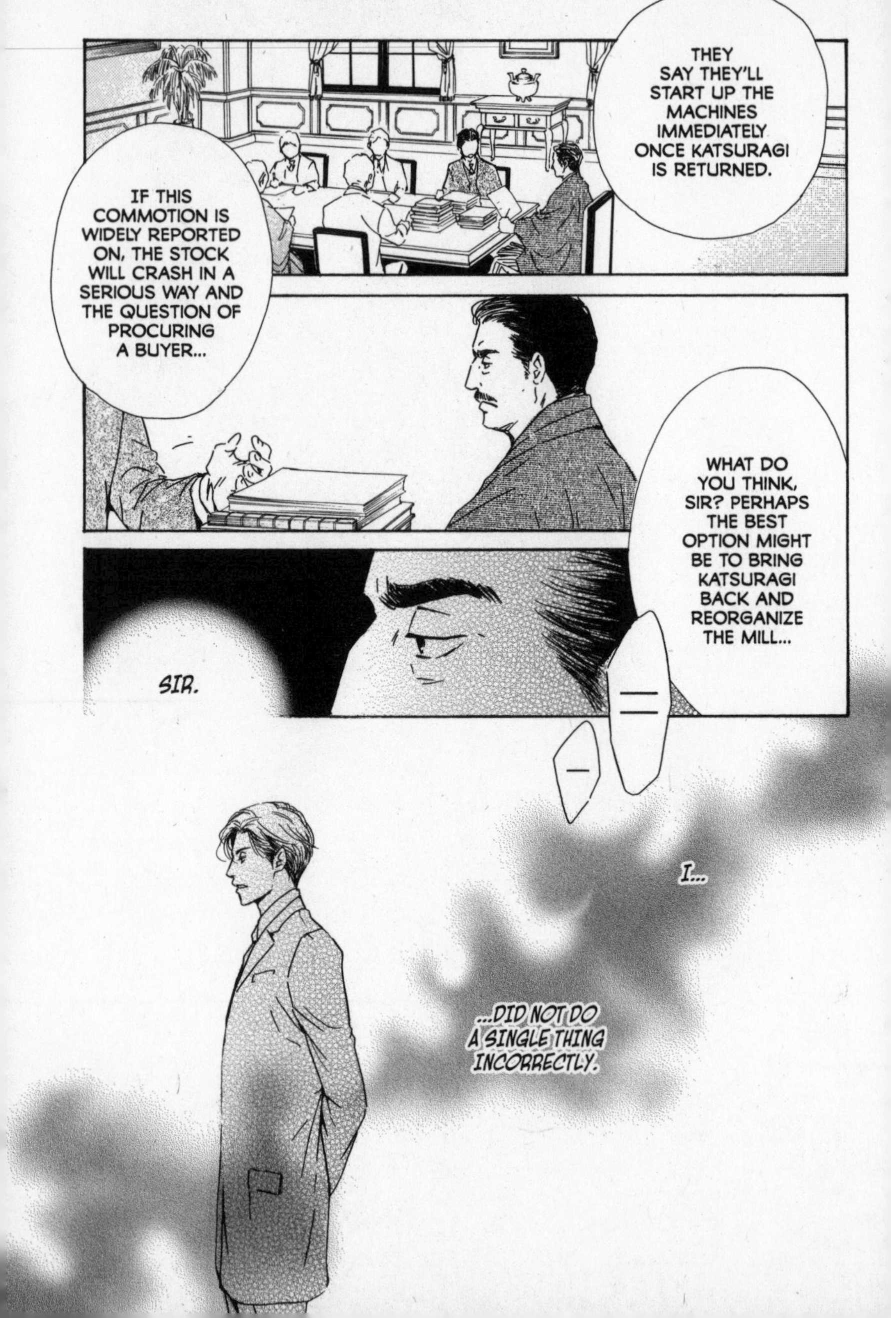
THEY SAY THEY'LL START UP THE MACHINES IMMEDIATELY ONCE KATSURAGI IS RETURNED.
IF THIS COMMOTION IS WIDELY REPORTED ON, THE STOCK WILL CRASH IN A SERIOUS WAY AND THE QUESTION OF PROCURING A BUYER...
WHAT DO YOU THINK, SIR? PERHAPS THE BEST OPTION MIGHT BE TO BRING KATSURAGI BACK AND REORGANIZE THE MILL...
SIR.
——
—
I...
...DID NOT DO A SINGLE THING INCORRECTLY.

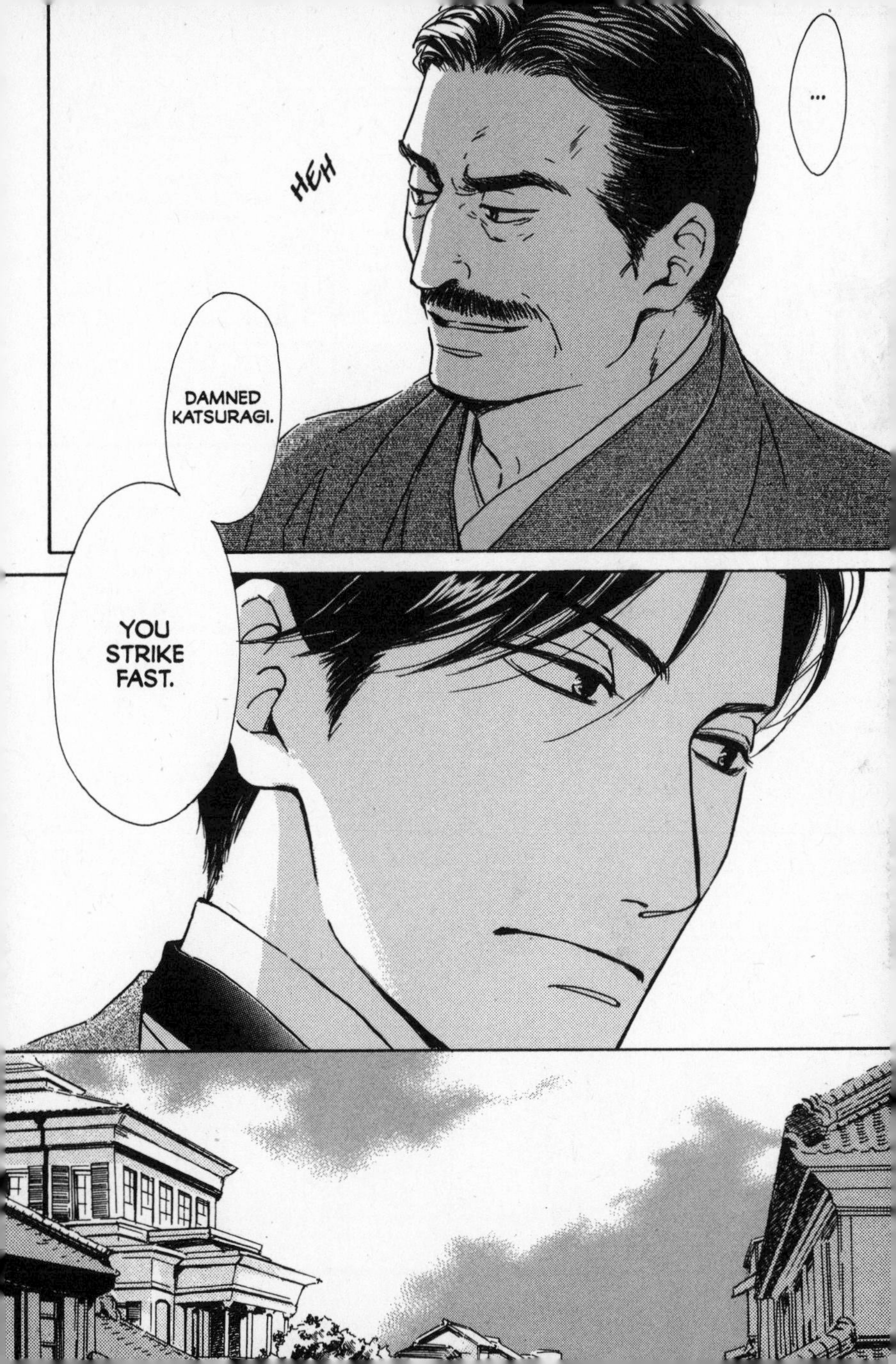
...
HEH
DAMNED KATSURAGI.
YOU STRIKE FAST.

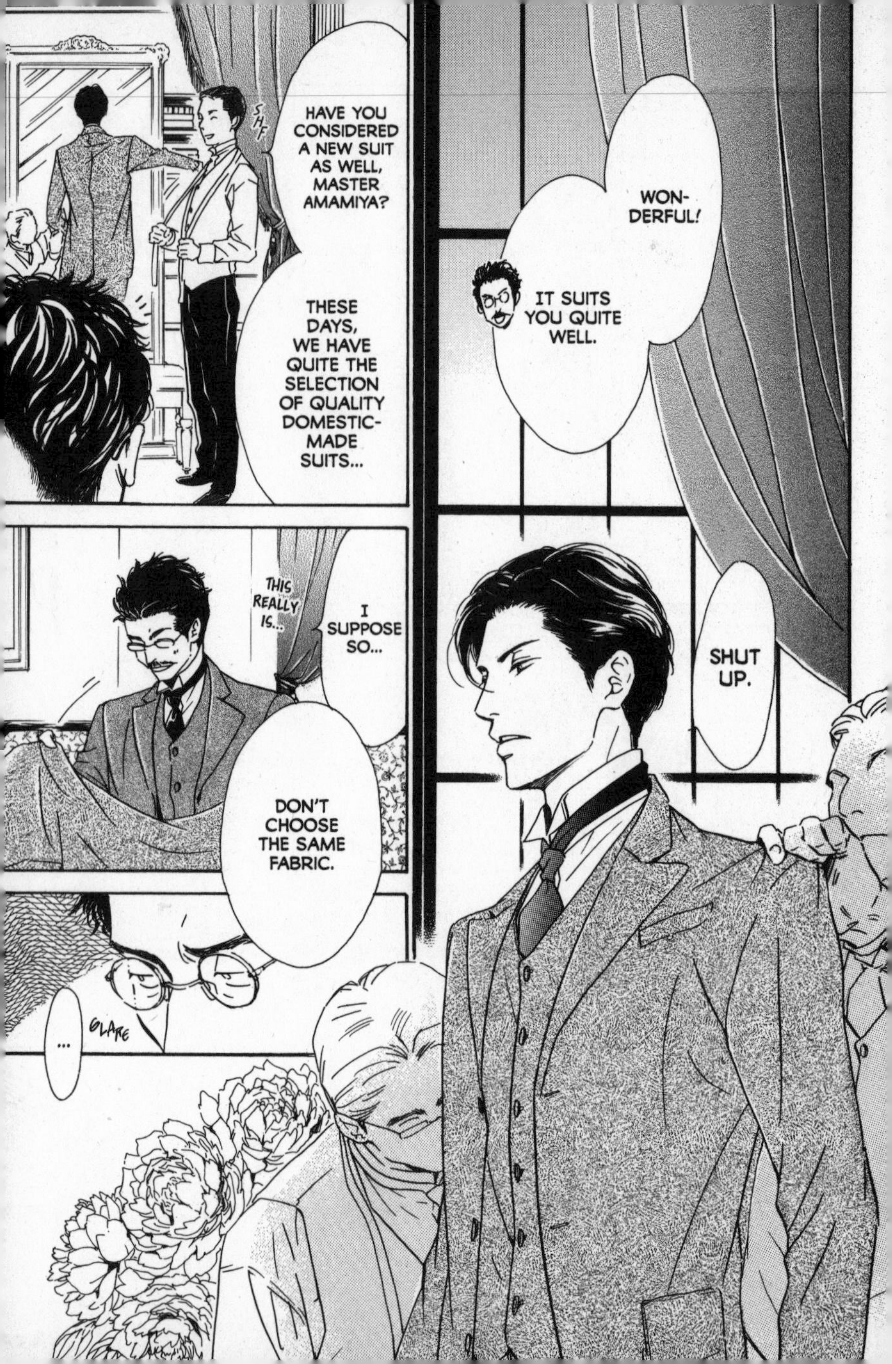
WON-DERFUL!
IT SUITS YOU QUITE WELL.
SHUT UP.
SHF
HAVE YOU CONSIDERED A NEW SUIT AS WELL, MASTER AMAMIYA?
THESE DAYS, WE HAVE QUITE THE SELECTION OF QUALITY DOMESTIC-MADE SUITS...
I SUPPOSE SO...
THIS REALLY IS...
DON'T CHOOSE THE SAME FABRIC.
GLARE
...

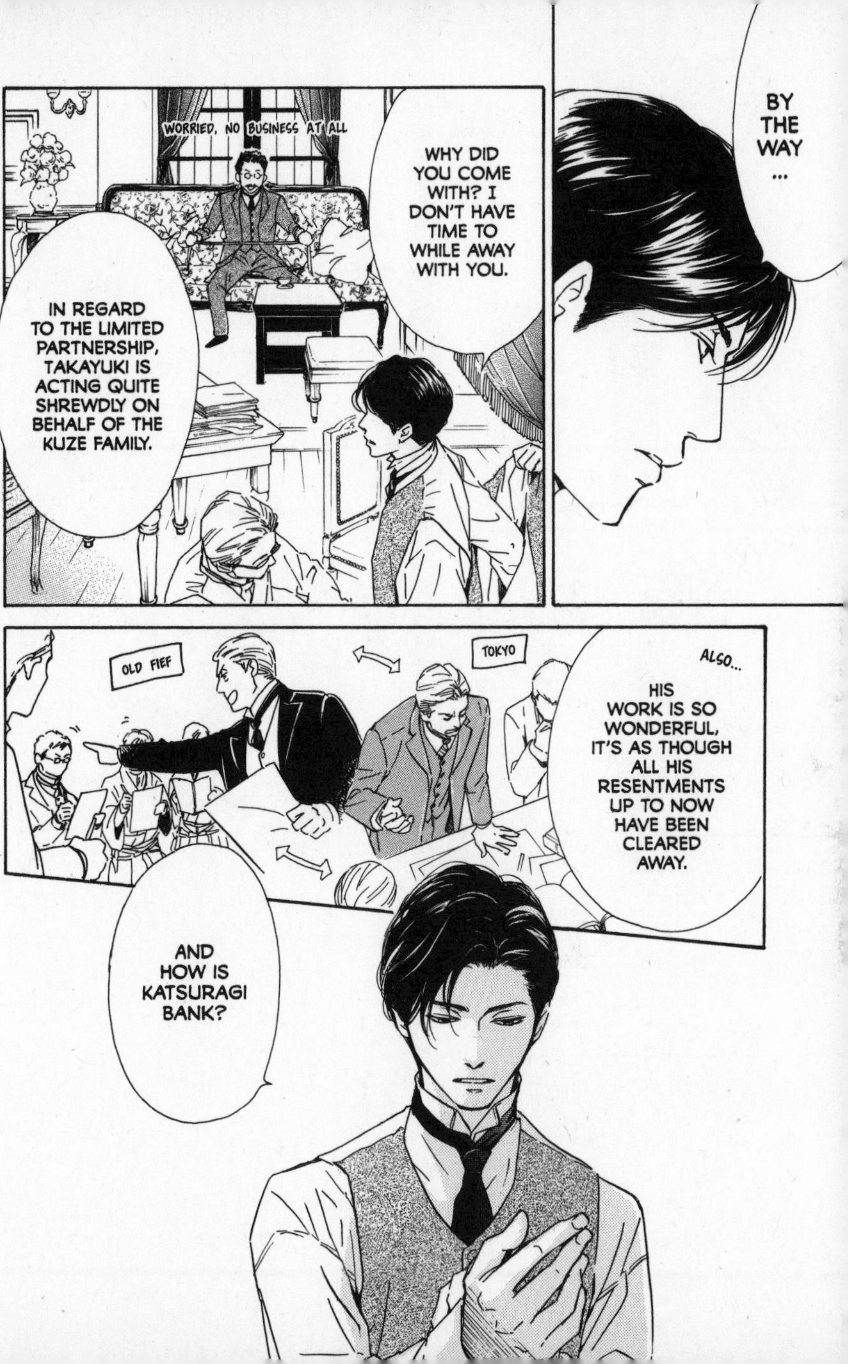
BY THE WAY ...
WHY DID YOU COME WITH? I DON'T HAVE TIME TO WHILE AWAY WITH YOU.
WORRIED, NO BUSINESS AT ALL
IN REGARD TO THE LIMITED PARTNERSHIP, TAKAYUKI IS ACTING QUITE SHREWDLY ON BEHALF OF THE KUZE FAMILY.
ALSO...
HIS WORK IS SO WONDERFUL, IT'S AS THOUGH ALL HIS RESENTMENTS UP TO NOW HAVE BEEN CLEARED AWAY.
TOKYO
OLD FIEF
AND HOW IS KATSURAGI BANK?

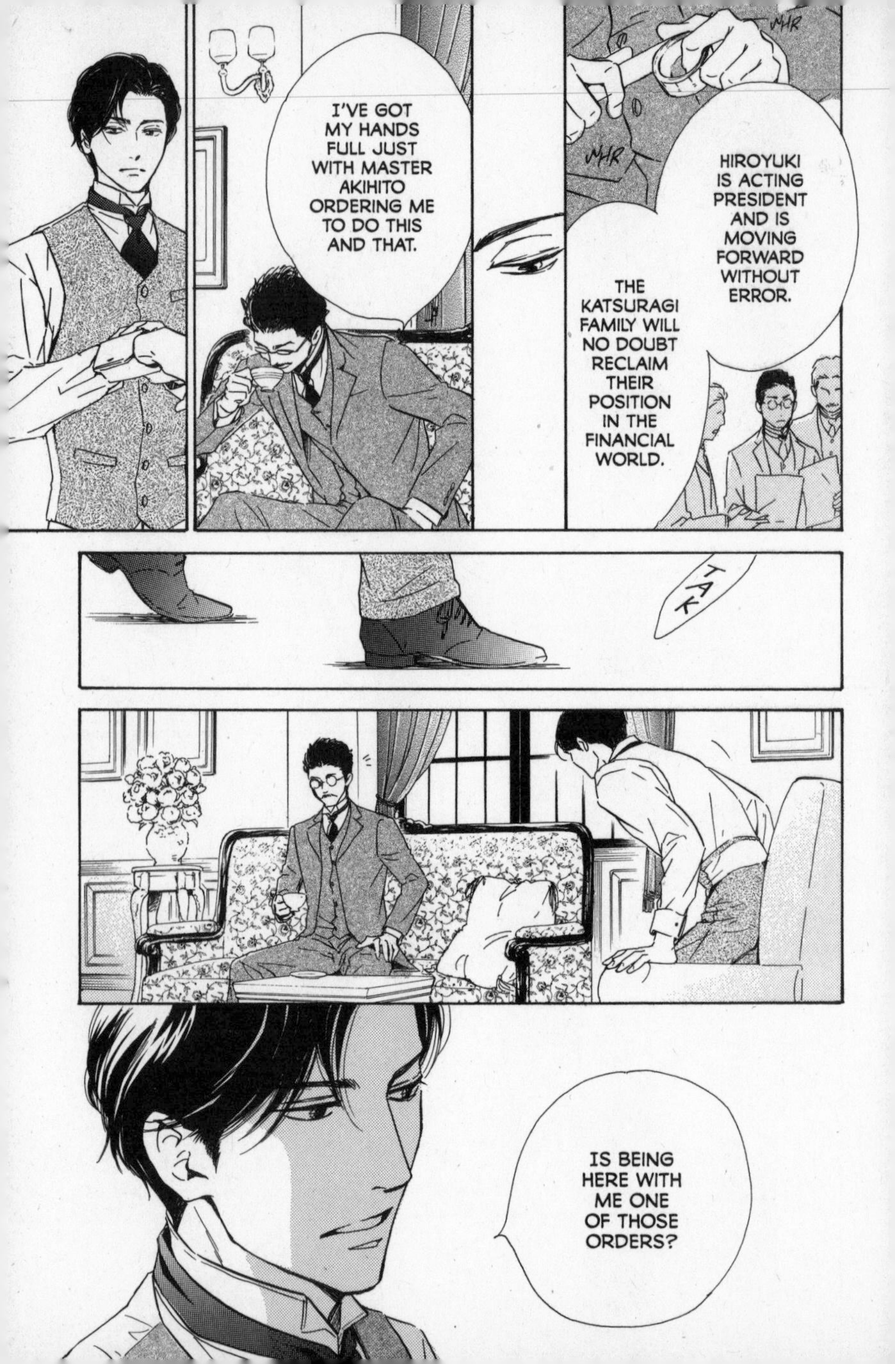
HIROYUKI IS ACTING PRESIDENT AND IS MOVING FORWARD WITHOUT ERROR.
THE KATSURAGI FAMILY WILL NO DOUBT RECLAIM THEIR POSITION IN THE FINANCIAL WORLD.
I'VE GOT MY HANDS FULL JUST WITH MASTER AKIHITO ORDERING ME TO DO THIS AND THAT.
TAK
IS BEING HERE WITH ME ONE OF THOSE ORDERS?

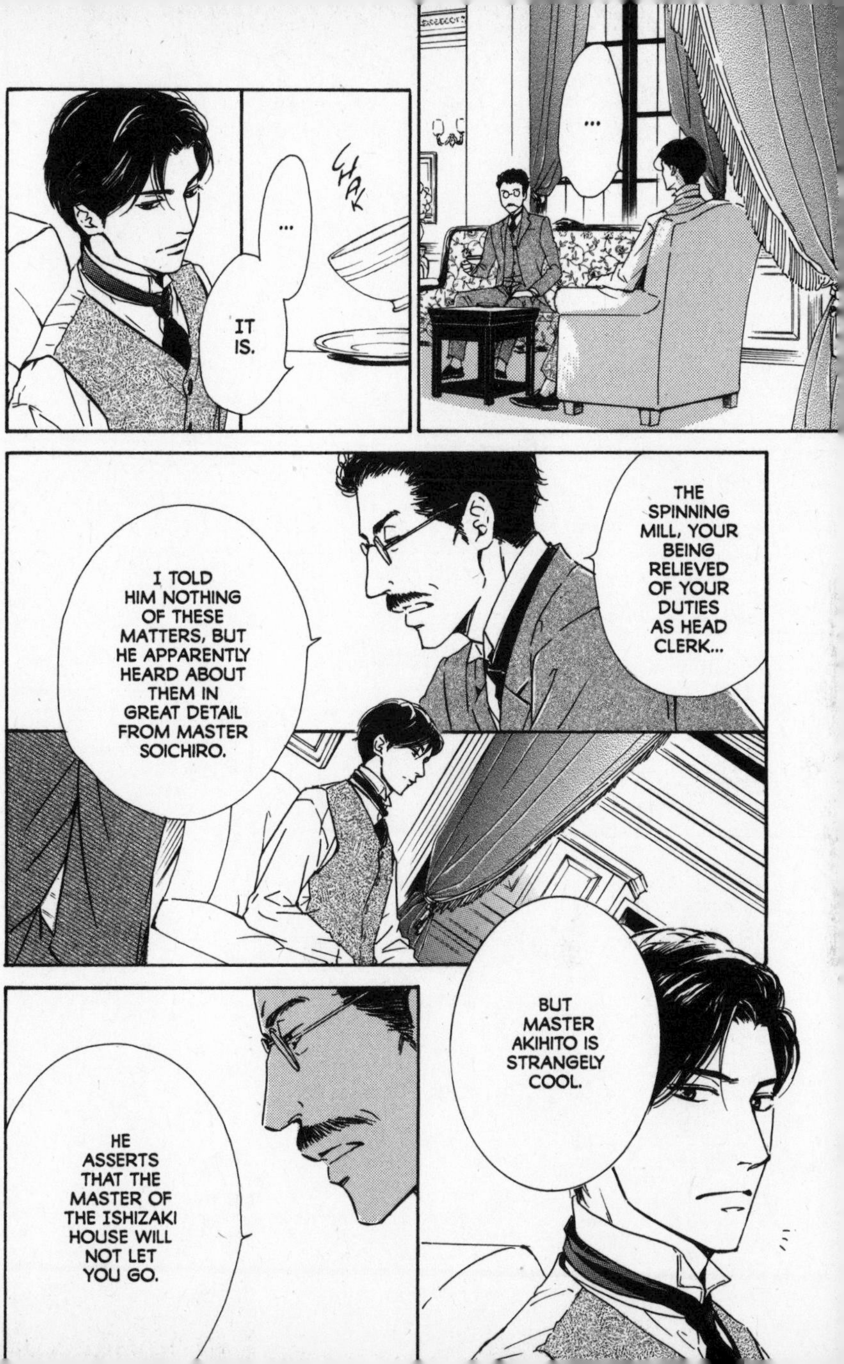
...
WHAK
...
IT IS.
THE SPINNING MILL, YOUR BEING RELIEVED OF YOUR DUTIES AS HEAD CLERK...
I TOLD HIM NOTHING OF THESE MATTERS, BUT HE APPARENTLY HEARD ABOUT THEM IN GREAT DETAIL FROM MASTER SOICHIRO.
BUT MASTER AKIHITO IS STRANGELY COOL.
HE ASSERTS THAT THE MASTER OF THE ISHIZAKI HOUSE WILL NOT LET YOU GO.

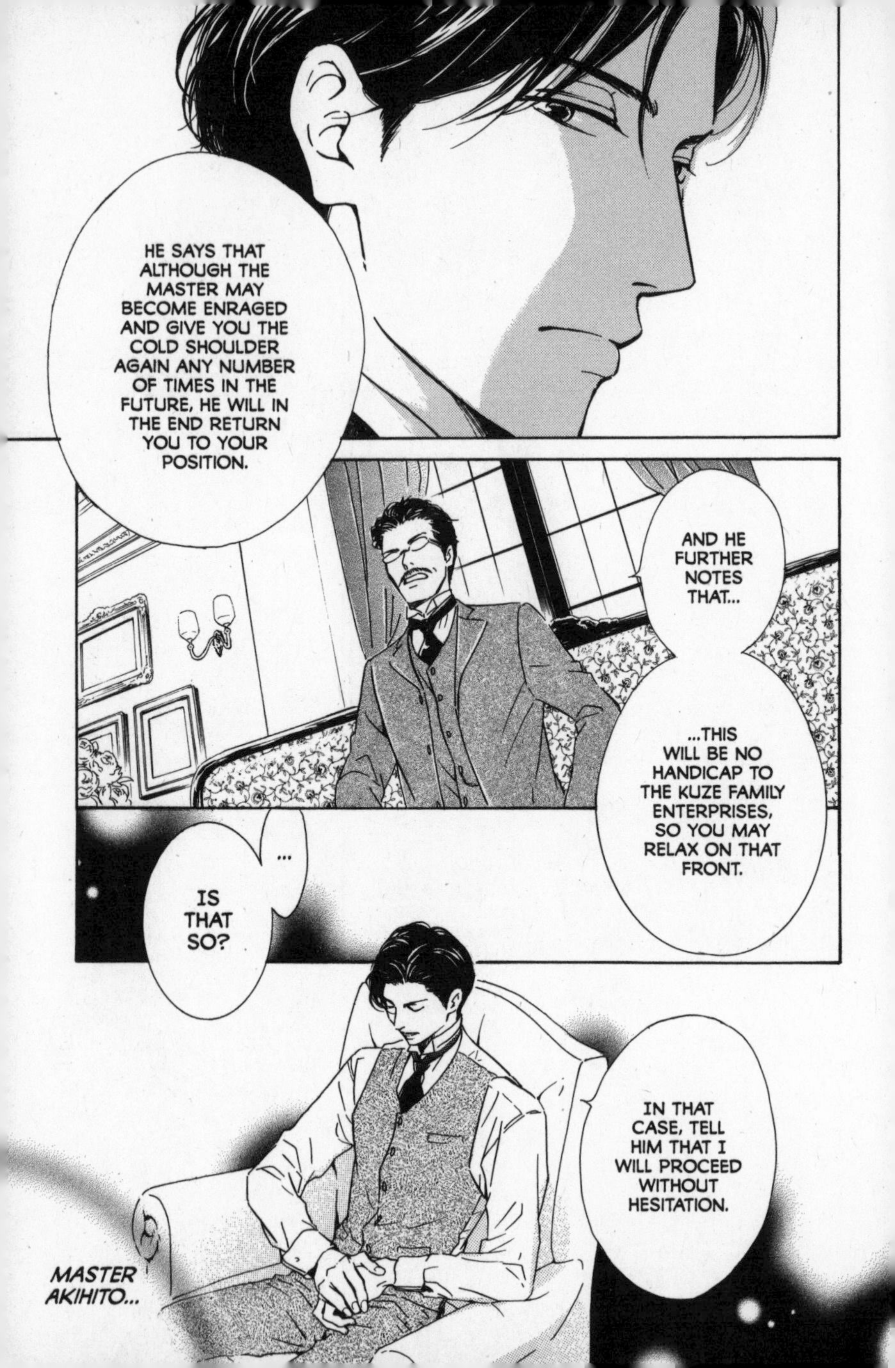
HE SAYS THAT ALTHOUGH THE MASTER MAY BECOME ENRAGED AND GIVE YOU THE COLD SHOULDER AGAIN ANY NUMBER OF TIMES IN THE FUTURE, HE WILL IN THE END RETURN YOU TO YOUR POSITION.
AND HE FURTHER NOTES THAT...
...THIS WILL BE NO HANDICAP TO THE KUZE FAMILY ENTERPRISES, SO YOU MAY RELAX ON THAT FRONT.
...
IS THAT SO?
IN THAT CASE, TELL HIM THAT I WILL PROCEED WITHOUT HESITATION.
MASTER AKIHITO...

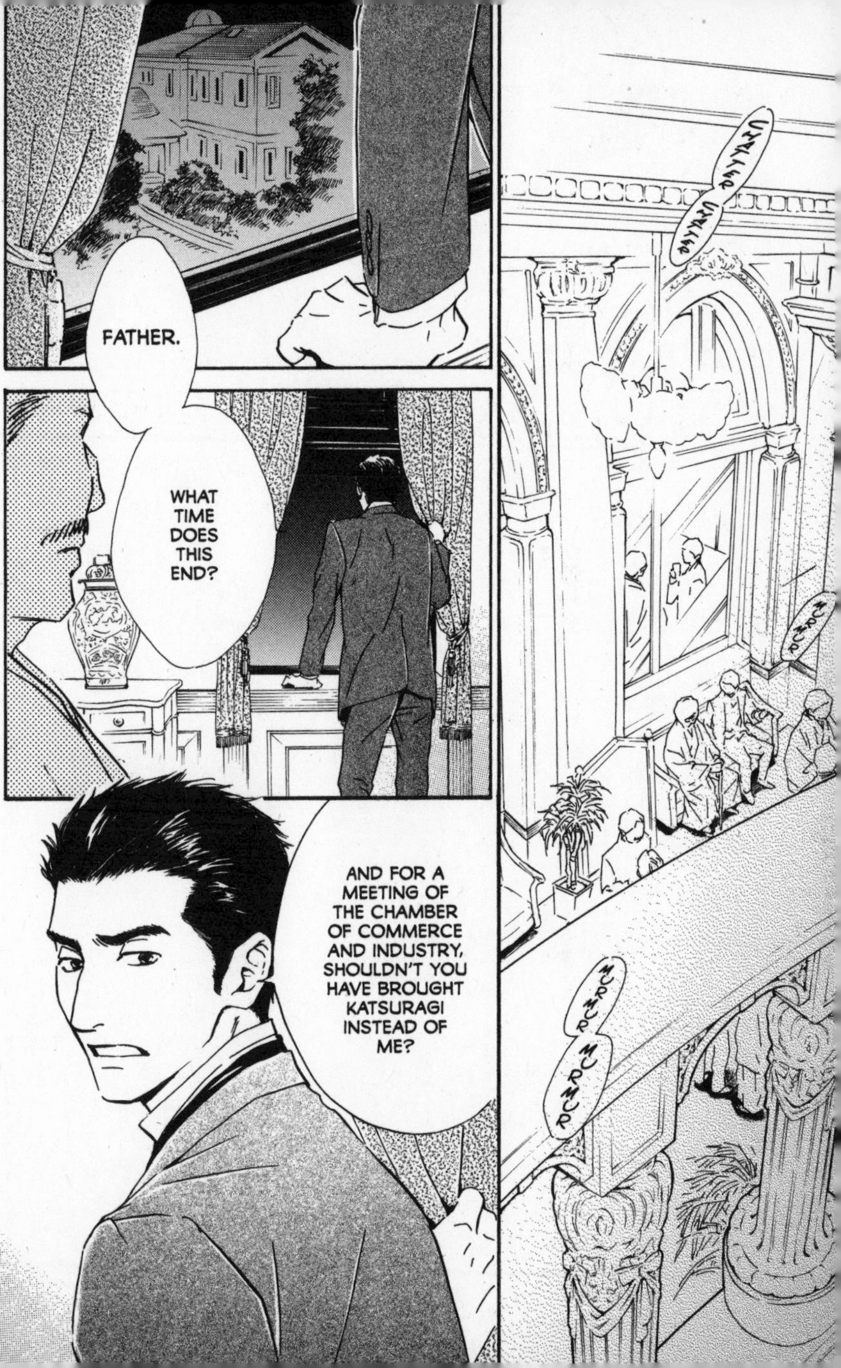
MURMUR MURMUR
MURMUR
MURMUR MURMUR
FATHER.
WHAT TIME DOES THIS END?
AND FOR A MEETING OF THE CHAMBER OF COMMERCE AND INDUSTRY, SHOULDN'T YOU HAVE BROUGHT KATSURAGI INSTEAD OF ME?

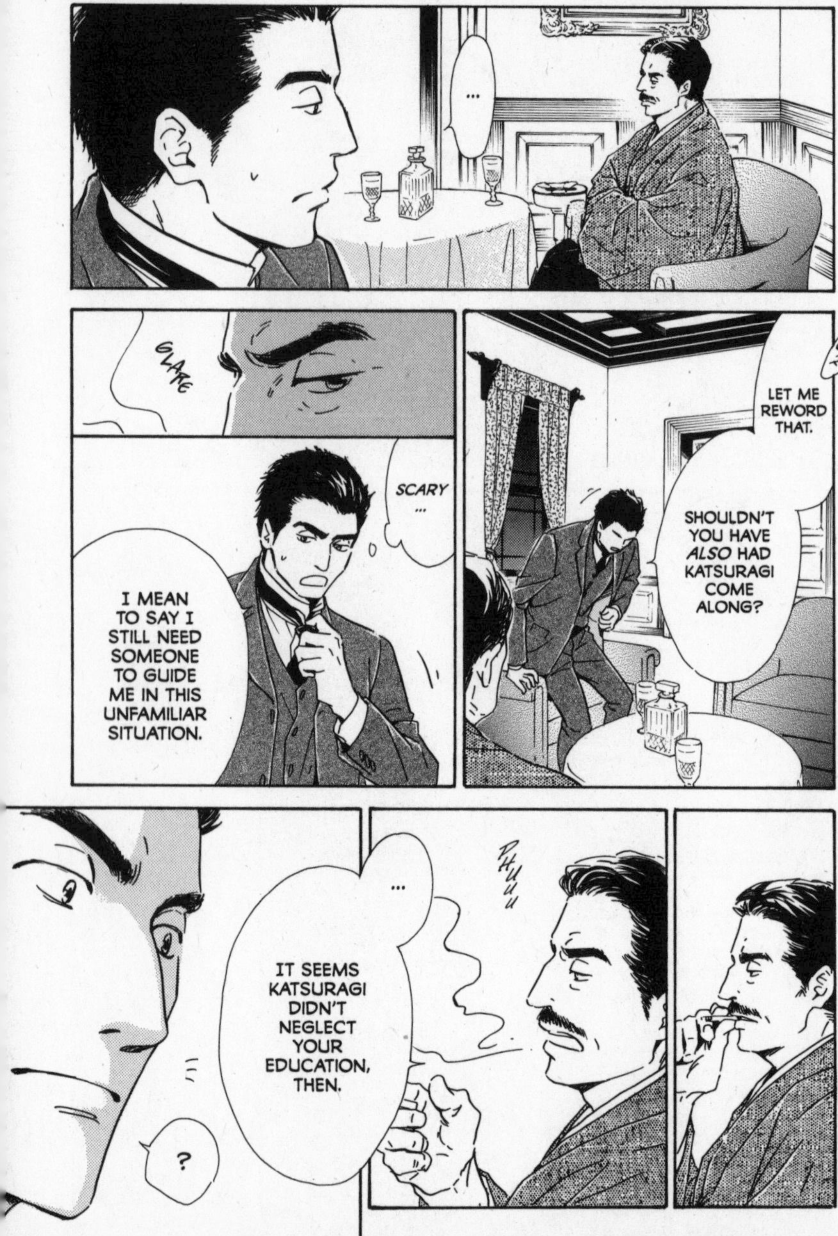
...
KOFF
LET ME REWORD THAT.
SHOULDN'T YOU HAVE *ALSO* HAD KATSURAGI COME ALONG?
GLARE
SCARY ...
I MEAN TO SAY I STILL NEED SOMEONE TO GUIDE ME IN THIS UNFAMILIAR SITUATION.
PHUUU
...
IT SEEMS KATSURAGI DIDN'T NEGLECT YOUR EDUCATION, THEN.
?

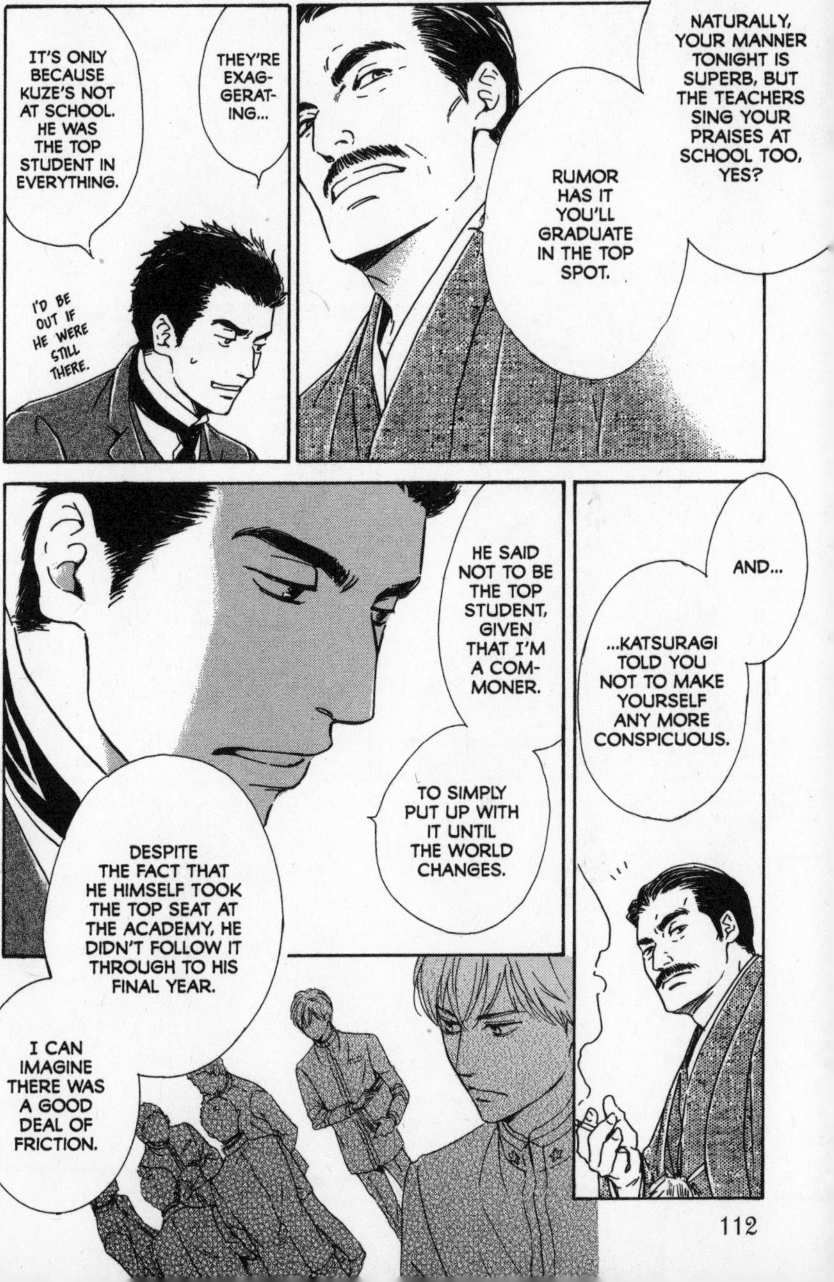
NATURALLY, YOUR MANNER TONIGHT IS SUPERB, BUT THE TEACHERS SING YOUR PRAISES AT SCHOOL TOO, YES?
RUMOR HAS IT YOU'LL GRADUATE IN THE TOP SPOT.
THEY'RE EXAG-GERAT-ING...
IT'S ONLY BECAUSE KUZE'S NOT AT SCHOOL. HE WAS THE TOP STUDENT IN EVERYTHING.
I'D BE OUT IF HE WERE STILL THERE.
AND...
...KATSURAGI TOLD YOU NOT TO MAKE YOURSELF ANY MORE CONSPICUOUS.
HE SAID NOT TO BE THE TOP STUDENT, GIVEN THAT I'M A COM-MONER.
TO SIMPLY PUT UP WITH IT UNTIL THE WORLD CHANGES.
DESPITE THE FACT THAT HE HIMSELF TOOK THE TOP SEAT AT THE ACADEMY, HE DIDN'T FOLLOW IT THROUGH TO HIS FINAL YEAR.
I CAN IMAGINE THERE WAS A GOOD DEAL OF FRICTION.

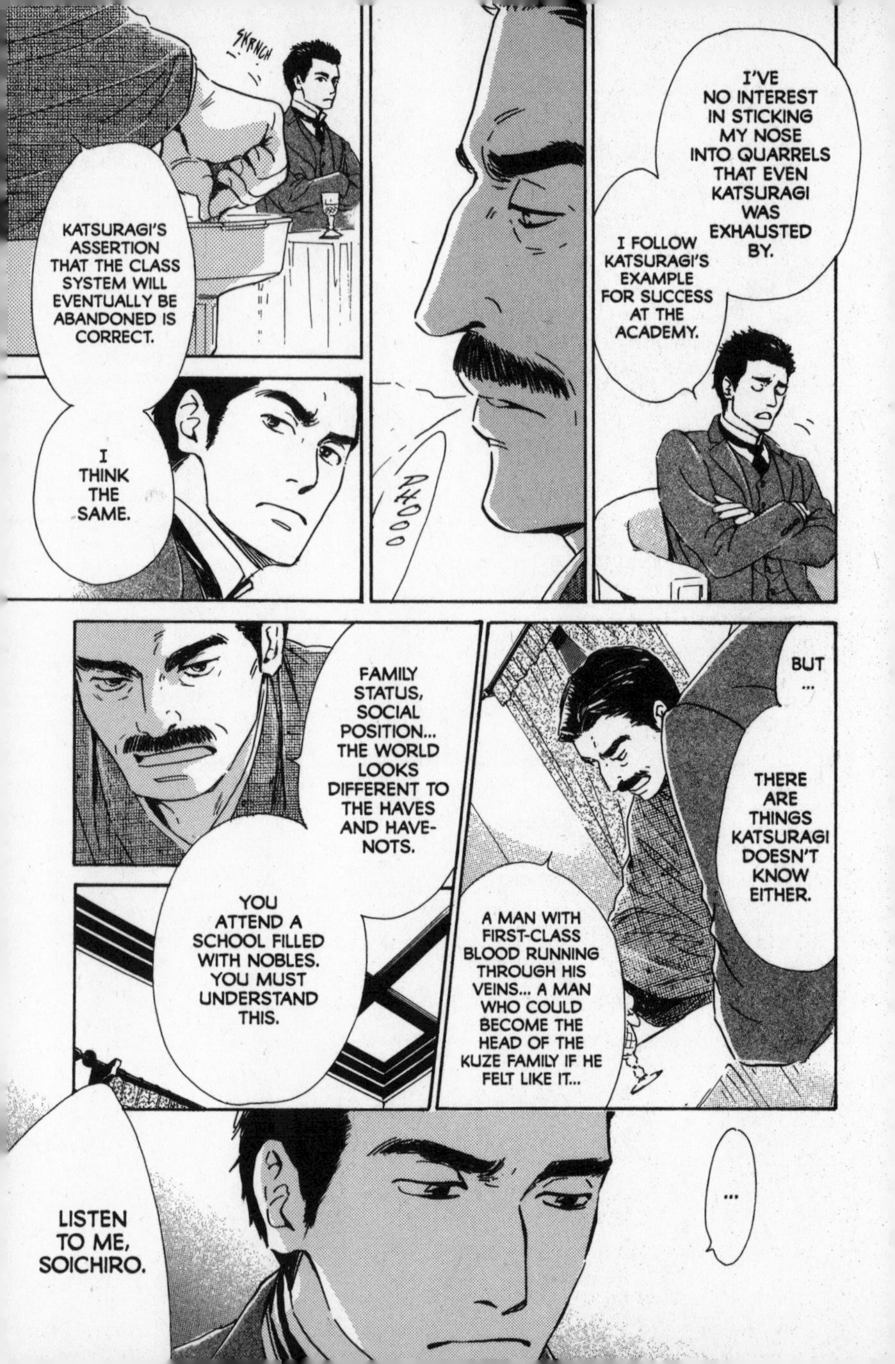
I'VE NO INTEREST IN STICKING MY NOSE INTO QUARRELS THAT EVEN KATSURAGI WAS EXHAUSTED BY.
I FOLLOW KATSURAGI'S EXAMPLE FOR SUCCESS AT THE ACADEMY.
PHOOO
SKRNCH
KATSURAGI'S ASSERTION THAT THE CLASS SYSTEM WILL EVENTUALLY BE ABANDONED IS CORRECT.
I THINK THE SAME.
BUT ...
THERE ARE THINGS KATSURAGI DOESN'T KNOW EITHER.
A MAN WITH FIRST-CLASS BLOOD RUNNING THROUGH HIS VEINS... A MAN WHO COULD BECOME THE HEAD OF THE KUZE FAMILY IF HE FELT LIKE IT...
FAMILY STATUS, SOCIAL POSITION... THE WORLD LOOKS DIFFERENT TO THE HAVES AND HAVE-NOTS.
YOU ATTEND A SCHOOL FILLED WITH NOBLES. YOU MUST UNDERSTAND THIS.
...
LISTEN TO ME, SOICHIRO.

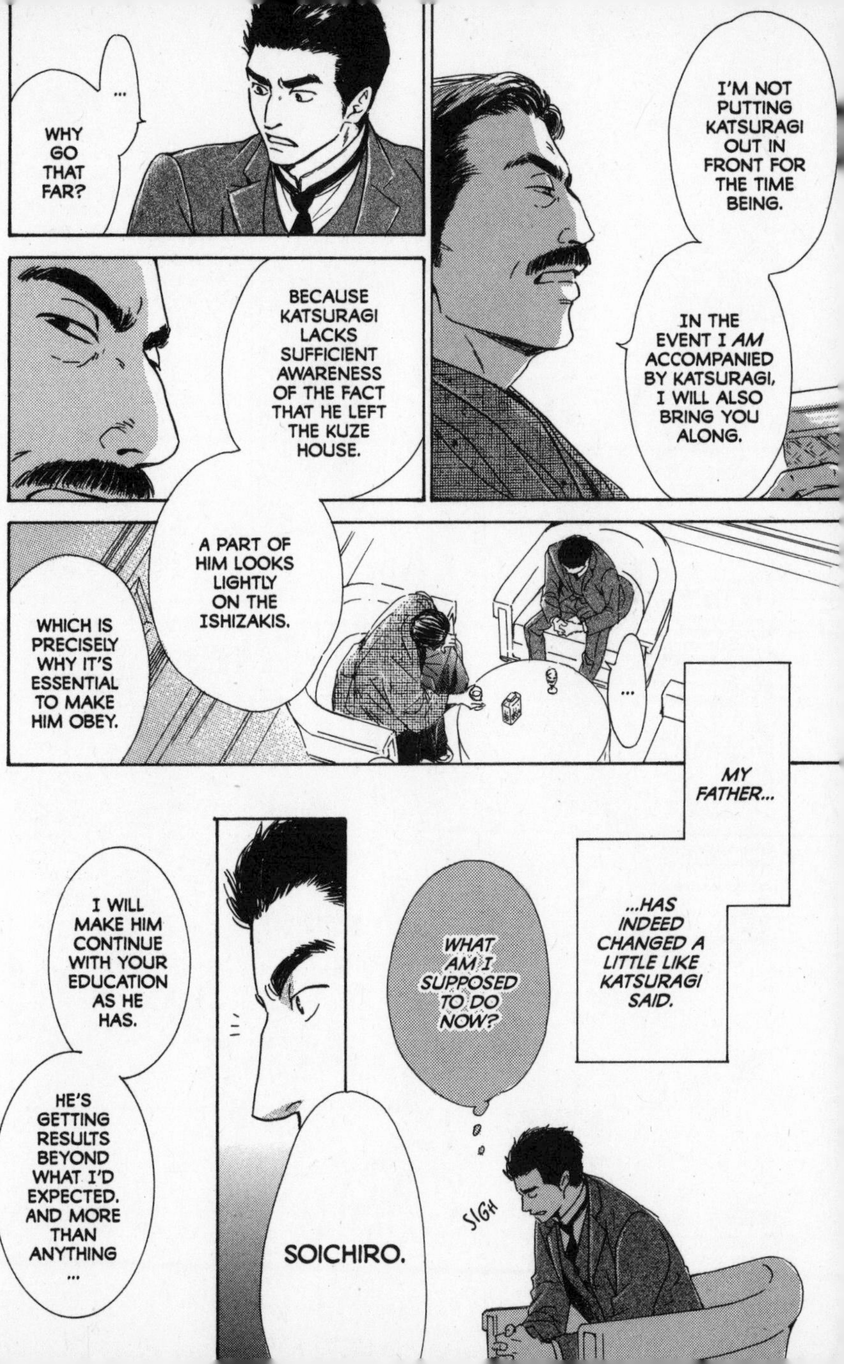
I'M NOT PUTTING KATSURAGI OUT IN FRONT FOR THE TIME BEING.
IN THE EVENT I *AM* ACCOMPANIED BY KATSURAGI, I WILL ALSO BRING YOU ALONG.
...
WHY GO THAT FAR?
BECAUSE KATSURAGI LACKS SUFFICIENT AWARENESS OF THE FACT THAT HE LEFT THE KUZE HOUSE.
A PART OF HIM LOOKS LIGHTLY ON THE ISHIZAKIS.
WHICH IS PRECISELY WHY IT'S ESSENTIAL TO MAKE HIM OBEY.
...
MY FATHER...
...HAS INDEED CHANGED A LITTLE LIKE KATSURAGI SAID.
WHAT AM I SUPPOSED TO DO NOW?
SIGH
I WILL MAKE HIM CONTINUE WITH YOUR EDUCATION AS HE HAS.
HE'S GETTING RESULTS BEYOND WHAT I'D EXPECTED. AND MORE THAN ANYTHING ...
SOICHIRO.

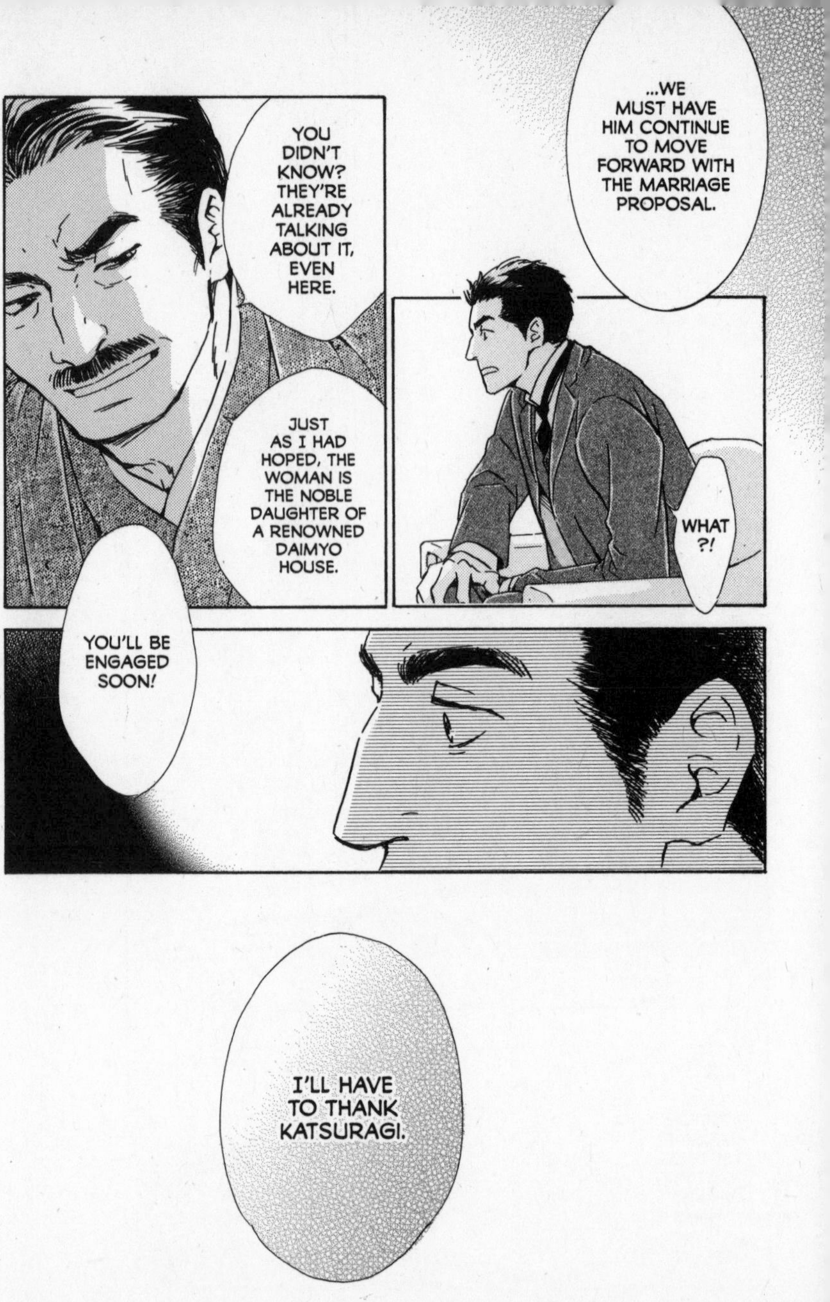
...WE MUST HAVE HIM CONTINUE TO MOVE FORWARD WITH THE MARRIAGE PROPOSAL.
WHAT?!
YOU DIDN'T KNOW? THEY'RE ALREADY TALKING ABOUT IT, EVEN HERE.
JUST AS I HAD HOPED, THE WOMAN IS THE NOBLE DAUGHTER OF A RENOWNED DAIMYO HOUSE.
YOU'LL BE ENGAGED SOON!
I'LL HAVE TO THANK KATSURAGI.

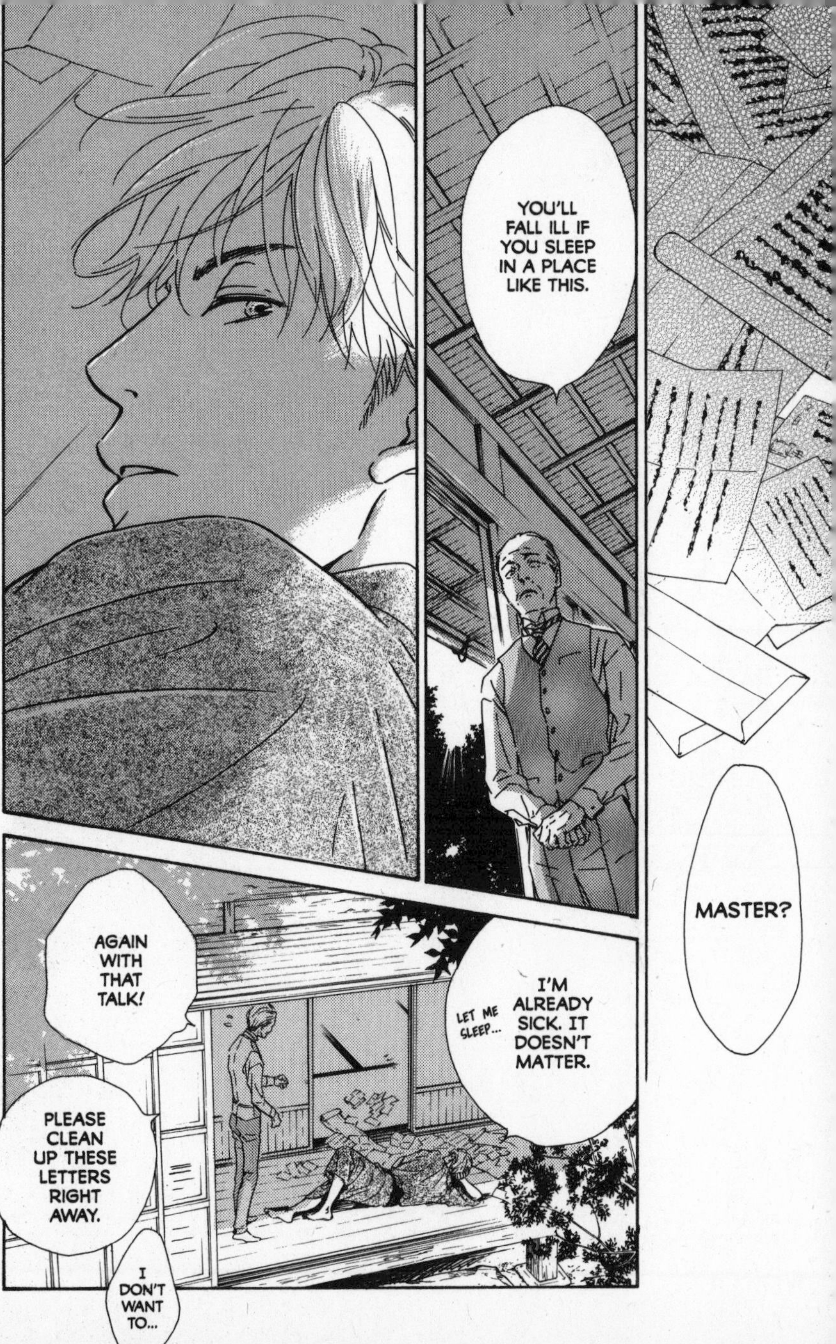
MASTER?
YOU'LL FALL ILL IF YOU SLEEP IN A PLACE LIKE THIS.
I'M ALREADY SICK. IT DOESN'T MATTER.
LET ME SLEEP...
AGAIN WITH THAT TALK!
PLEASE CLEAN UP THESE LETTERS RIGHT AWAY.
I DON'T WANT TO...

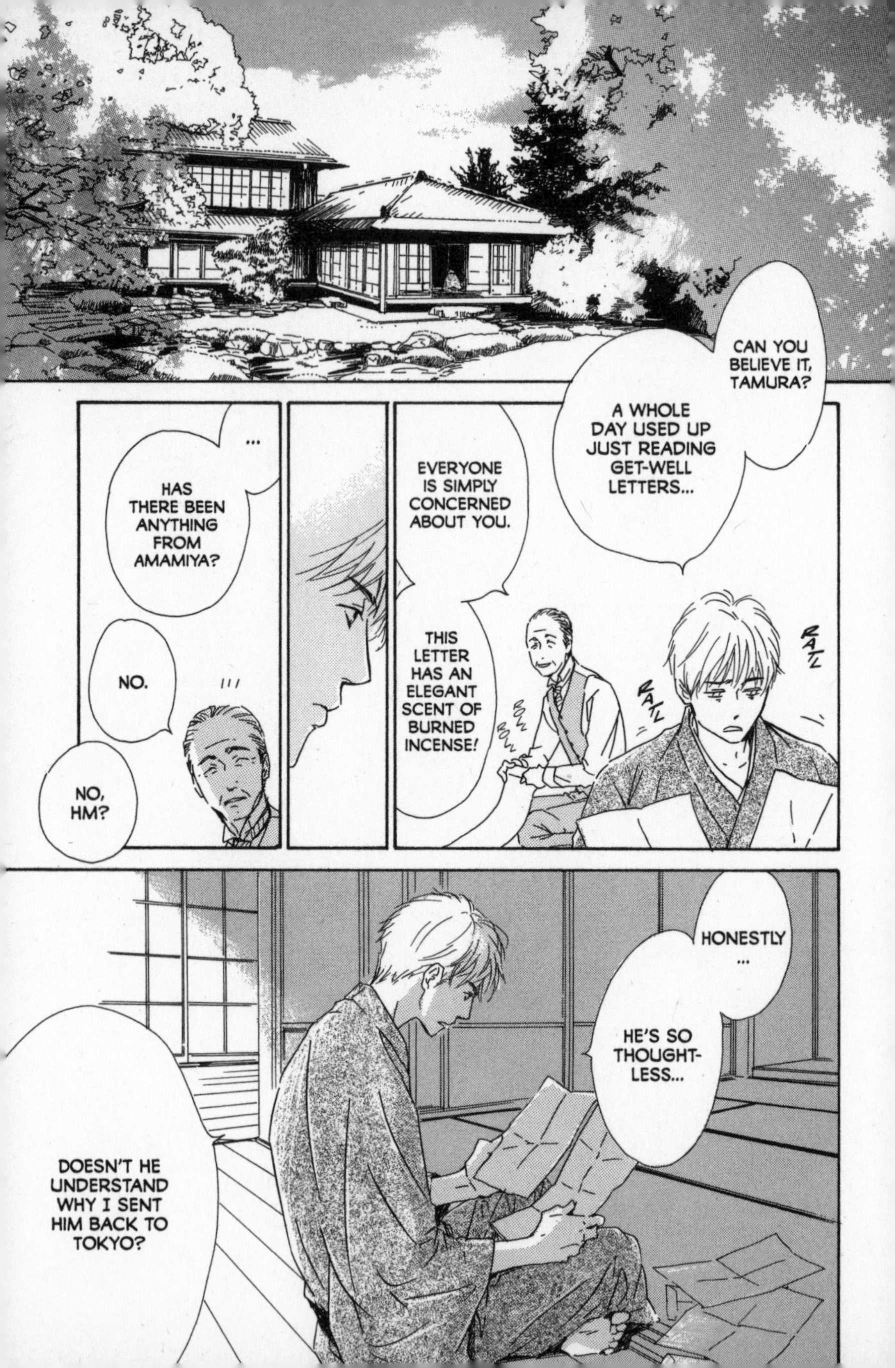

CAN YOU BELIEVE IT, TAMURA?
A WHOLE DAY USED UP JUST READING GET-WELL LETTERS...
RATL
RATL
EVERYONE IS SIMPLY CONCERNED ABOUT YOU.
THIS LETTER HAS AN ELEGANT SCENT OF BURNED INCENSE!
...
HAS THERE BEEN ANYTHING FROM AMAMIYA?
NO.
NO, HM?
HONESTLY ...
HE'S SO THOUGHT-LESS...
DOESN'T HE UNDERSTAND WHY I SENT HIM BACK TO TOKYO?

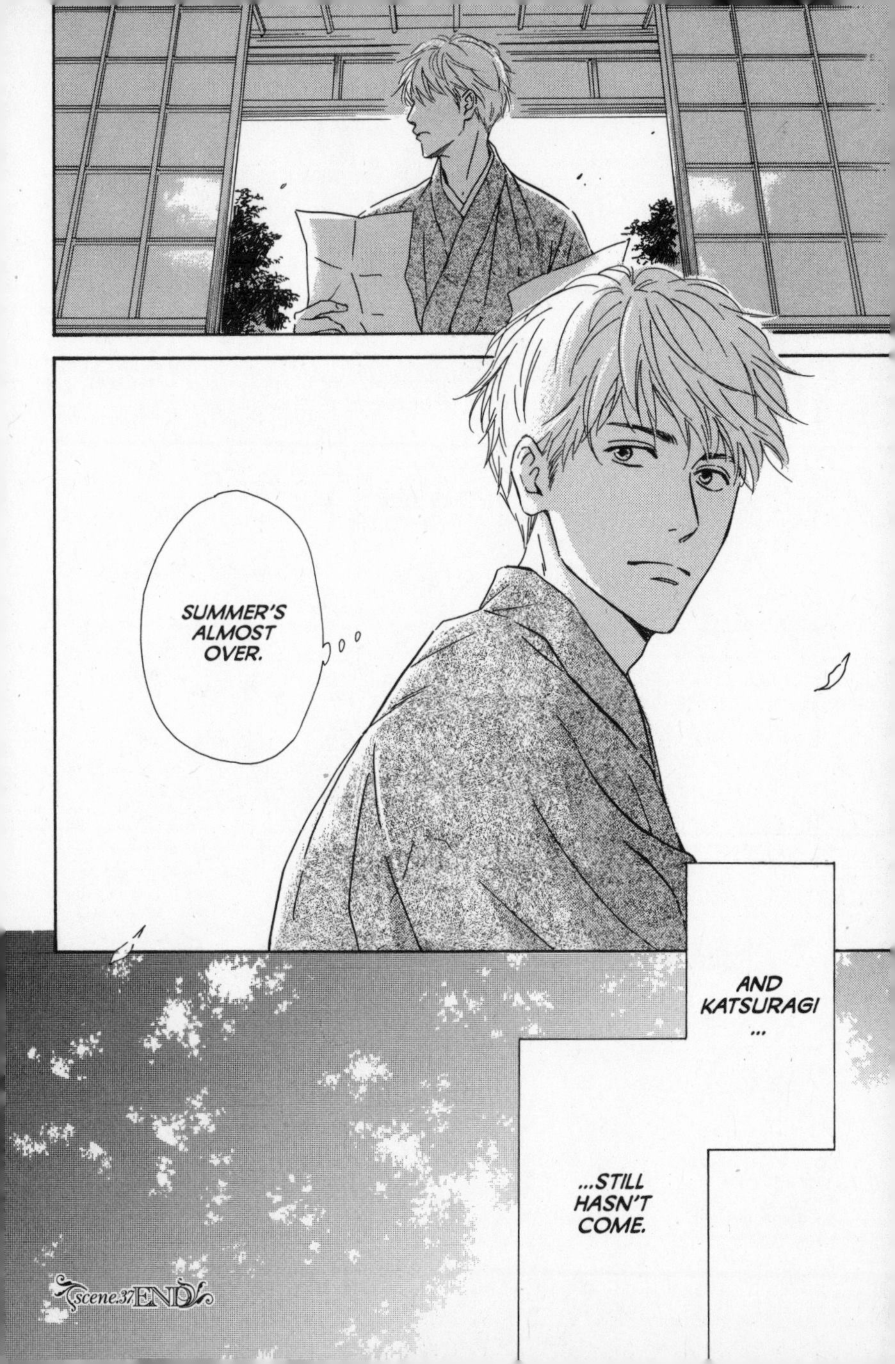
SUMMER'S ALMOST OVER.
AND KATSURAGI ...
...STILL HASN'T COME.
scene.37 END

憂鬱な朝

Blue Morning

憂鬱な朝

Blue Morning

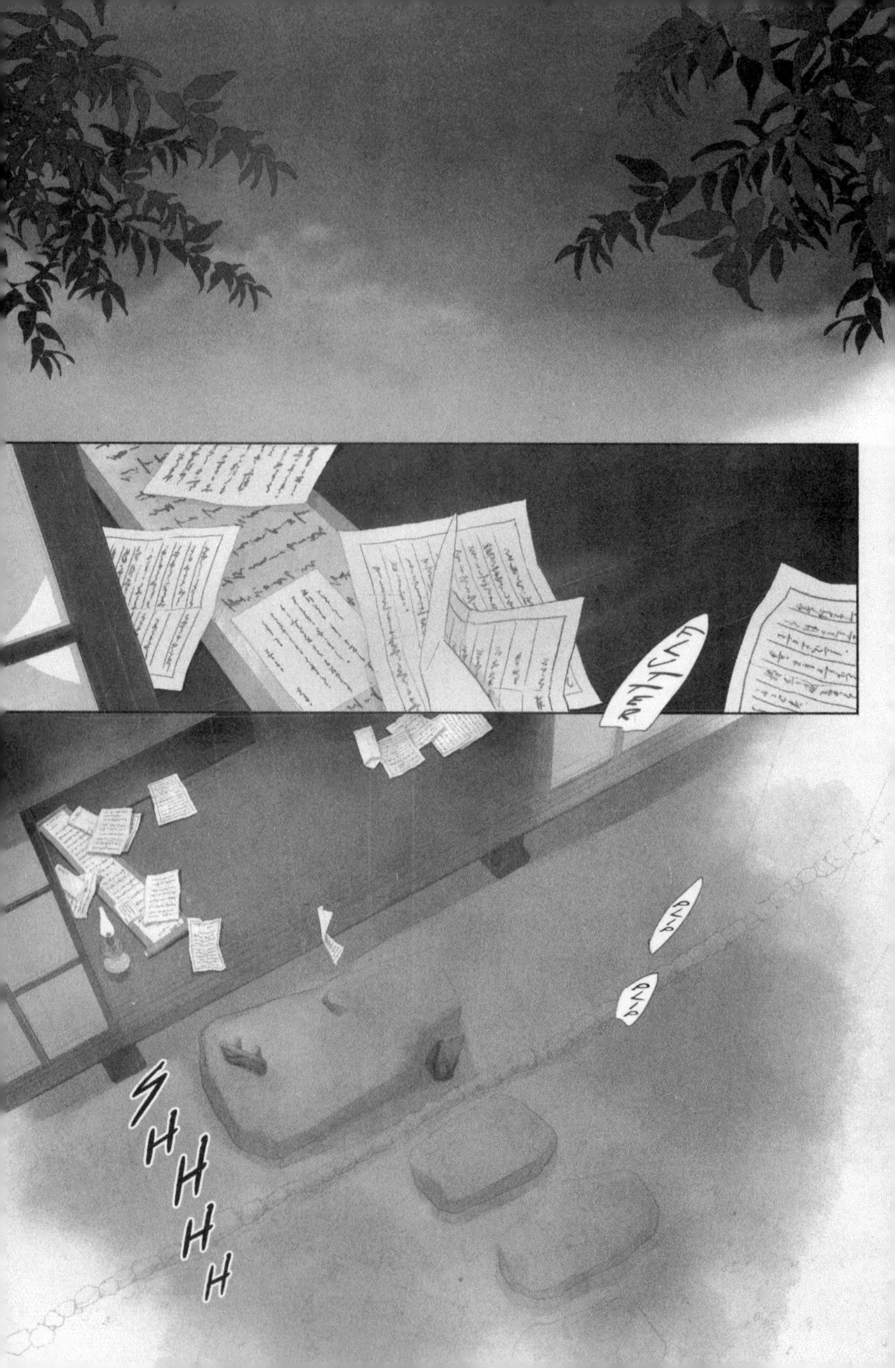
FLUTTER
flip
flip
SHHHHH

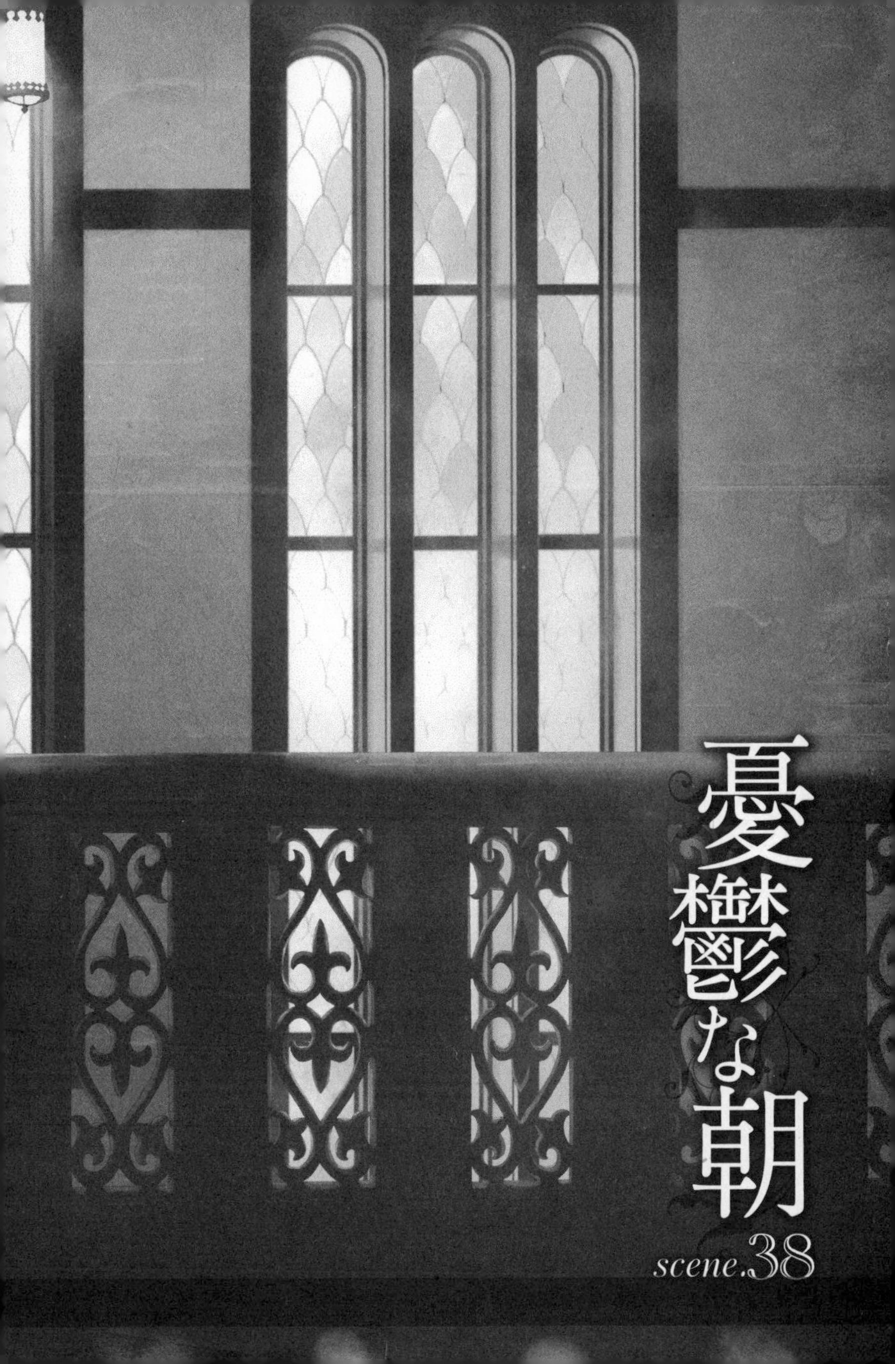
憂鬱な朝
scene.38

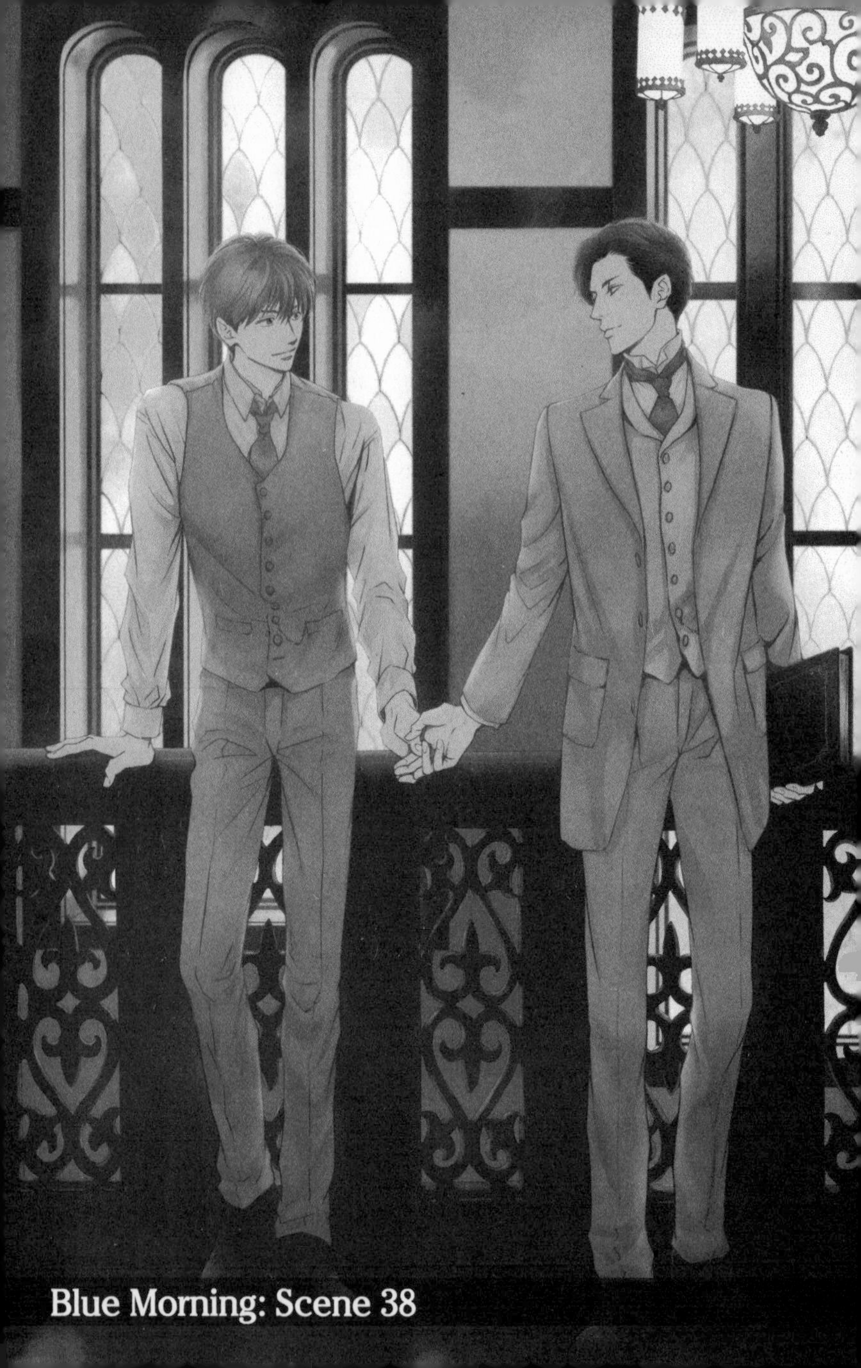

Blue Morning: Scene 38

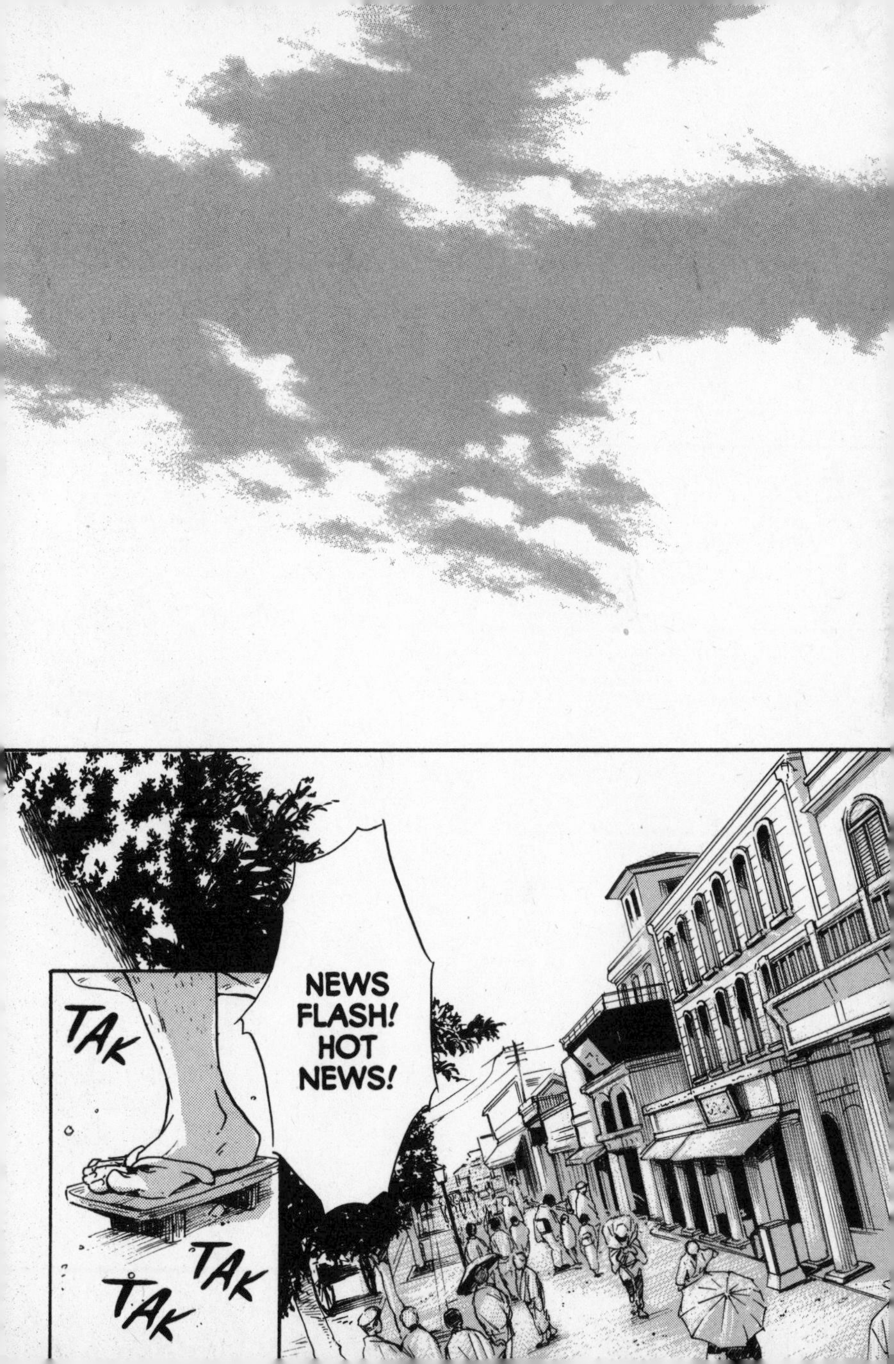
NEWS FLASH! HOT NEWS!
TAK
TAK
TAK

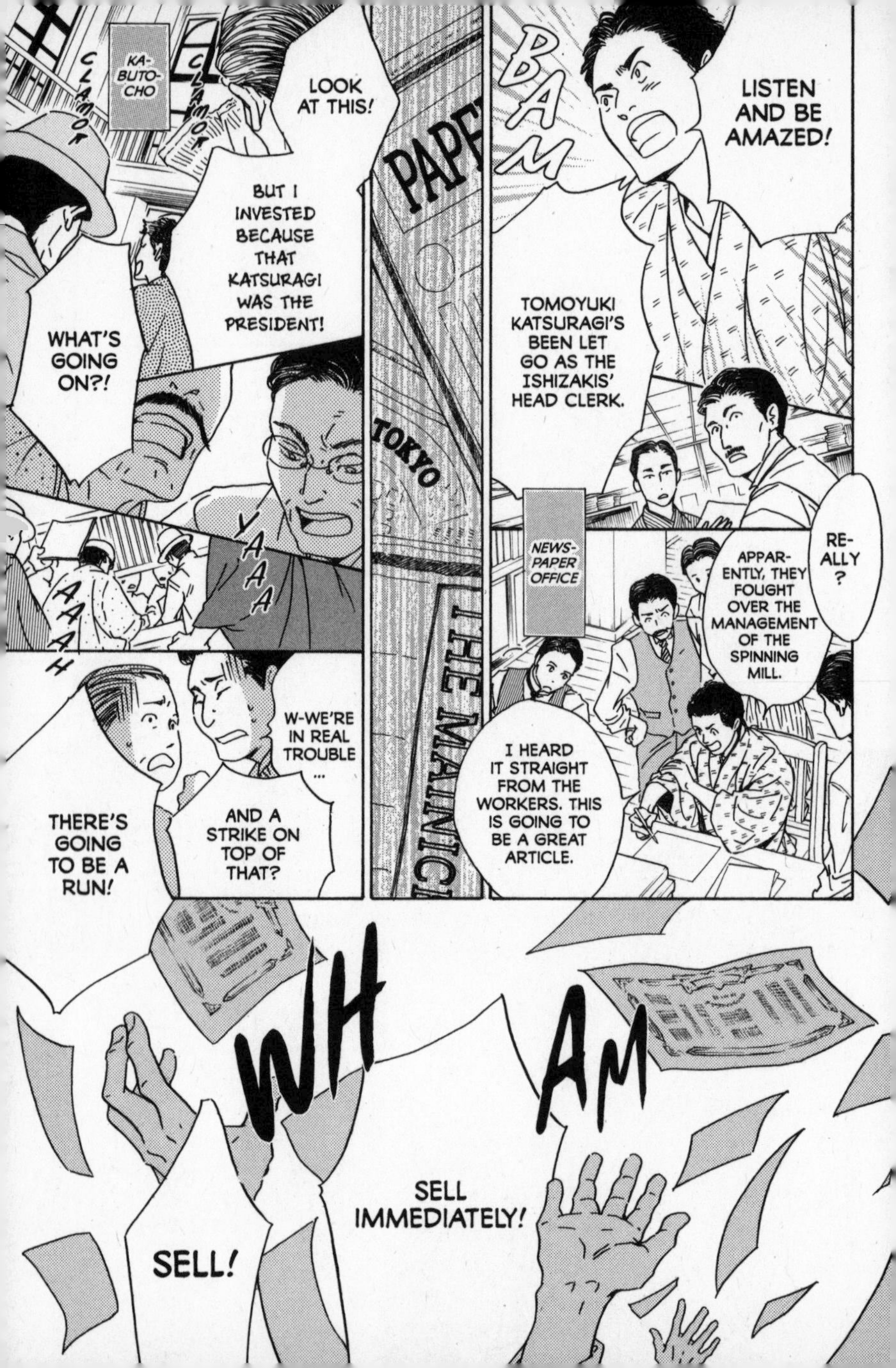
BAM
LISTEN AND BE AMAZED!
TOMOYUKI KATSURAGI'S BEEN LET GO AS THE ISHIZAKIS' HEAD CLERK.
NEWS-PAPER OFFICE
RE-ALLY?
APPAR-ENTLY, THEY FOUGHT OVER THE MANAGEMENT OF THE SPINNING MILL.
I HEARD IT STRAIGHT FROM THE WORKERS. THIS IS GOING TO BE A GREAT ARTICLE.
TOKYO
KA-BUTO-CHO
CLAMOR
CLAMOR
LOOK AT THIS!
BUT I INVESTED BECAUSE THAT KATSURAGI WAS THE PRESIDENT!
WHAT'S GOING ON?!
YAAAAAAH
W-WE'RE IN REAL TROUBLE...
AND A STRIKE ON TOP OF THAT?
THERE'S GOING TO BE A RUN!
WHAM
SELL IMMEDIATELY!
SELL!

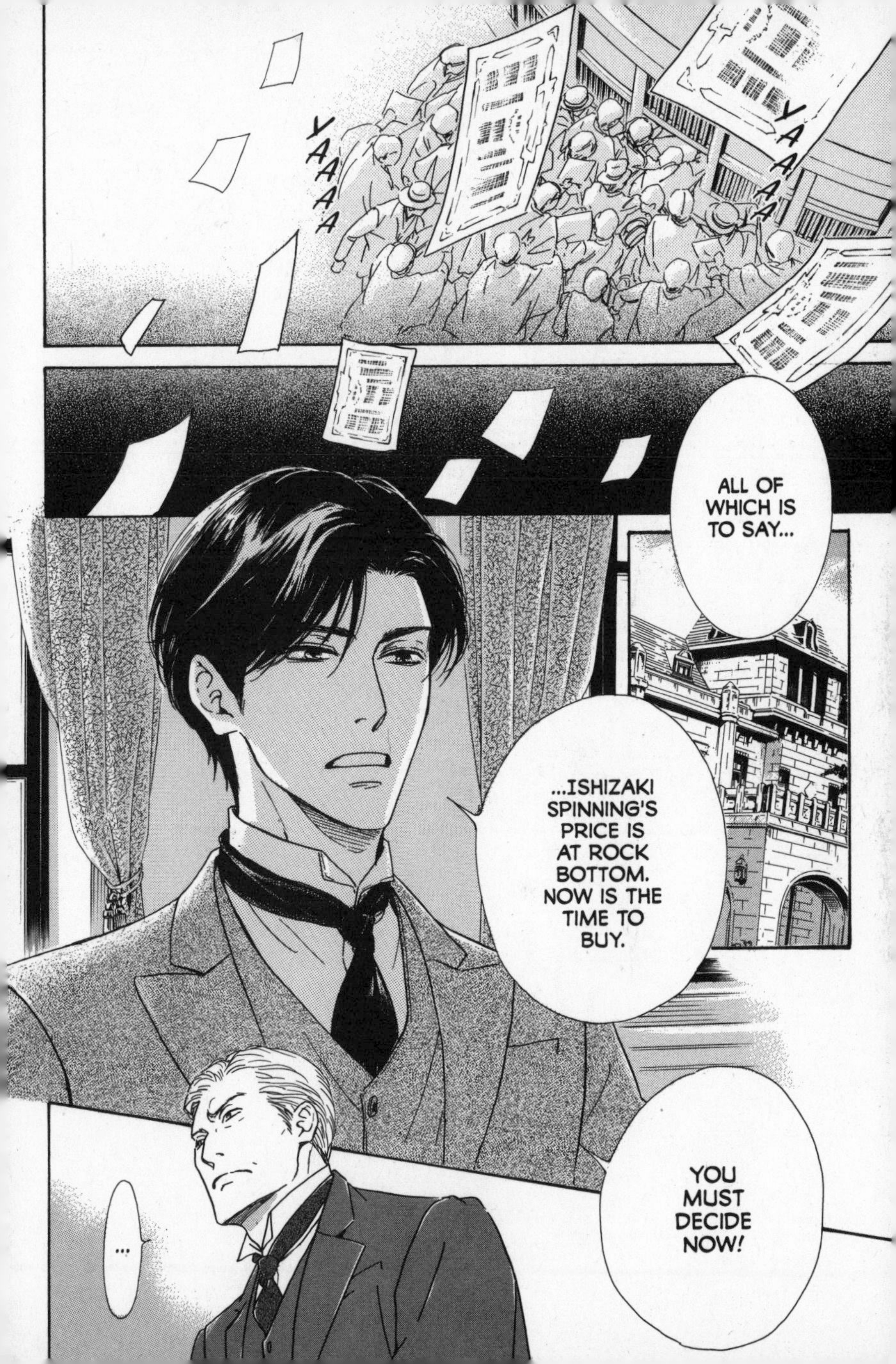
YAAAAA
YAAAAA
ALL OF WHICH IS TO SAY...
...ISHIZAKI SPINNING'S PRICE IS AT ROCK BOTTOM. NOW IS THE TIME TO BUY.
YOU MUST DECIDE NOW!
...

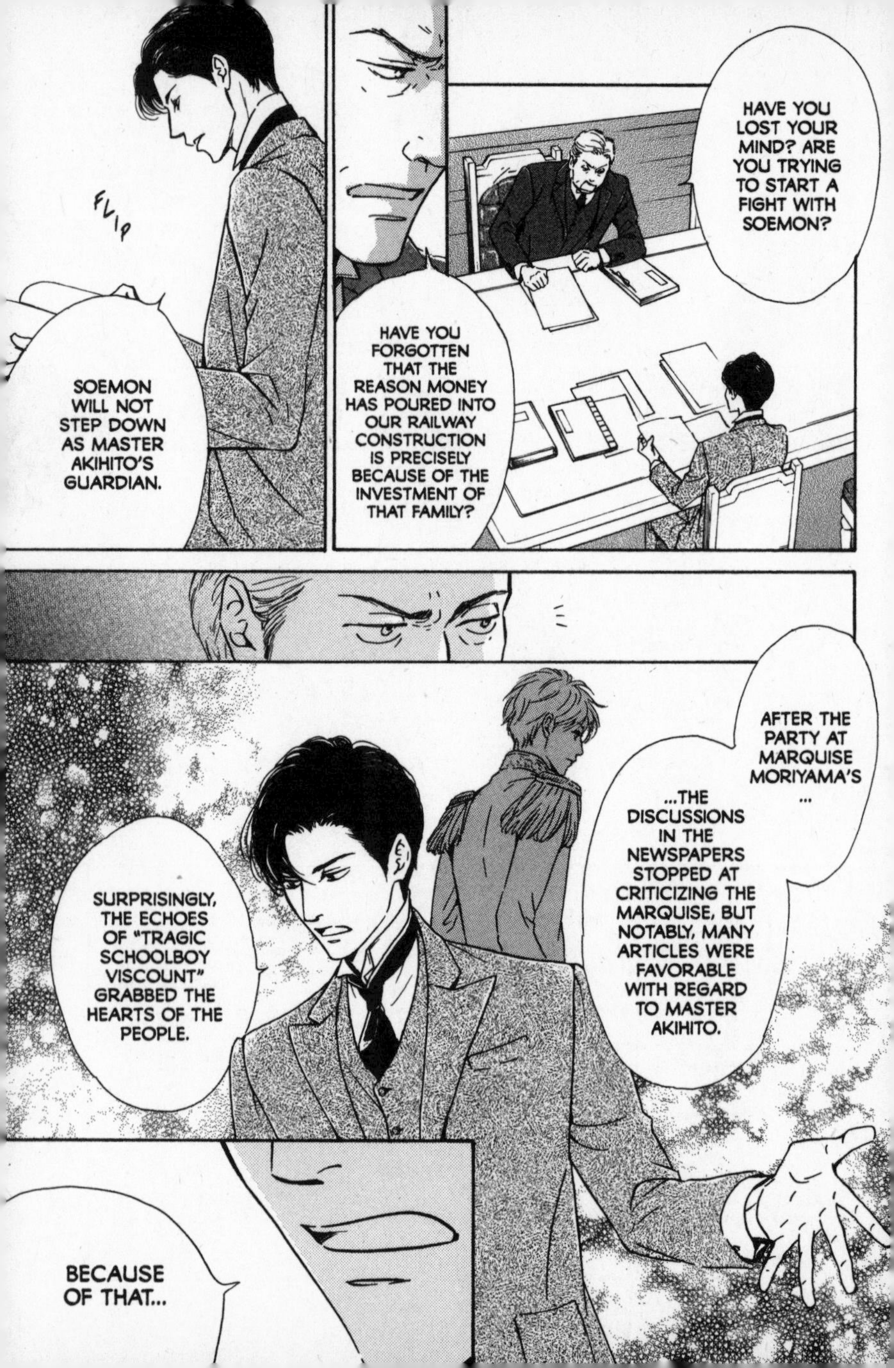
HAVE YOU LOST YOUR MIND? ARE YOU TRYING TO START A FIGHT WITH SOEMON?
HAVE YOU FORGOTTEN THAT THE REASON MONEY HAS POURED INTO OUR RAILWAY CONSTRUCTION IS PRECISELY BECAUSE OF THE INVESTMENT OF THAT FAMILY?
FLIP
SOEMON WILL NOT STEP DOWN AS MASTER AKIHITO'S GUARDIAN.
AFTER THE PARTY AT MARQUISE MORIYAMA'S ...
...THE DISCUSSIONS IN THE NEWSPAPERS STOPPED AT CRITICIZING THE MARQUISE, BUT NOTABLY, MANY ARTICLES WERE FAVORABLE WITH REGARD TO MASTER AKIHITO.
SURPRISINGLY, THE ECHOES OF "TRAGIC SCHOOLBOY VISCOUNT" GRABBED THE HEARTS OF THE PEOPLE.
BECAUSE OF THAT...

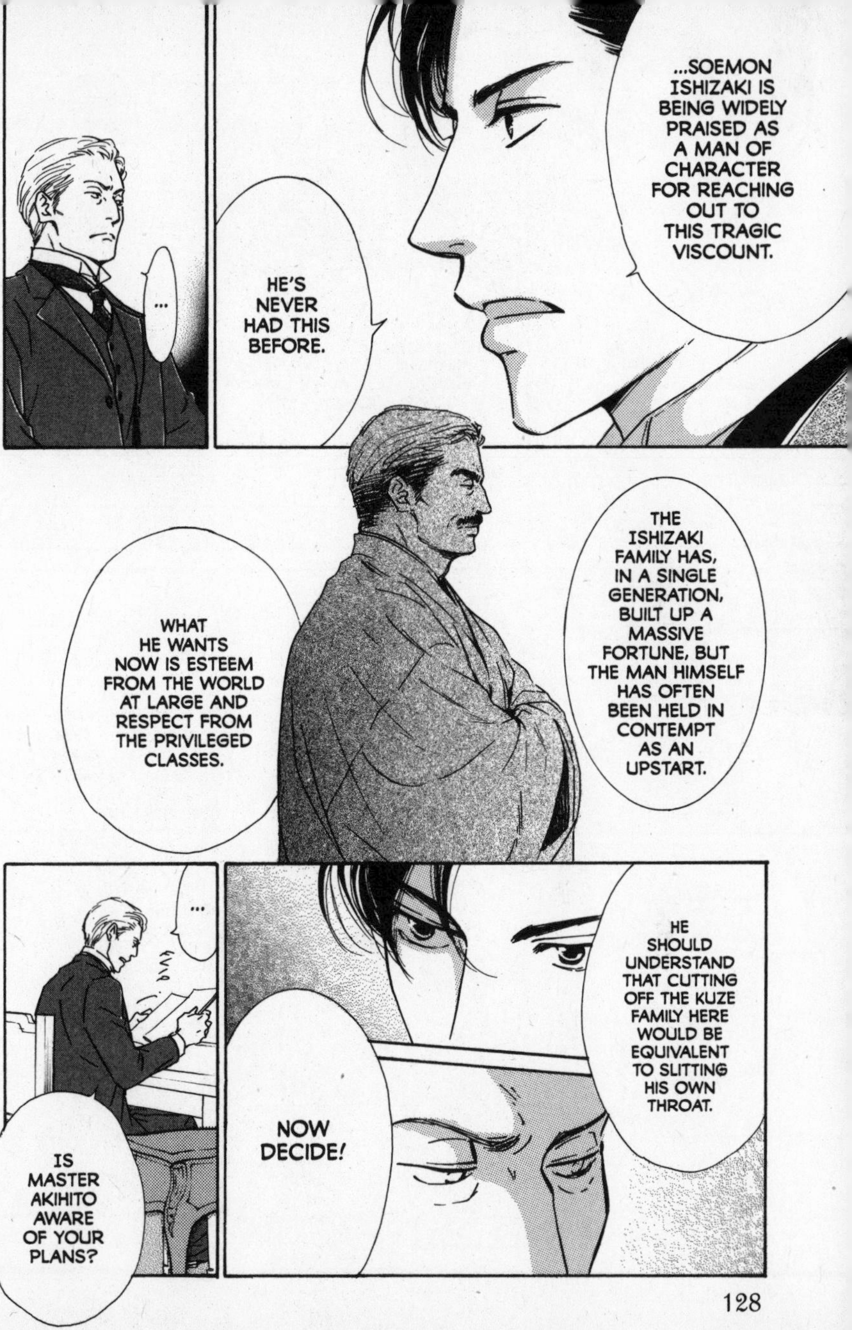
...SOEMON ISHIZAKI IS BEING WIDELY PRAISED AS A MAN OF CHARACTER FOR REACHING OUT TO THIS TRAGIC VISCOUNT.
HE'S NEVER HAD THIS BEFORE.
...
THE ISHIZAKI FAMILY HAS, IN A SINGLE GENERATION, BUILT UP A MASSIVE FORTUNE, BUT THE MAN HIMSELF HAS OFTEN BEEN HELD IN CONTEMPT AS AN UPSTART.
WHAT HE WANTS NOW IS ESTEEM FROM THE WORLD AT LARGE AND RESPECT FROM THE PRIVILEGED CLASSES.
HE SHOULD UNDERSTAND THAT CUTTING OFF THE KUZE FAMILY HERE WOULD BE EQUIVALENT TO SLITTING HIS OWN THROAT.
NOW DECIDE!
...
IS MASTER AKIHITO AWARE OF YOUR PLANS?

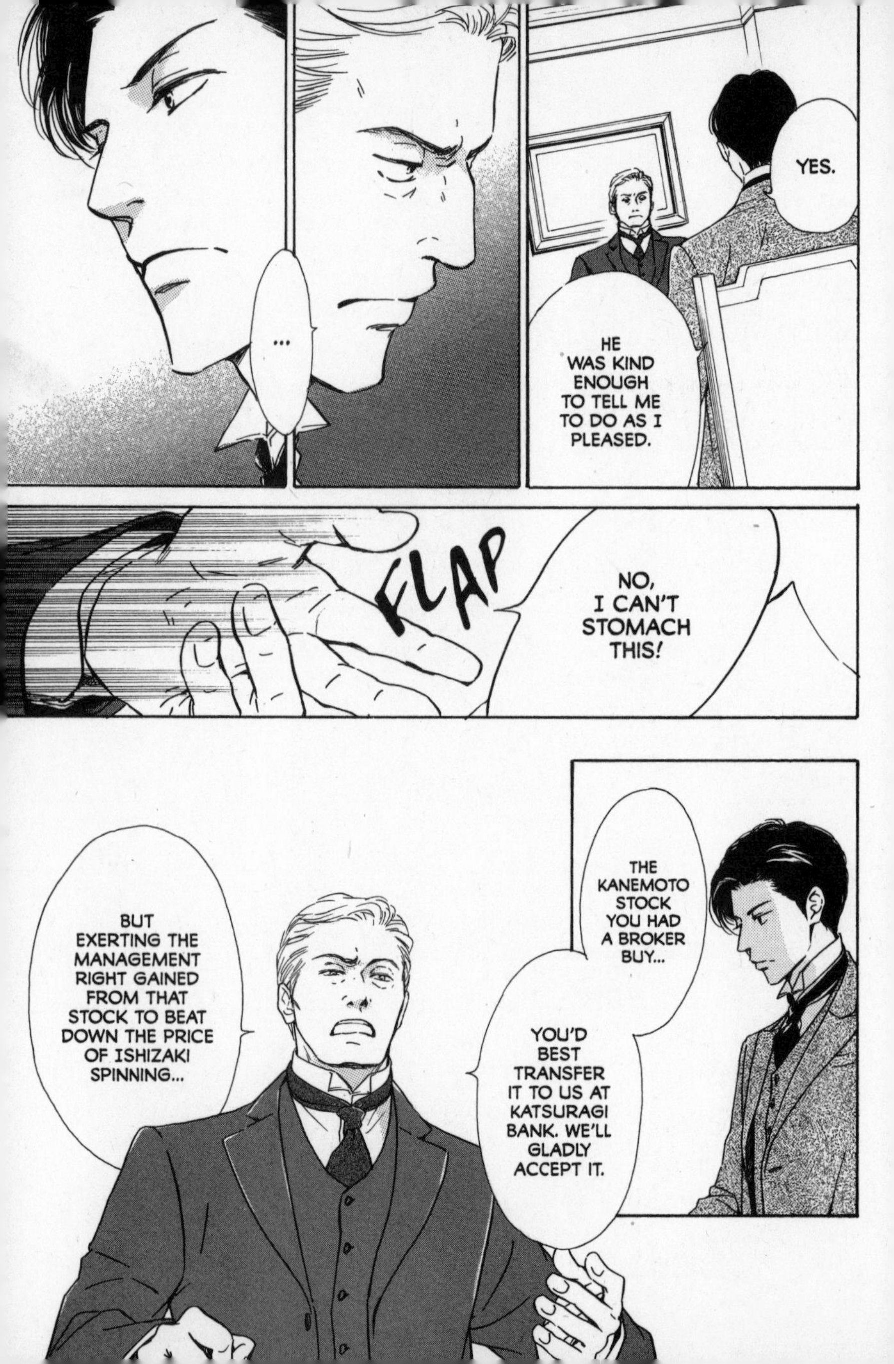
YES.
HE WAS KIND ENOUGH TO TELL ME TO DO AS I PLEASED.
...
NO, I CAN'T STOMACH THIS!
FLAP
THE KANEMOTO STOCK YOU HAD A BROKER BUY...
YOU'D BEST TRANSFER IT TO US AT KATSURAGI BANK. WE'LL GLADLY ACCEPT IT.
BUT EXERTING THE MANAGEMENT RIGHT GAINED FROM THAT STOCK TO BEAT DOWN THE PRICE OF ISHIZAKI SPINNING...

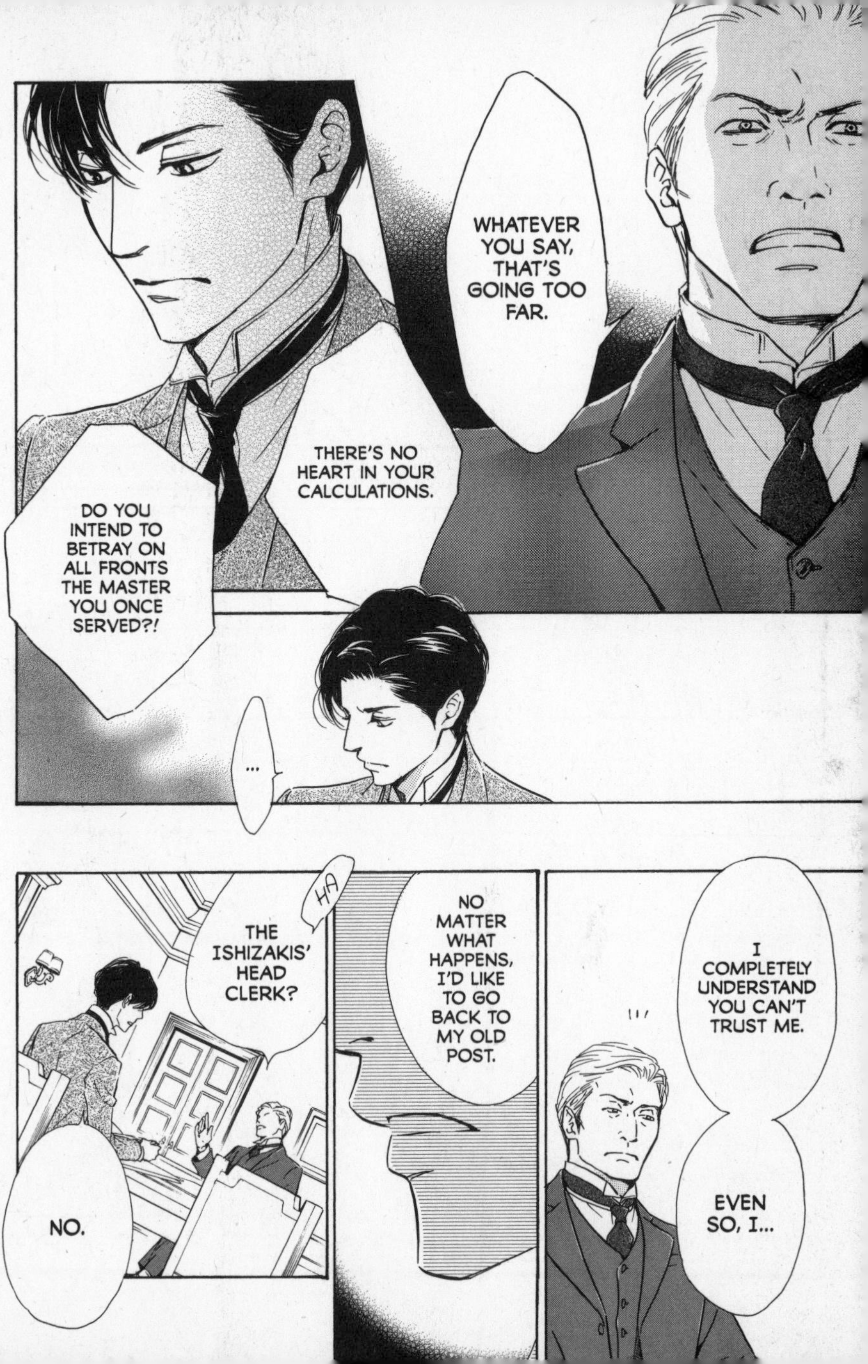
WHATEVER YOU SAY, THAT'S GOING TOO FAR.
THERE'S NO HEART IN YOUR CALCULATIONS.
DO YOU INTEND TO BETRAY ON ALL FRONTS THE MASTER YOU ONCE SERVED?!
...
I COMPLETELY UNDERSTAND YOU CAN'T TRUST ME.
EVEN SO, I...
NO MATTER WHAT HAPPENS, I'D LIKE TO GO BACK TO MY OLD POST.
HA
THE ISHIZAKIS' HEAD CLERK?
NO.

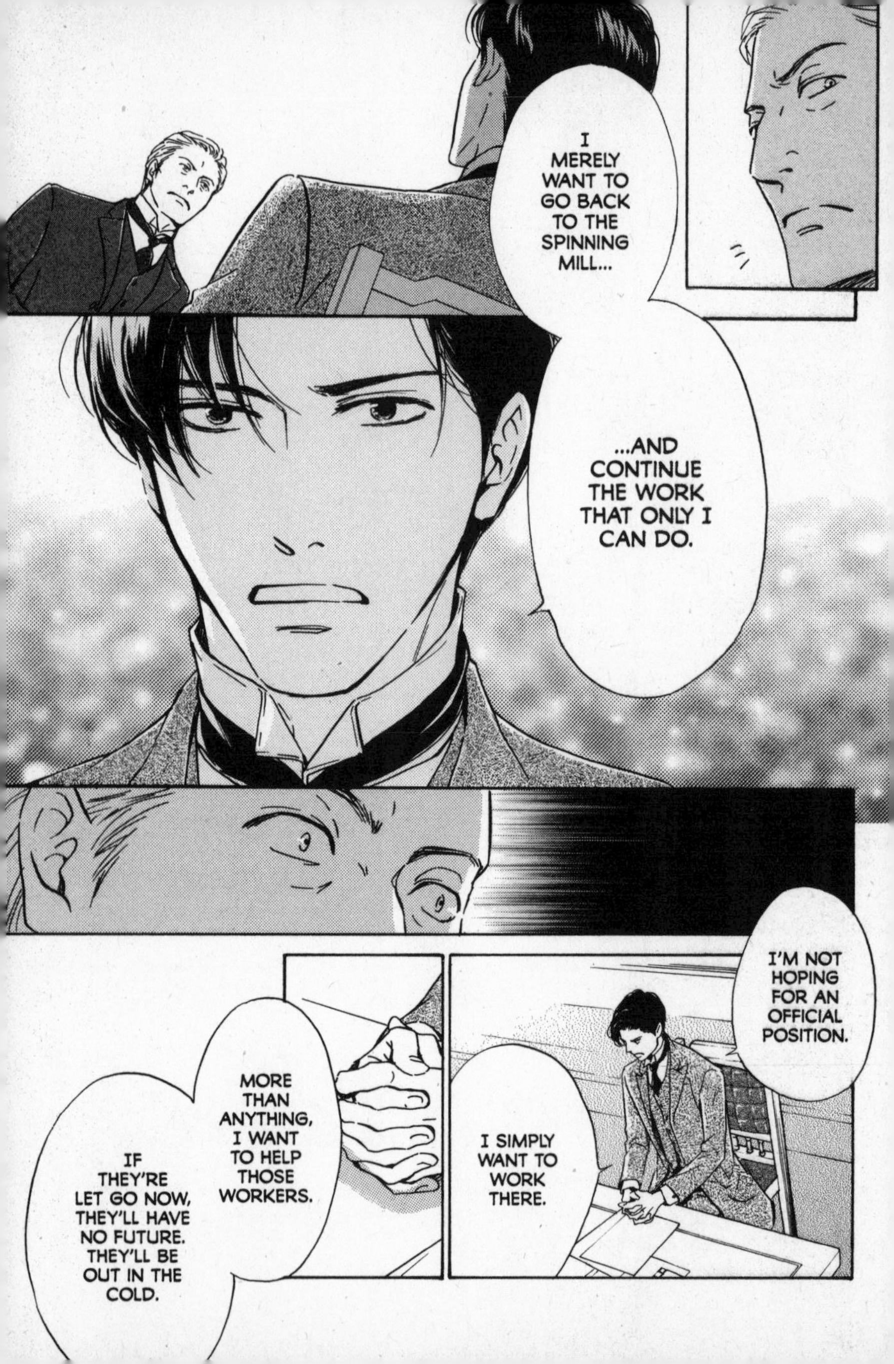
I MERELY WANT TO GO BACK TO THE SPINNING MILL...
...AND CONTINUE THE WORK THAT ONLY I CAN DO.
I'M NOT HOPING FOR AN OFFICIAL POSITION.
I SIMPLY WANT TO WORK THERE.
MORE THAN ANYTHING, I WANT TO HELP THOSE WORKERS.
IF THEY'RE LET GO NOW, THEY'LL HAVE NO FUTURE. THEY'LL BE OUT IN THE COLD.

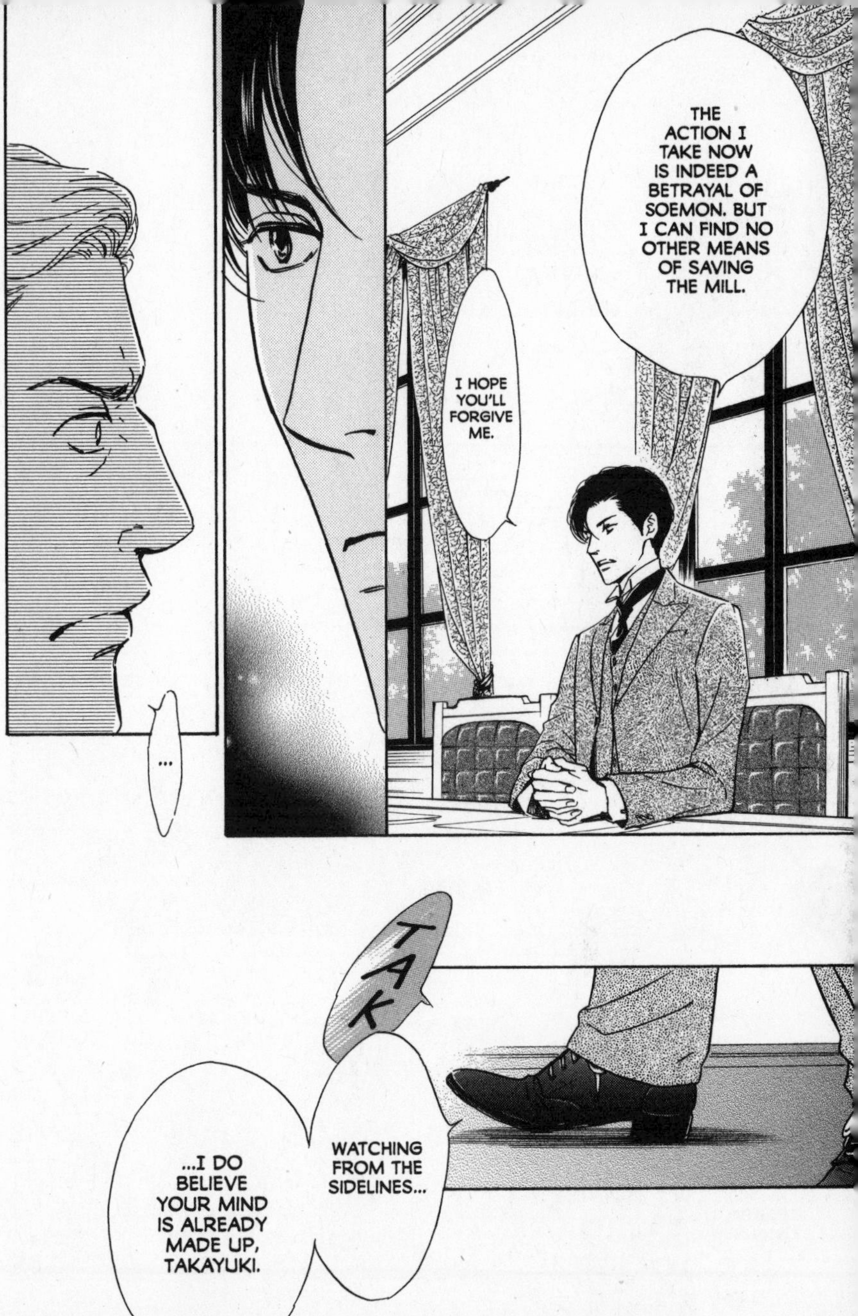
THE ACTION I TAKE NOW IS INDEED A BETRAYAL OF SOEMON. BUT I CAN FIND NO OTHER MEANS OF SAVING THE MILL.
I HOPE YOU'LL FORGIVE ME.
...
TAK
WATCHING FROM THE SIDELINES...
...I DO BELIEVE YOUR MIND IS ALREADY MADE UP, TAKAYUKI.

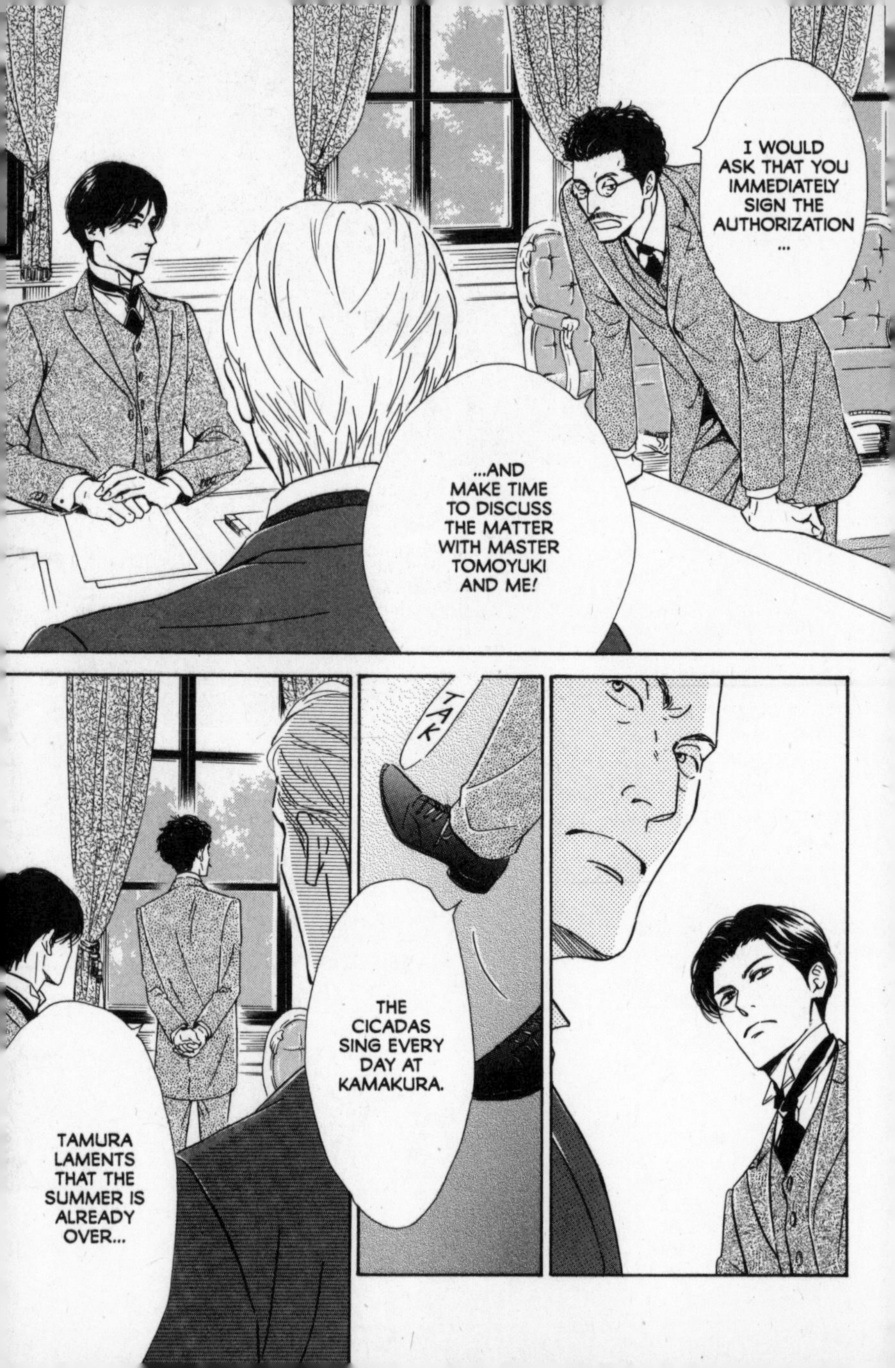
I WOULD ASK THAT YOU IMMEDIATELY SIGN THE AUTHORIZATION ...
...AND MAKE TIME TO DISCUSS THE MATTER WITH MASTER TOMOYUKI AND ME!
TAK
THE CICADAS SING EVERY DAY AT KAMAKURA.
TAMURA LAMENTS THAT THE SUMMER IS ALREADY OVER...

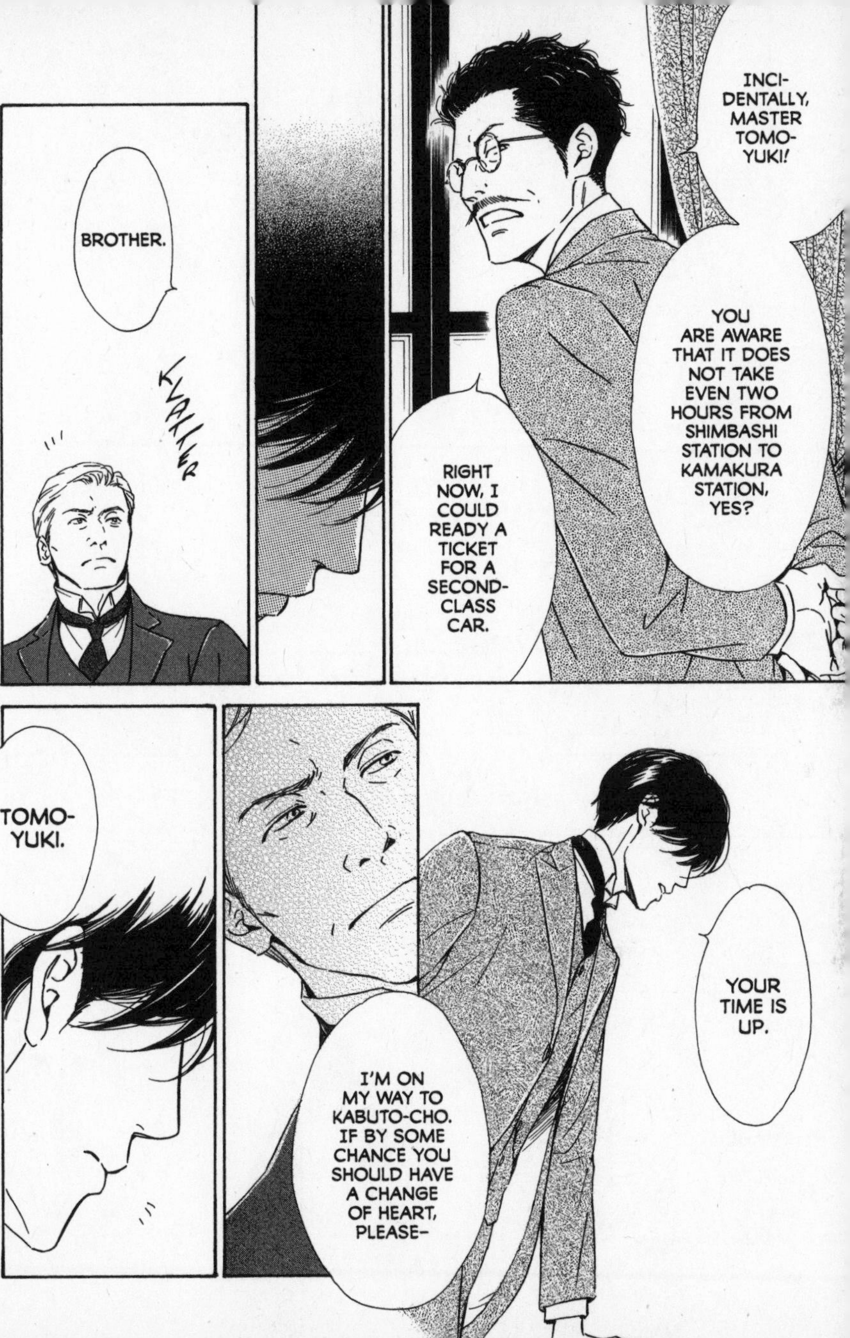
INCI-DENTALLY, MASTER TOMO-YUKI!
YOU ARE AWARE THAT IT DOES NOT TAKE EVEN TWO HOURS FROM SHIMBASHI STATION TO KAMAKURA STATION, YES?
RIGHT NOW, I COULD READY A TICKET FOR A SECOND-CLASS CAR.
KLATTER
BROTHER.
YOUR TIME IS UP.
I'M ON MY WAY TO KABUTO-CHO. IF BY SOME CHANCE YOU SHOULD HAVE A CHANGE OF HEART, PLEASE-
TOMO-YUKI.

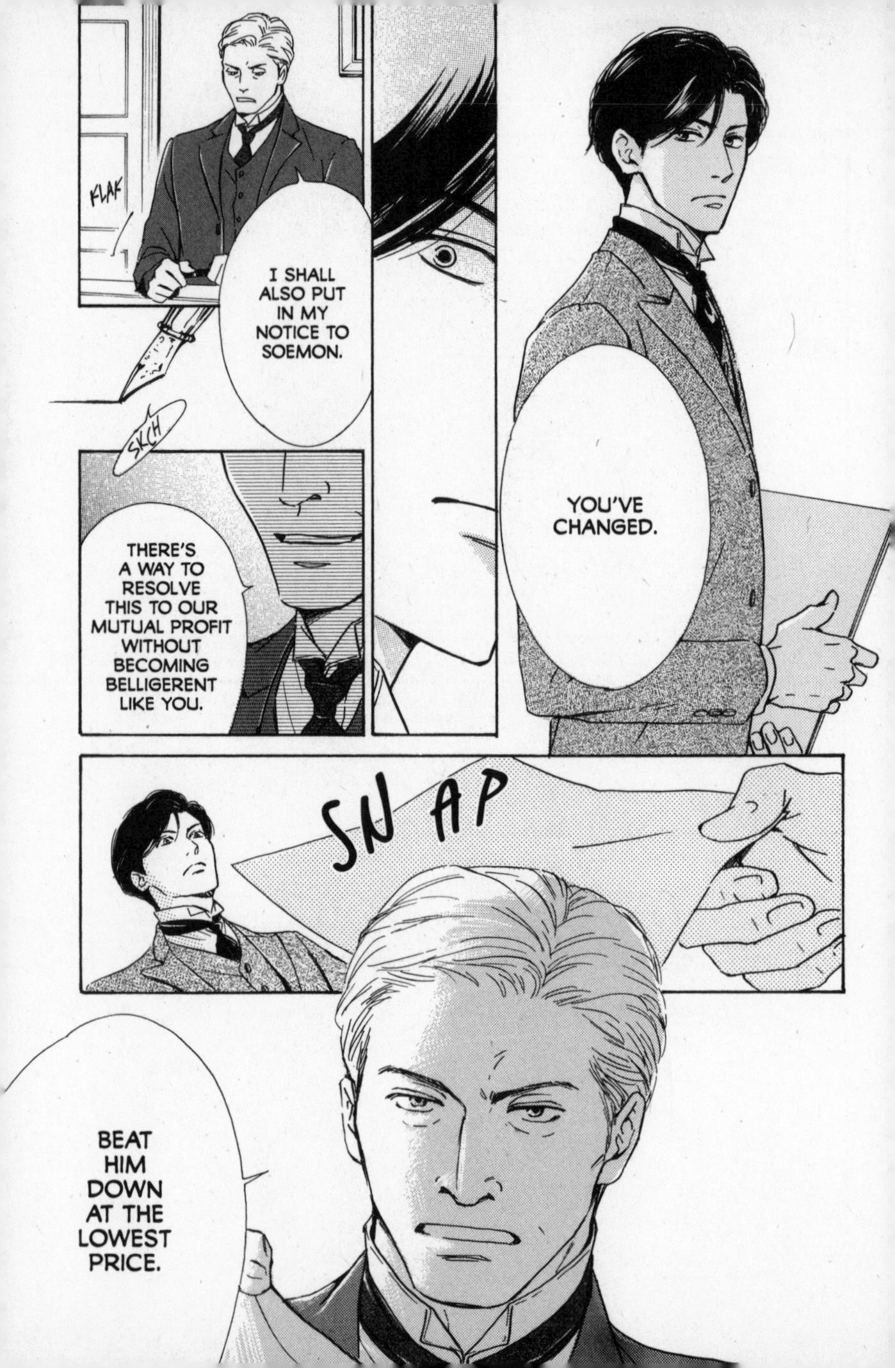
YOU'VE CHANGED.
I SHALL ALSO PUT IN MY NOTICE TO SOEMON.
KLAK
SKCH
THERE'S A WAY TO RESOLVE THIS TO OUR MUTUAL PROFIT WITHOUT BECOMING BELLIGERENT LIKE YOU.
SNAP
BEAT HIM DOWN AT THE LOWEST PRICE.

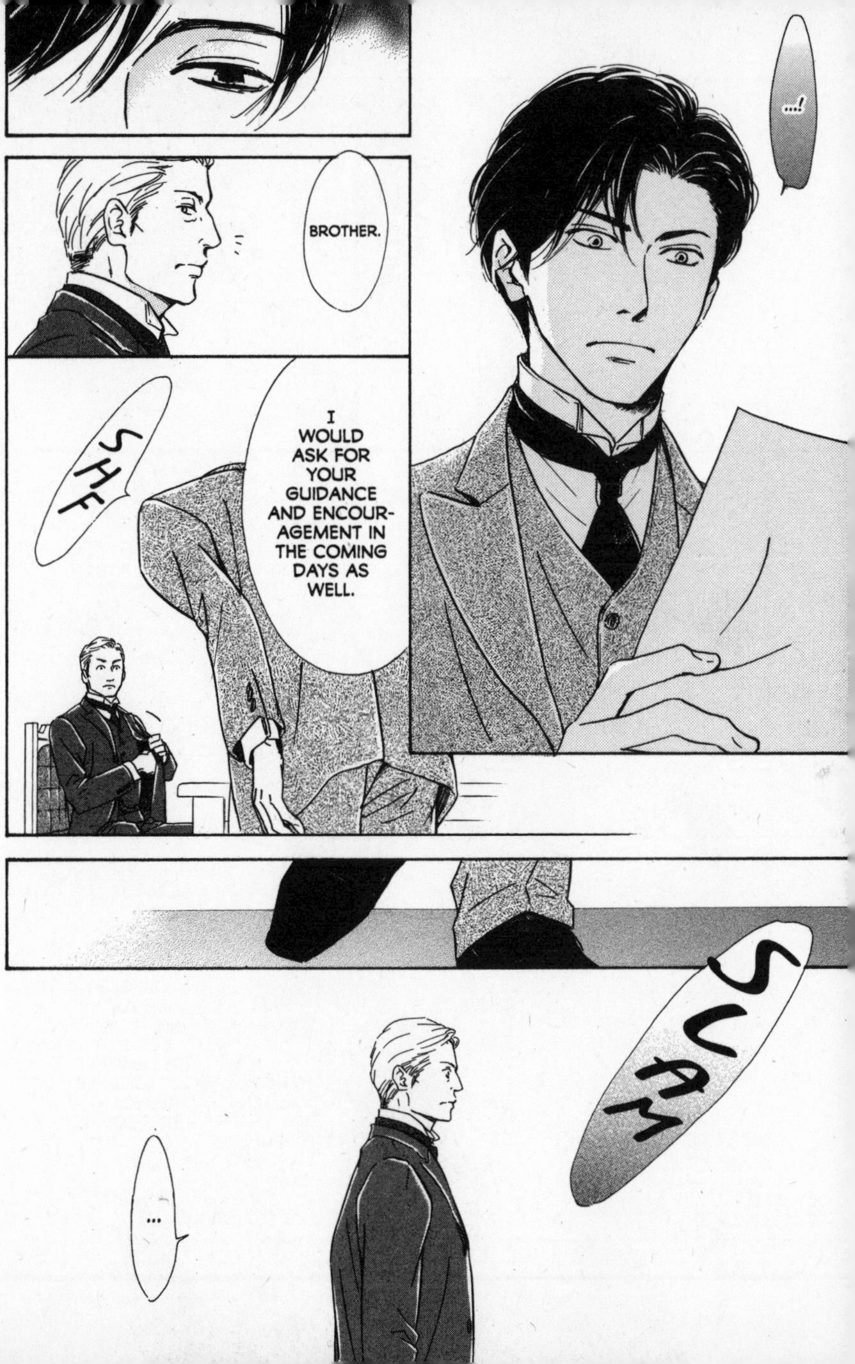
...!
BROTHER.
I WOULD ASK FOR YOUR GUIDANCE AND ENCOURAGEMENT IN THE COMING DAYS AS WELL.
SHF
SLAM
...

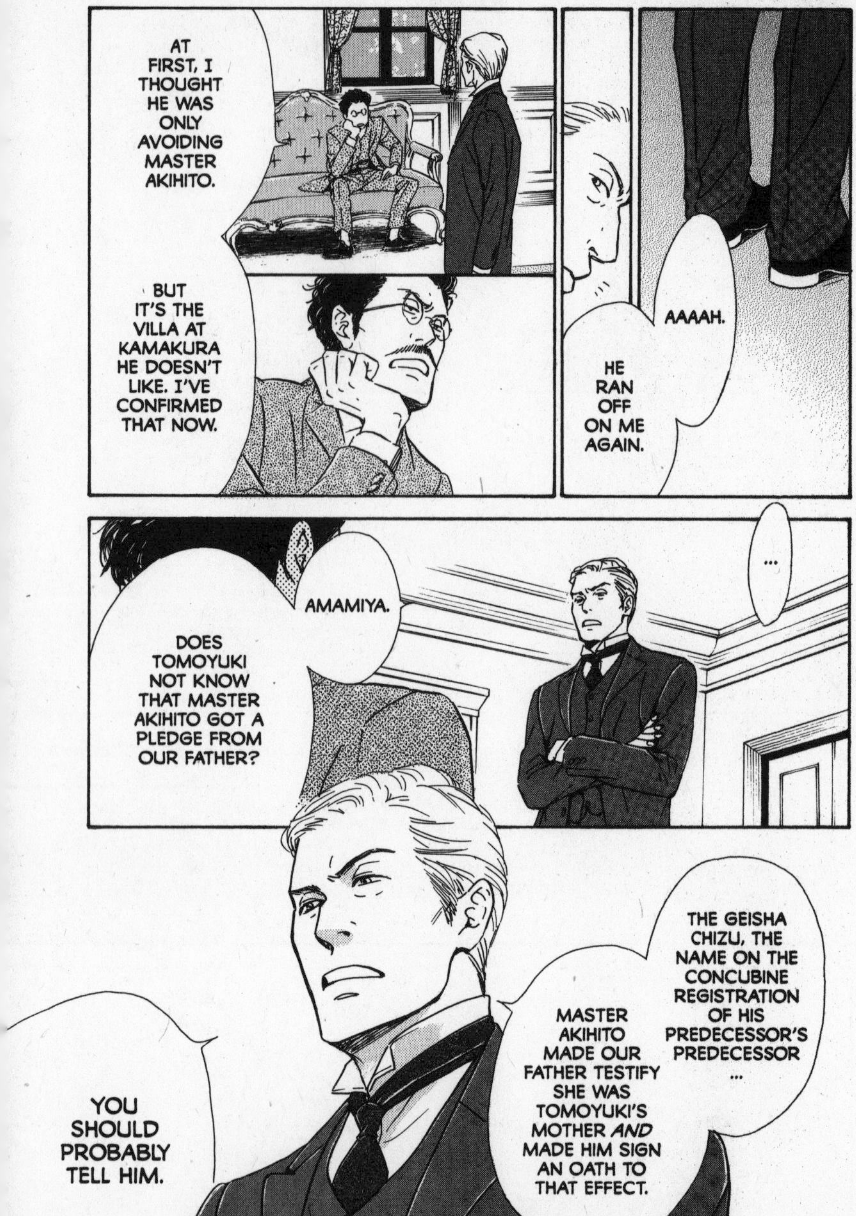
AAAAH.
HE RAN OFF ON ME AGAIN.
AT FIRST, I THOUGHT HE WAS ONLY AVOIDING MASTER AKIHITO.
BUT IT'S THE VILLA AT KAMAKURA HE DOESN'T LIKE. I'VE CONFIRMED THAT NOW.
...
AMAMIYA.
DOES TOMOYUKI NOT KNOW THAT MASTER AKIHITO GOT A PLEDGE FROM OUR FATHER?
THE GEISHA CHIZU, THE NAME ON THE CONCUBINE REGISTRATION OF HIS PREDECESSOR'S PREDECESSOR ...
MASTER AKIHITO MADE OUR FATHER TESTIFY SHE WAS TOMOYUKI'S MOTHER *AND* MADE HIM SIGN AN OATH TO THAT EFFECT.
YOU SHOULD PROBABLY TELL HIM.

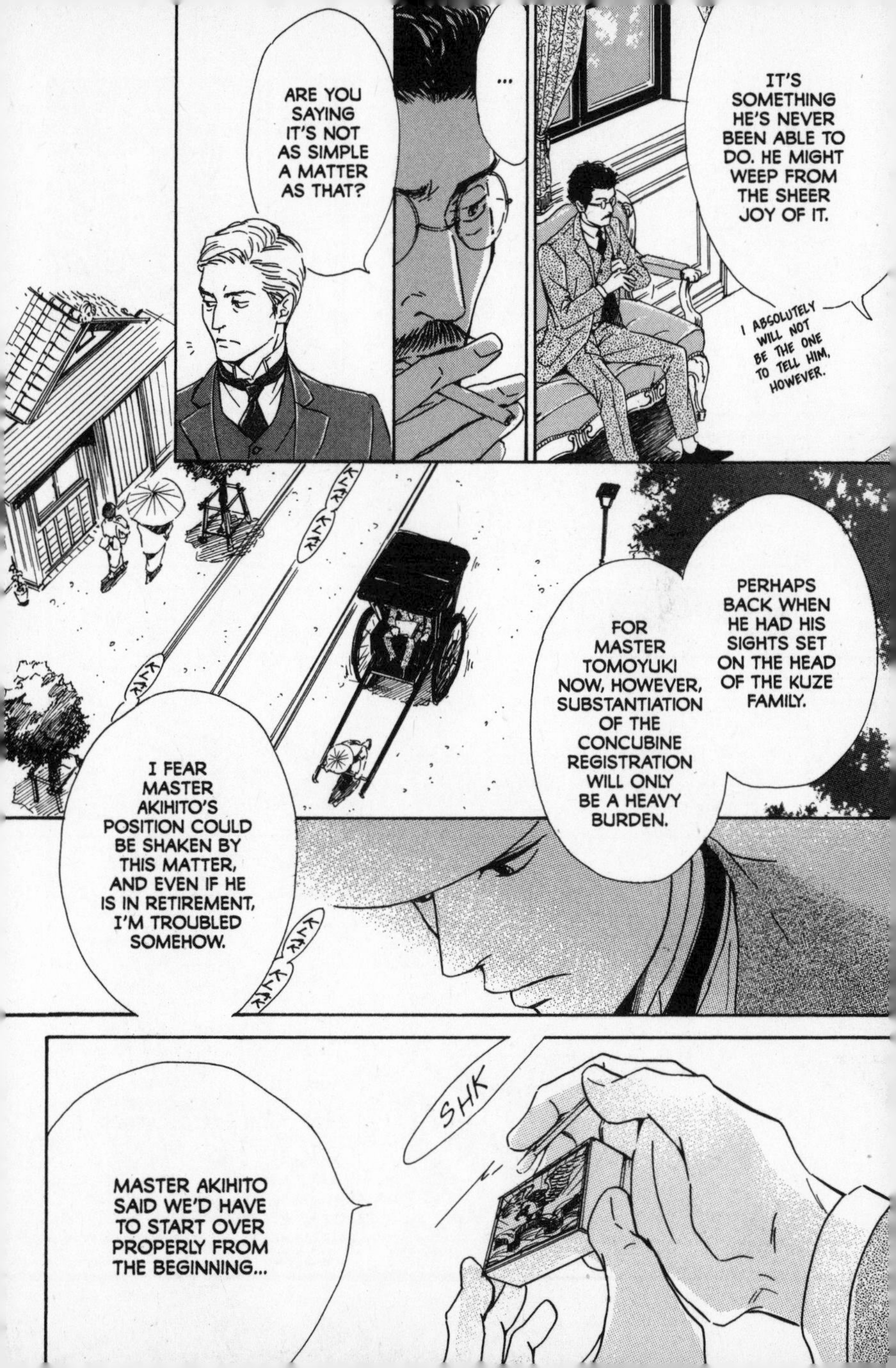
IT'S SOMETHING HE'S NEVER BEEN ABLE TO DO. HE MIGHT WEEP FROM THE SHEER JOY OF IT.
I ABSOLUTELY WILL NOT BE THE ONE TO TELL HIM, HOWEVER.
...
ARE YOU SAYING IT'S NOT AS SIMPLE A MATTER AS THAT?
KLAK KLAK
PERHAPS BACK WHEN HE HAD HIS SIGHTS SET ON THE HEAD OF THE KUZE FAMILY.
FOR MASTER TOMOYUKI NOW, HOWEVER, SUBSTANTIATION OF THE CONCUBINE REGISTRATION WILL ONLY BE A HEAVY BURDEN.
KLAK
I FEAR MASTER AKIHITO'S POSITION COULD BE SHAKEN BY THIS MATTER, AND EVEN IF HE IS IN RETIREMENT, I'M TROUBLED SOMEHOW.
KLAK KLAK
SHK
MASTER AKIHITO SAID WE'D HAVE TO START OVER PROPERLY FROM THE BEGINNING...

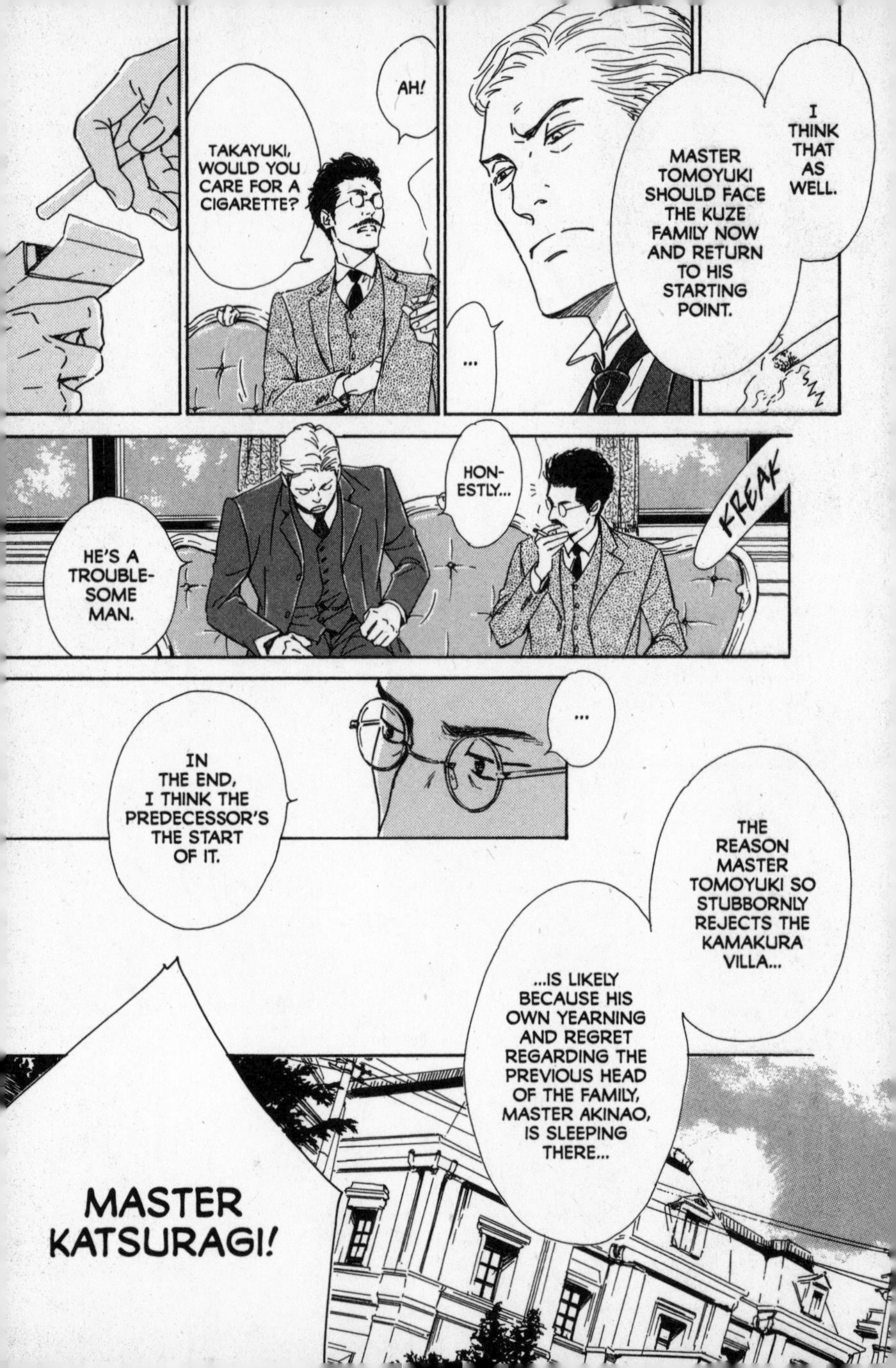
I THINK THAT AS WELL.
MASTER TOMOYUKI SHOULD FACE THE KUZE FAMILY NOW AND RETURN TO HIS STARTING POINT.
...
AH!
TAKAYUKI, WOULD YOU CARE FOR A CIGARETTE?
KREAK
HON-ESTLY...
HE'S A TROUBLE-SOME MAN.
...
IN THE END, I THINK THE PREDECESSOR'S THE START OF IT.
THE REASON MASTER TOMOYUKI SO STUBBORNLY REJECTS THE KAMAKURA VILLA...
...IS LIKELY BECAUSE HIS OWN YEARNING AND REGRET REGARDING THE PREVIOUS HEAD OF THE FAMILY, MASTER AKINAO, IS SLEEPING THERE...
MASTER KATSURAGI!

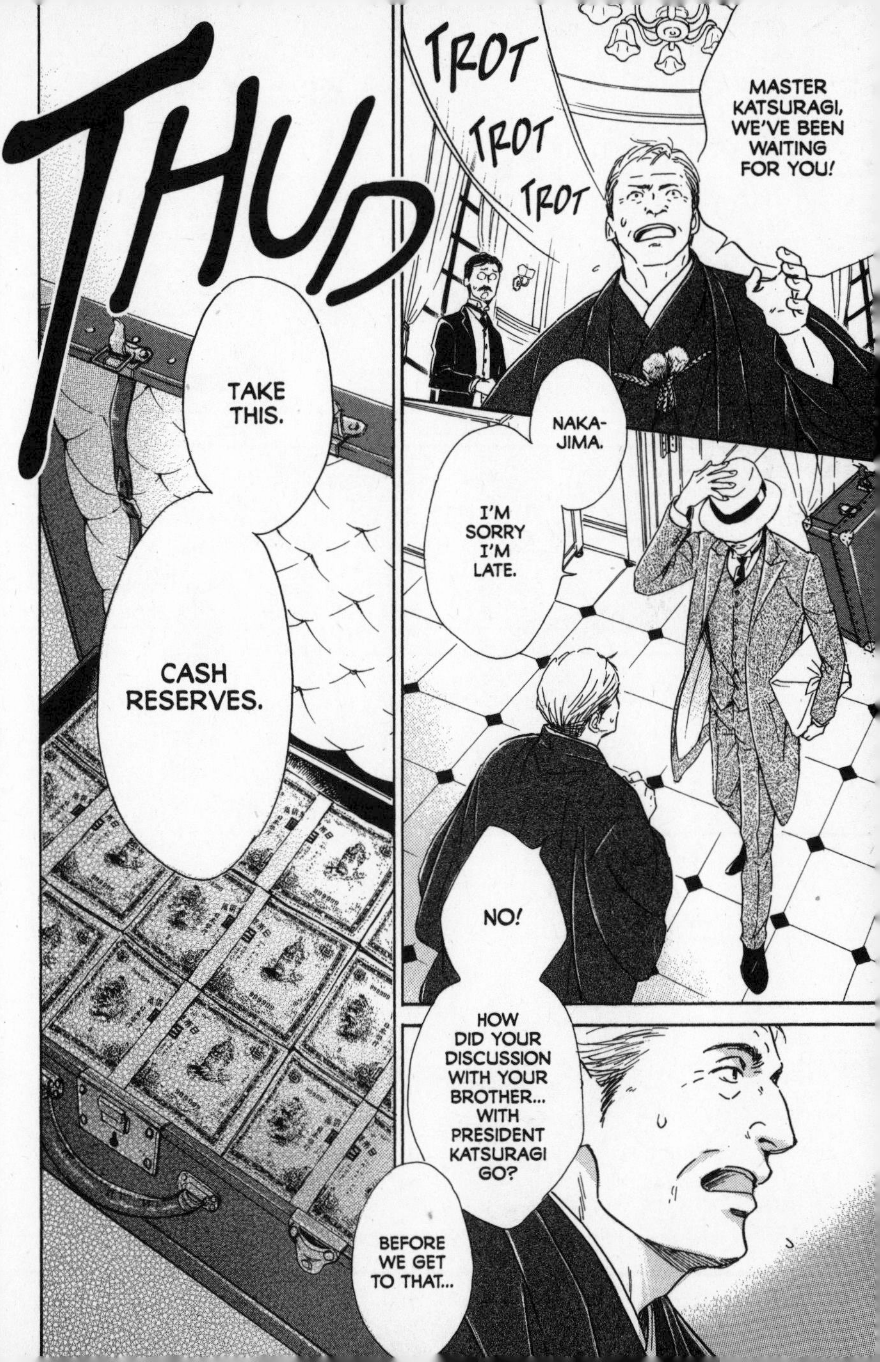
TROT
TROT
TROT
MASTER KATSURAGI, WE'VE BEEN WAITING FOR YOU!
NAKA-JIMA.
I'M SORRY I'M LATE.
NO!
HOW DID YOUR DISCUSSION WITH YOUR BROTHER... WITH PRESIDENT KATSURAGI GO?
BEFORE WE GET TO THAT...
THUD
TAKE THIS.
CASH RESERVES.

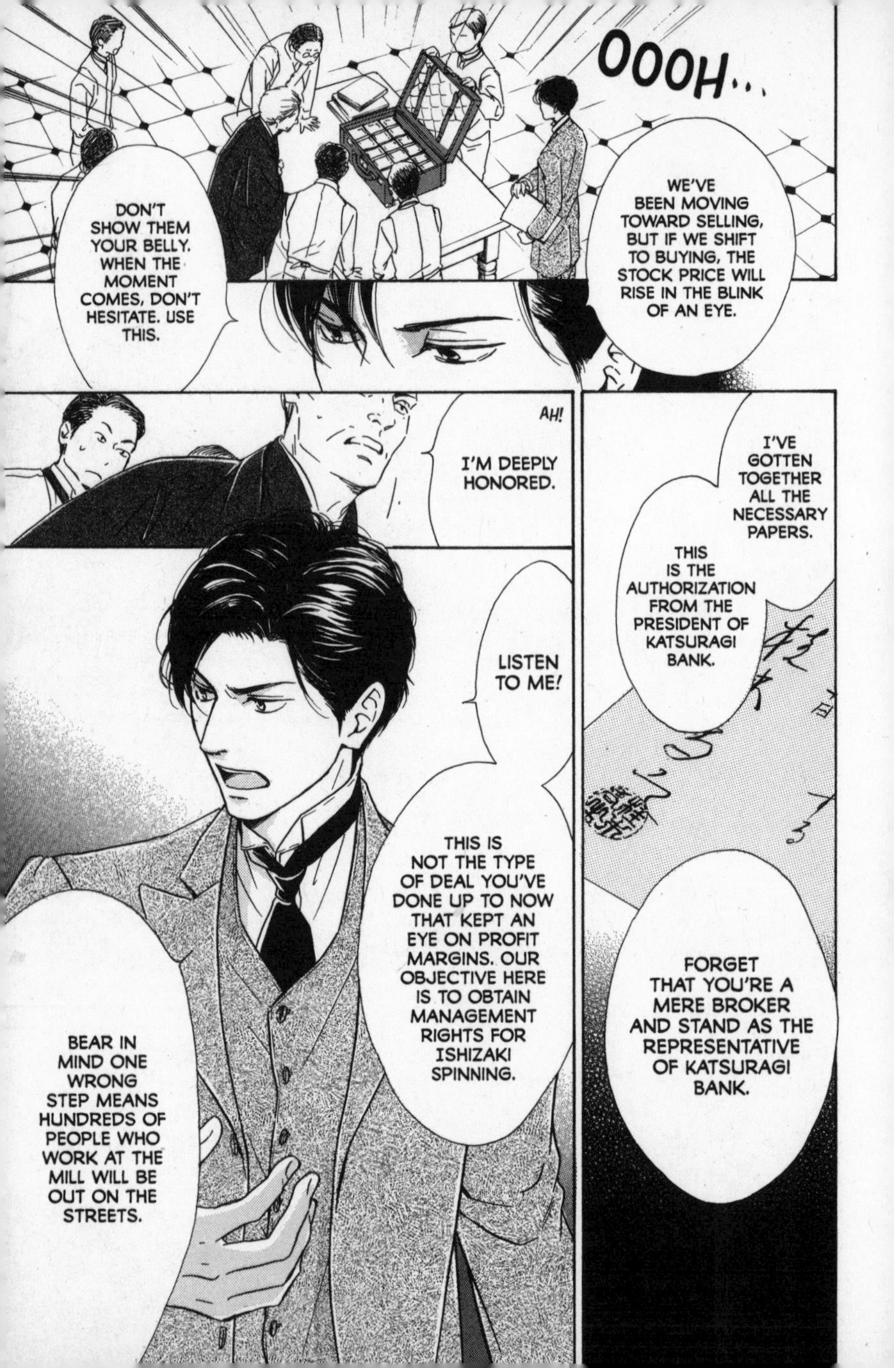
OOOH...
WE'VE BEEN MOVING TOWARD SELLING, BUT IF WE SHIFT TO BUYING, THE STOCK PRICE WILL RISE IN THE BLINK OF AN EYE.
DON'T SHOW THEM YOUR BELLY. WHEN THE MOMENT COMES, DON'T HESITATE. USE THIS.
I'VE GOTTEN TOGETHER ALL THE NECESSARY PAPERS.
THIS IS THE AUTHORIZATION FROM THE PRESIDENT OF KATSURAGI BANK.
FORGET THAT YOU'RE A MERE BROKER AND STAND AS THE REPRESENTATIVE OF KATSURAGI BANK.
AH!
I'M DEEPLY HONORED.
LISTEN TO ME!
THIS IS NOT THE TYPE OF DEAL YOU'VE DONE UP TO NOW THAT KEPT AN EYE ON PROFIT MARGINS. OUR OBJECTIVE HERE IS TO OBTAIN MANAGEMENT RIGHTS FOR ISHIZAKI SPINNING.
BEAR IN MIND ONE WRONG STEP MEANS HUNDREDS OF PEOPLE WHO WORK AT THE MILL WILL BE OUT ON THE STREETS.

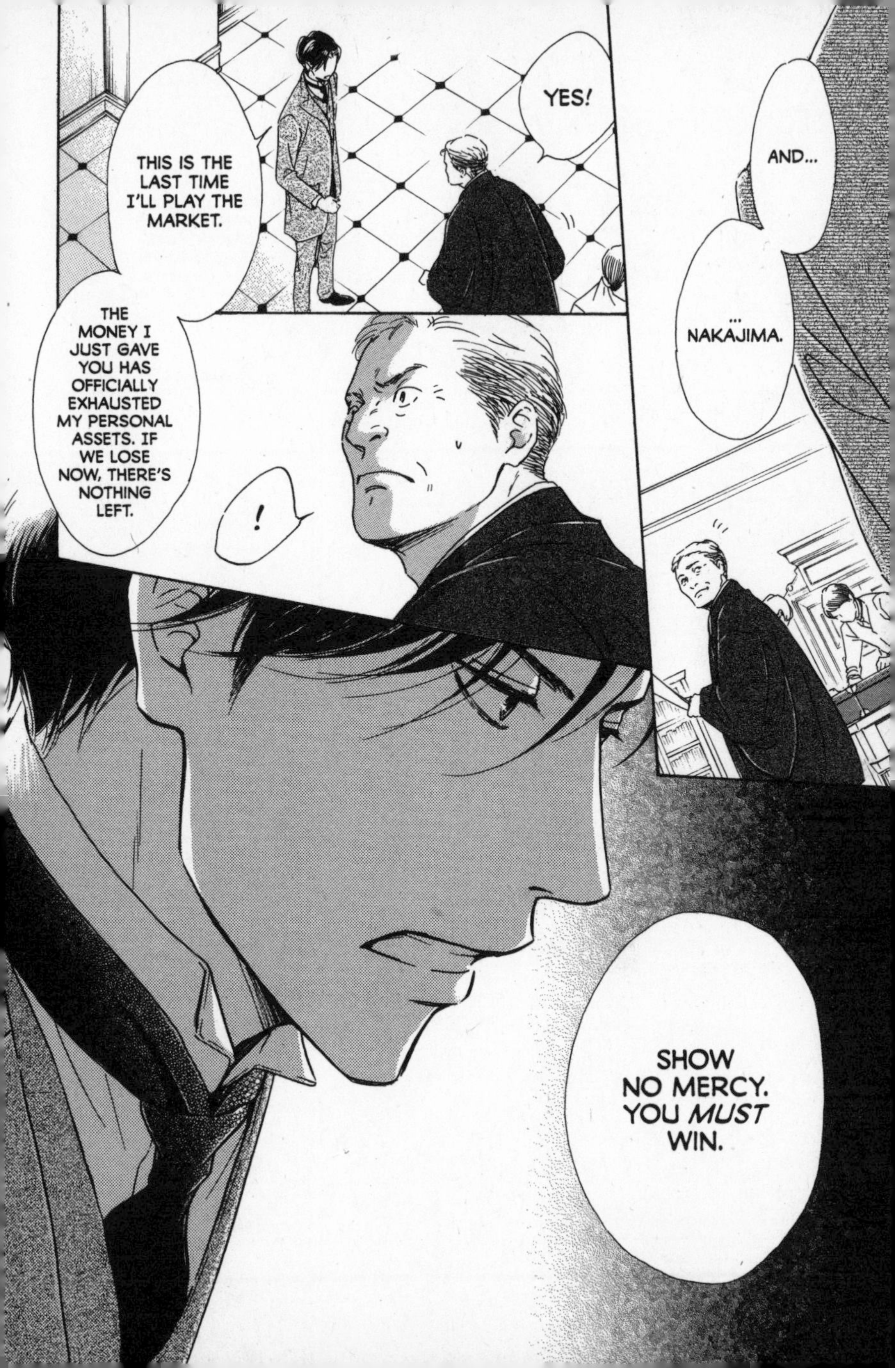
AND...
...NAKAJIMA.
YES!
THIS IS THE LAST TIME I'LL PLAY THE MARKET.
THE MONEY I JUST GAVE YOU HAS OFFICIALLY EXHAUSTED MY PERSONAL ASSETS. IF WE LOSE NOW, THERE'S NOTHING LEFT.
!
SHOW NO MERCY. YOU *MUST* WIN.

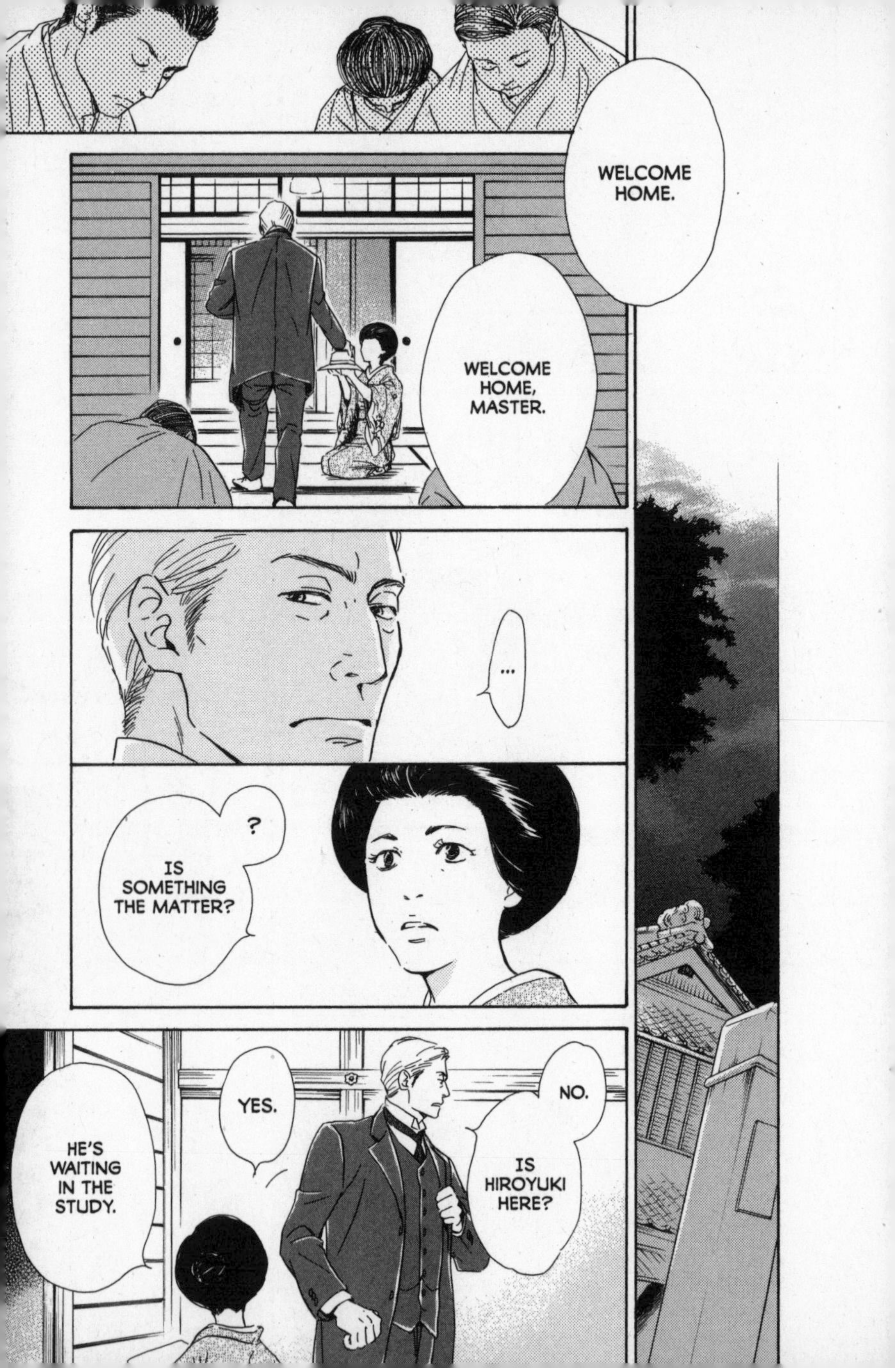
WELCOME HOME.
WELCOME HOME, MASTER.
...
?
IS SOMETHING THE MATTER?
NO.
IS HIROYUKI HERE?
YES.
HE'S WAITING IN THE STUDY.

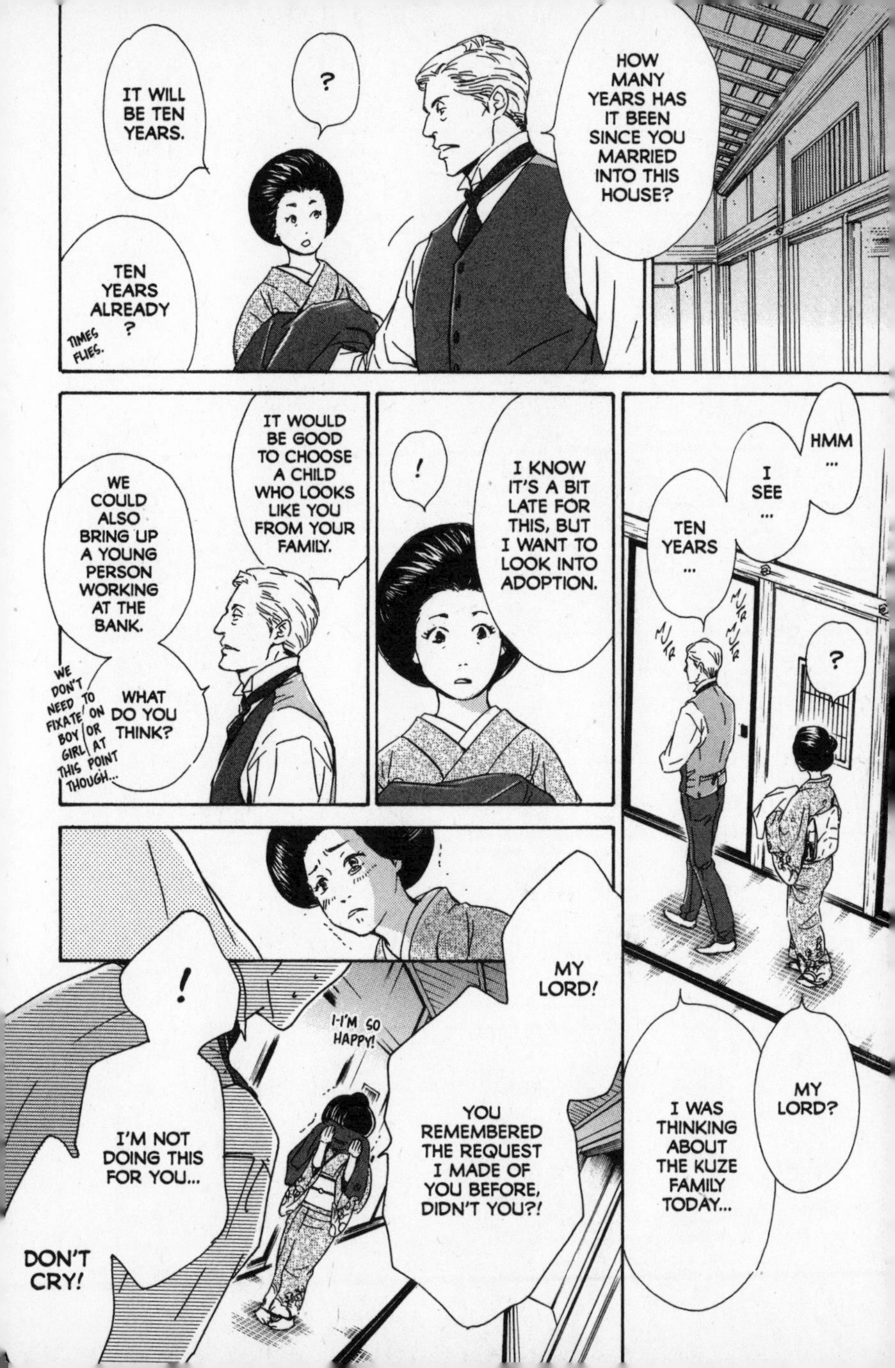
HOW MANY YEARS HAS IT BEEN SINCE YOU MARRIED INTO THIS HOUSE?
?
IT WILL BE TEN YEARS.
TEN YEARS ALREADY?
TIMES FLIES.
HMM...
I SEE...
TEN YEARS...
?
I KNOW IT'S A BIT LATE FOR THIS, BUT I WANT TO LOOK INTO ADOPTION.
!
IT WOULD BE GOOD TO CHOOSE A CHILD WHO LOOKS LIKE YOU FROM YOUR FAMILY.
WE COULD ALSO BRING UP A YOUNG PERSON WORKING AT THE BANK.
WHAT DO YOU THINK?
WE DON'T NEED TO FIXATE ON BOY OR GIRL AT THIS POINT THOUGH...
MY LORD?
I WAS THINKING ABOUT THE KUZE FAMILY TODAY...
MY LORD!
YOU REMEMBERED THE REQUEST I MADE OF YOU BEFORE, DIDN'T YOU?!
I-I'M SO HAPPY!
!
I'M NOT DOING THIS FOR YOU...
DON'T CRY!

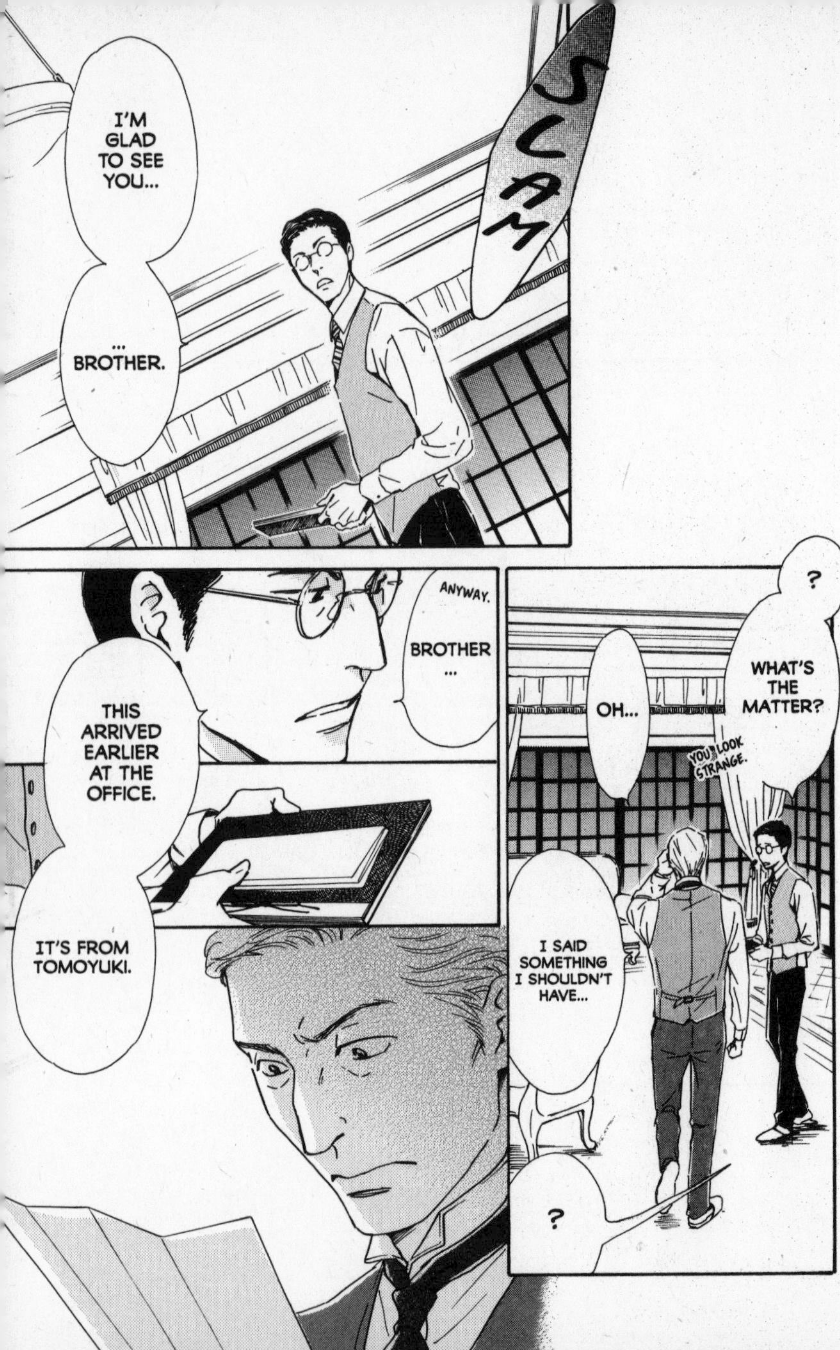
SLAM
I'M GLAD TO SEE YOU...
... BROTHER.
?
WHAT'S THE MATTER?
YOU LOOK STRANGE.
OH...
I SAID SOMETHING I SHOULDN'T HAVE...
?
ANYWAY.
BROTHER ...
THIS ARRIVED EARLIER AT THE OFFICE.
IT'S FROM TOMOYUKI.

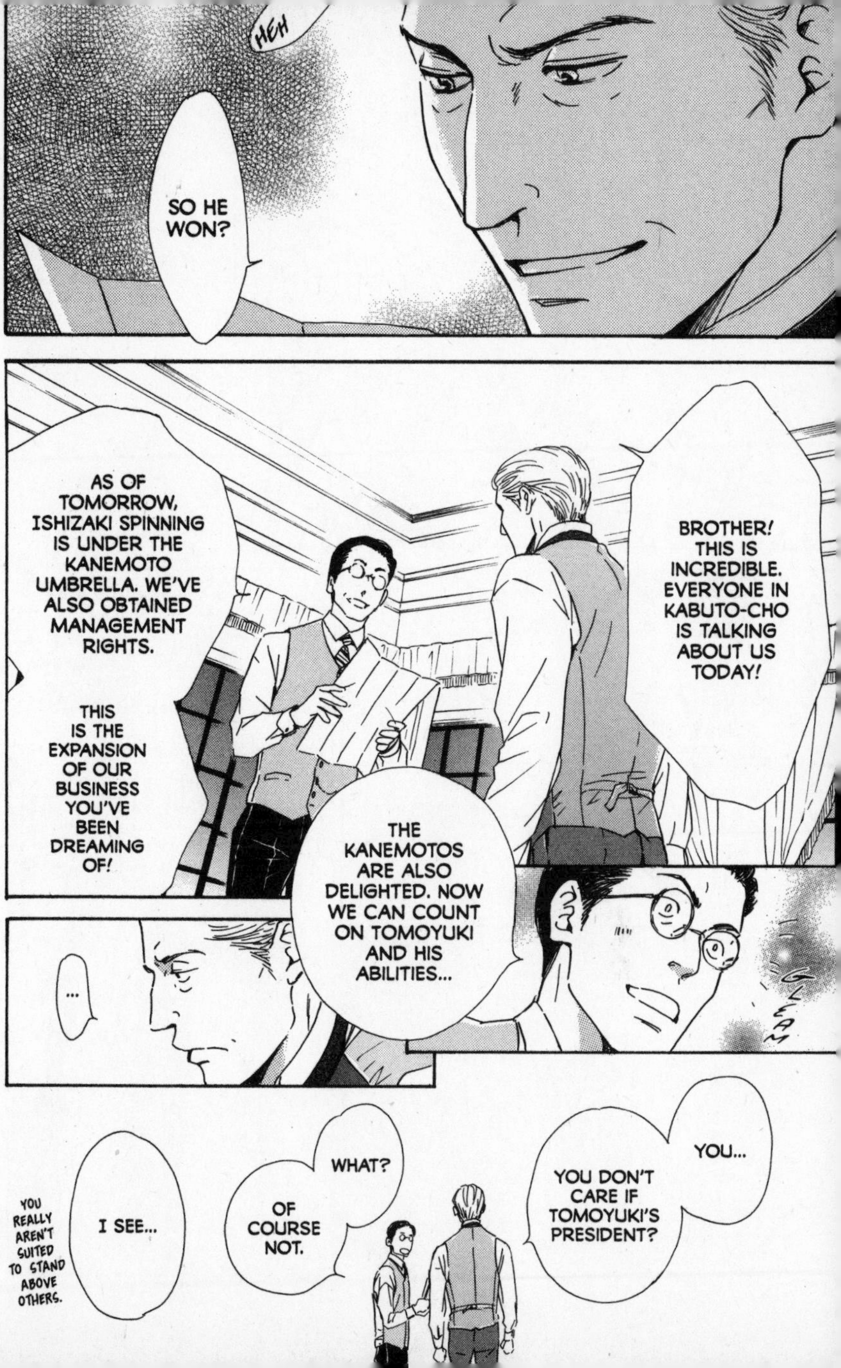
HEH
SO HE WON?
BROTHER! THIS IS INCREDIBLE. EVERYONE IN KABUTO-CHO IS TALKING ABOUT US TODAY!
AS OF TOMORROW, ISHIZAKI SPINNING IS UNDER THE KANEMOTO UMBRELLA. WE'VE ALSO OBTAINED MANAGEMENT RIGHTS.
THIS IS THE EXPANSION OF OUR BUSINESS YOU'VE BEEN DREAMING OF!
THE KANEMOTOS ARE ALSO DELIGHTED. NOW WE CAN COUNT ON TOMOYUKI AND HIS ABILITIES...
GLEAM
...
YOU...
YOU DON'T CARE IF TOMOYUKI'S PRESIDENT?
WHAT?
OF COURSE NOT.
I SEE...
YOU REALLY AREN'T SUITED TO STAND ABOVE OTHERS.

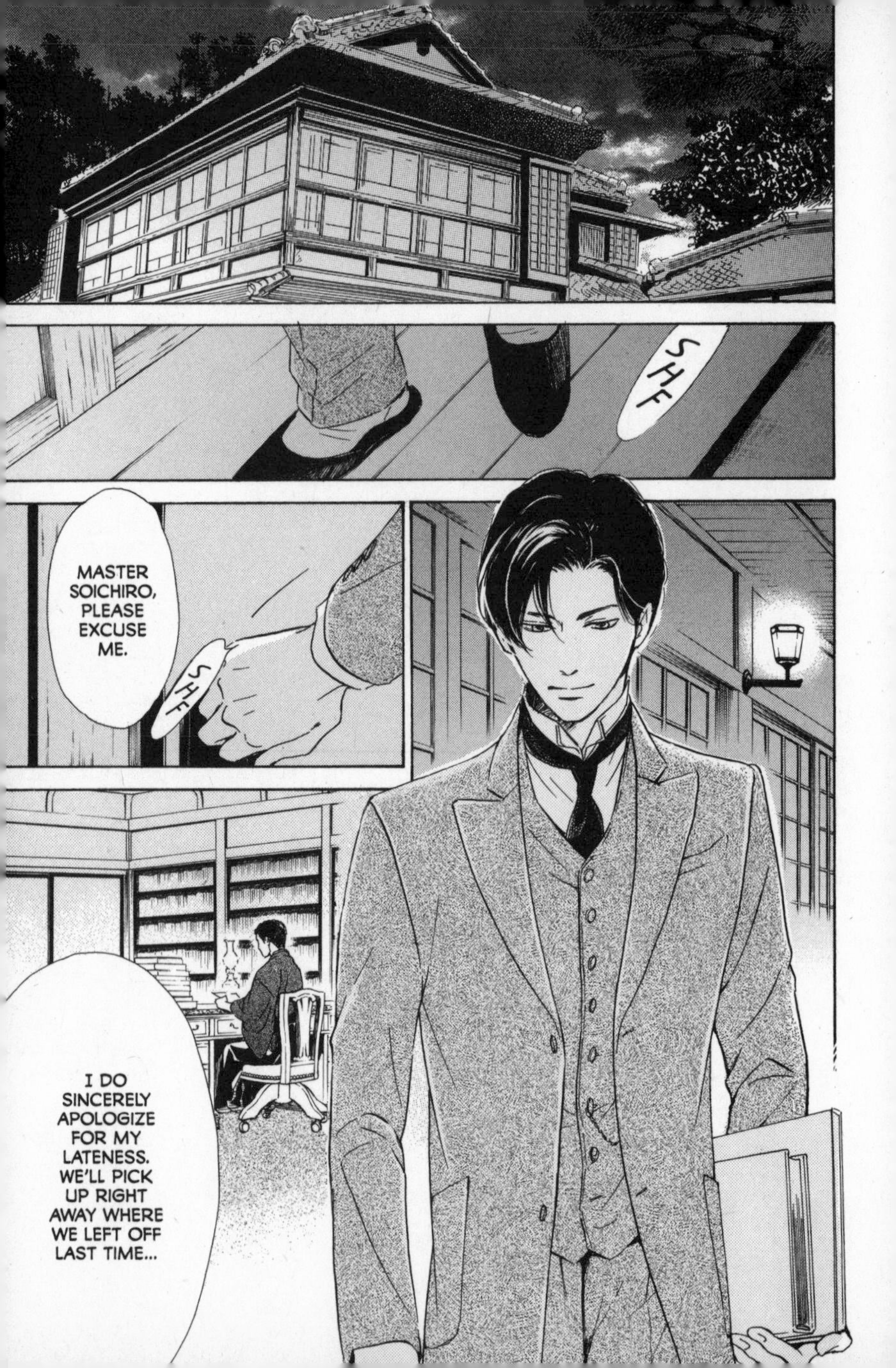
SHF
MASTER SOICHIRO, PLEASE EXCUSE ME.
SHF
I DO SINCERELY APOLOGIZE FOR MY LATENESS. WE'LL PICK UP RIGHT AWAY WHERE WE LEFT OFF LAST TIME...

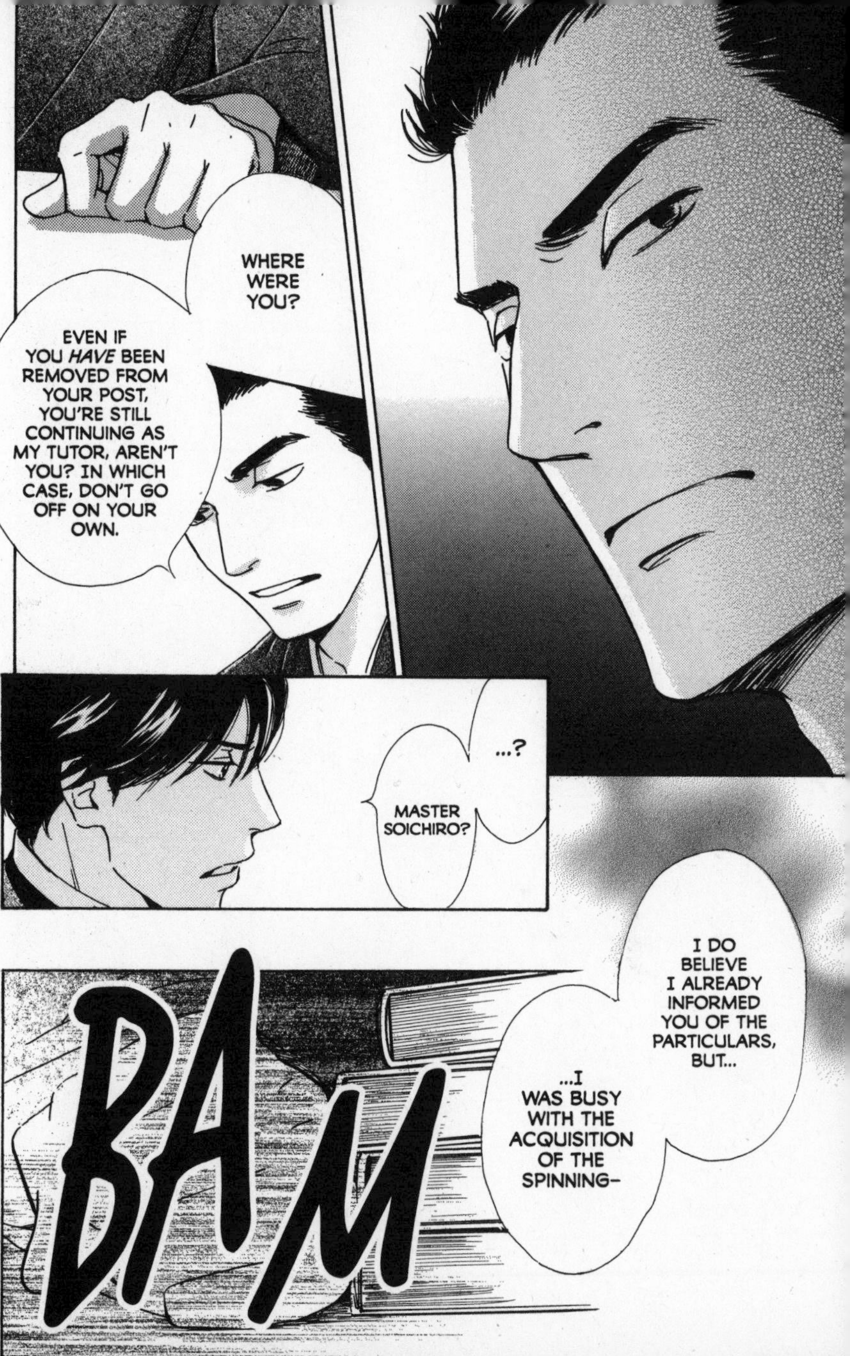
WHERE WERE YOU?
EVEN IF YOU *HAVE* BEEN REMOVED FROM YOUR POST, YOU'RE STILL CONTINUING AS MY TUTOR, AREN'T YOU? IN WHICH CASE, DON'T GO OFF ON YOUR OWN.
...?
MASTER SOICHIRO?
I DO BELIEVE I ALREADY INFORMED YOU OF THE PARTICULARS, BUT...
...I WAS BUSY WITH THE ACQUISITION OF THE SPINNING–
BAM

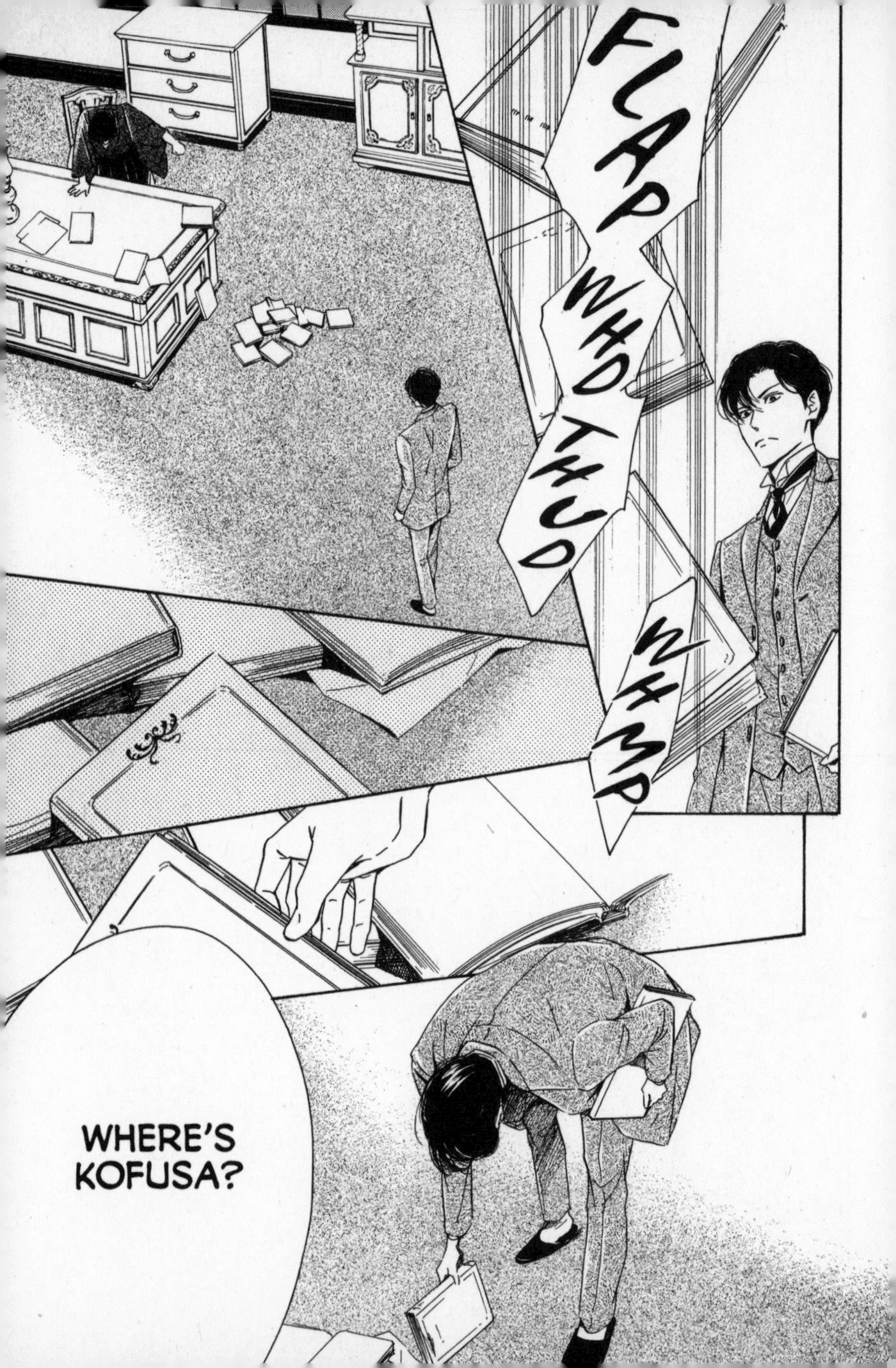
FLAP
WHAP
THUD
WHMP
WHERE'S KOFUSA?

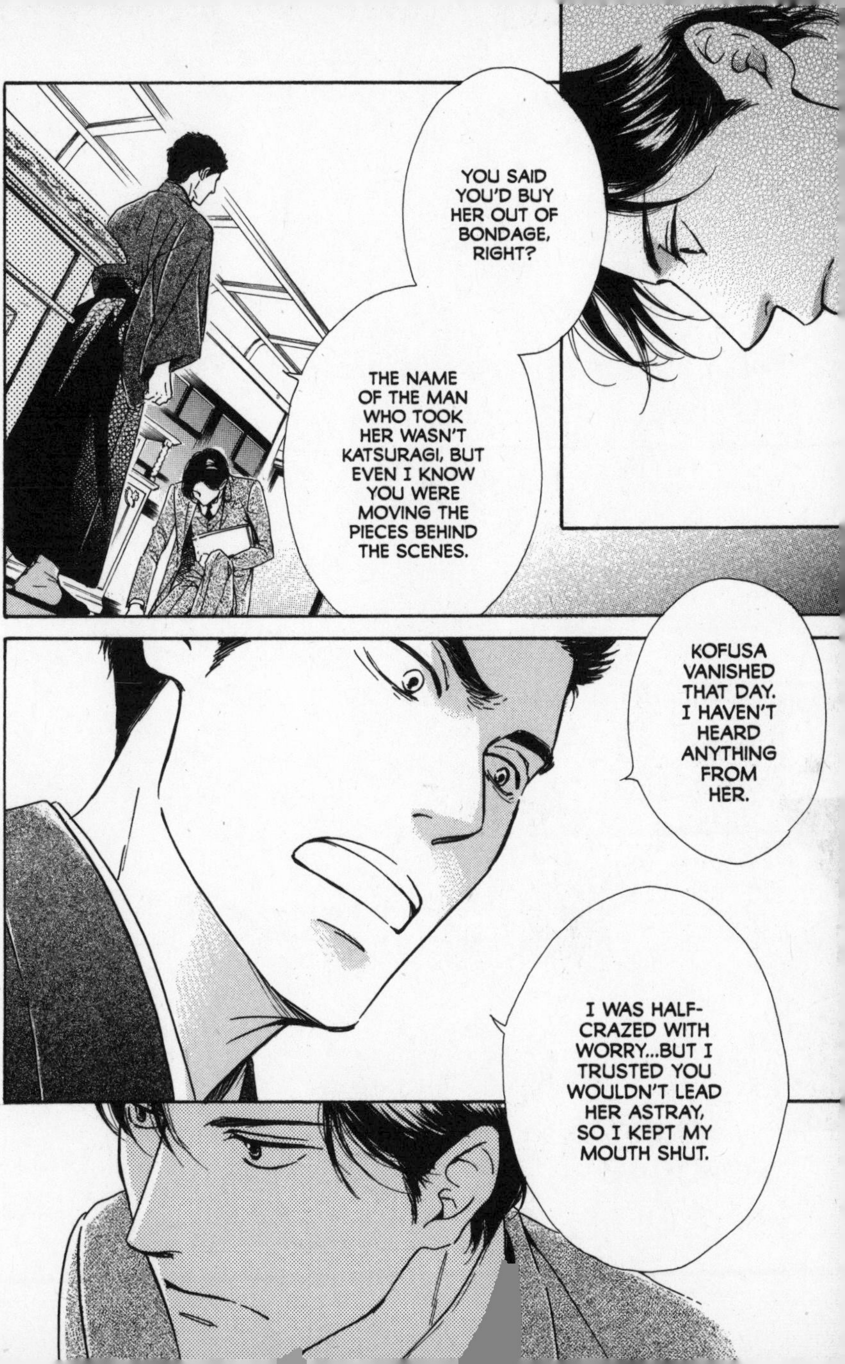
YOU SAID YOU'D BUY HER OUT OF BONDAGE, RIGHT?
THE NAME OF THE MAN WHO TOOK HER WASN'T KATSURAGI, BUT EVEN I KNOW YOU WERE MOVING THE PIECES BEHIND THE SCENES.
KOFUSA VANISHED THAT DAY. I HAVEN'T HEARD ANYTHING FROM HER.
I WAS HALF-CRAZED WITH WORRY...BUT I TRUSTED YOU WOULDN'T LEAD HER ASTRAY, SO I KEPT MY MOUTH SHUT.

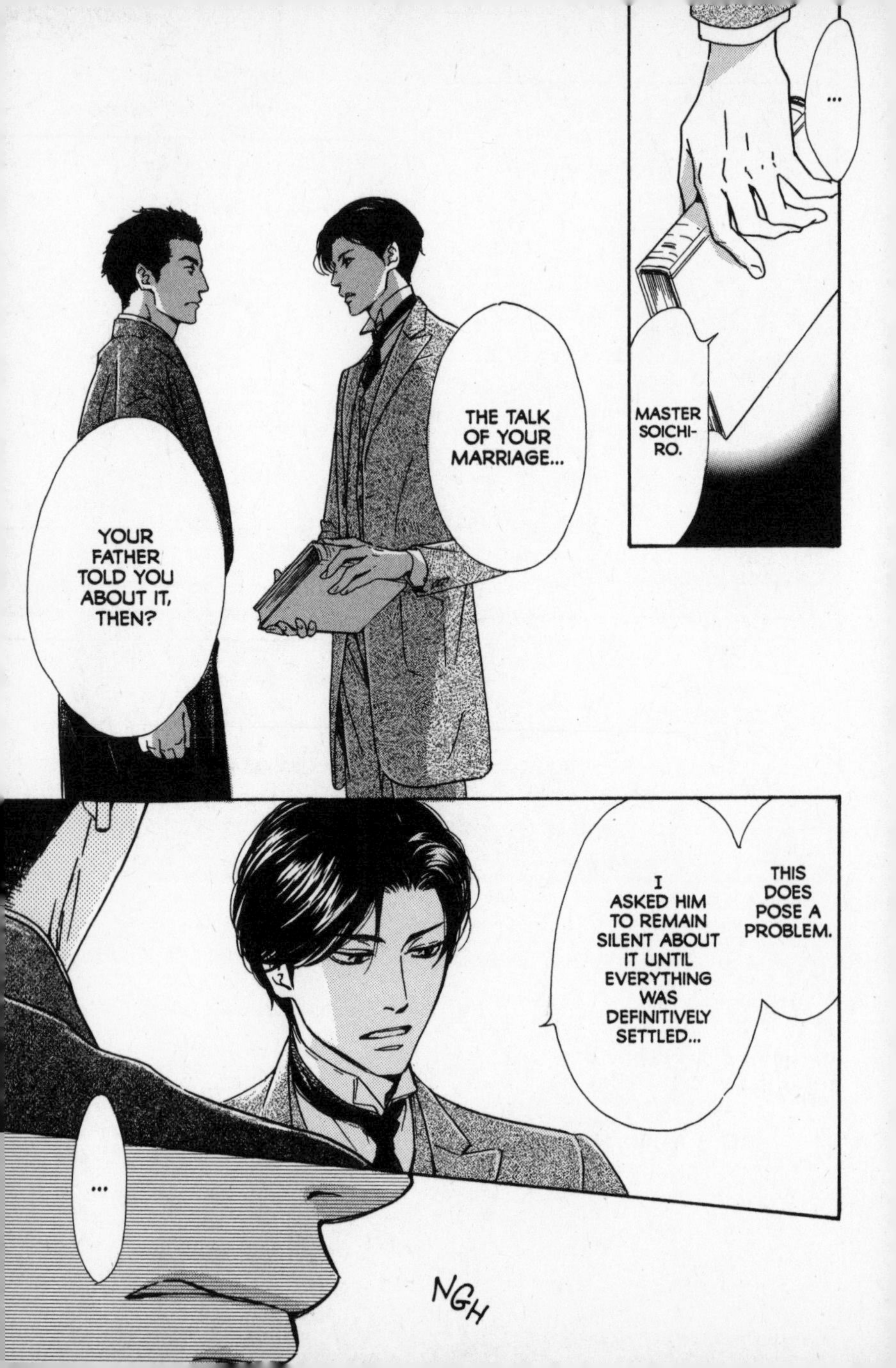
...
MASTER SOICHI-RO.
THE TALK OF YOUR MARRIAGE...
YOUR FATHER TOLD YOU ABOUT IT, THEN?
THIS DOES POSE A PROBLEM.
I ASKED HIM TO REMAIN SILENT ABOUT IT UNTIL EVERYTHING WAS DEFINITIVELY SETTLED...
...
NGH

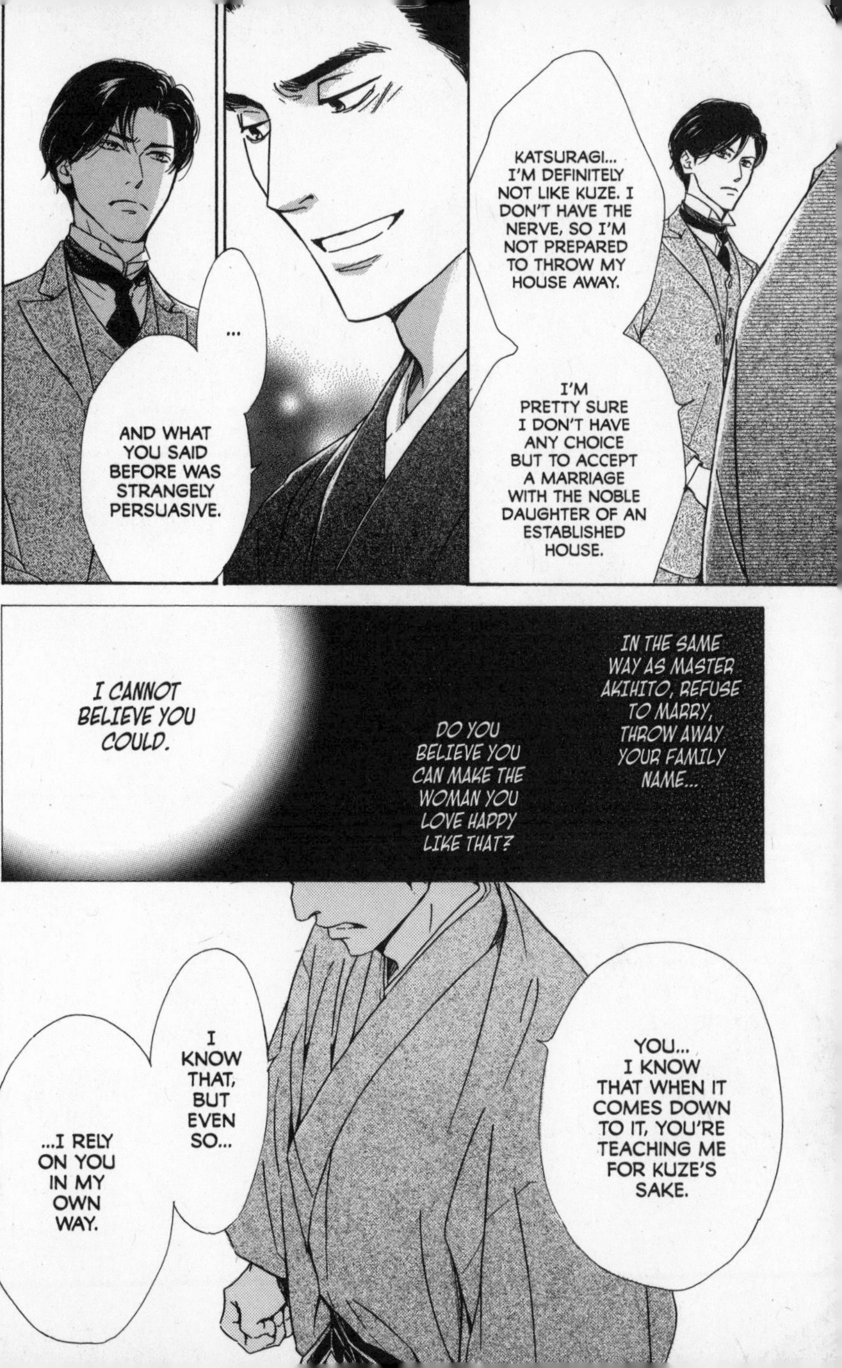
KATSURAGI... I'M DEFINITELY NOT LIKE KUZE. I DON'T HAVE THE NERVE, SO I'M NOT PREPARED TO THROW MY HOUSE AWAY.
I'M PRETTY SURE I DON'T HAVE ANY CHOICE BUT TO ACCEPT A MARRIAGE WITH THE NOBLE DAUGHTER OF AN ESTABLISHED HOUSE.
...
AND WHAT YOU SAID BEFORE WAS STRANGELY PERSUASIVE.
IN THE SAME WAY AS MASTER AKIHITO, REFUSE TO MARRY, THROW AWAY YOUR FAMILY NAME...
DO YOU BELIEVE YOU CAN MAKE THE WOMAN YOU LOVE HAPPY LIKE THAT?
I CANNOT BELIEVE YOU COULD.
YOU... I KNOW THAT WHEN IT COMES DOWN TO IT, YOU'RE TEACHING ME FOR KUZE'S SAKE.
I KNOW THAT, BUT EVEN SO...
...I RELY ON YOU IN MY OWN WAY.

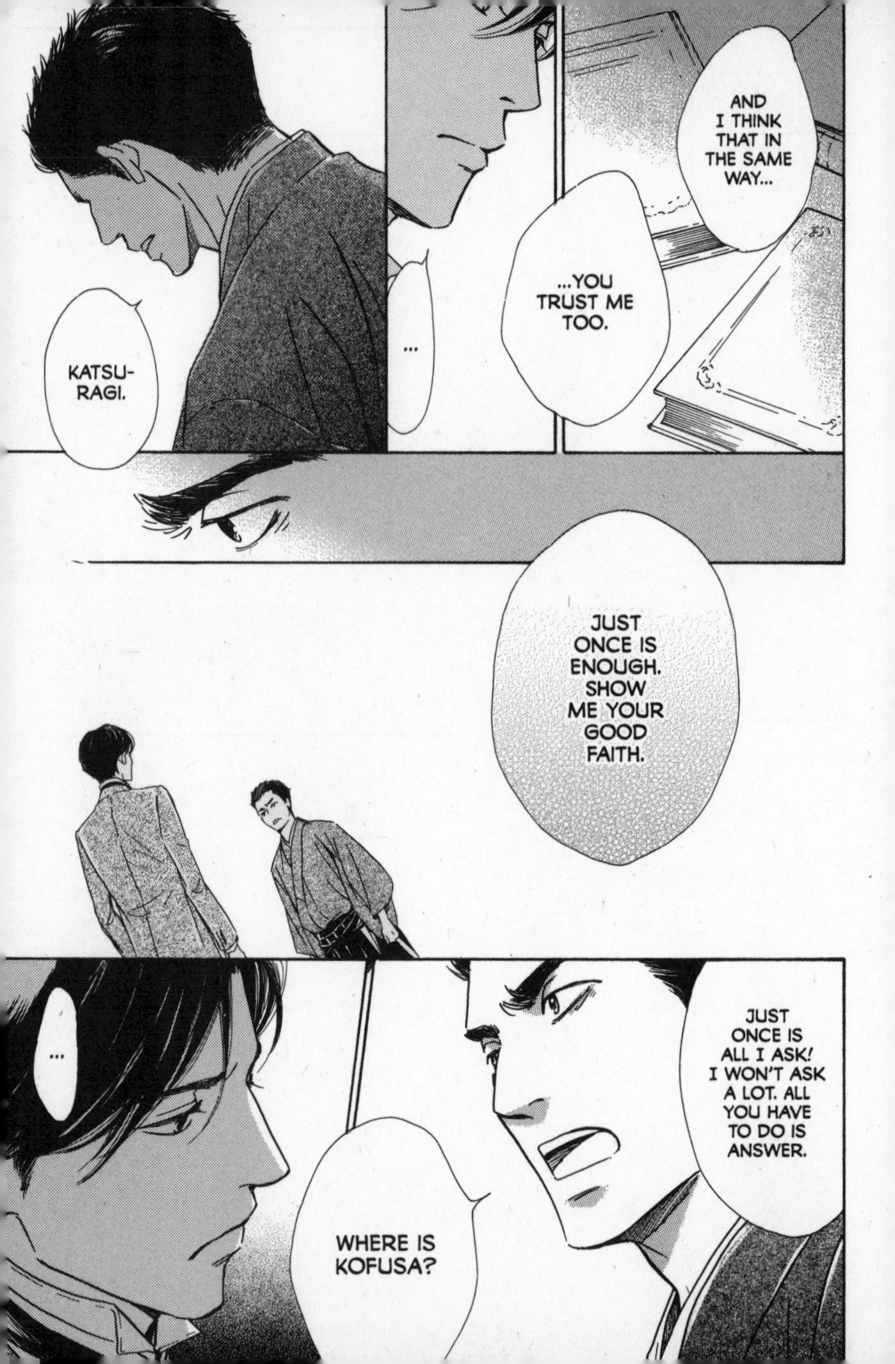
AND I THINK THAT IN THE SAME WAY...
...YOU TRUST ME TOO.
...
KATSU-RAGI.
JUST ONCE IS ENOUGH. SHOW ME YOUR GOOD FAITH.
JUST ONCE IS ALL I ASK! I WON'T ASK A LOT. ALL YOU HAVE TO DO IS ANSWER.
WHERE IS KOFUSA?
...

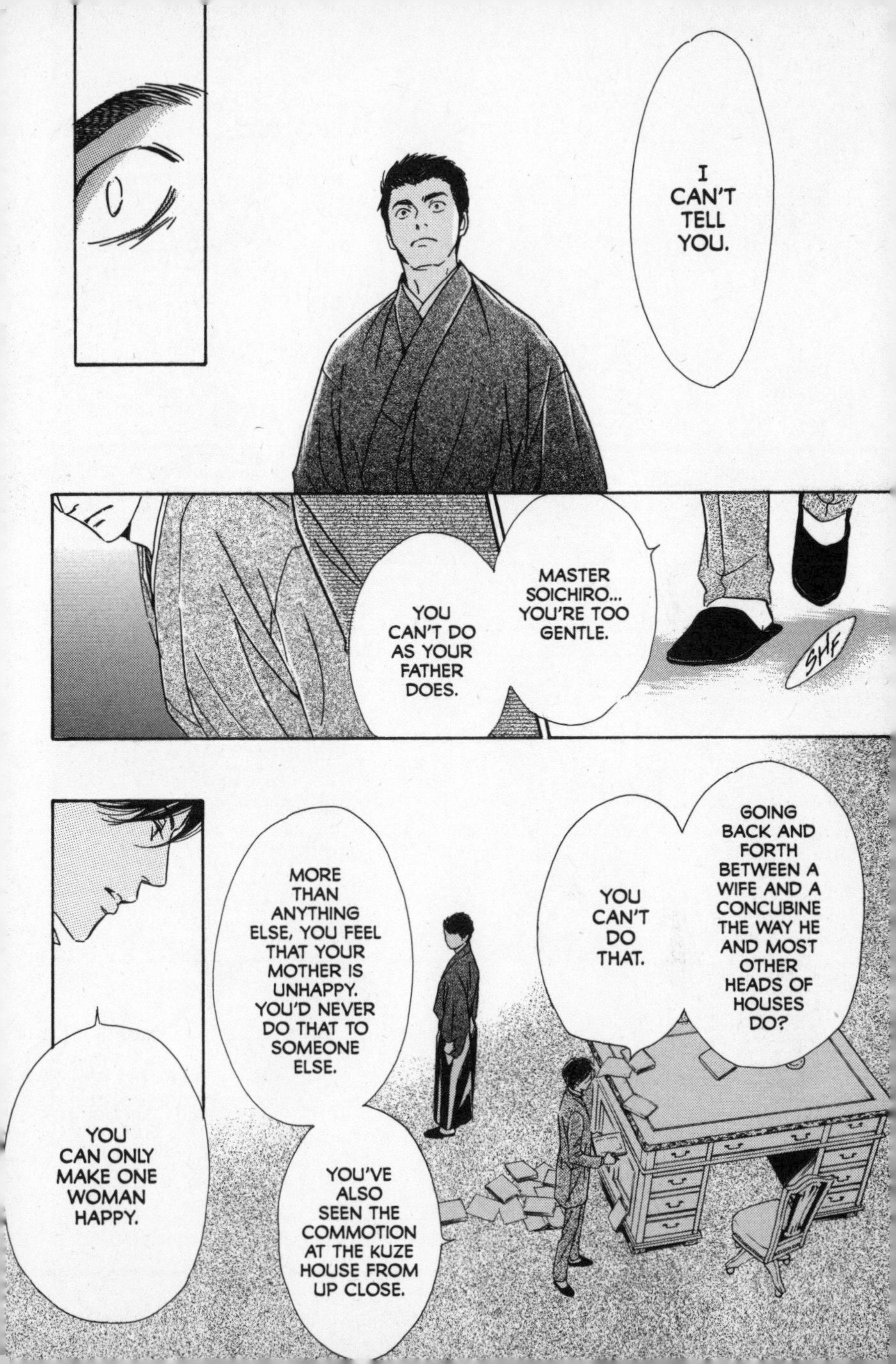
I CAN'T TELL YOU.
SHF
MASTER SOICHIRO... YOU'RE TOO GENTLE.
YOU CAN'T DO AS YOUR FATHER DOES.
GOING BACK AND FORTH BETWEEN A WIFE AND A CONCUBINE THE WAY HE AND MOST OTHER HEADS OF HOUSES DO?
YOU CAN'T DO THAT.
MORE THAN ANYTHING ELSE, YOU FEEL THAT YOUR MOTHER IS UNHAPPY. YOU'D NEVER DO THAT TO SOMEONE ELSE.
YOU'VE ALSO SEEN THE COMMOTION AT THE KUZE HOUSE FROM UP CLOSE.
YOU CAN ONLY MAKE ONE WOMAN HAPPY.

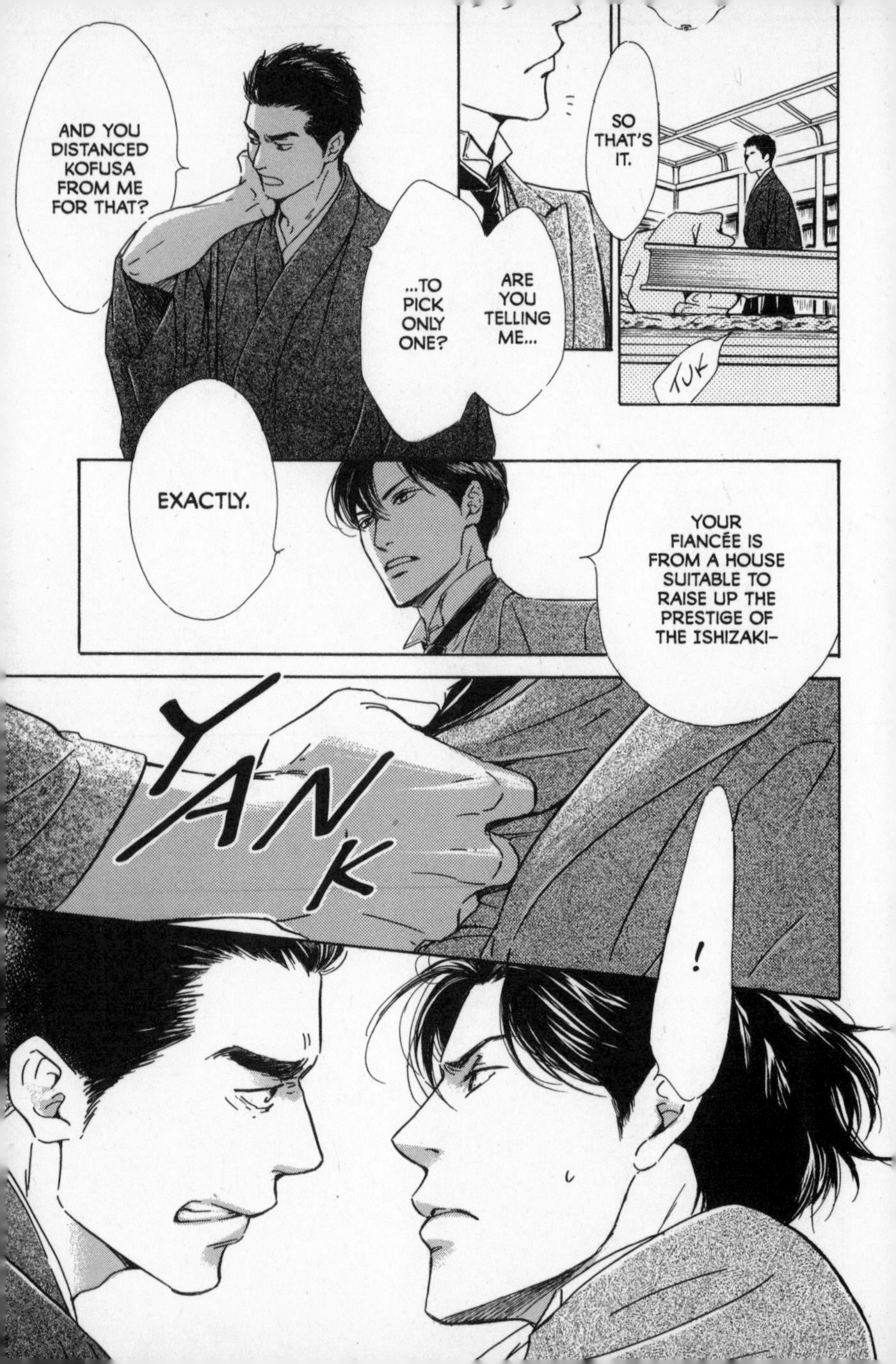
TUK
SO THAT'S IT.
ARE YOU TELLING ME...
...TO PICK ONLY ONE?
AND YOU DISTANCED KOFUSA FROM ME FOR THAT?
EXACTLY.
YOUR FIANCÉE IS FROM A HOUSE SUITABLE TO RAISE UP THE PRESTIGE OF THE ISHIZAKI-
YANK
!

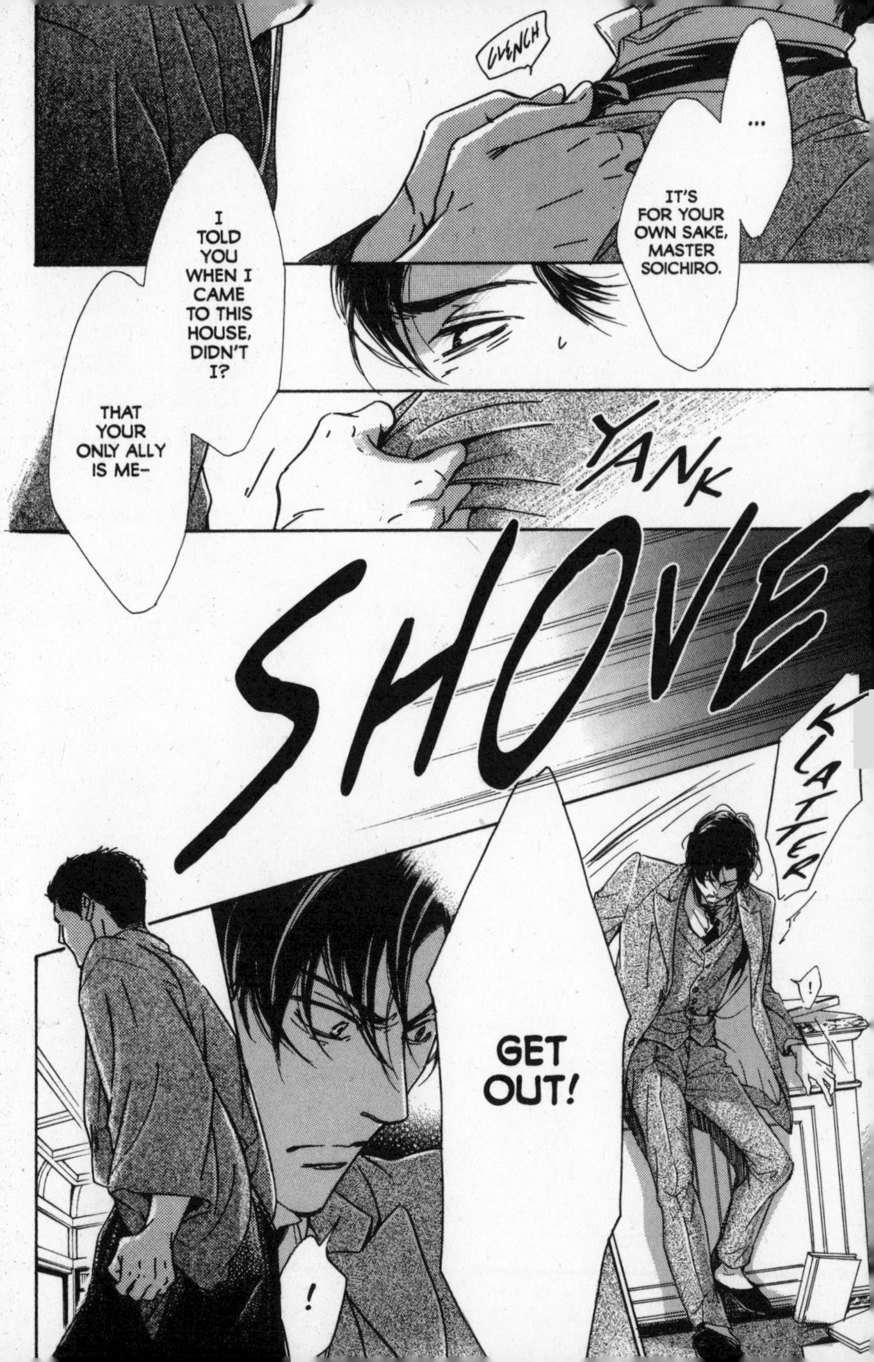
CLENCH
...
IT'S FOR YOUR OWN SAKE, MASTER SOICHIRO.
I TOLD YOU WHEN I CAME TO THIS HOUSE, DIDN'T I?
THAT YOUR ONLY ALLY IS ME-
YANK
SHOVE
KLATTER
!
GET OUT!
!

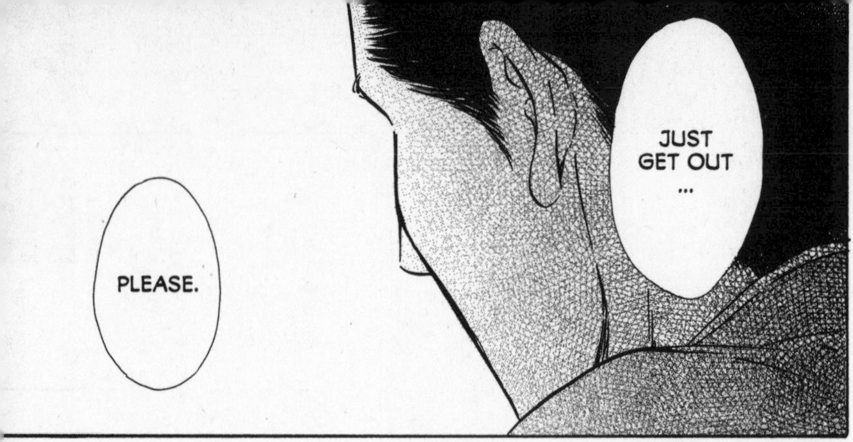
JUST GET OUT ...
PLEASE.

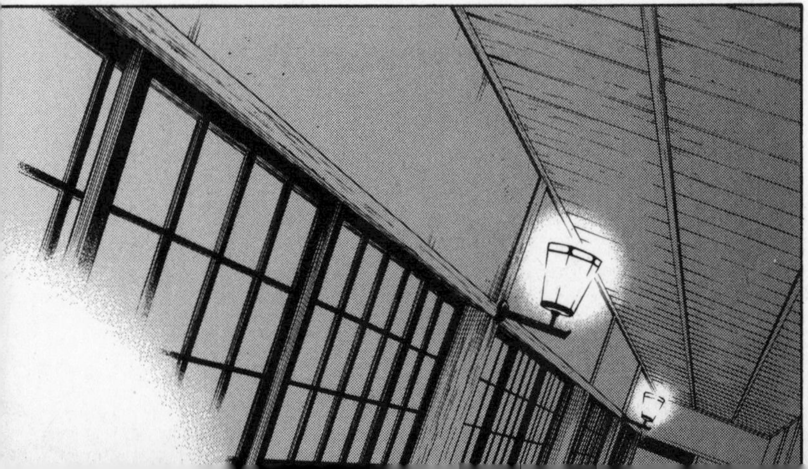

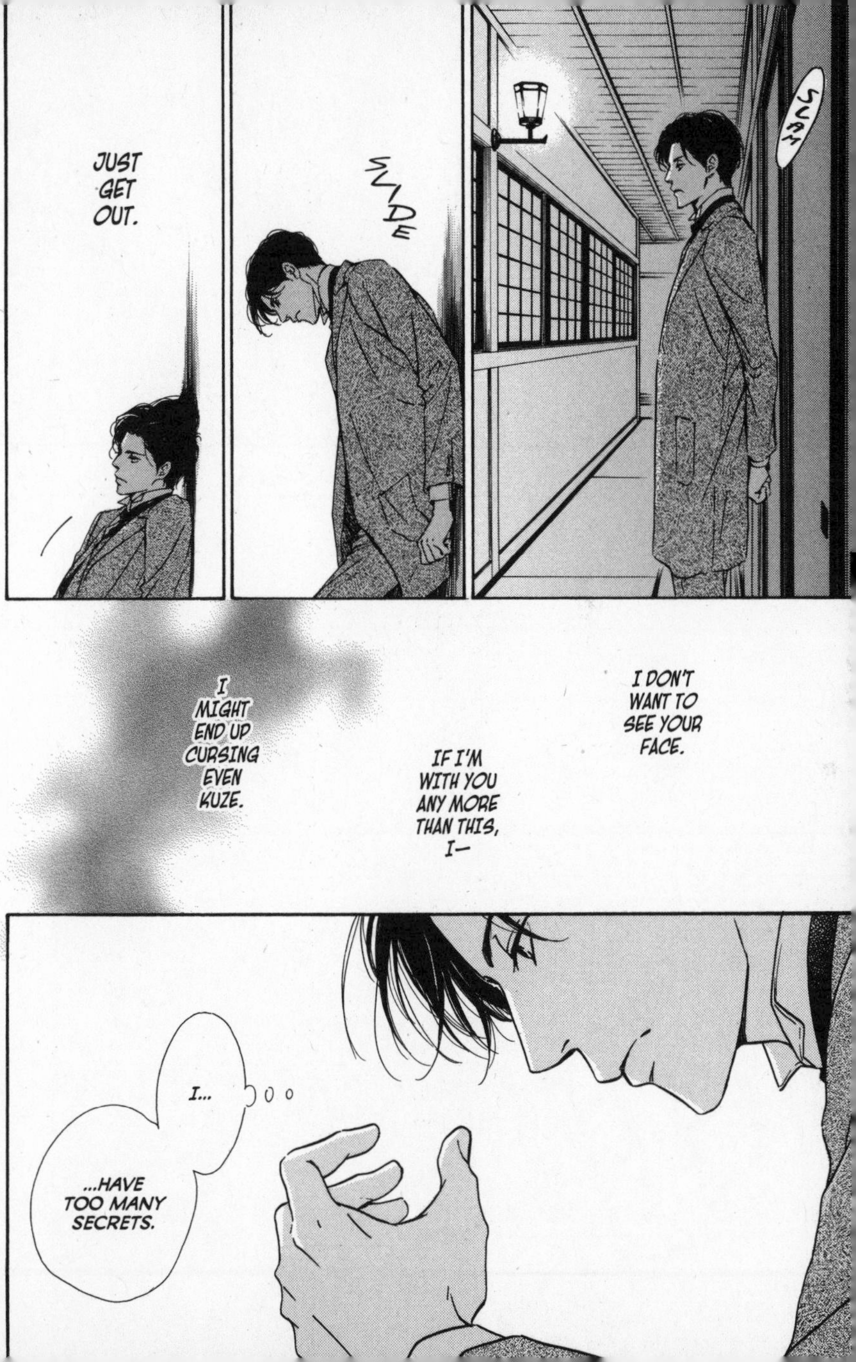
SLAM
SLIDE
JUST GET OUT.
I DON'T WANT TO SEE YOUR FACE.
IF I'M WITH YOU ANY MORE THAN THIS, I—
I MIGHT END UP CURSING EVEN KUZE.
I...
...HAVE TOO MANY SECRETS.

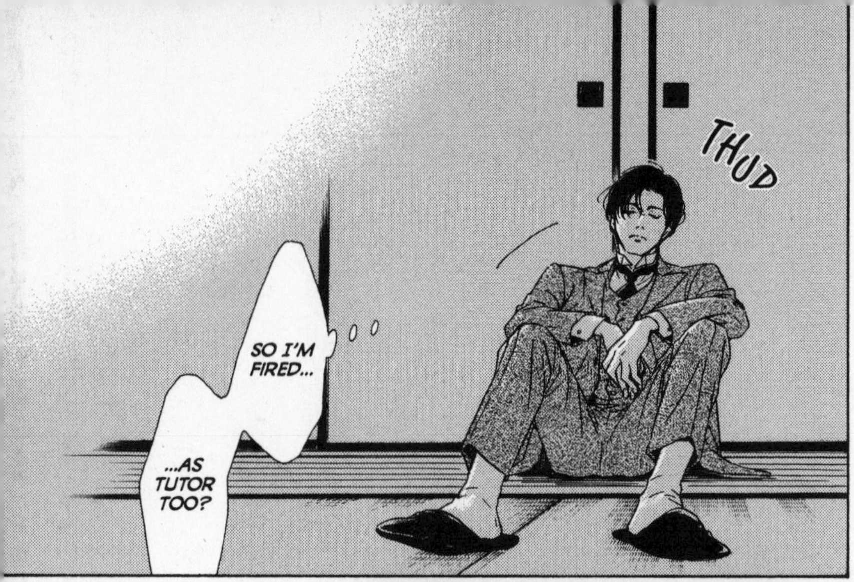
THUD
SO I'M FIRED...
...AS TUTOR TOO?
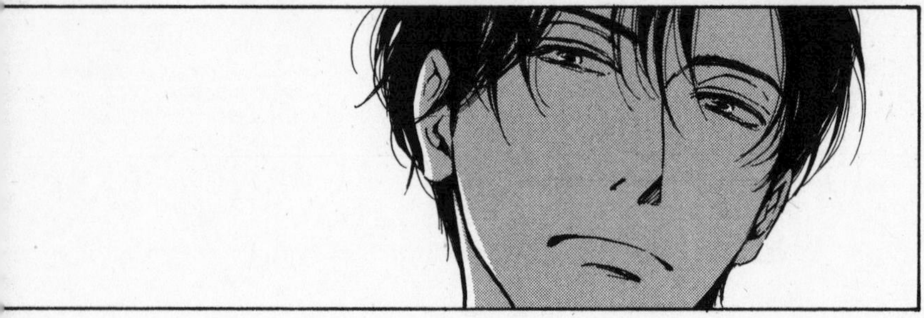

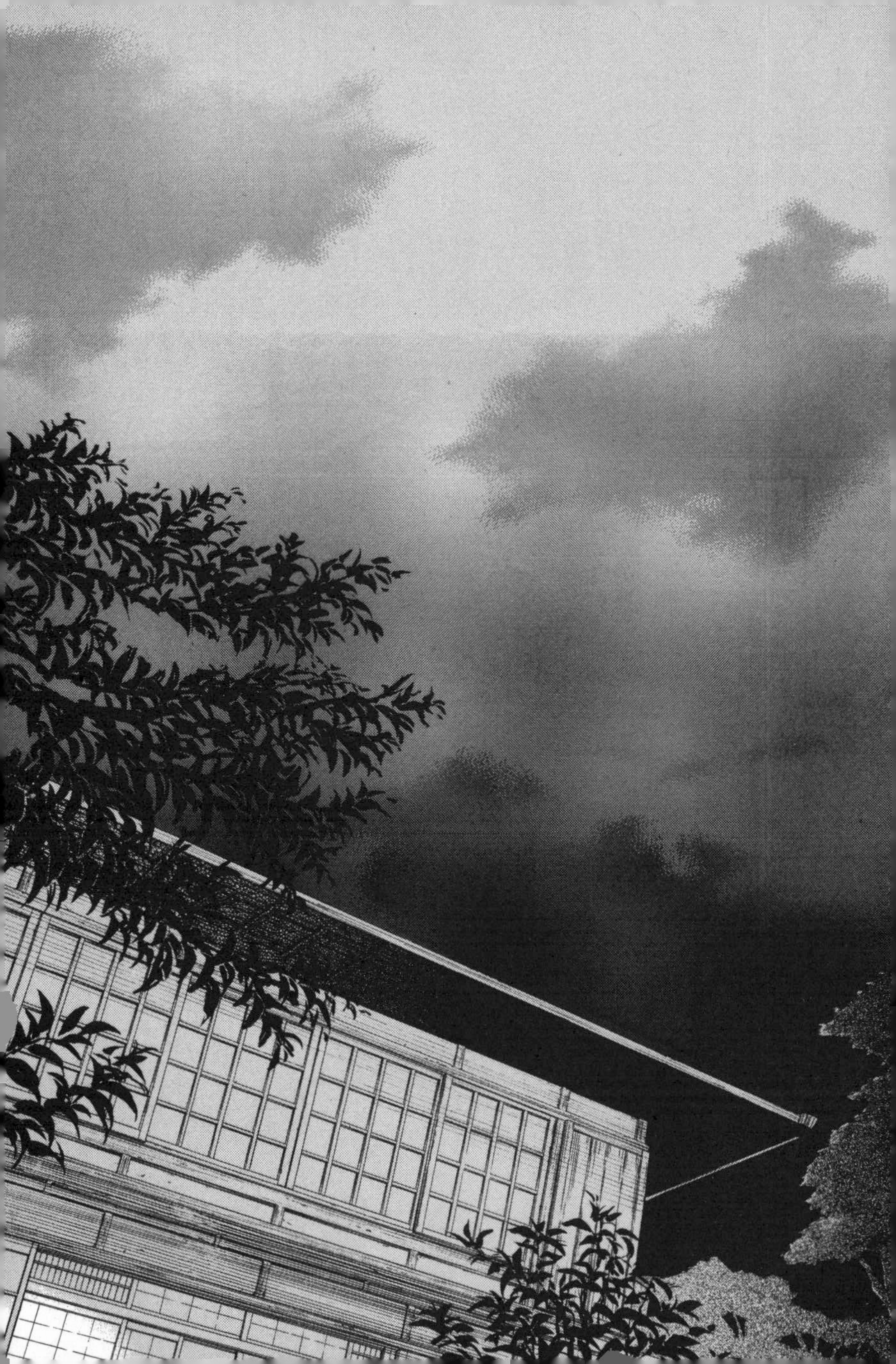

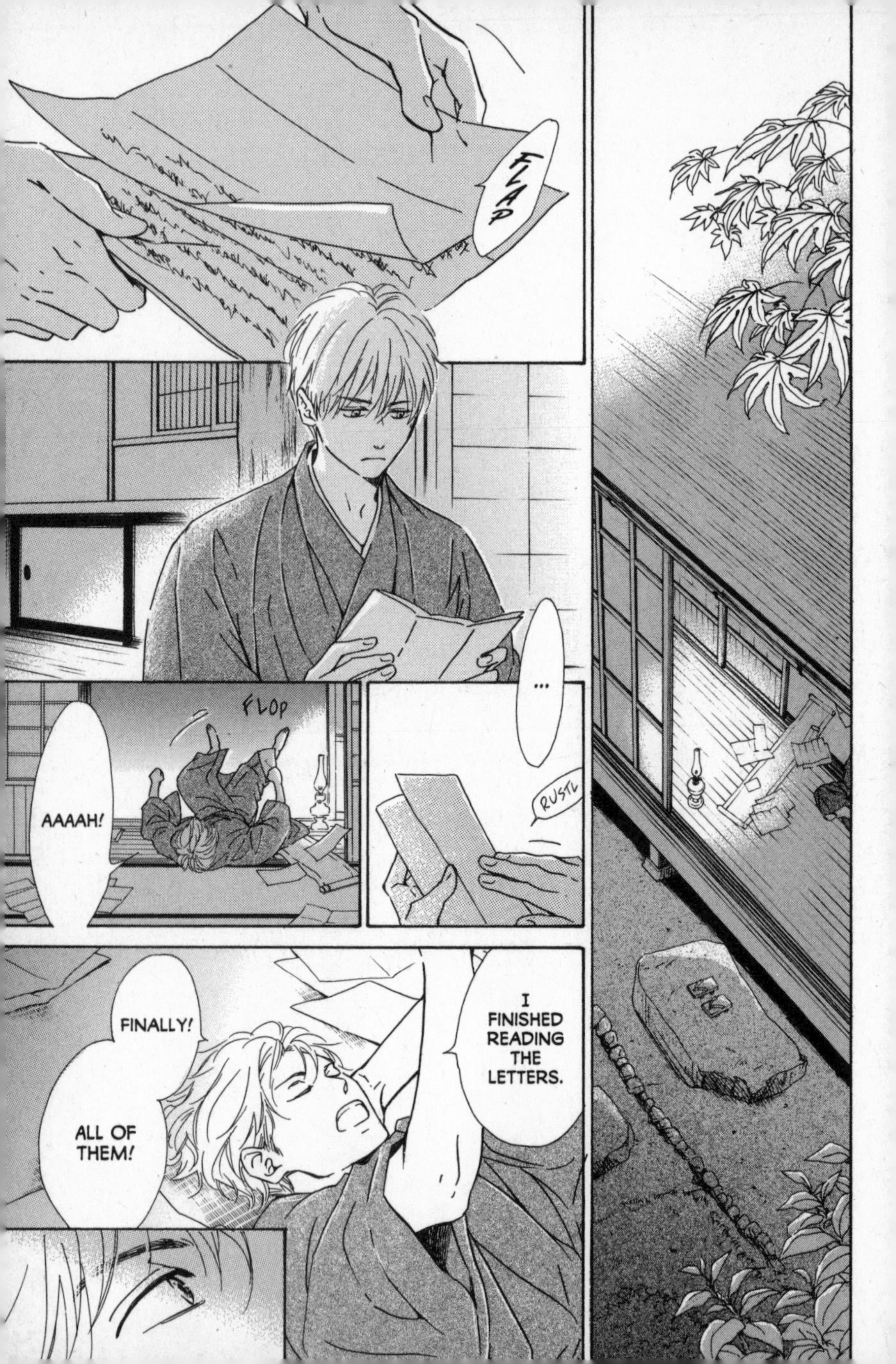
FLAP
...
RUSTL
FLOP
AAAAH!
I FINISHED READING THE LETTERS.
FINALLY!
ALL OF THEM!

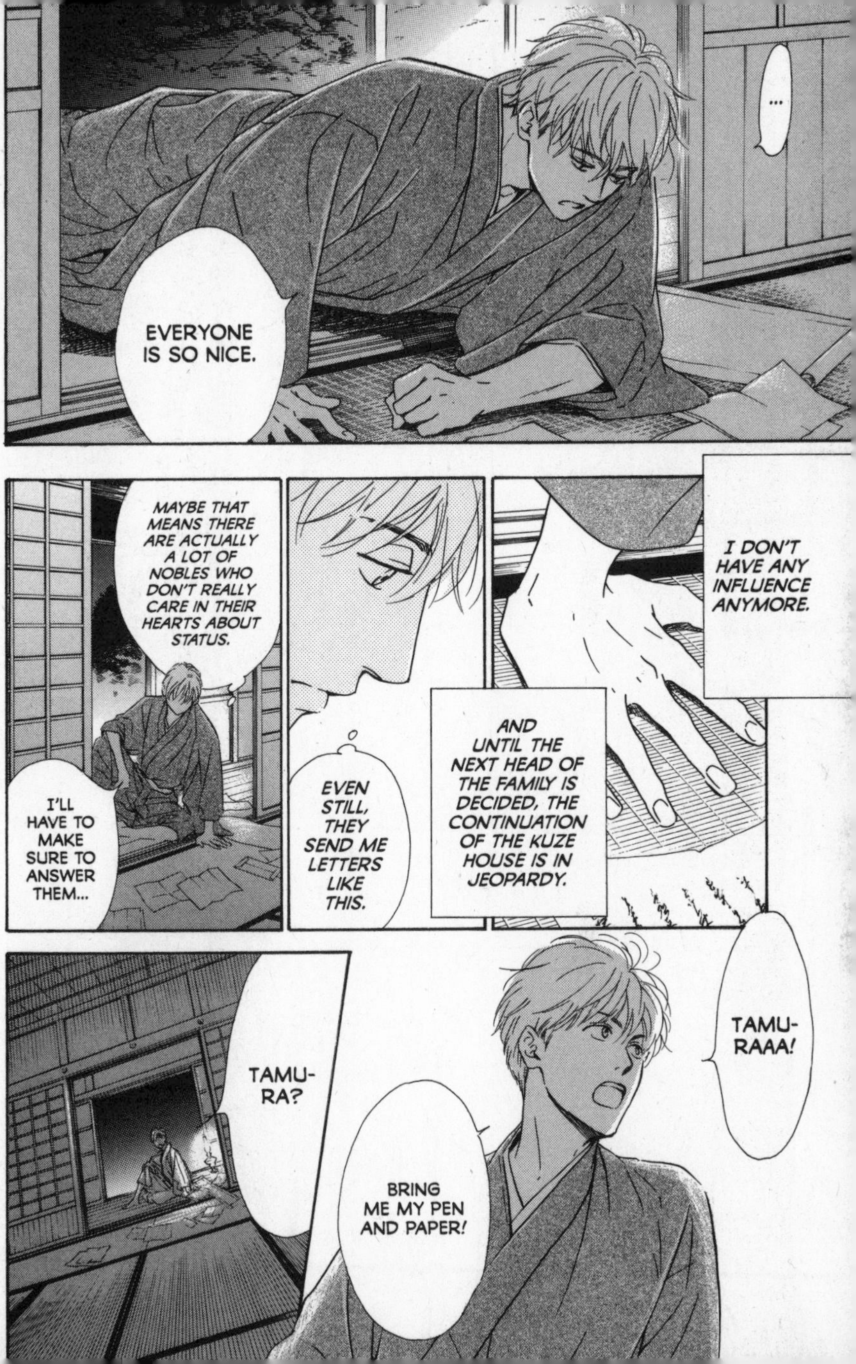
...
EVERYONE IS SO NICE.
I DON'T HAVE ANY INFLUENCE ANYMORE.
AND UNTIL THE NEXT HEAD OF THE FAMILY IS DECIDED, THE CONTINUATION OF THE KUZE HOUSE IS IN JEOPARDY.
EVEN STILL, THEY SEND ME LETTERS LIKE THIS.
MAYBE THAT MEANS THERE ARE ACTUALLY A LOT OF NOBLES WHO DON'T REALLY CARE IN THEIR HEARTS ABOUT STATUS.
I'LL HAVE TO MAKE SURE TO ANSWER THEM...
TAMU-RAAA!
BRING ME MY PEN AND PAPER!
TAMU-RA?

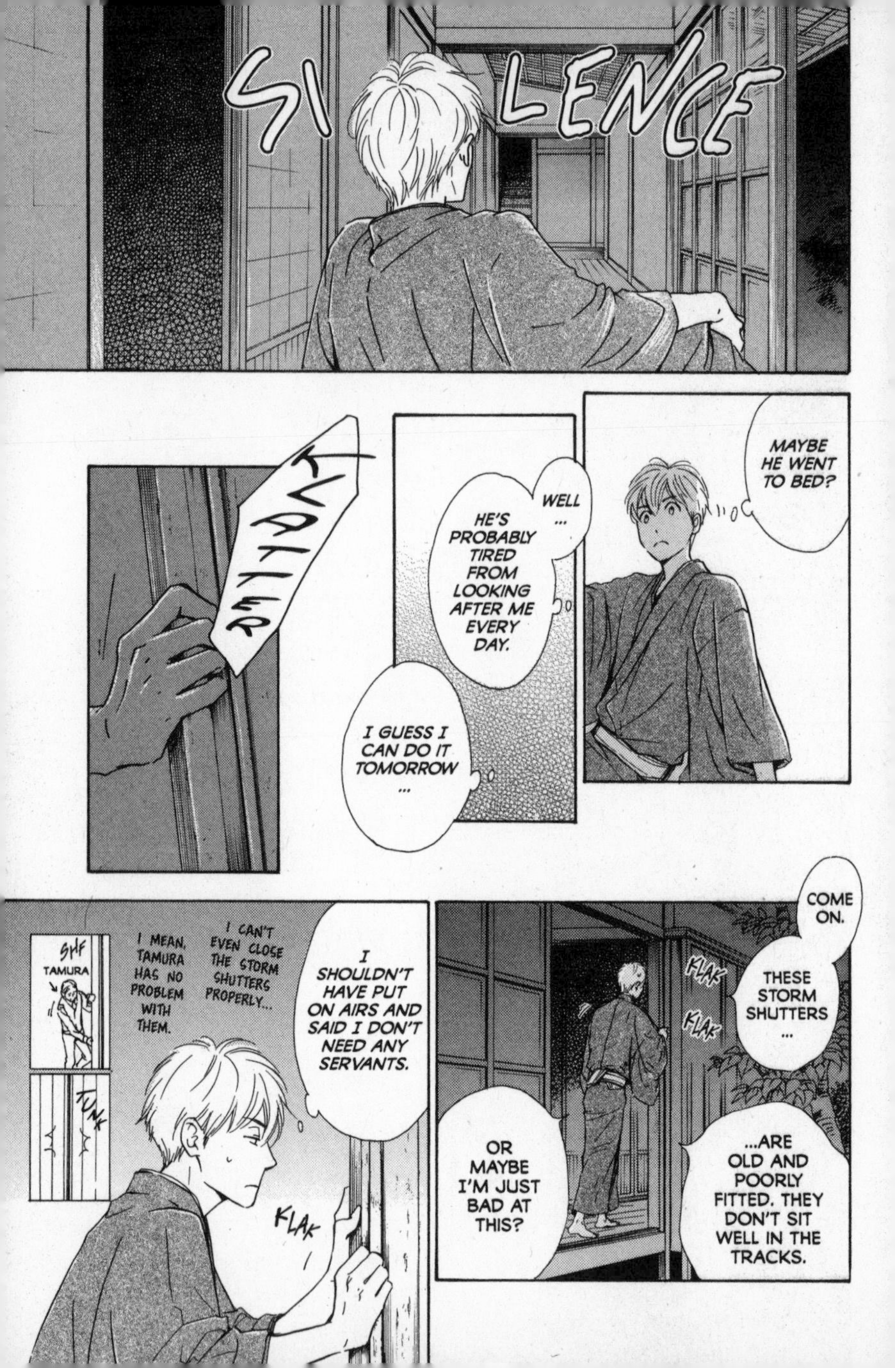
SILENCE
MAYBE HE WENT TO BED?
WELL ...
HE'S PROBABLY TIRED FROM LOOKING AFTER ME EVERY DAY.
I GUESS I CAN DO IT TOMORROW ...
KLATTER
COME ON.
KLAK
KLAK
THESE STORM SHUTTERS ...
...ARE OLD AND POORLY FITTED. THEY DON'T SIT WELL IN THE TRACKS.
OR MAYBE I'M JUST BAD AT THIS?
I SHOULDN'T HAVE PUT ON AIRS AND SAID I DON'T NEED ANY SERVANTS.
KLAK
I CAN'T EVEN CLOSE THE STORM SHUTTERS PROPERLY...
I MEAN, TAMURA HAS NO PROBLEM WITH THEM.
SHF
TAMURA
TUNK

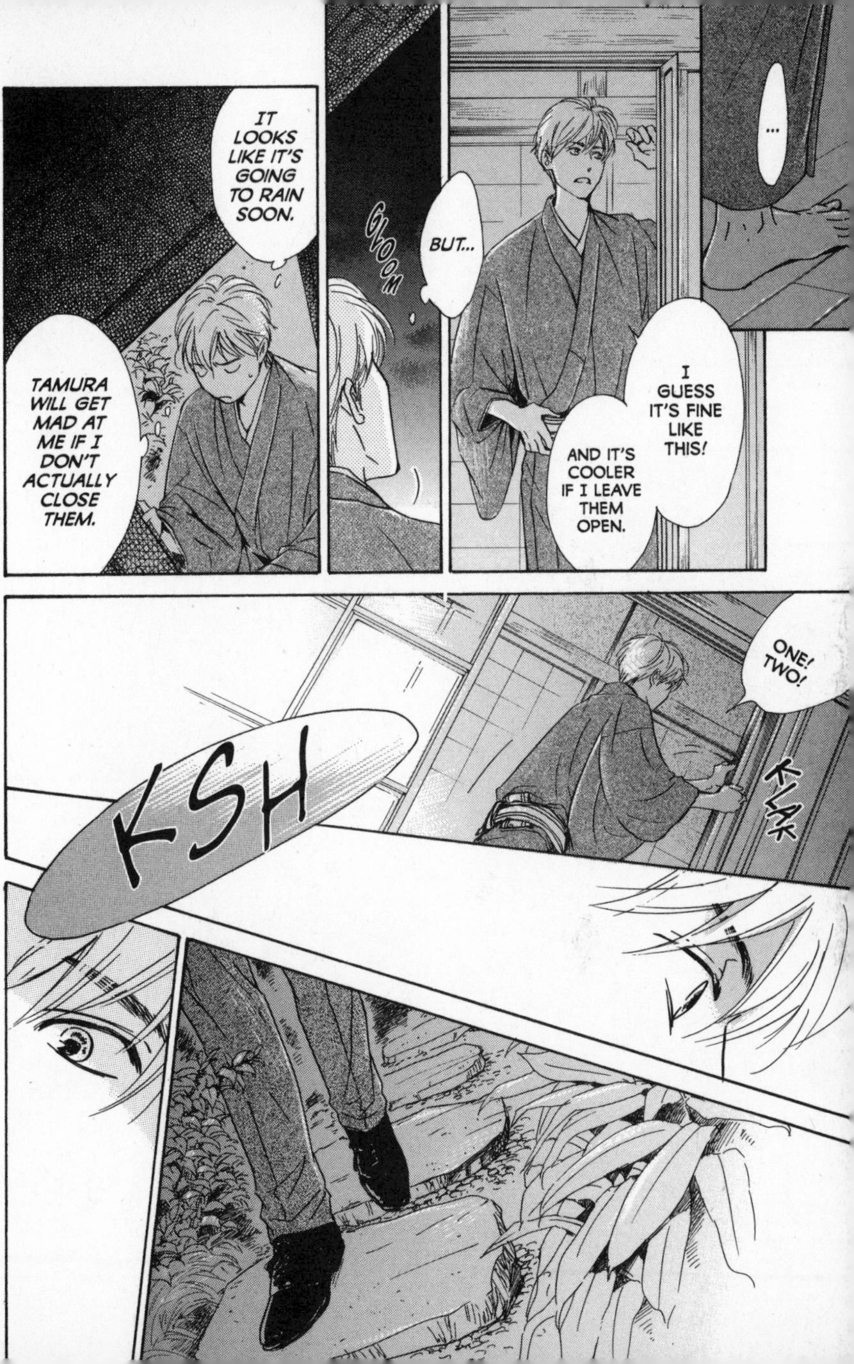
...
BUT...
I GUESS IT'S FINE LIKE THIS!
AND IT'S COOLER IF I LEAVE THEM OPEN.
GLOOM
IT LOOKS LIKE IT'S GOING TO RAIN SOON.
TAMURA WILL GET MAD AT ME IF I DON'T ACTUALLY CLOSE THEM.
ONE! TWO!
KLAK
KSH

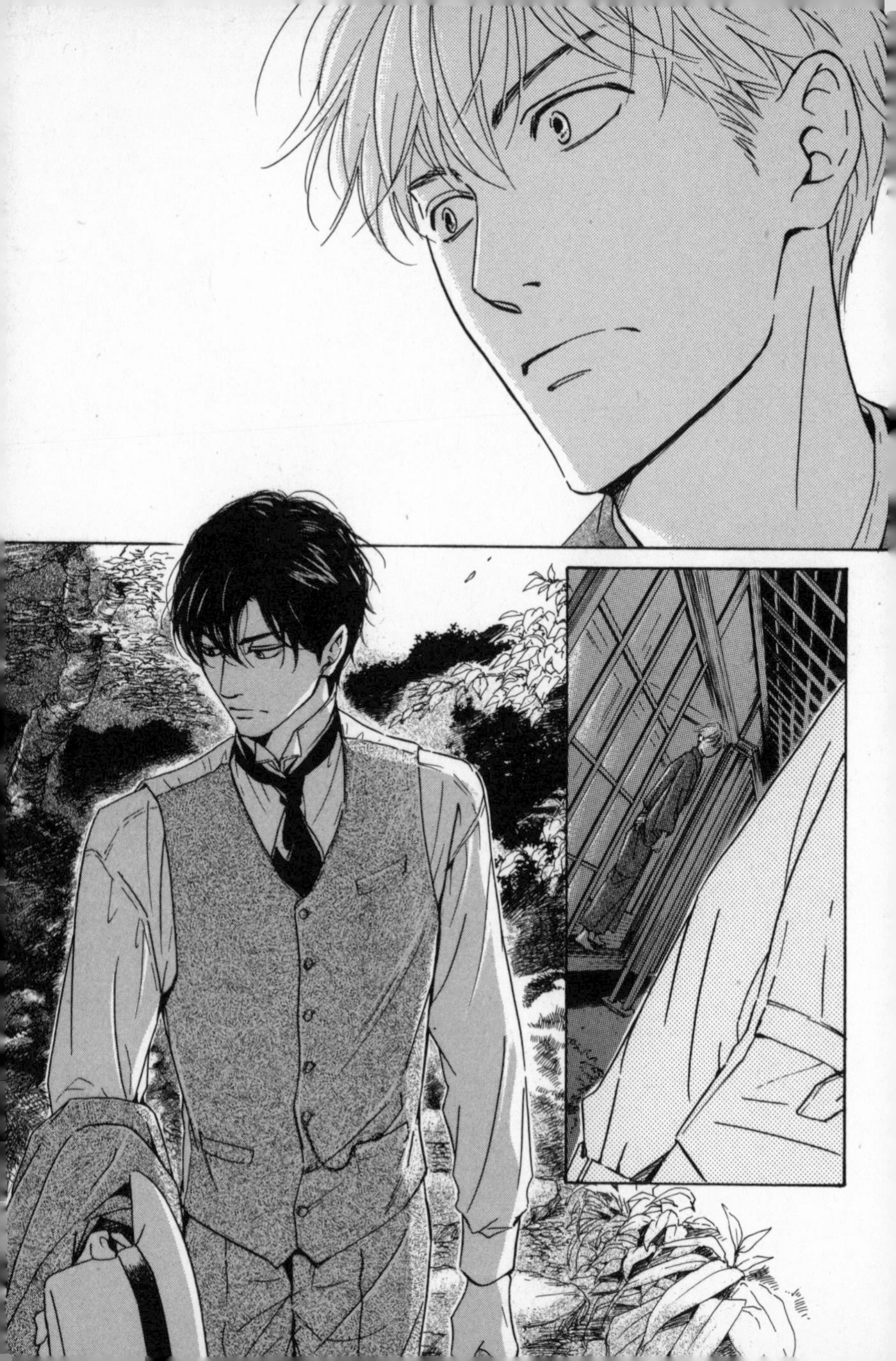

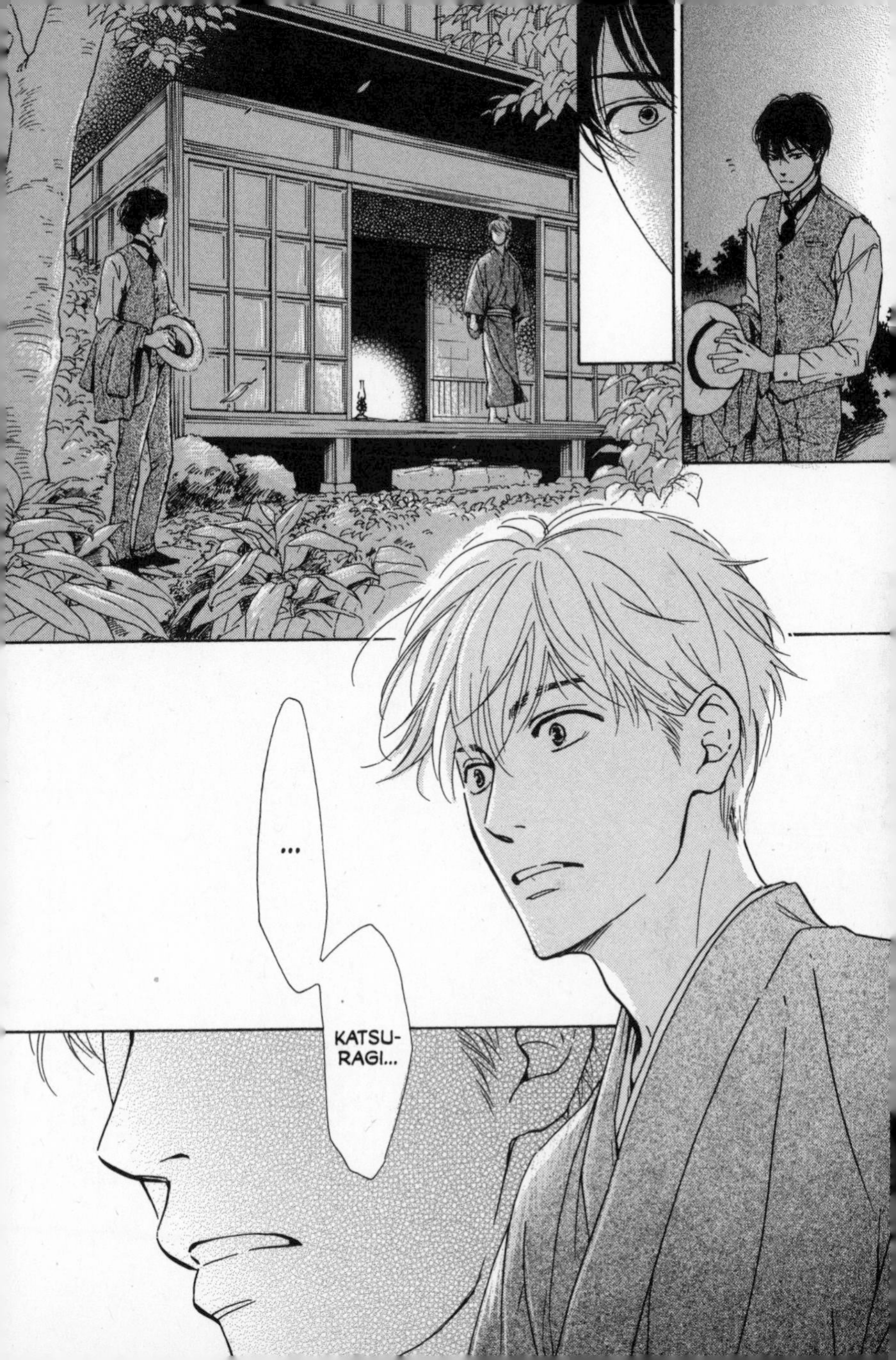
...
KATSU-RAGI...

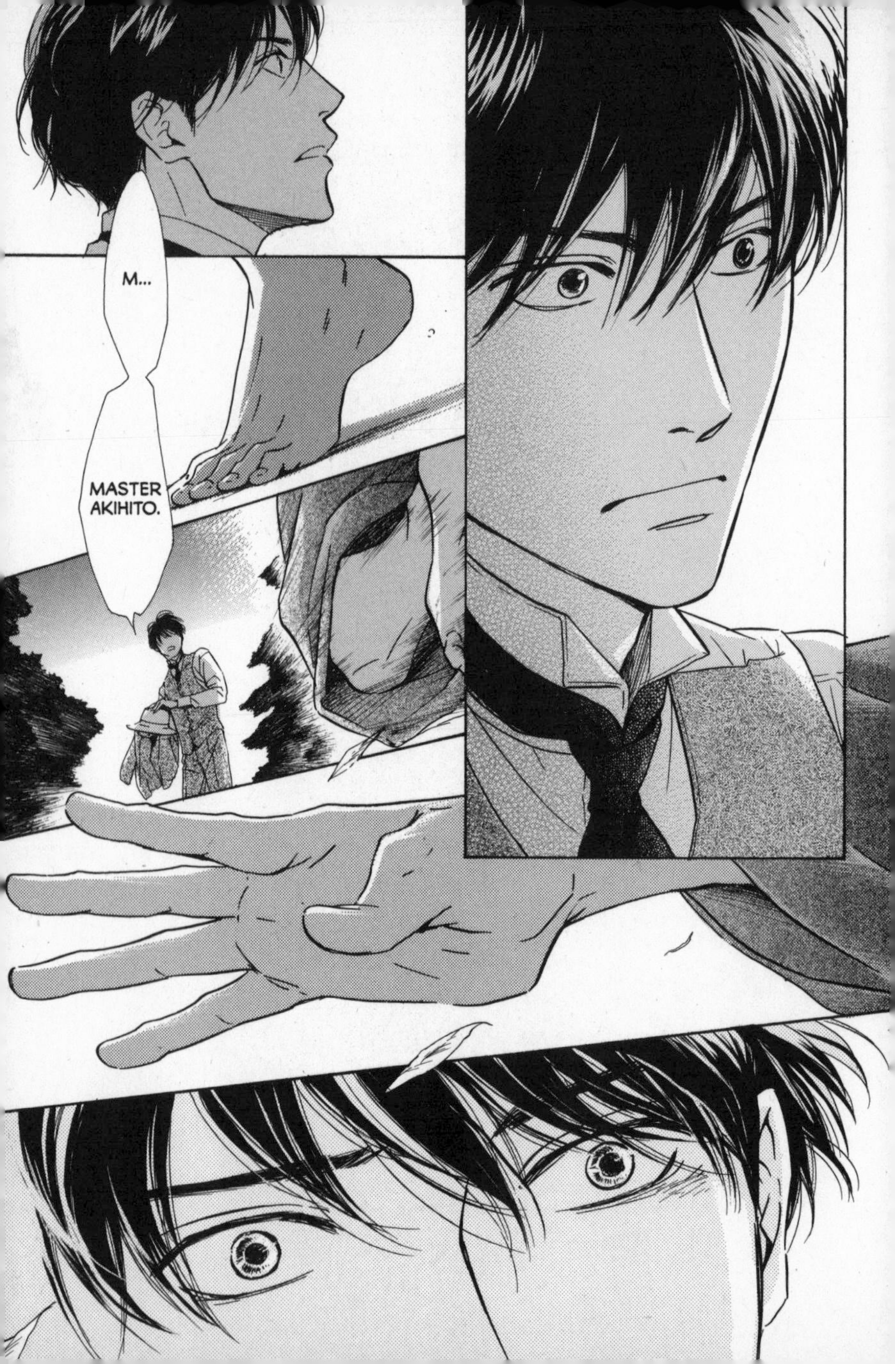
M...
MASTER AKIHITO.

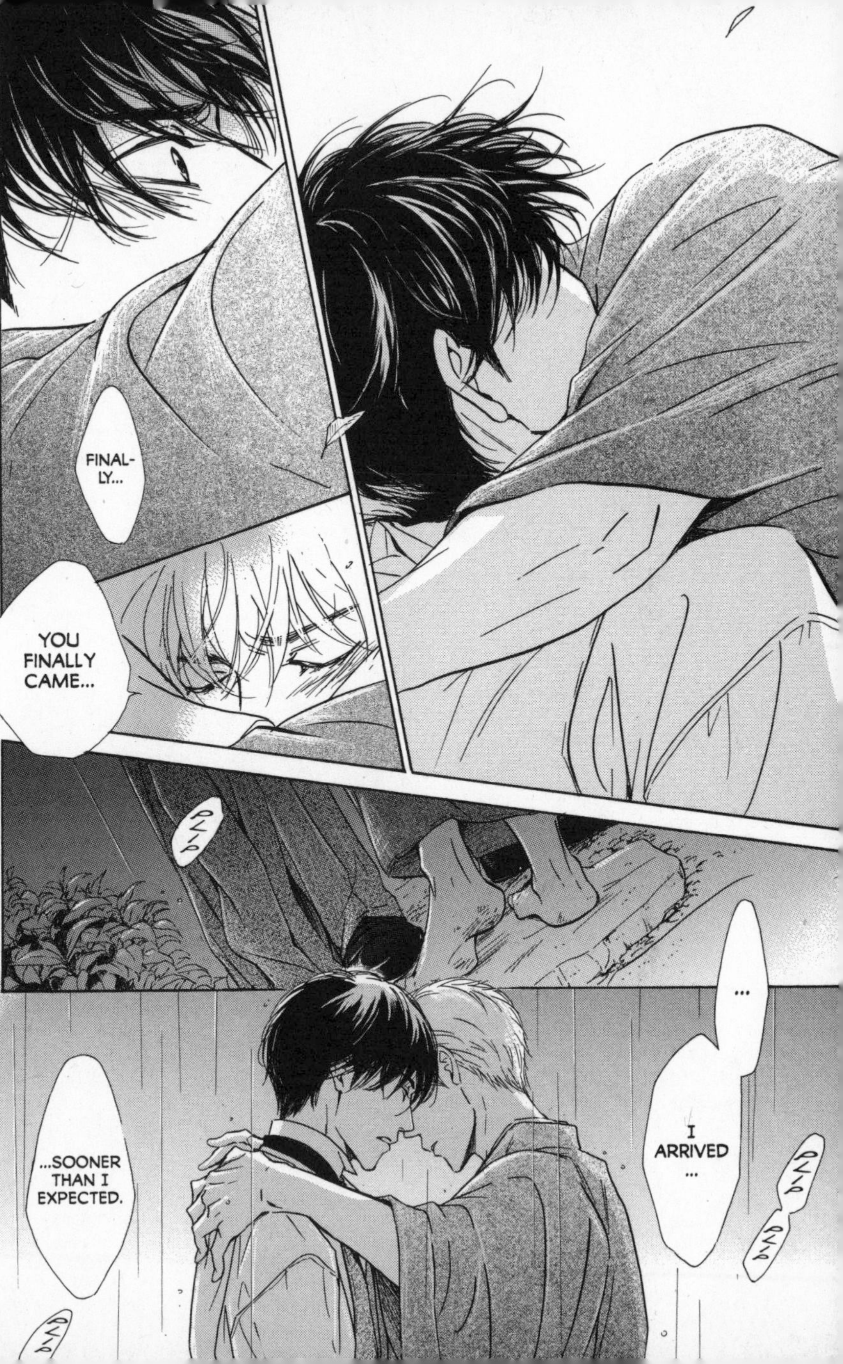
FINAL-LY...
YOU FINALLY CAME...
...
I ARRIVED ...
...SOONER THAN I EXPECTED.

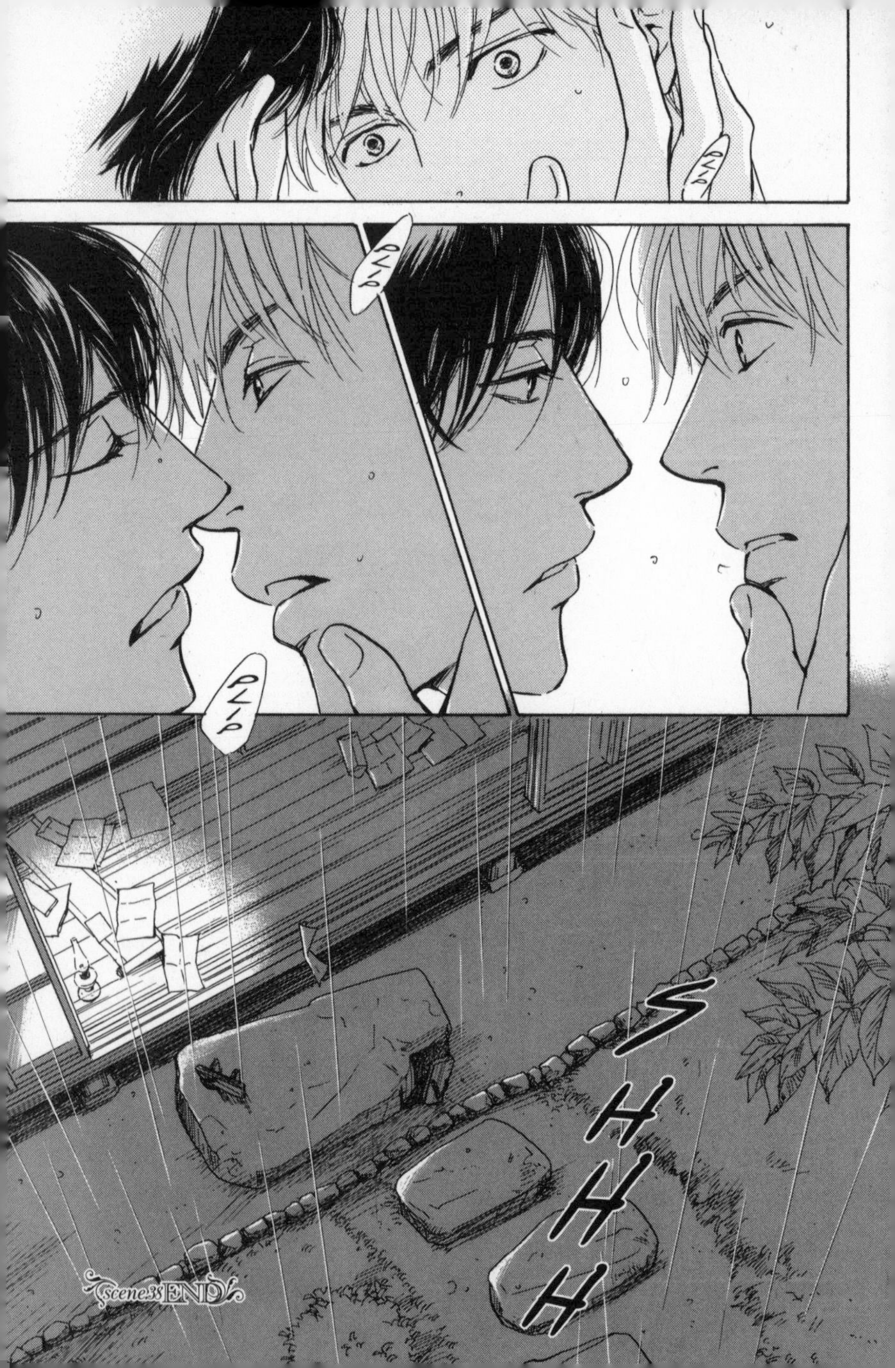
plip
plip
plip
SHHHH
scene 38 END

憂鬱な朝

Blue Morning

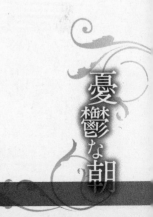

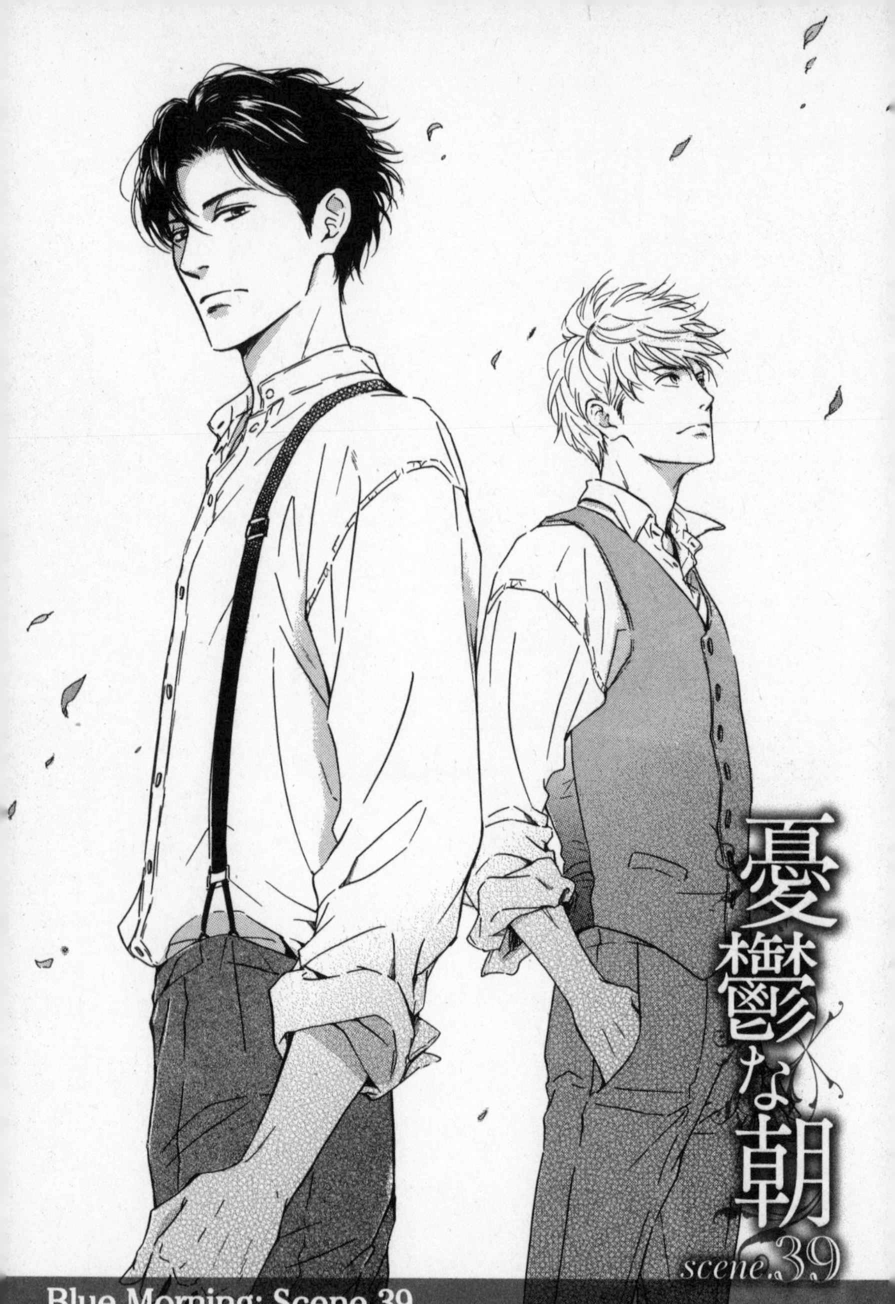
憂鬱な朝
scene.39

Blue Morning: Scene 39

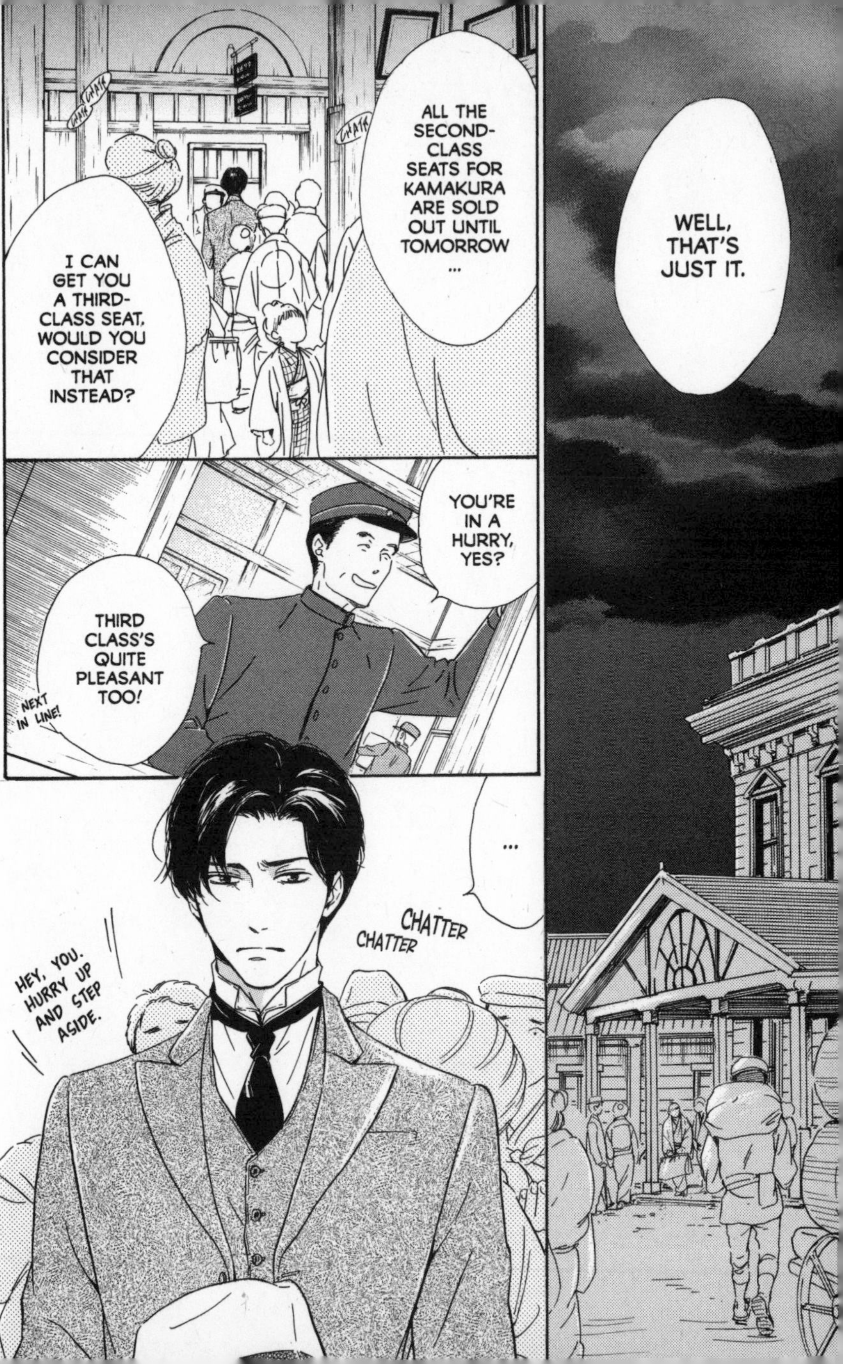
WELL, THAT'S JUST IT.
ALL THE SECOND-CLASS SEATS FOR KAMAKURA ARE SOLD OUT UNTIL TOMORROW ...
I CAN GET YOU A THIRD-CLASS SEAT. WOULD YOU CONSIDER THAT INSTEAD?
YOU'RE IN A HURRY, YES?
THIRD CLASS'S QUITE PLEASANT TOO!
NEXT IN LINE!
...
CHATTER
CHATTER
HEY, YOU. HURRY UP AND STEP ASIDE.

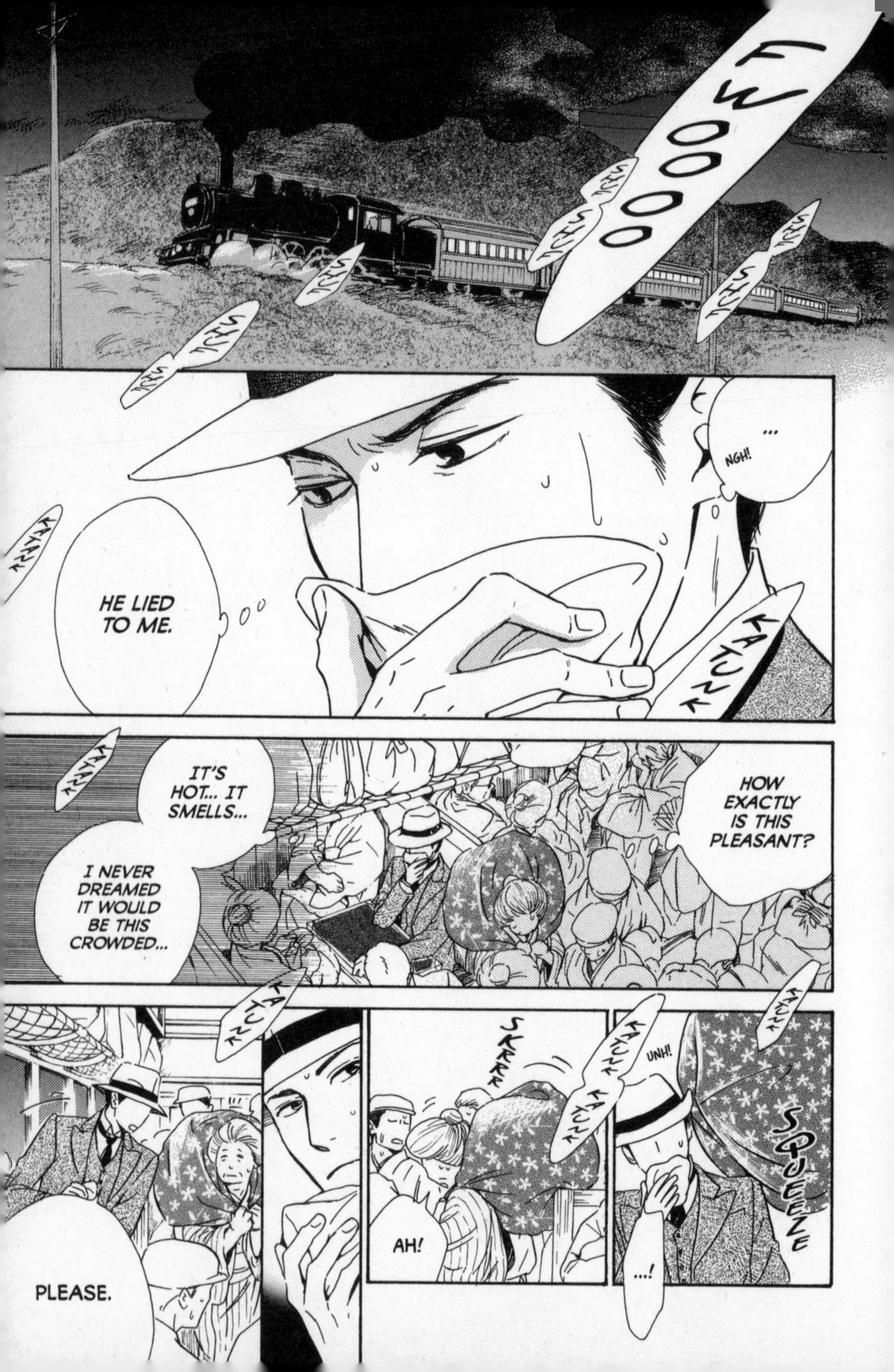
FWOOOO
SHUL SHUL
SHUL
SHUL
SHUL SHUL
...
NGH!
HE LIED TO ME.
KATUNK
KATUNK
HOW EXACTLY IS THIS PLEASANT?
IT'S HOT... IT SMELLS...
I NEVER DREAMED IT WOULD BE THIS CROWDED...
KATUNK
KATUNK
UNH!
SQUEEZE
...!
KATUNK KATUNK
SKRRR
AH!
KATUNK
PLEASE.

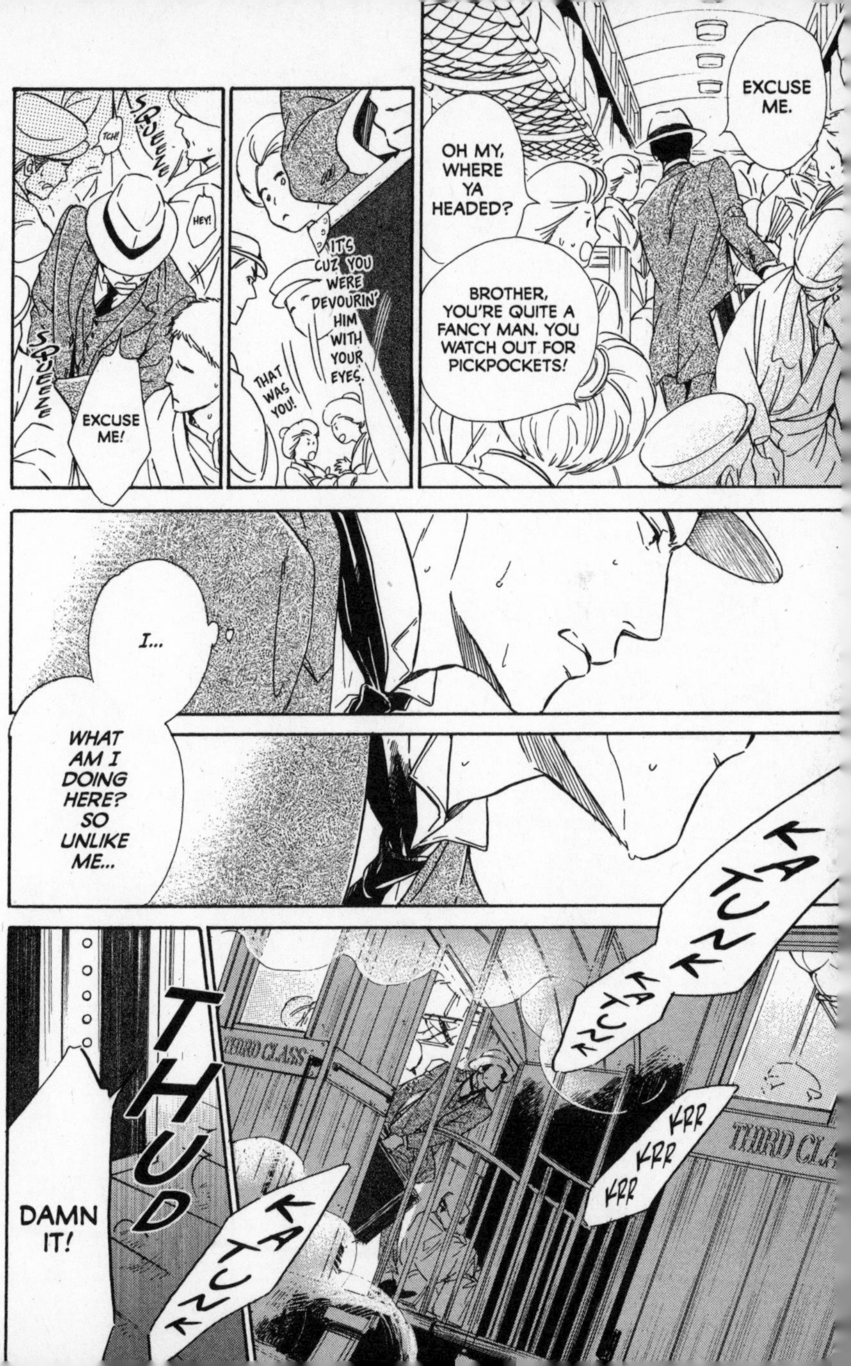
EXCUSE ME.
OH MY, WHERE YA HEADED?
BROTHER, YOU'RE QUITE A FANCY MAN. YOU WATCH OUT FOR PICKPOCKETS!
IT'S CUZ YOU WERE DEVOURIN' HIM WITH YOUR EYES.
THAT WAS YOU!
SQUEEZE
TCH!
HEY!
SQUEEZE
EXCUSE ME!
I...
WHAT AM I DOING HERE? SO UNLIKE ME...
KATUNK
KATUNK
THIRD CLASS
KRR KRR KRR
THIRD CLA
THUD
DAMN IT!
KATUNK

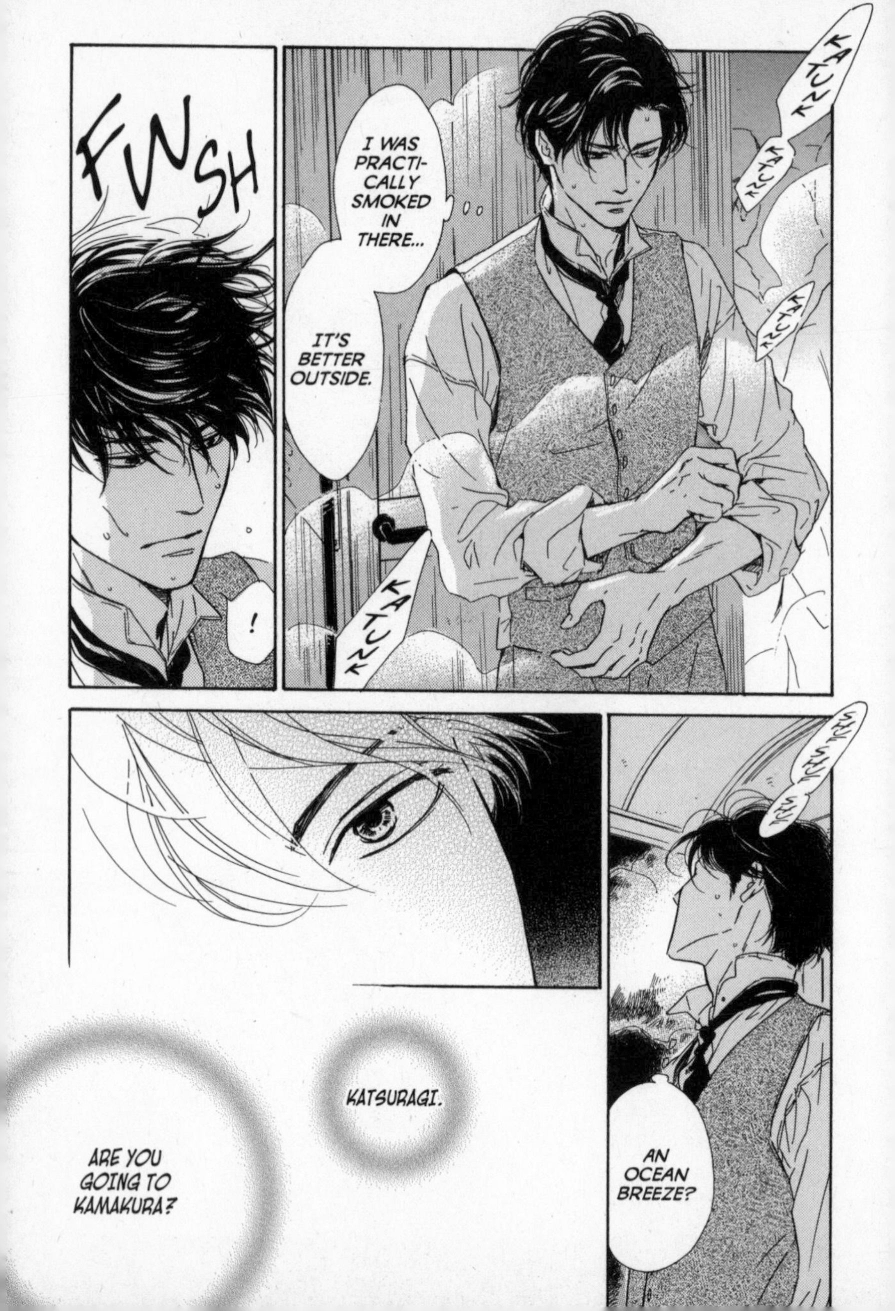

KATUNK
KATUNK
KATUNK
I WAS PRACTICALLY SMOKED IN THERE...
IT'S BETTER OUTSIDE.
KATUNK
FWSH
!
SHU SHU SHU
AN OCEAN BREEZE?
KATSURAGI.
ARE YOU GOING TO KAMAKURA?

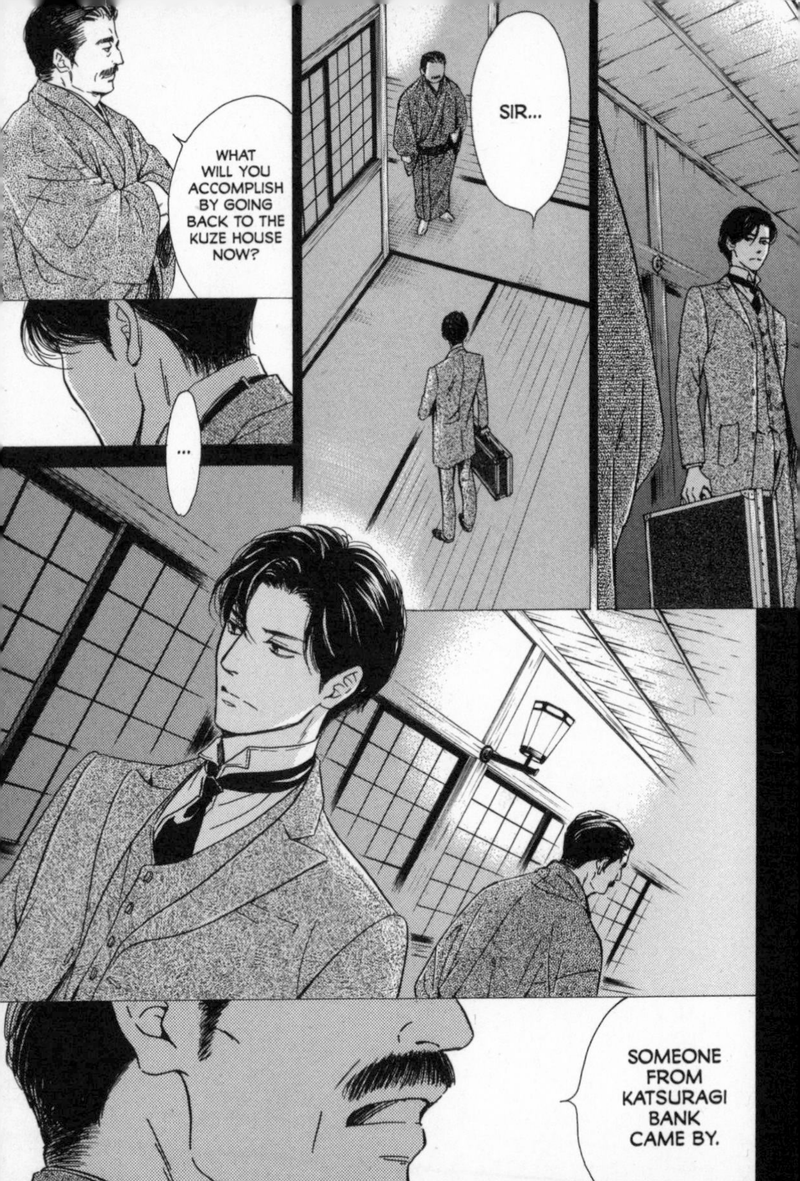
SIR...
WHAT WILL YOU ACCOMPLISH BY GOING BACK TO THE KUZE HOUSE NOW?
...
SOMEONE FROM KATSURAGI BANK CAME BY.

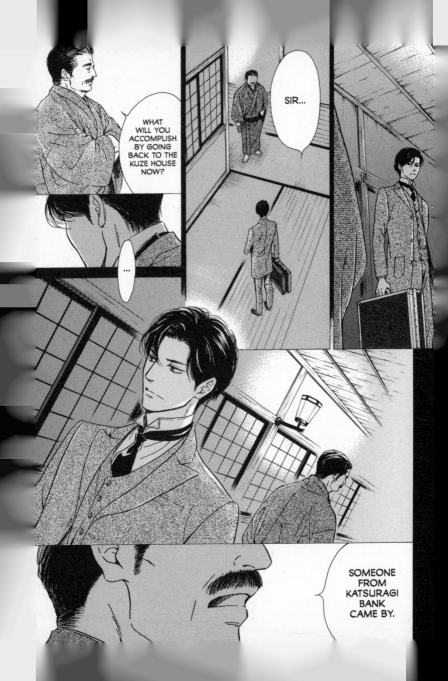

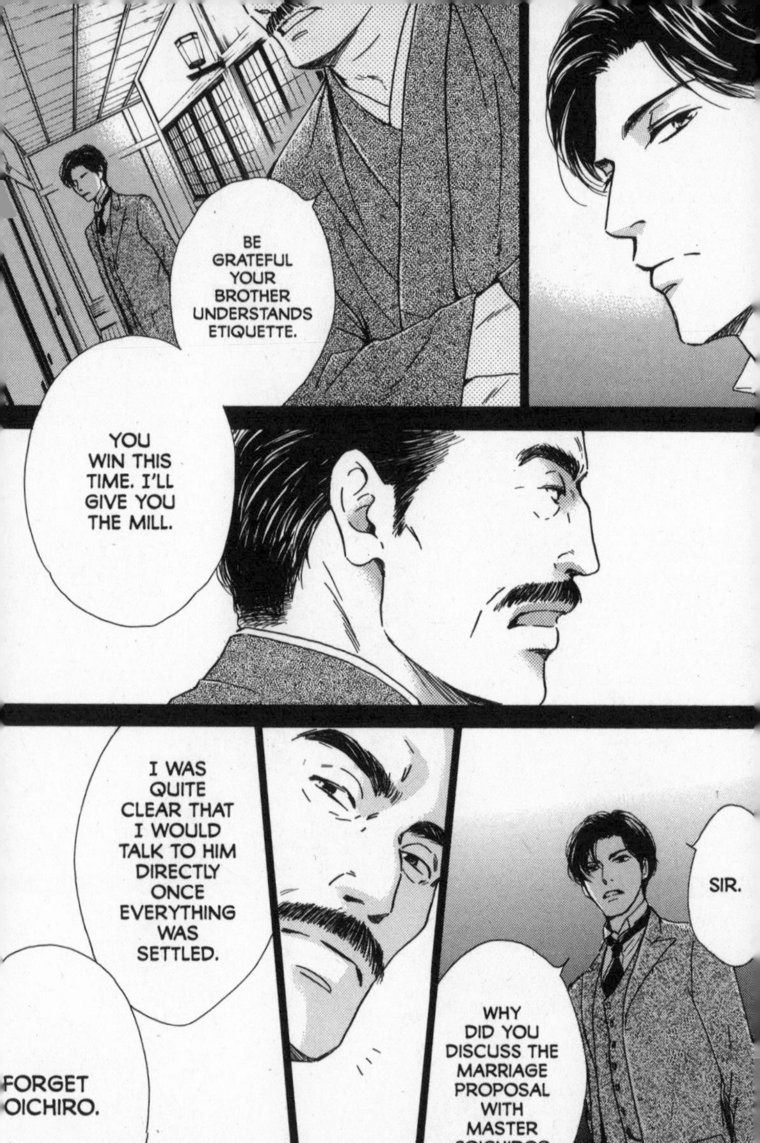
BE GRATEFUL YOUR BROTHER UNDERSTANDS ETIQUETTE.
YOU WIN THIS TIME. I'LL GIVE YOU THE MILL.
SIR.
WHY DID YOU DISCUSS THE MARRIAGE PROPOSAL WITH MASTER SOICHIRO?
I WAS QUITE CLEAR THAT I WOULD TALK TO HIM DIRECTLY ONCE EVERYTHING WAS SETTLED.
FORGET SOICHIRO.

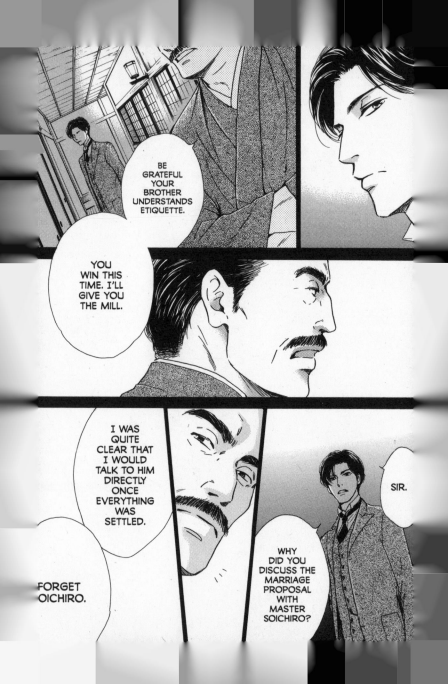

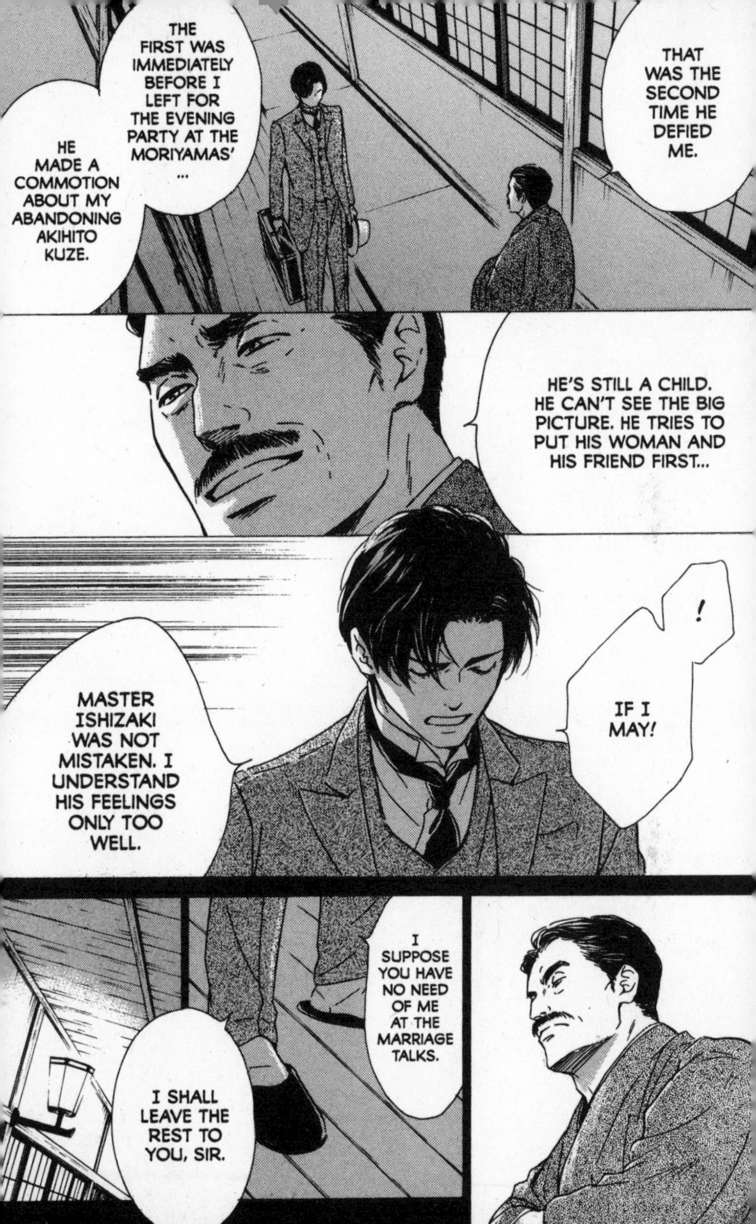
THAT WAS THE SECOND TIME HE DEFIED ME.
THE FIRST WAS IMMEDIATELY BEFORE I LEFT FOR THE EVENING PARTY AT THE MORIYAMAS' ...
HE MADE A COMMOTION ABOUT MY ABANDONING AKIHITO KUZE.
HE'S STILL A CHILD. HE CAN'T SEE THE BIG PICTURE. HE TRIES TO PUT HIS WOMAN AND HIS FRIEND FIRST...
!
IF I MAY!
MASTER ISHIZAKI WAS NOT MISTAKEN. I UNDERSTAND HIS FEELINGS ONLY TOO WELL.
I SUPPOSE YOU HAVE NO NEED OF ME AT THE MARRIAGE TALKS.
I SHALL LEAVE THE REST TO YOU, SIR.

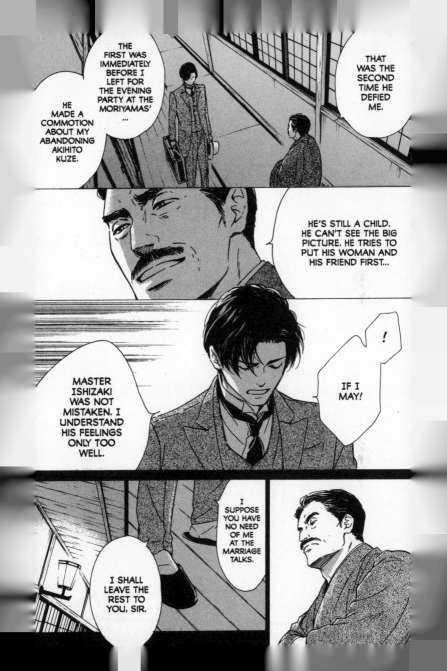

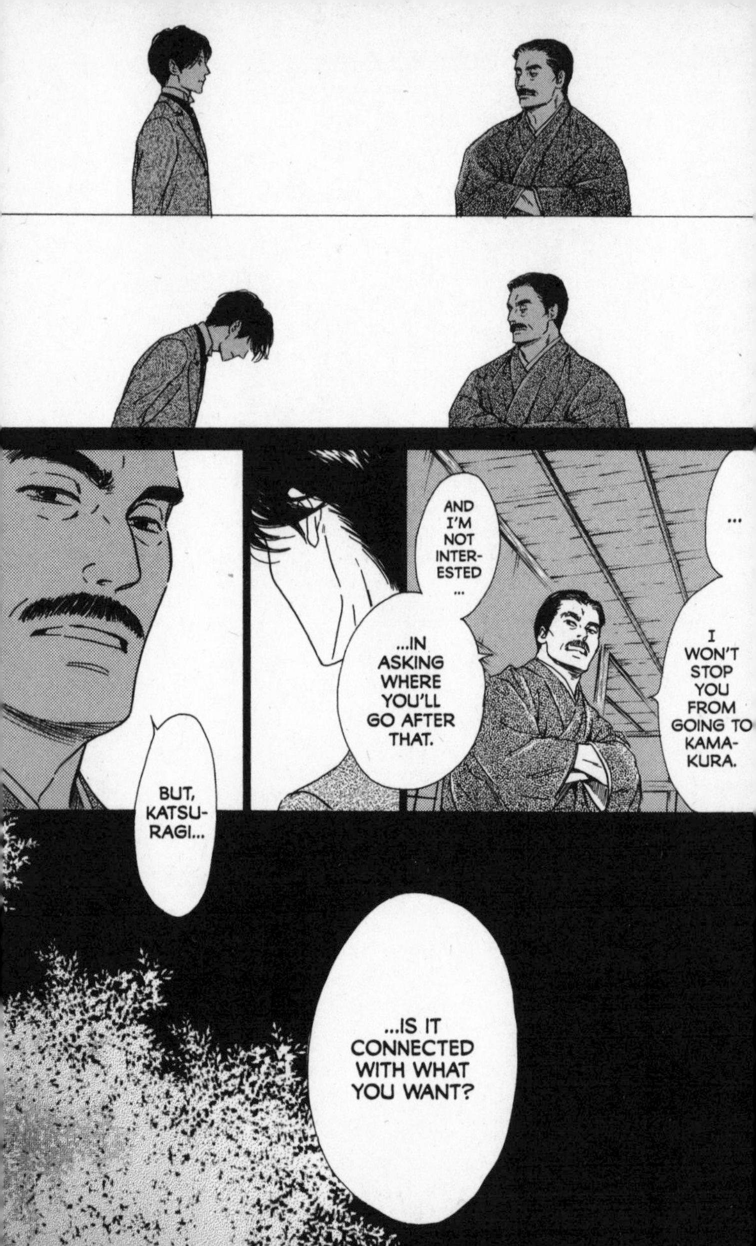
...
I WON'T STOP YOU FROM GOING TO KAMAKURA.
AND I'M NOT INTERESTED...
...IN ASKING WHERE YOU'LL GO AFTER THAT.
BUT, KATSURAGI...
...IS IT CONNECTED WITH WHAT YOU WANT?

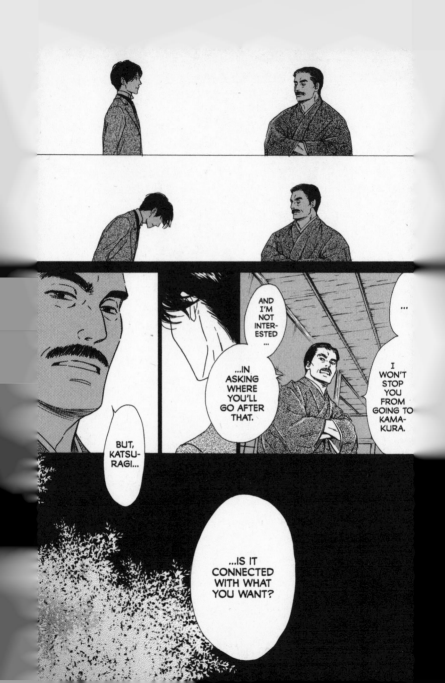

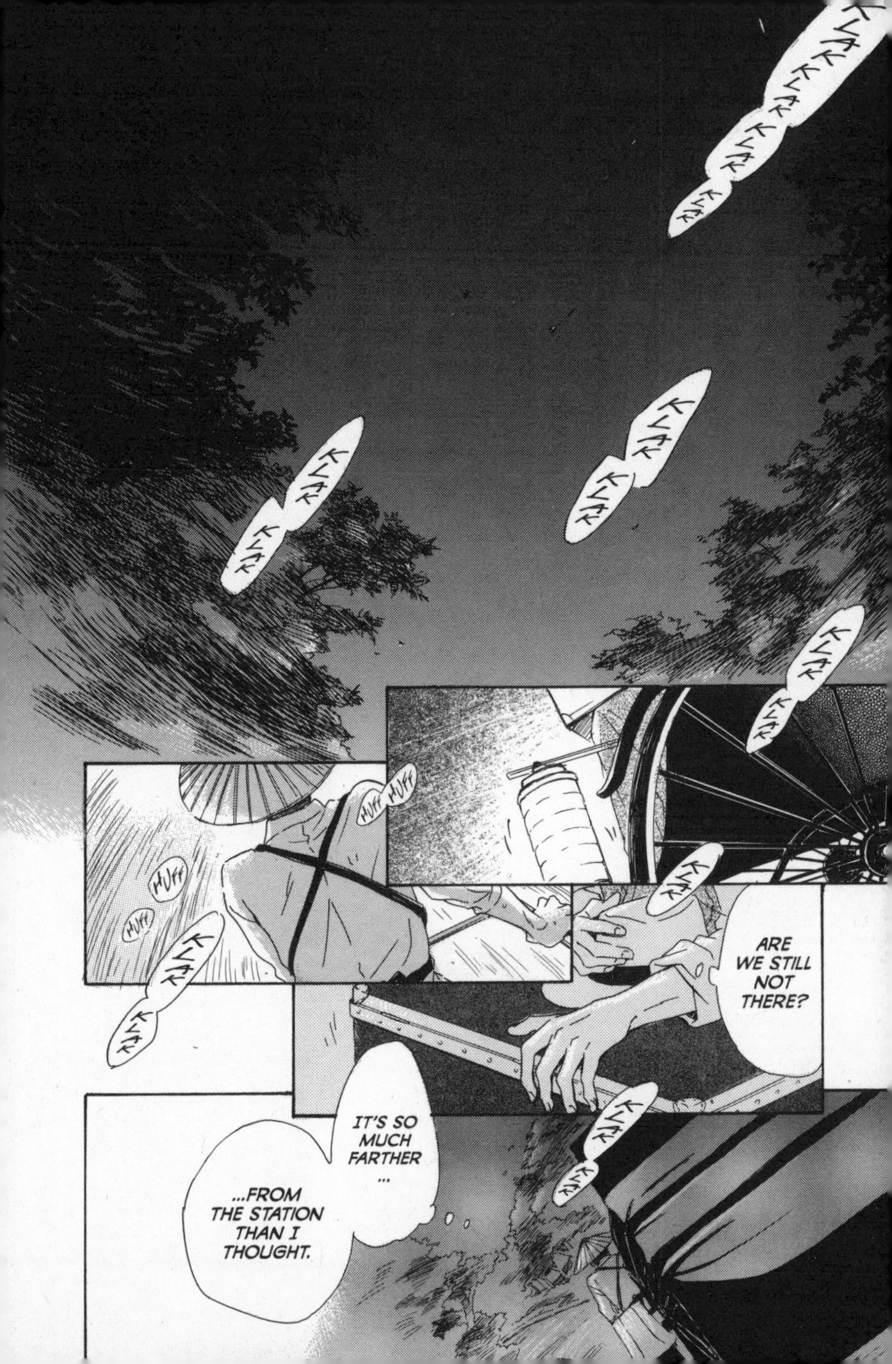
KLAK KLAK KLAK KLAK KLAK KLAK
KLAK KLAK
KLAK KLAK
KLAK KLAK
HUFF HUFF
HUFF
HUFF
KLAK KLAK
KLAK
ARE WE STILL NOT THERE?
KLAK KLAK
IT'S SO MUCH FARTHER ...
...FROM THE STATION THAN I THOUGHT.

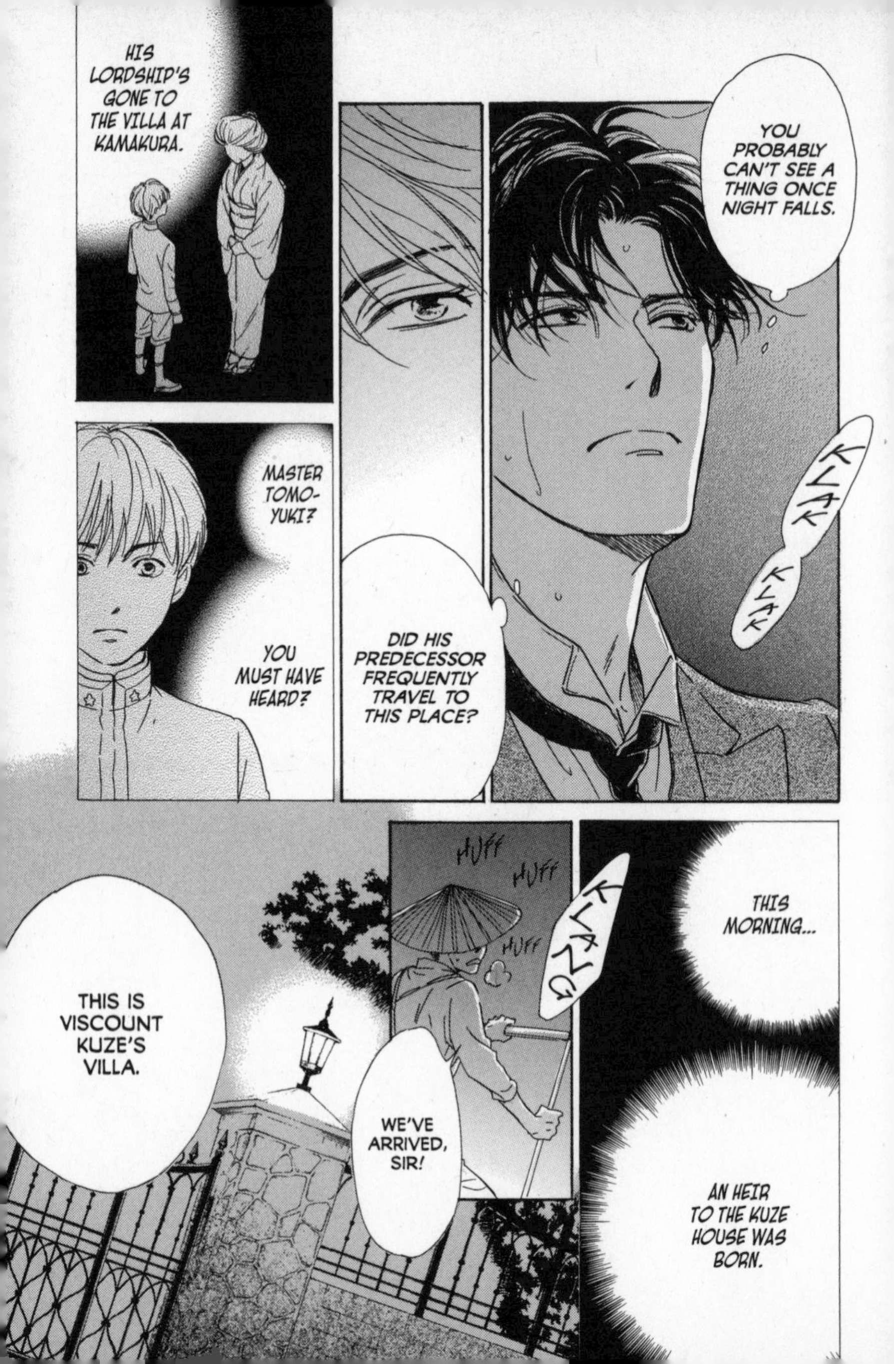
YOU PROBABLY CAN'T SEE A THING ONCE NIGHT FALLS.
KLAK KLAK KLAK
DID HIS PREDECESSOR FREQUENTLY TRAVEL TO THIS PLACE?
HIS LORDSHIP'S GONE TO THE VILLA AT KAMAKURA.
MASTER TOMO-YUKI?
YOU MUST HAVE HEARD?
THIS MORNING...
AN HEIR TO THE KUZE HOUSE WAS BORN.
HUFF
HUFF
HUFF
KLANG
WE'VE ARRIVED, SIR!
THIS IS VISCOUNT KUZE'S VILLA.

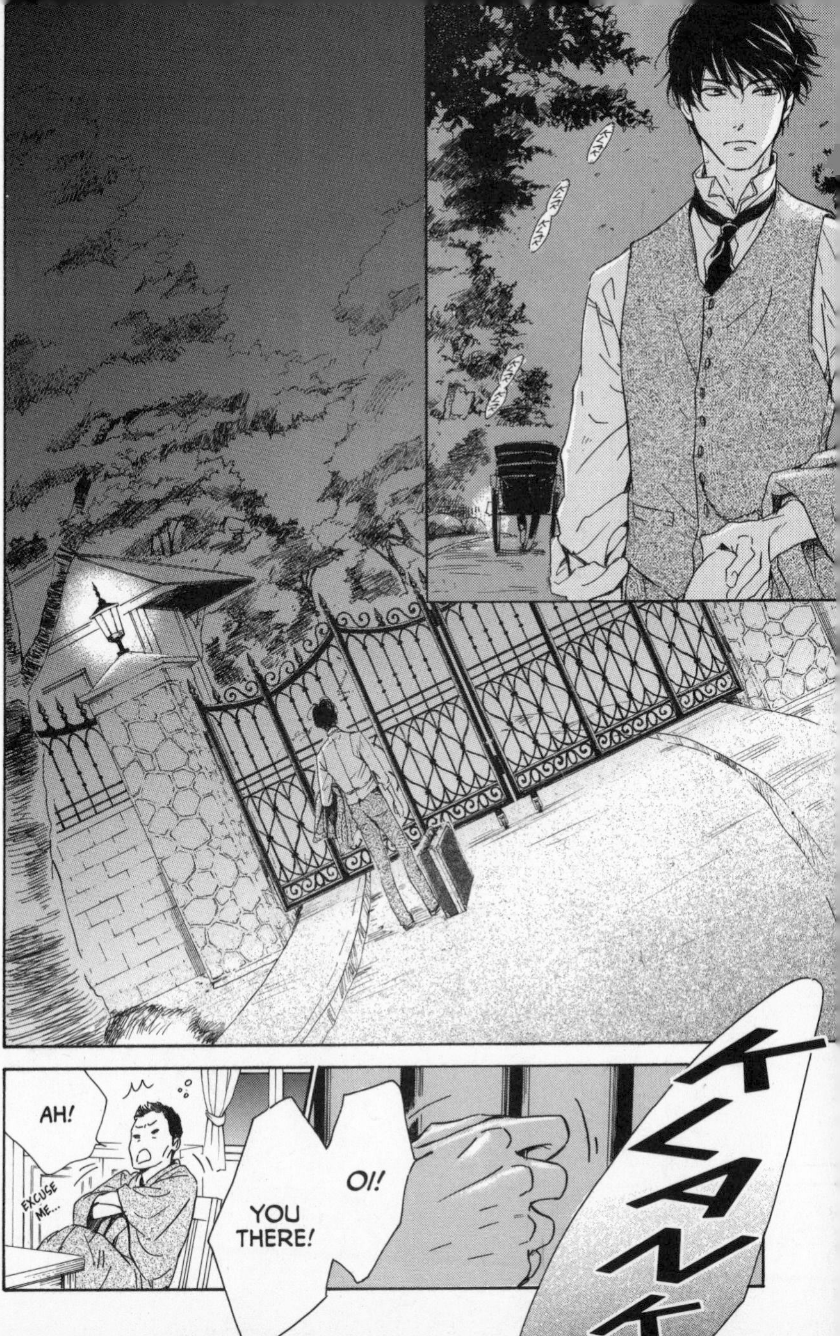
KIRK
KIRK KIRK
KIRK KIRK
KLANK
OI!
YOU THERE!
AH!
EXCUSE ME...

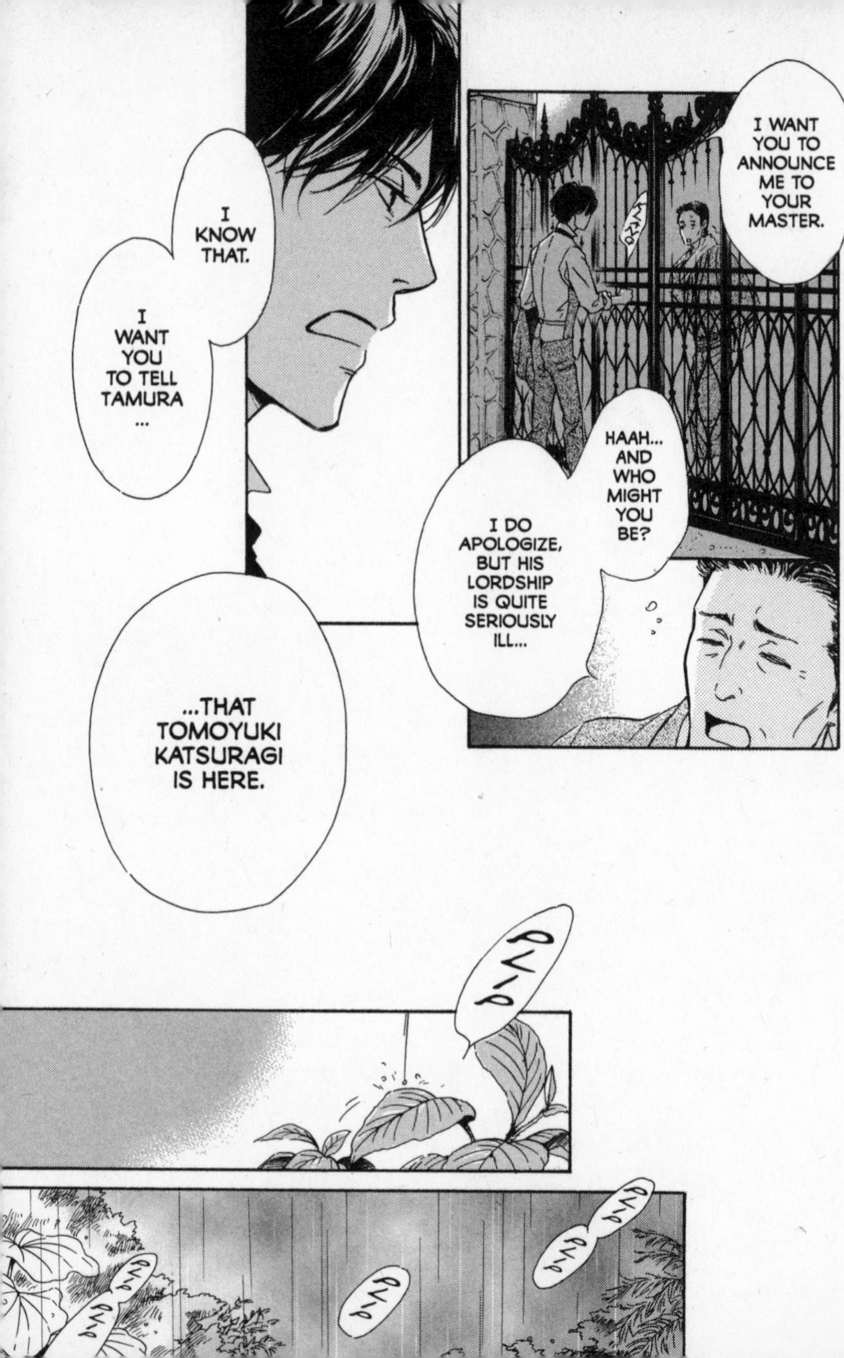
I WANT YOU TO ANNOUNCE ME TO YOUR MASTER.
HAAH... AND WHO MIGHT YOU BE?
I DO APOLOGIZE, BUT HIS LORDSHIP IS QUITE SERIOUSLY ILL...
I KNOW THAT.
I WANT YOU TO TELL TAMURA...
...THAT TOMOYUKI KATSURAGI IS HERE.

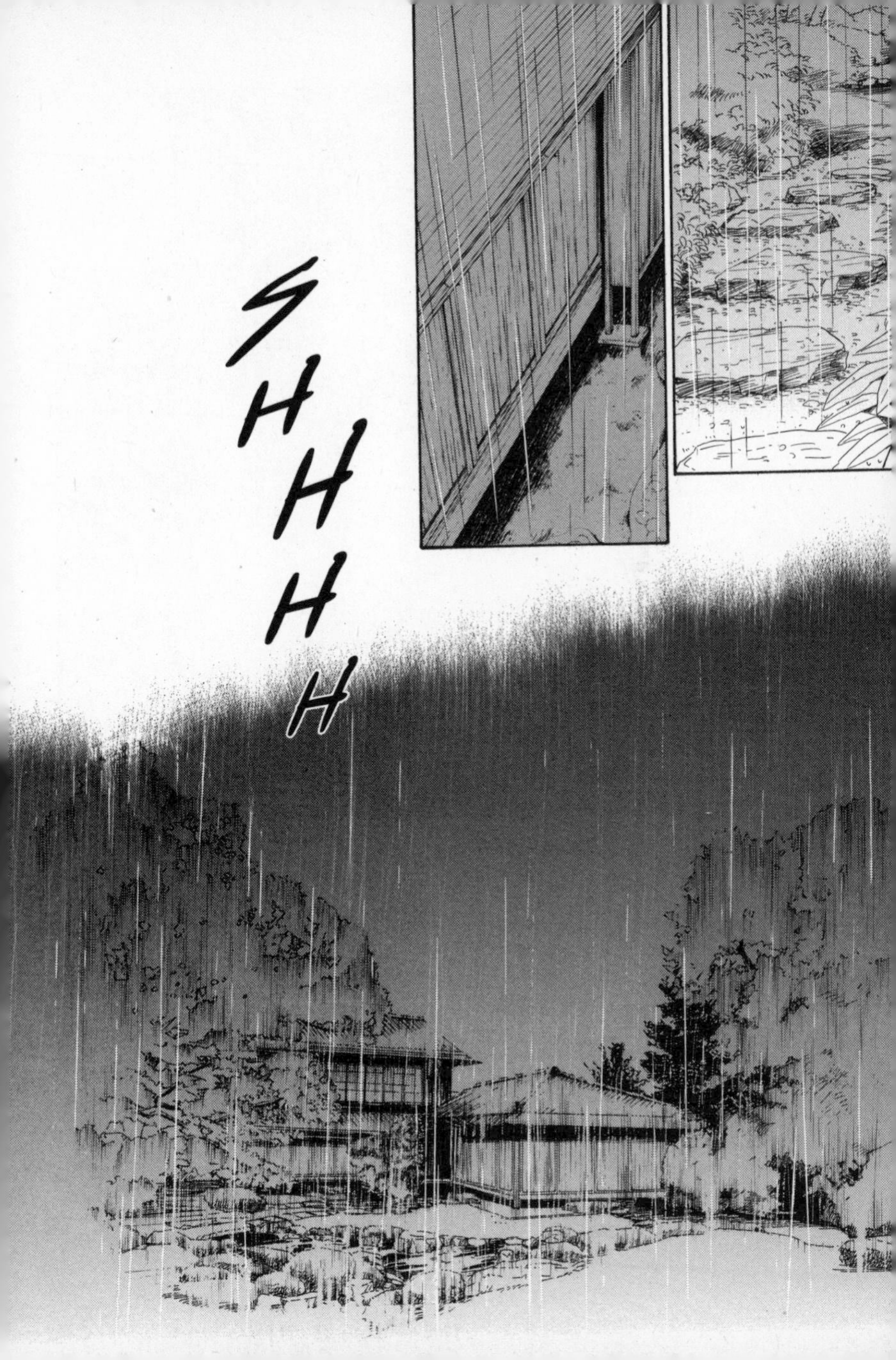
SHHHH

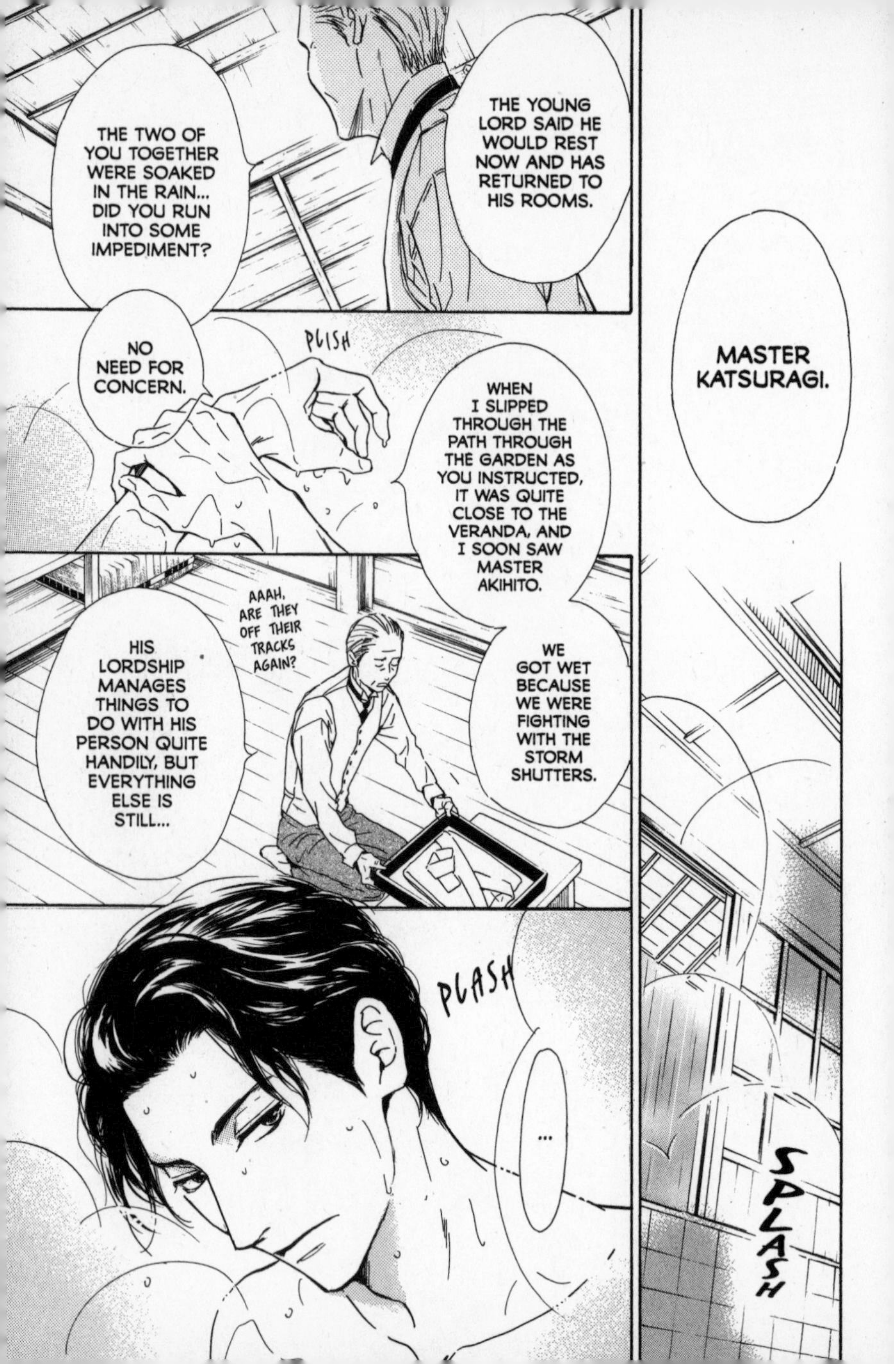
MASTER KATSURAGI.
SPLASH
THE YOUNG LORD SAID HE WOULD REST NOW AND HAS RETURNED TO HIS ROOMS.
THE TWO OF YOU TOGETHER WERE SOAKED IN THE RAIN... DID YOU RUN INTO SOME IMPEDIMENT?
PLISH
NO NEED FOR CONCERN.
WHEN I SLIPPED THROUGH THE PATH THROUGH THE GARDEN AS YOU INSTRUCTED, IT WAS QUITE CLOSE TO THE VERANDA, AND I SOON SAW MASTER AKIHITO.
WE GOT WET BECAUSE WE WERE FIGHTING WITH THE STORM SHUTTERS.
AAAH, ARE THEY OFF THEIR TRACKS AGAIN?
HIS LORDSHIP MANAGES THINGS TO DO WITH HIS PERSON QUITE HANDILY, BUT EVERYTHING ELSE IS STILL...
PLASH
...

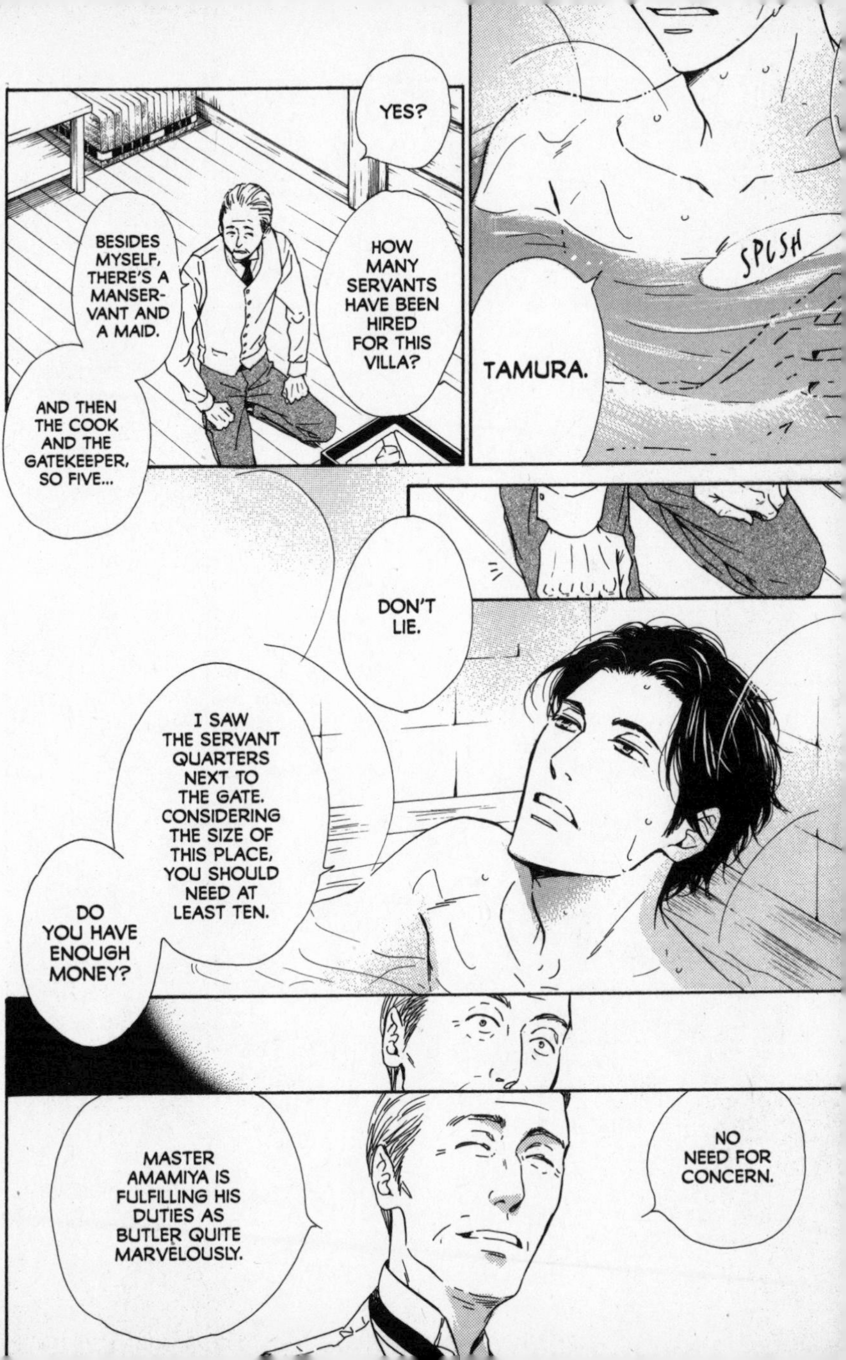
SPLSH
TAMURA.
YES?
HOW MANY SERVANTS HAVE BEEN HIRED FOR THIS VILLA?
BESIDES MYSELF, THERE'S A MANSERVANT AND A MAID.
AND THEN THE COOK AND THE GATEKEEPER, SO FIVE...
DON'T LIE.
I SAW THE SERVANT QUARTERS NEXT TO THE GATE. CONSIDERING THE SIZE OF THIS PLACE, YOU SHOULD NEED AT LEAST TEN.
DO YOU HAVE ENOUGH MONEY?
NO NEED FOR CONCERN.
MASTER AMAMIYA IS FULFILLING HIS DUTIES AS BUTLER QUITE MARVELOUSLY.

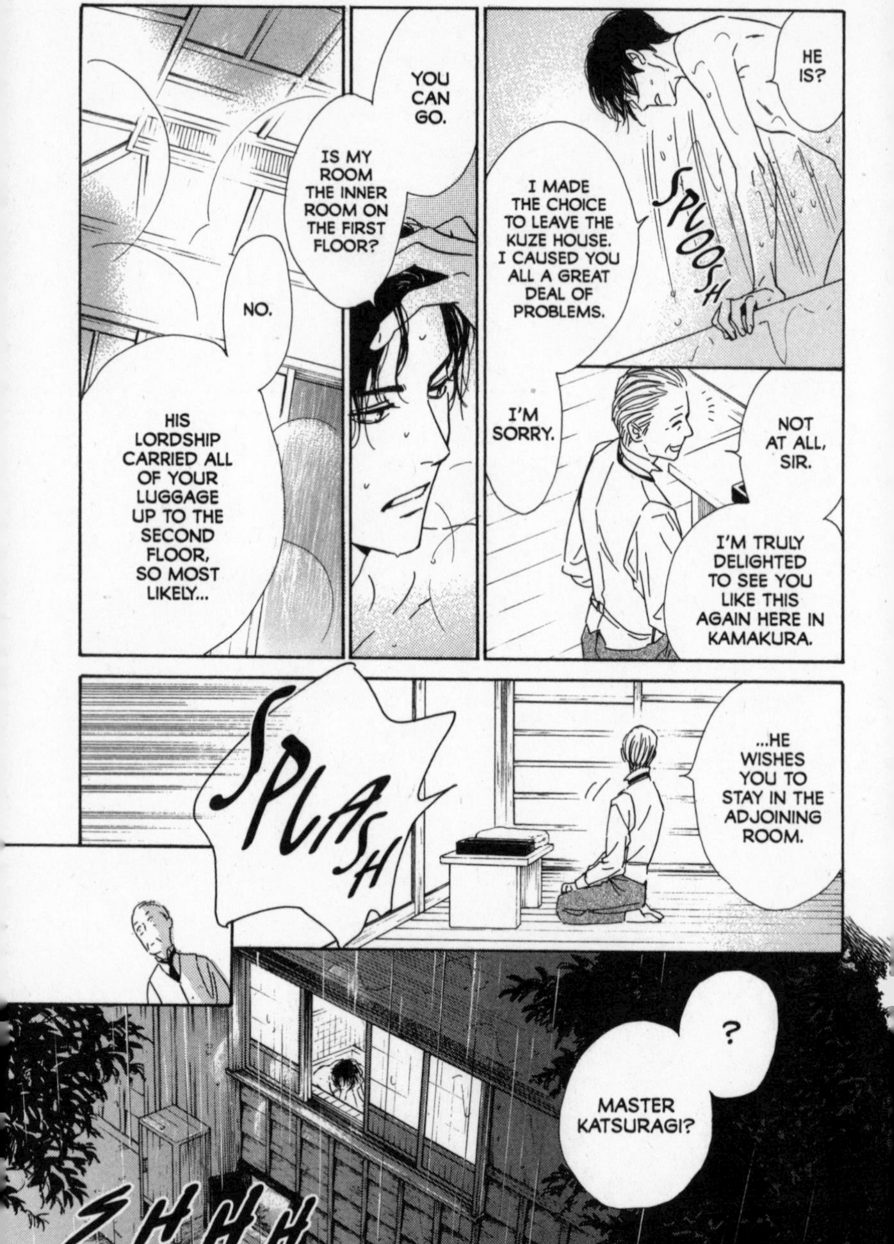
HE IS?
SPLOOSH
I MADE THE CHOICE TO LEAVE THE KUZE HOUSE. I CAUSED YOU ALL A GREAT DEAL OF PROBLEMS.
I'M SORRY.
NOT AT ALL, SIR.
I'M TRULY DELIGHTED TO SEE YOU LIKE THIS AGAIN HERE IN KAMAKURA.
YOU CAN GO.
IS MY ROOM THE INNER ROOM ON THE FIRST FLOOR?
NO.
HIS LORDSHIP CARRIED ALL OF YOUR LUGGAGE UP TO THE SECOND FLOOR, SO MOST LIKELY...
...HE WISHES YOU TO STAY IN THE ADJOINING ROOM.
SPLASH
?
MASTER KATSURAGI?
SHHH

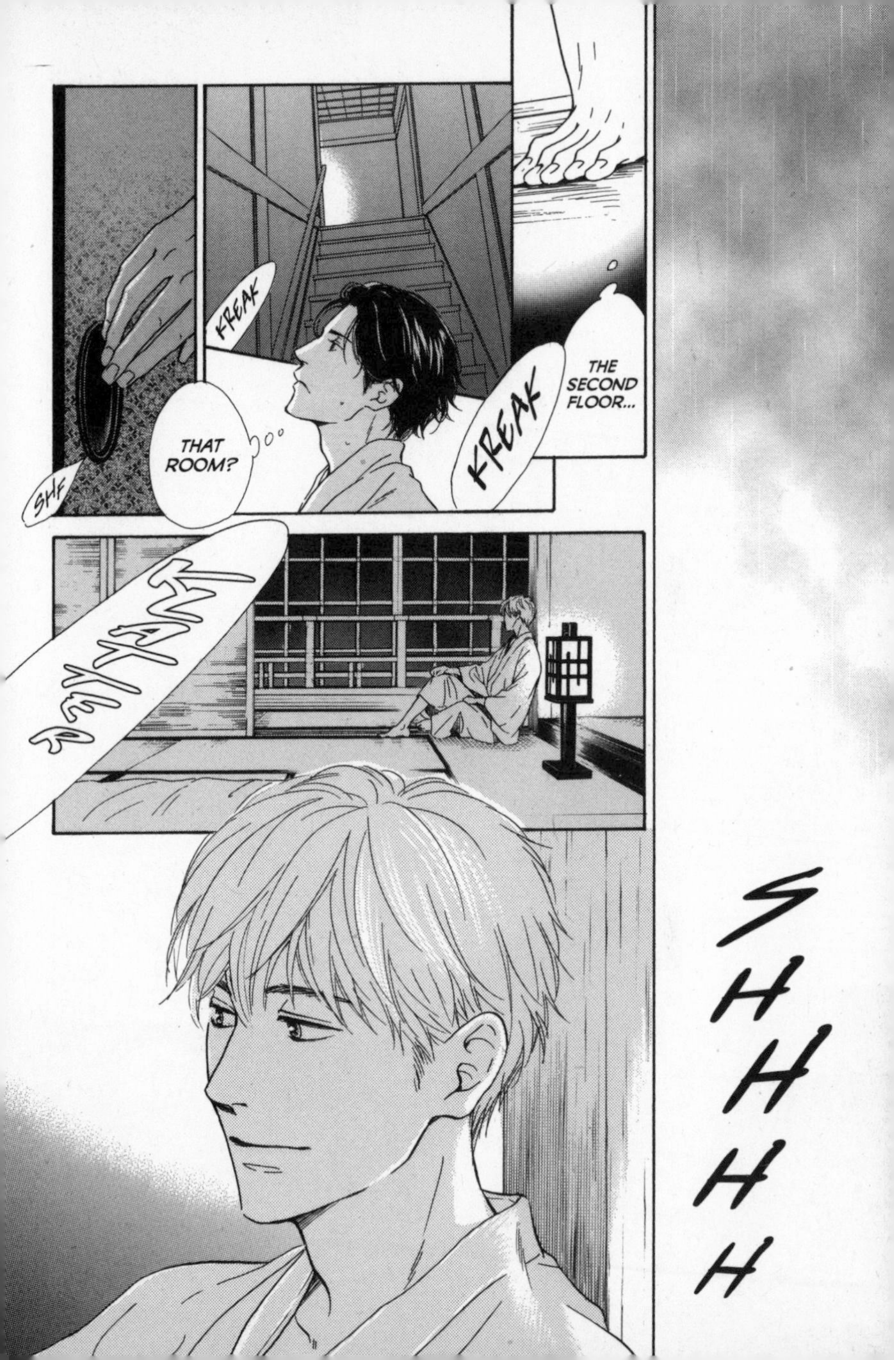

THE SECOND FLOOR...
KREAK
KREAK
THAT ROOM?
SHF
RATTLE
SHHHH

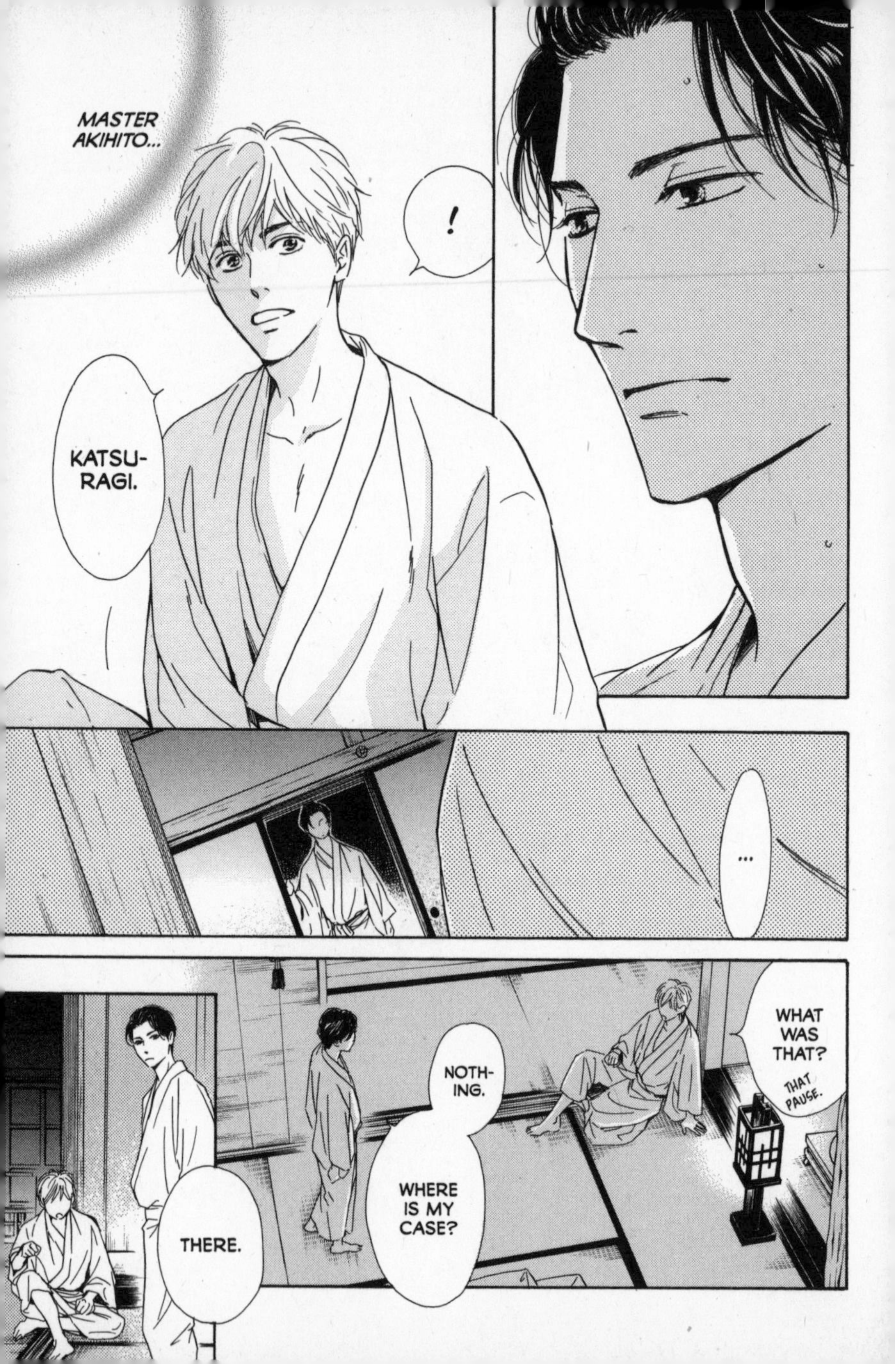
MASTER AKIHITO...
!
KATSU-RAGI.
...
WHAT WAS THAT?
THAT PAUSE.
NOTH-ING.
WHERE IS MY CASE?
THERE.

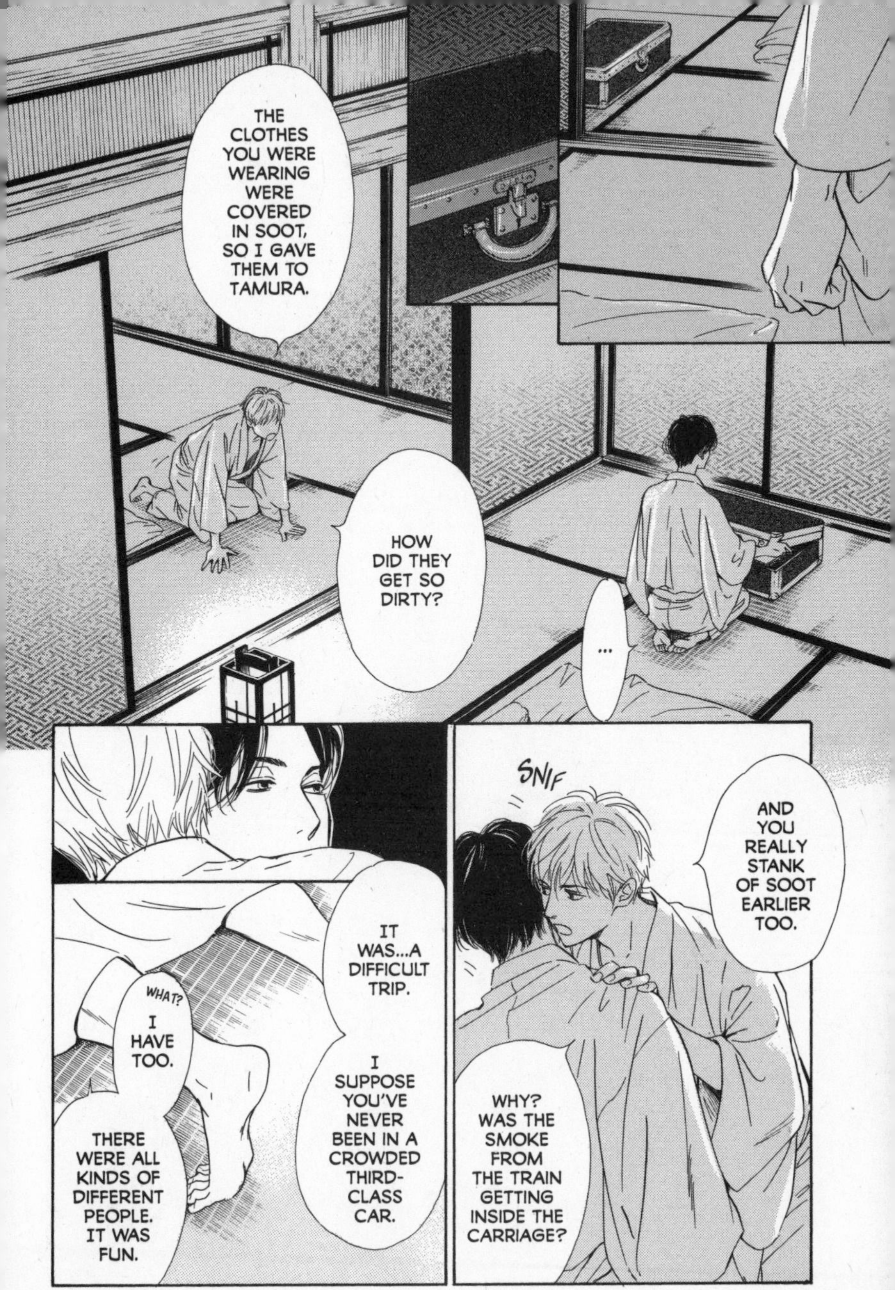
THE CLOTHES YOU WERE WEARING WERE COVERED IN SOOT, SO I GAVE THEM TO TAMURA.
HOW DID THEY GET SO DIRTY?
...
SNIF
AND YOU REALLY STANK OF SOOT EARLIER TOO.
WHY? WAS THE SMOKE FROM THE TRAIN GETTING INSIDE THE CARRIAGE?
IT WAS...A DIFFICULT TRIP.
I SUPPOSE YOU'VE NEVER BEEN IN A CROWDED THIRD-CLASS CAR.
WHAT?
I HAVE TOO.
THERE WERE ALL KINDS OF DIFFERENT PEOPLE. IT WAS FUN.

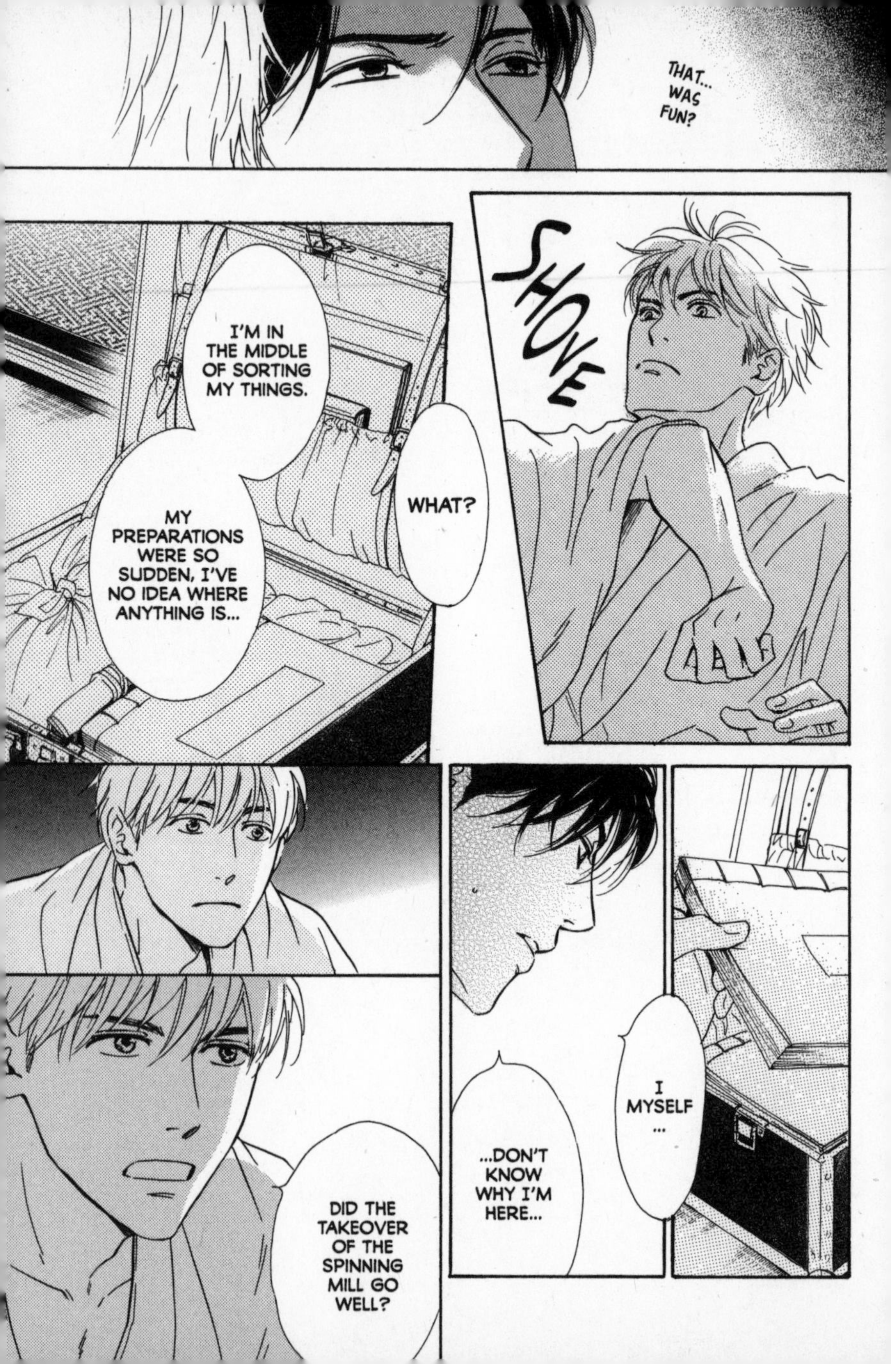
THAT... WAS FUN?
SHOVE
WHAT?
I'M IN THE MIDDLE OF SORTING MY THINGS.
MY PREPARATIONS WERE SO SUDDEN, I'VE NO IDEA WHERE ANYTHING IS...
I MYSELF ...
...DON'T KNOW WHY I'M HERE...
DID THE TAKEOVER OF THE SPINNING MILL GO WELL?

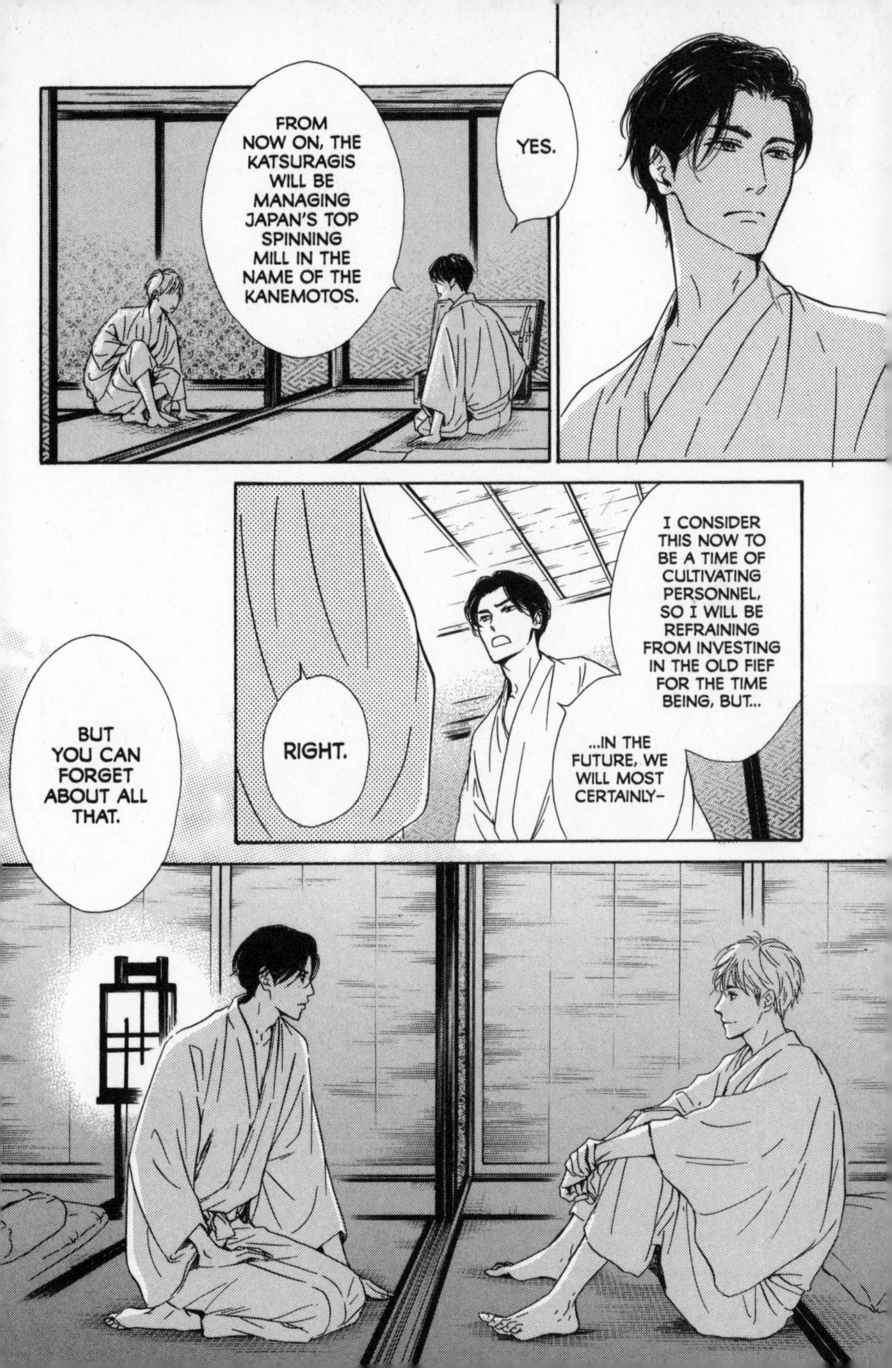
FROM NOW ON, THE KATSURAGIS WILL BE MANAGING JAPAN'S TOP SPINNING MILL IN THE NAME OF THE KANEMOTOS.
YES.
I CONSIDER THIS NOW TO BE A TIME OF CULTIVATING PERSONNEL, SO I WILL BE REFRAINING FROM INVESTING IN THE OLD FIEF FOR THE TIME BEING, BUT...
RIGHT.
...IN THE FUTURE, WE WILL MOST CERTAINLY–
BUT YOU CAN FORGET ABOUT ALL THAT.

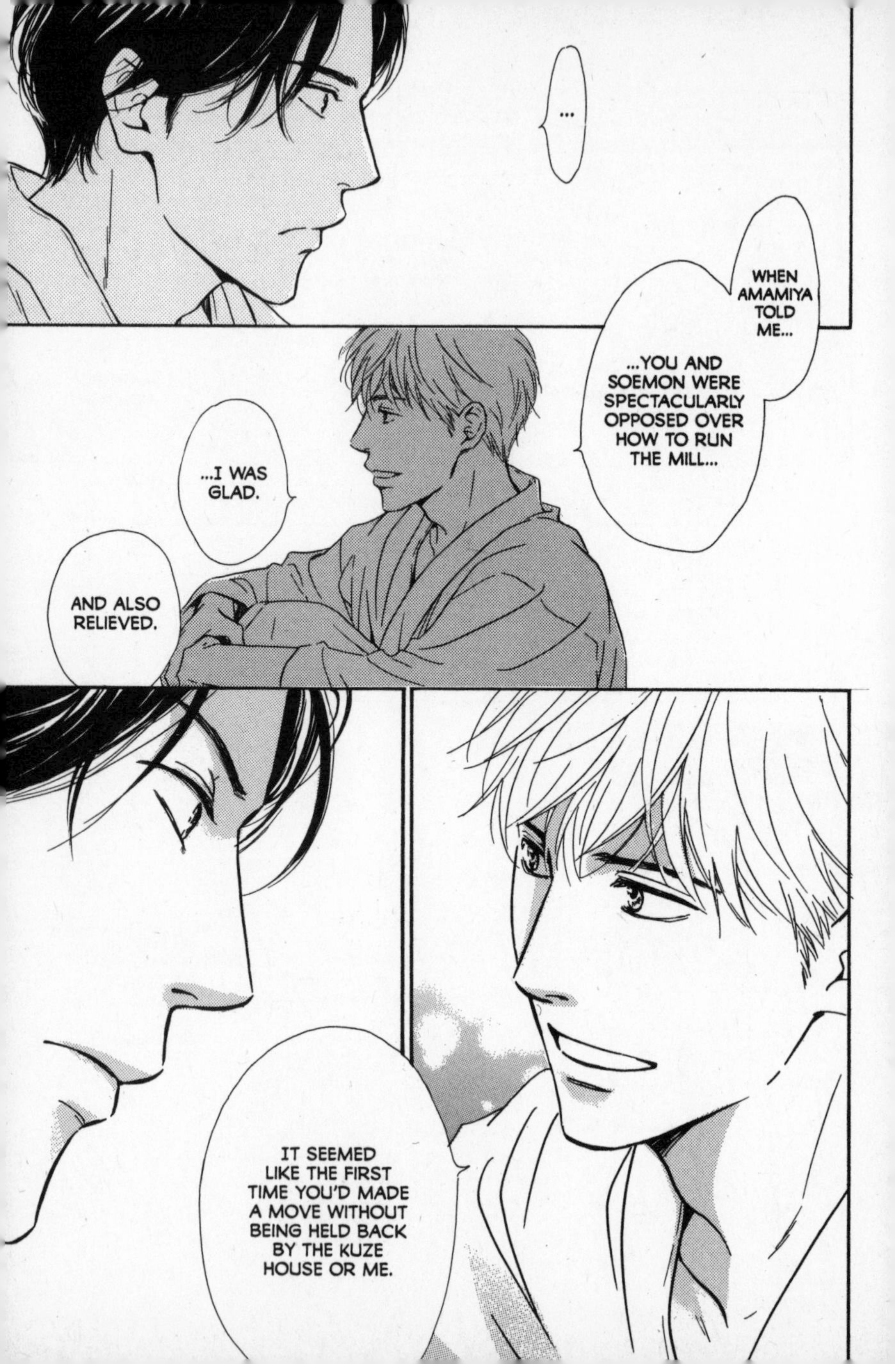
...
WHEN AMAMIYA TOLD ME...
...YOU AND SOEMON WERE SPECTACULARLY OPPOSED OVER HOW TO RUN THE MILL...
...I WAS GLAD.
AND ALSO RELIEVED.
IT SEEMED LIKE THE FIRST TIME YOU'D MADE A MOVE WITHOUT BEING HELD BACK BY THE KUZE HOUSE OR ME.

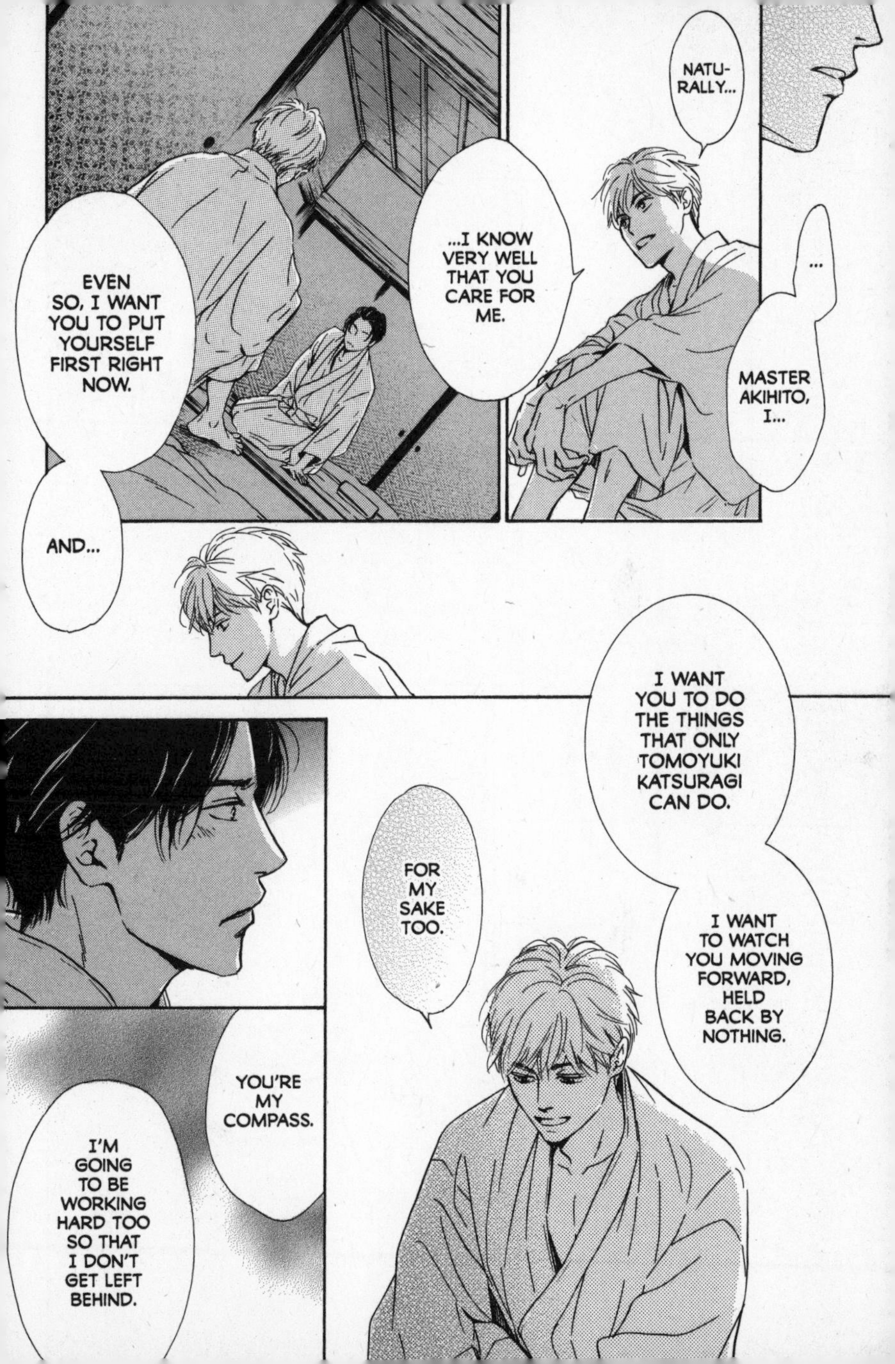
NATU-RALLY...
...I KNOW VERY WELL THAT YOU CARE FOR ME.
...
MASTER AKIHITO, I...
EVEN SO, I WANT YOU TO PUT YOURSELF FIRST RIGHT NOW.
AND...
I WANT YOU TO DO THE THINGS THAT ONLY TOMOYUKI KATSURAGI CAN DO.
I WANT TO WATCH YOU MOVING FORWARD, HELD BACK BY NOTHING.
FOR MY SAKE TOO.
YOU'RE MY COMPASS.
I'M GOING TO BE WORKING HARD TOO SO THAT I DON'T GET LEFT BEHIND.

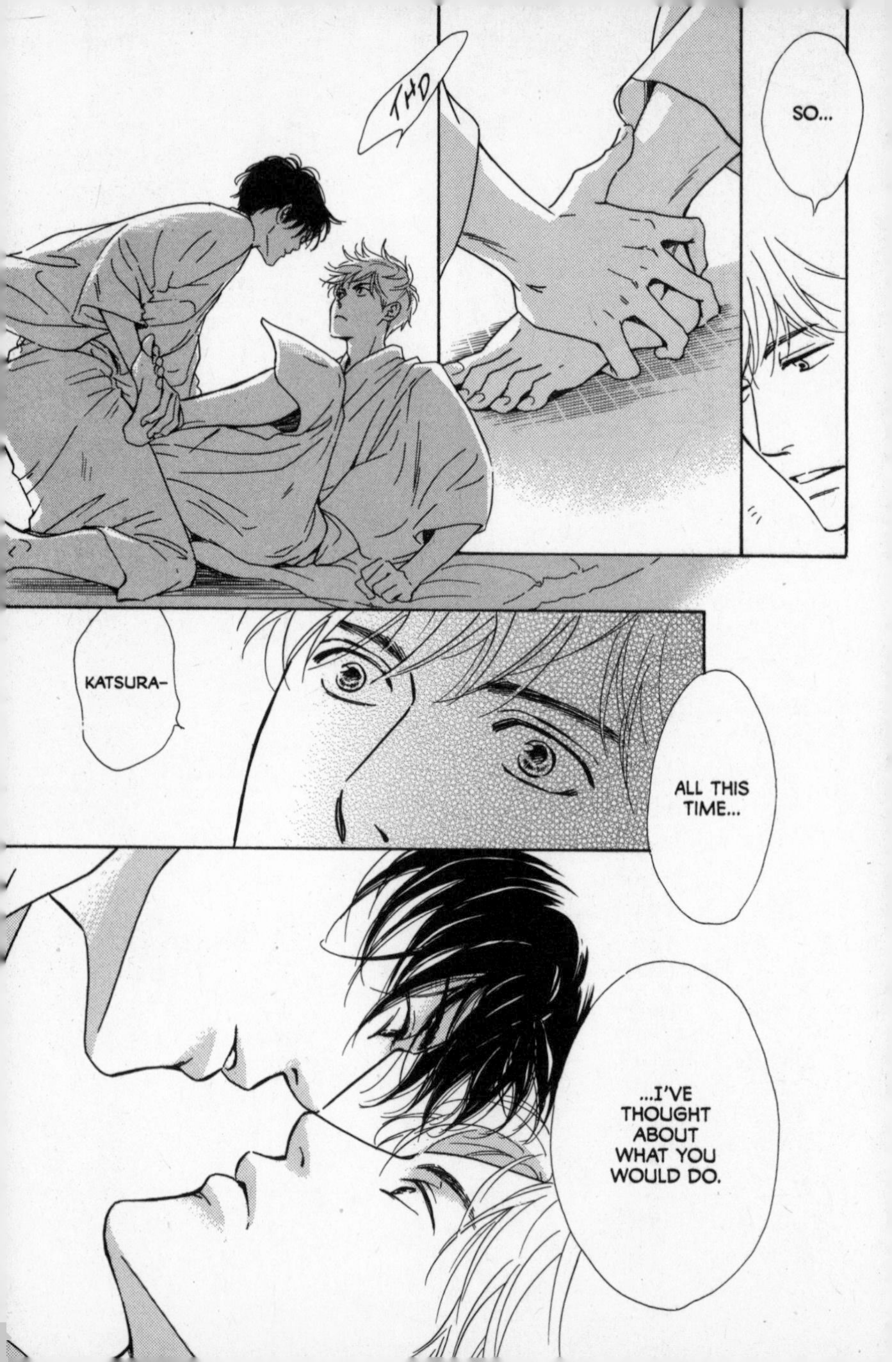
SO...
THD
KATSURA-
ALL THIS TIME...
...I'VE THOUGHT ABOUT WHAT YOU WOULD DO.

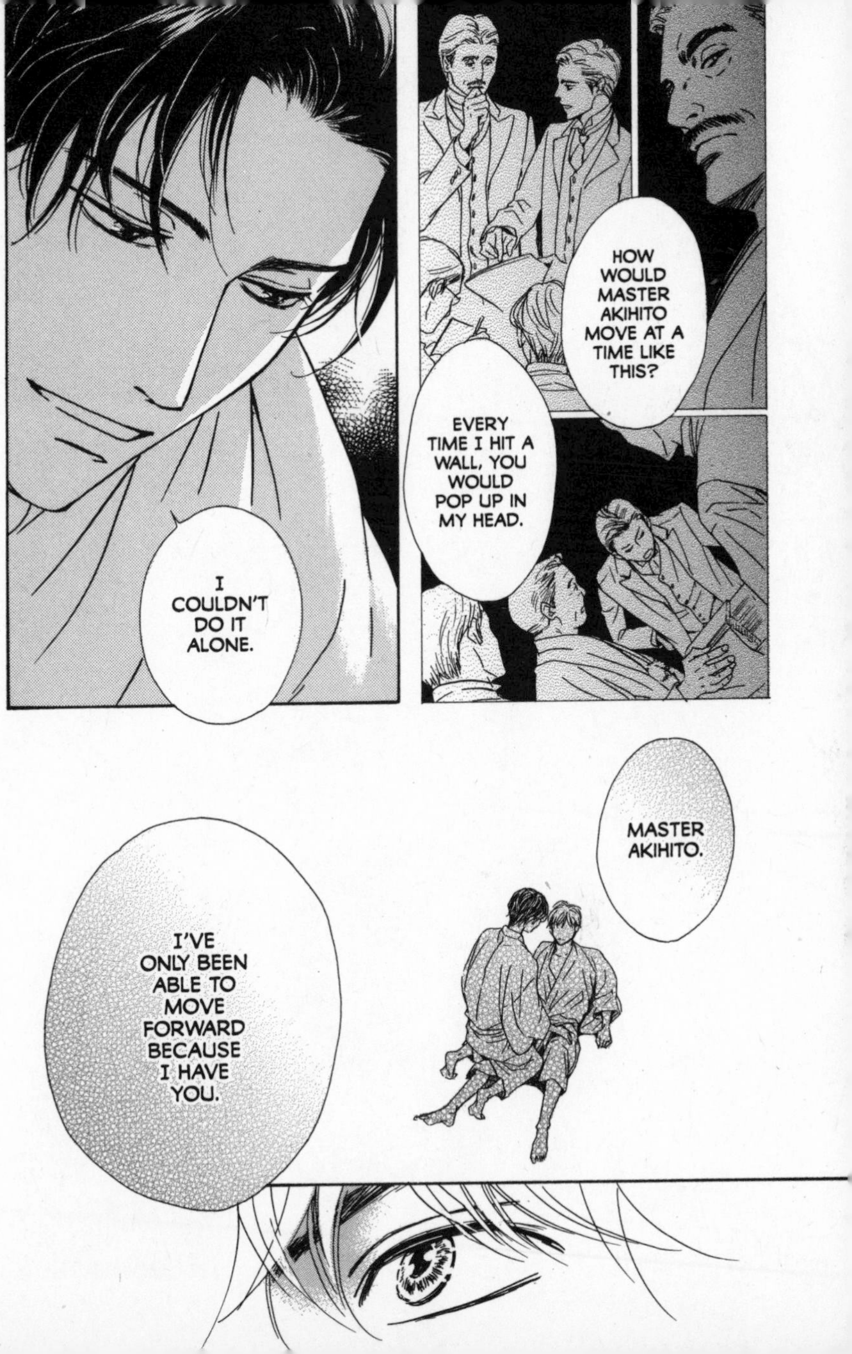
HOW WOULD MASTER AKIHITO MOVE AT A TIME LIKE THIS?
EVERY TIME I HIT A WALL, YOU WOULD POP UP IN MY HEAD.
I COULDN'T DO IT ALONE.
MASTER AKIHITO.
I'VE ONLY BEEN ABLE TO MOVE FORWARD BECAUSE I HAVE YOU.

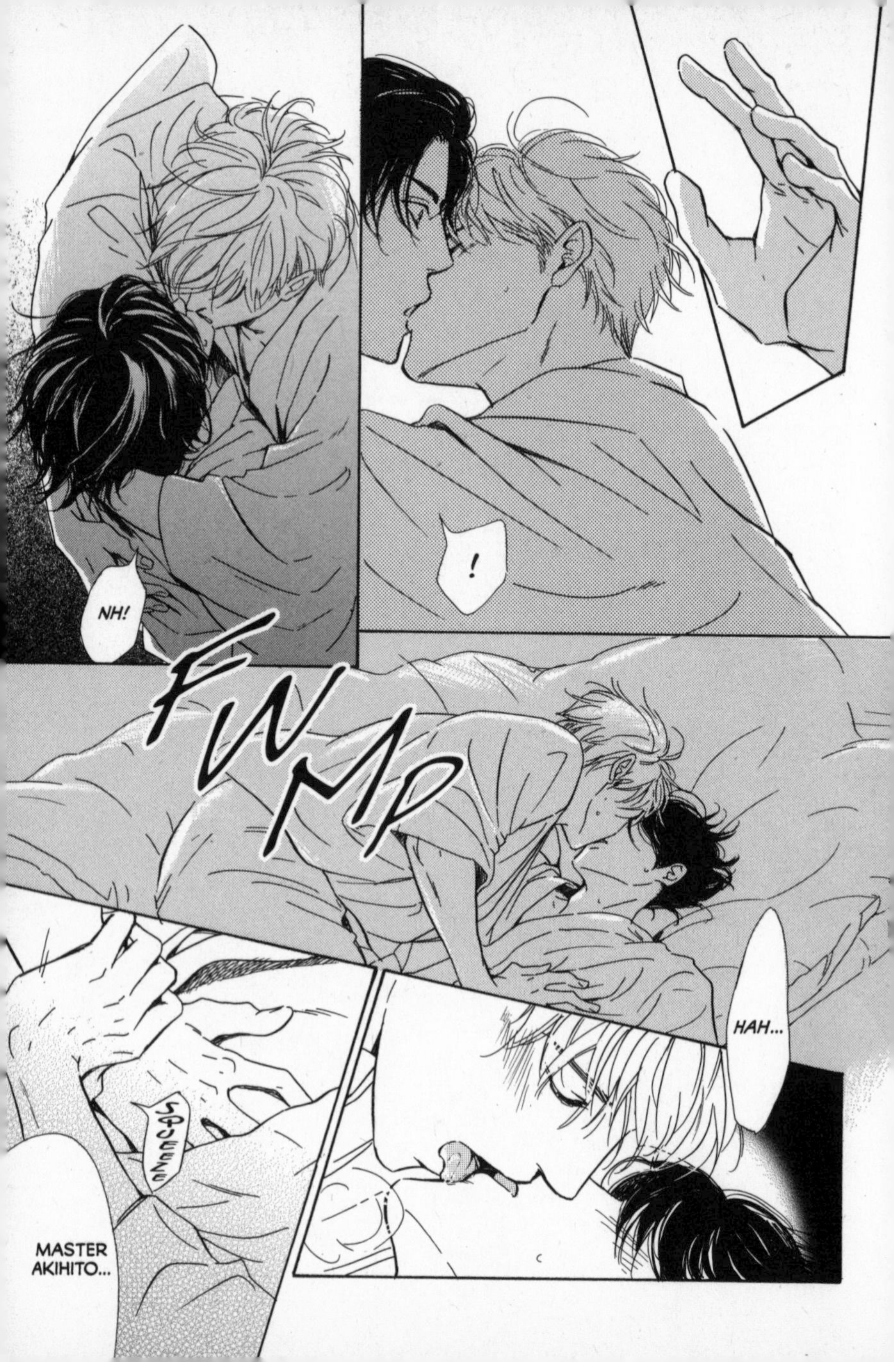
!
NH!
FWMP
HAH...
SQUEEZE
MASTER AKIHITO...

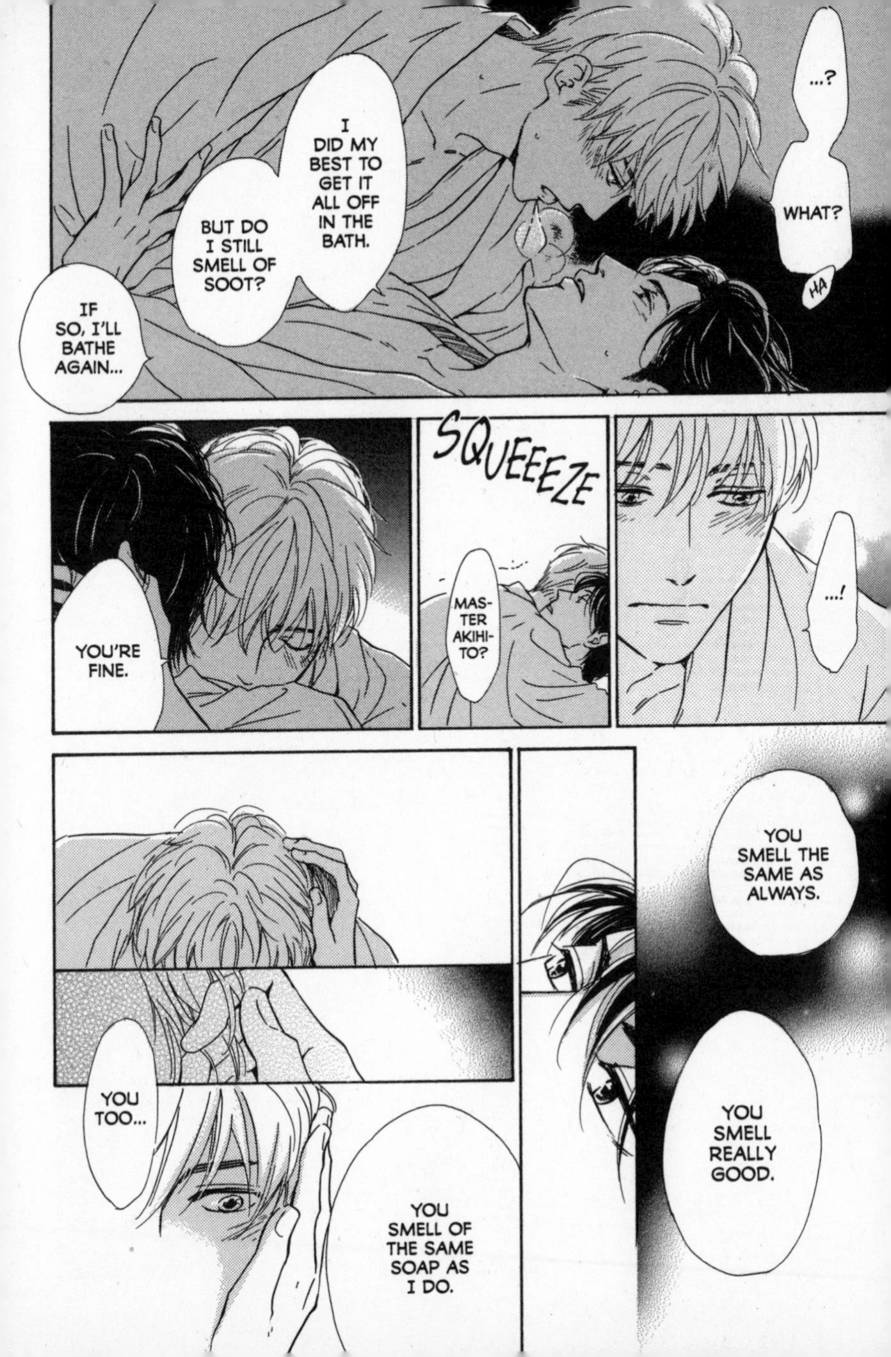
...?
WHAT?
HA
I DID MY BEST TO GET IT ALL OFF IN THE BATH.
BUT DO I STILL SMELL OF SOOT?
IF SO, I'LL BATHE AGAIN...
...!
SQUEEEZE
MASTER AKIHITO?
YOU'RE FINE.
YOU SMELL THE SAME AS ALWAYS.
YOU SMELL REALLY GOOD.
YOU SMELL OF THE SAME SOAP AS I DO.
YOU TOO...

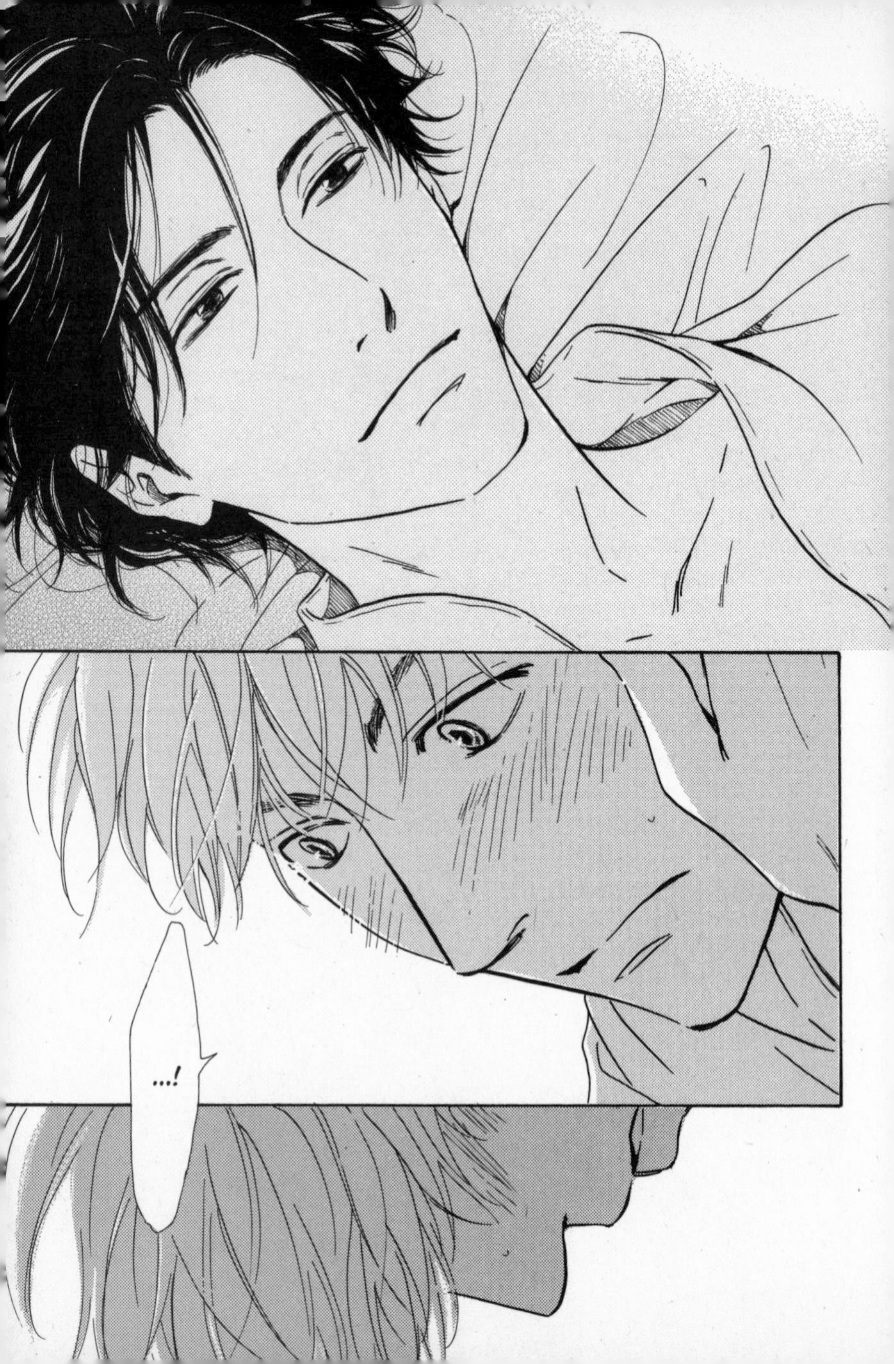
...!

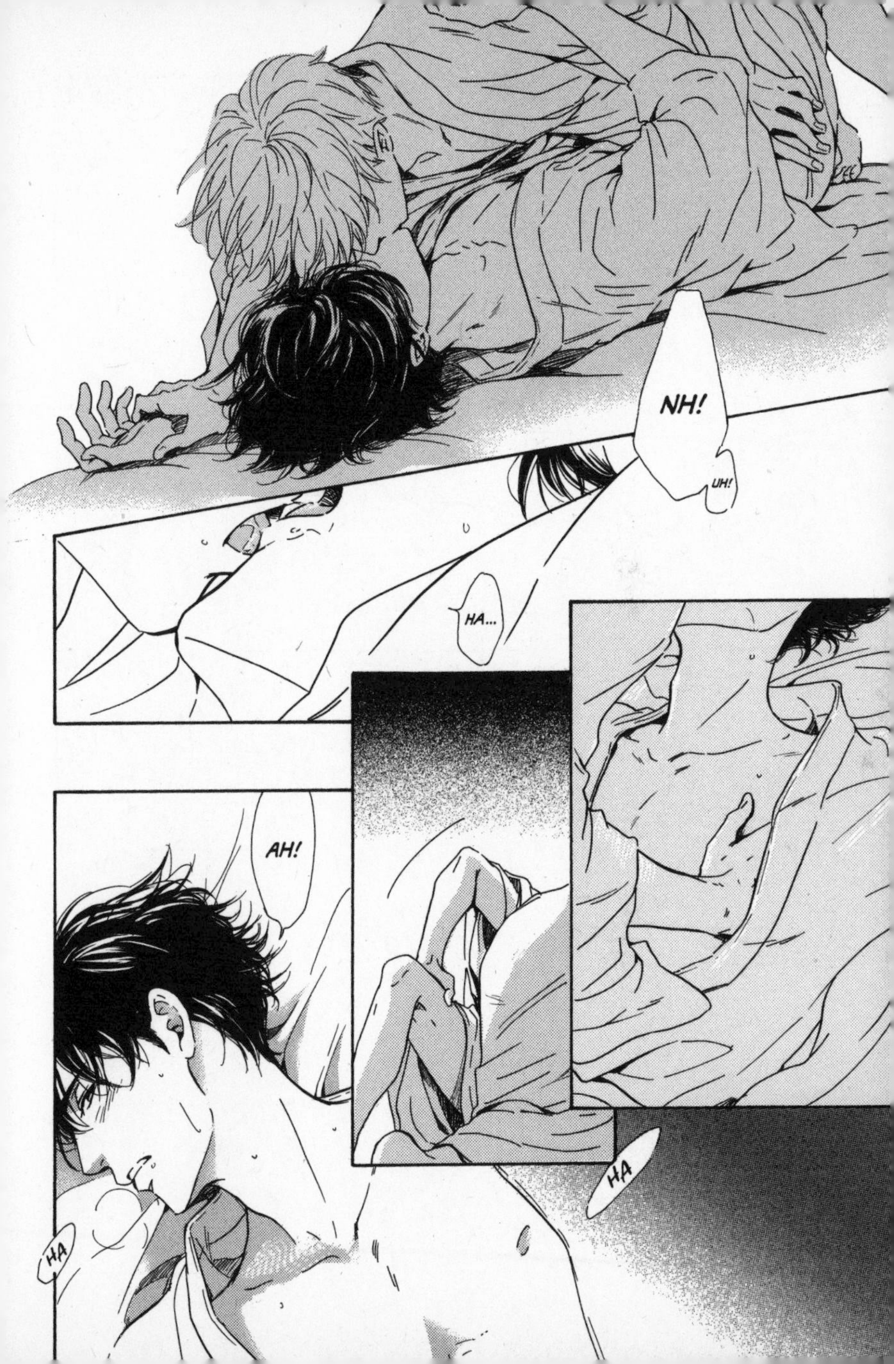
NH!
UH!
HA...
HA
AH!
HA

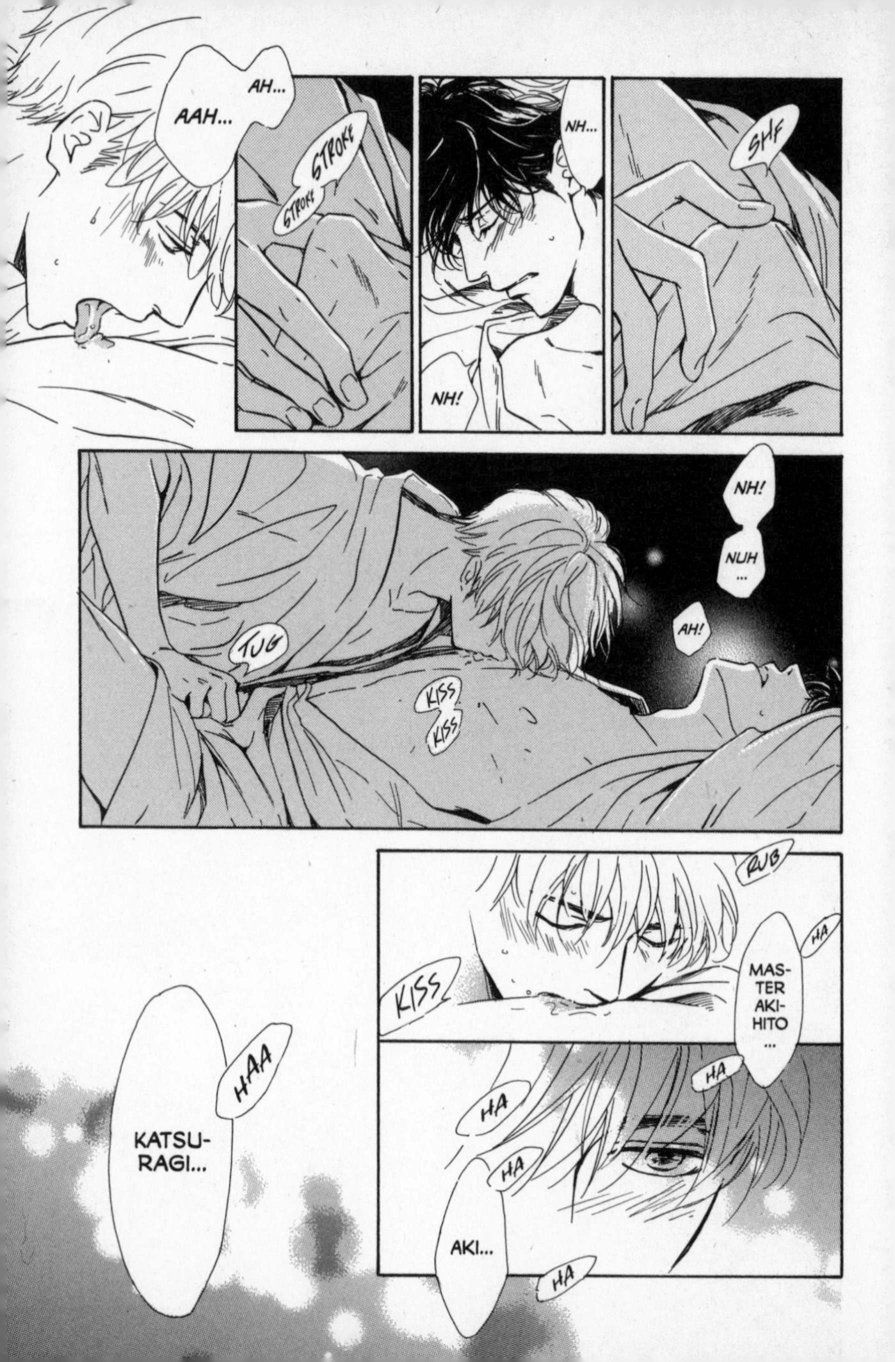
SHF
NH...
NH!
STROKE STROKE
AH... AAH...
NH!
NUH...
AH!
KISS KISS
TUG
RUB
HA
MASTER AKIHITO...
KISS
HA
HA
HA
AKI...
HA
HAA
KATSURAGI...

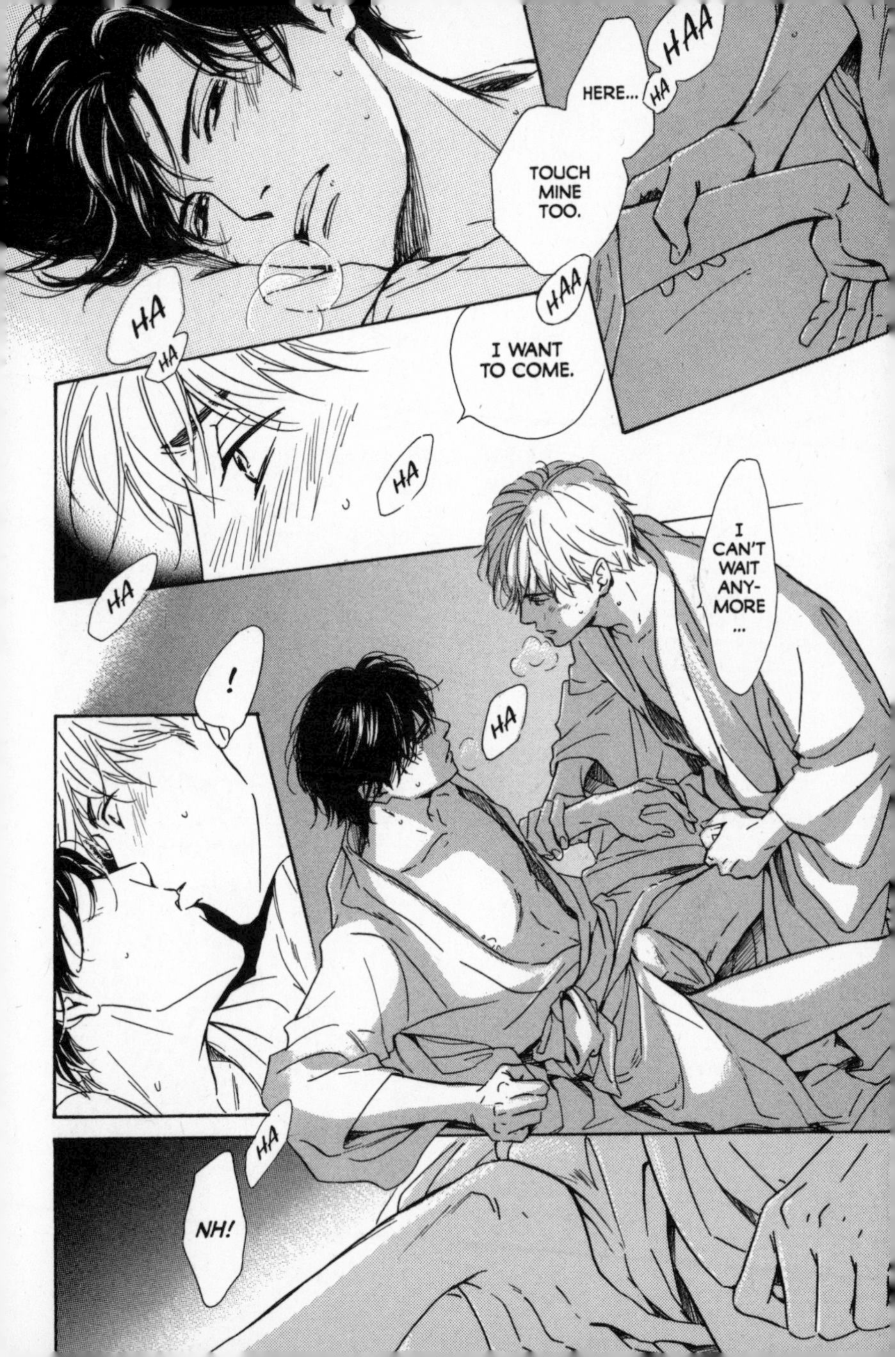
HAA
HERE...
HA
TOUCH MINE TOO.
HAA
I WANT TO COME.
HA
HA
HA
I CAN'T WAIT ANY-MORE...
HA
HA
!
HA
NH!

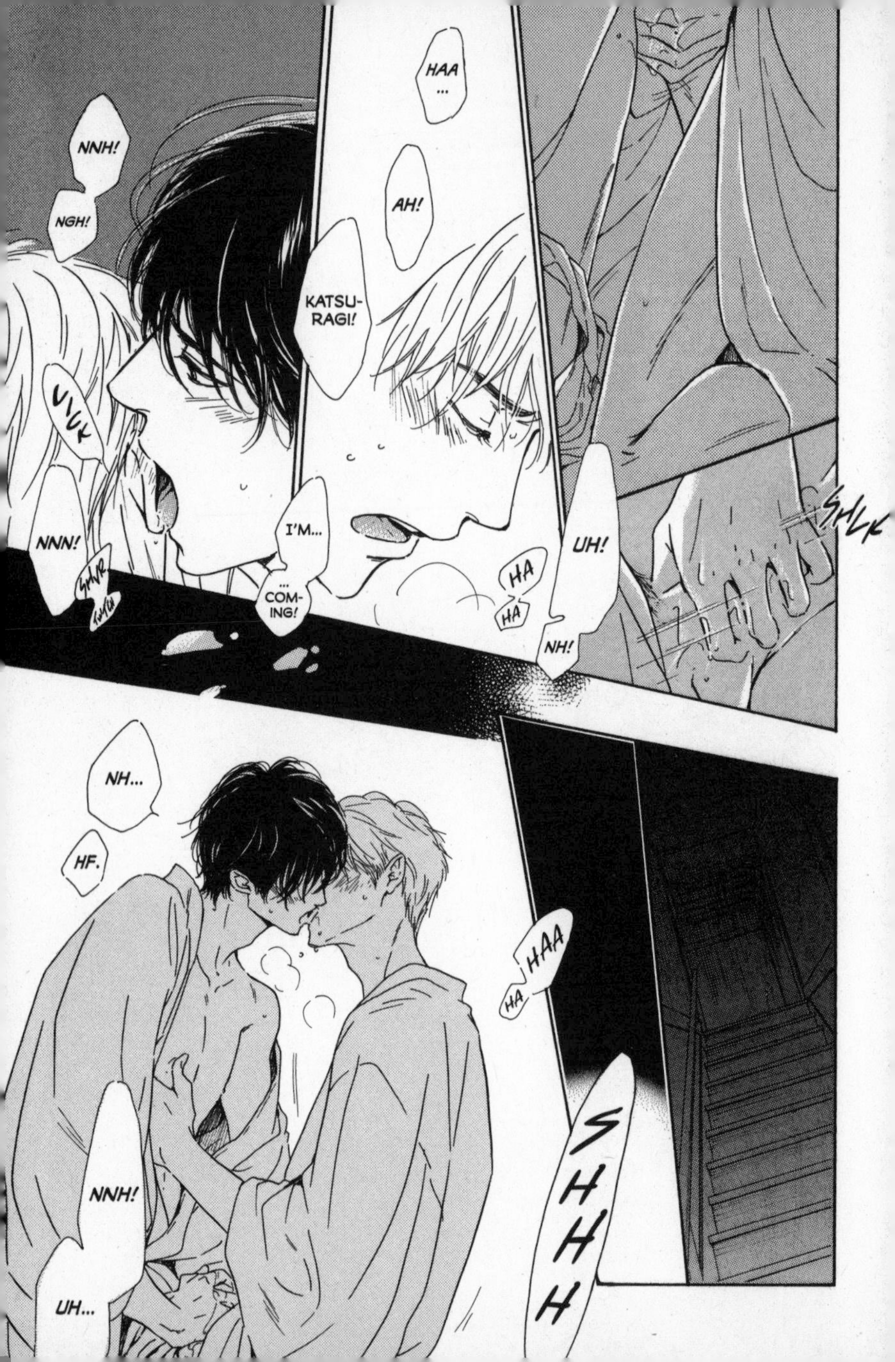
HAA...
AH!
KATSURAGI!
I'M...
...COMING!
HA
HA
UH!
NH!
NNH!
NGH!
NNN!
HAA
HA
SHHHH
NH...
HF.
NNH!
UH...

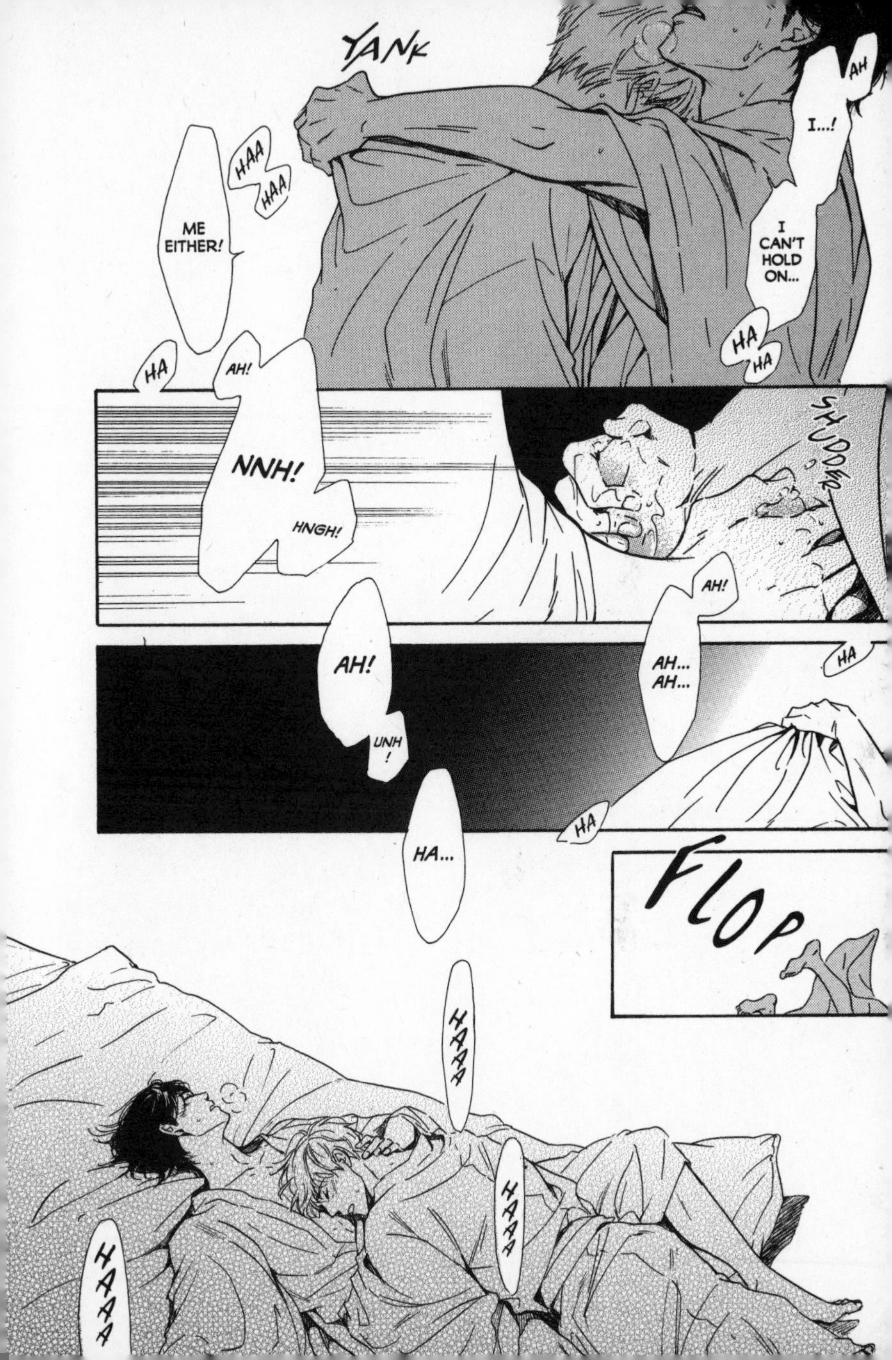
AH
I...!
I CAN'T HOLD ON...
HA HA
YANK
HAA HAA
ME EITHER!
HA
SHUDDER
AH!
NNH!
HNGH!
HA
AH!
AH... AH...
AH!
UNH!
HA
HA...
FLOP
HAAAA
HAAAA
HAAAA

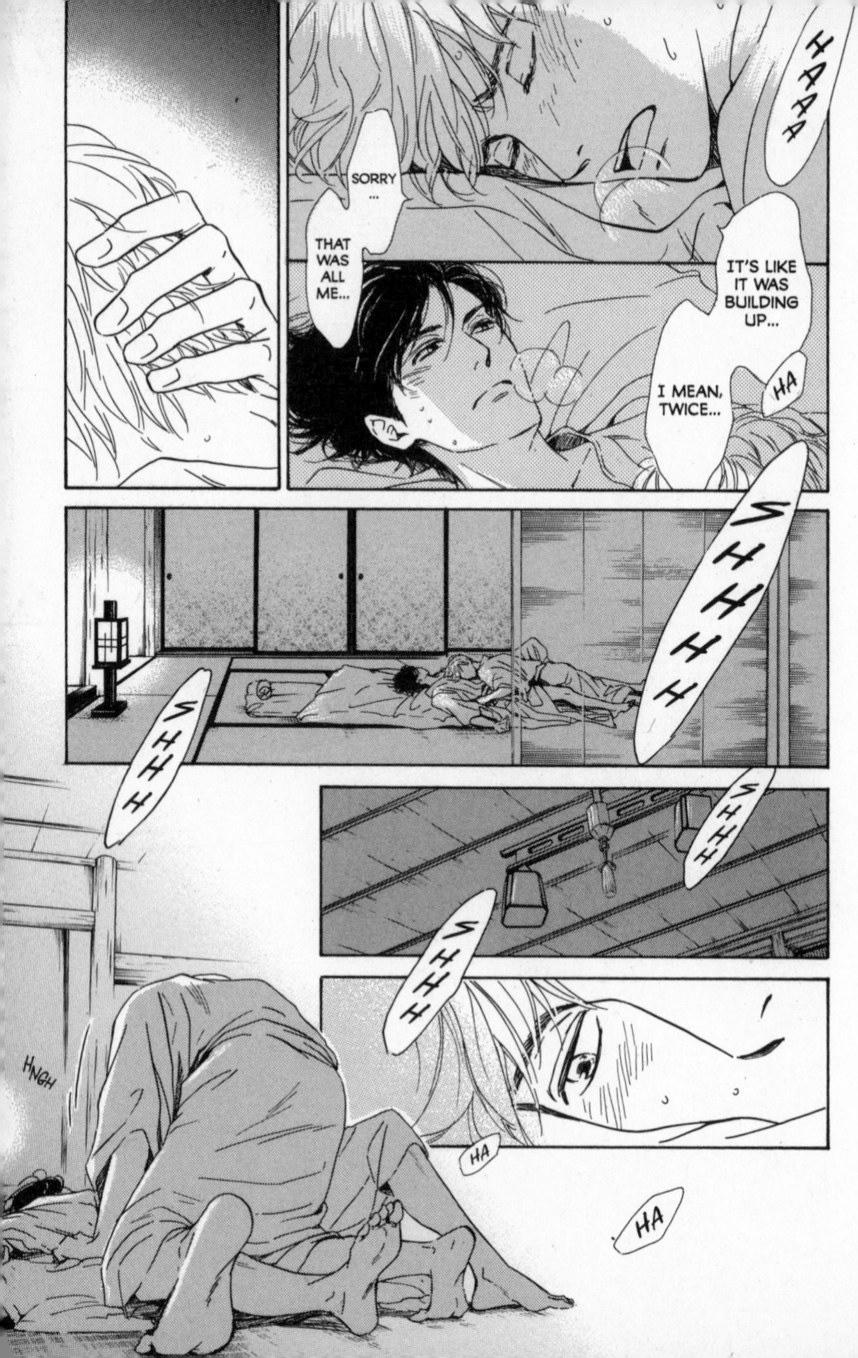
HAAAA
IT'S LIKE IT WAS BUILDING UP...
I MEAN, TWICE...
HA
SORRY... THAT WAS ALL ME...
SHHHHH
SHHHH
SHHHH
HA
HA
SHHHH
HNGH

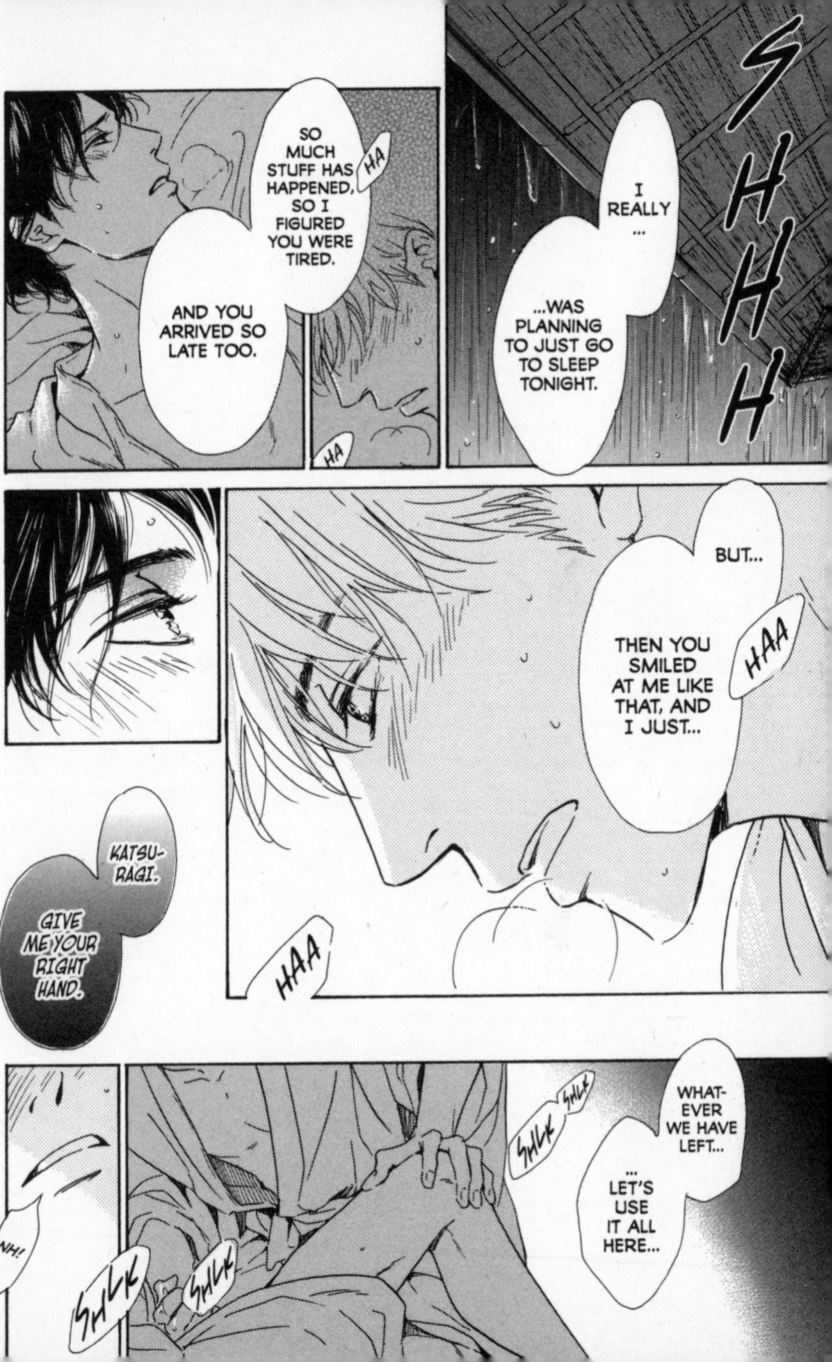
SHHHH
I REALLY ...
...WAS PLANNING TO JUST GO TO SLEEP TONIGHT.
SO MUCH STUFF HAS HAPPENED, SO I FIGURED YOU WERE TIRED.
HA
AND YOU ARRIVED SO LATE TOO.
HA
BUT...
THEN YOU SMILED AT ME LIKE THAT, AND I JUST...
HAA
HAA
KATSU-RAGI.
GIVE ME YOUR RIGHT HAND.
WHAT-EVER WE HAVE LEFT...
... LET'S USE IT ALL HERE...
SHLK SHLK
SHLK
SHLK
NH!

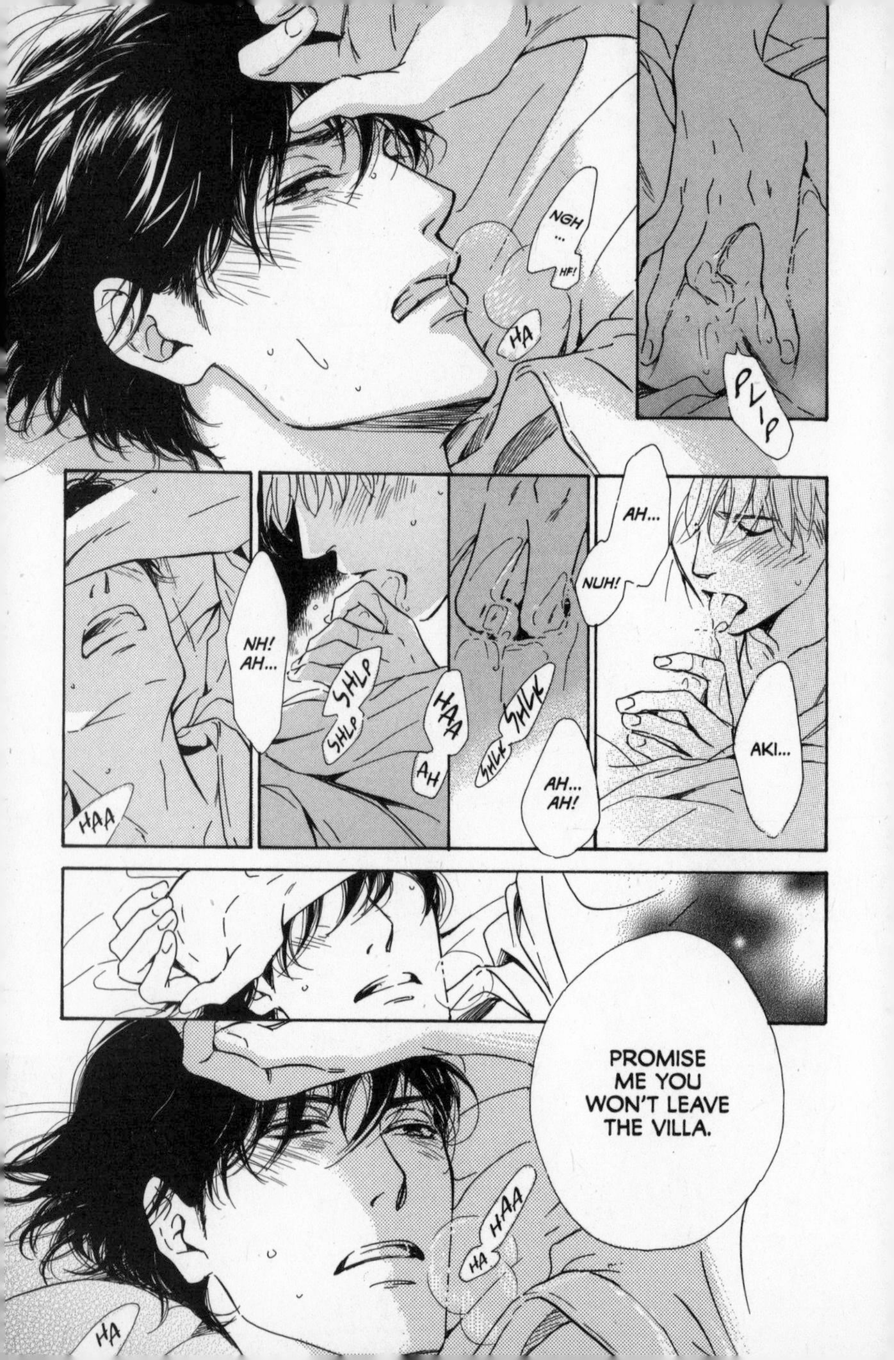
NGH... HF!
HA
AH... NUH!
AKI...
AH... AH!
SHLK SHLK
SHLP SHLP
HAA
AH
NH! AH...
HAA
PROMISE ME YOU WON'T LEAVE THE VILLA.
HAA HA
HA

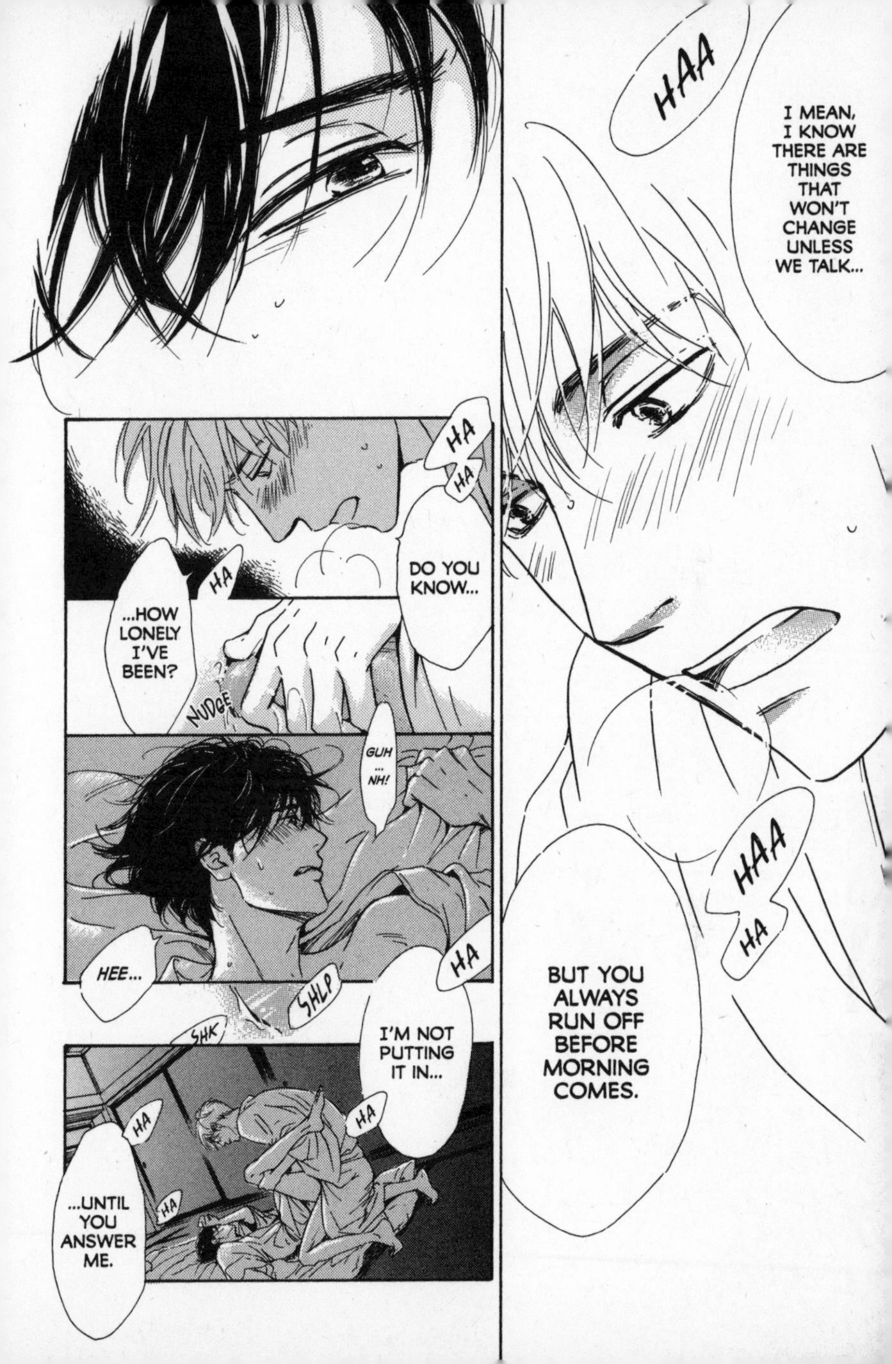
HAA
I MEAN, I KNOW THERE ARE THINGS THAT WON'T CHANGE UNLESS WE TALK...
HAA
HA
BUT YOU ALWAYS RUN OFF BEFORE MORNING COMES.
HA
HA
DO YOU KNOW...
HA
...HOW LONELY I'VE BEEN?
NUDGE
GUH ... NH!
HEE...
HA
SHLP
SHK
I'M NOT PUTTING IT IN...
HA
HA
...UNTIL YOU ANSWER ME.
HA

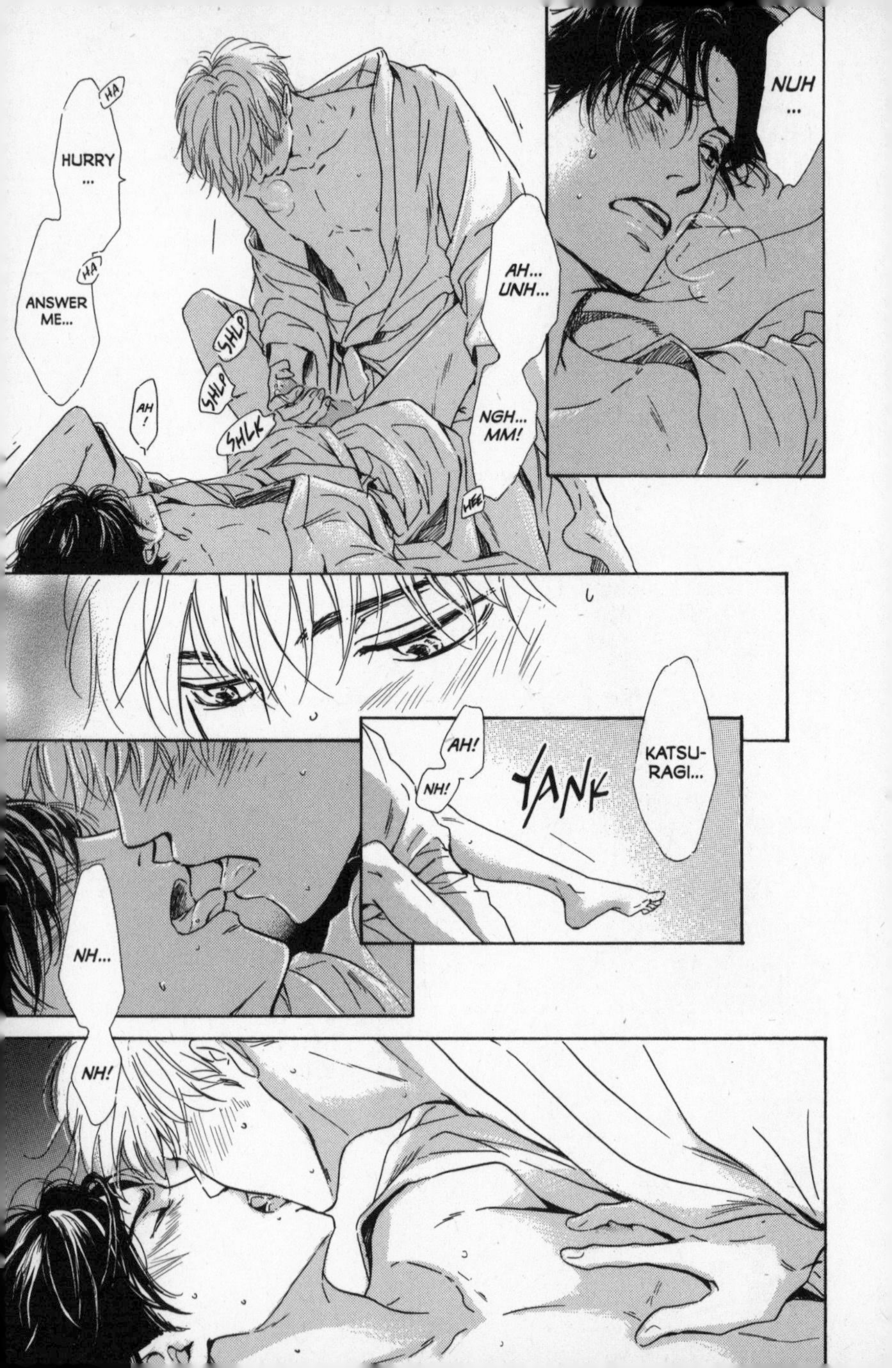
NUH ...
AH... UNH...
NGH... MM!
HEE
HA
HURRY ...
HA
ANSWER ME...
SHLP
SHLP
SHLK
AH!
KATSU-RAGI...
YANK
AH!
NH!
NH...
NH!

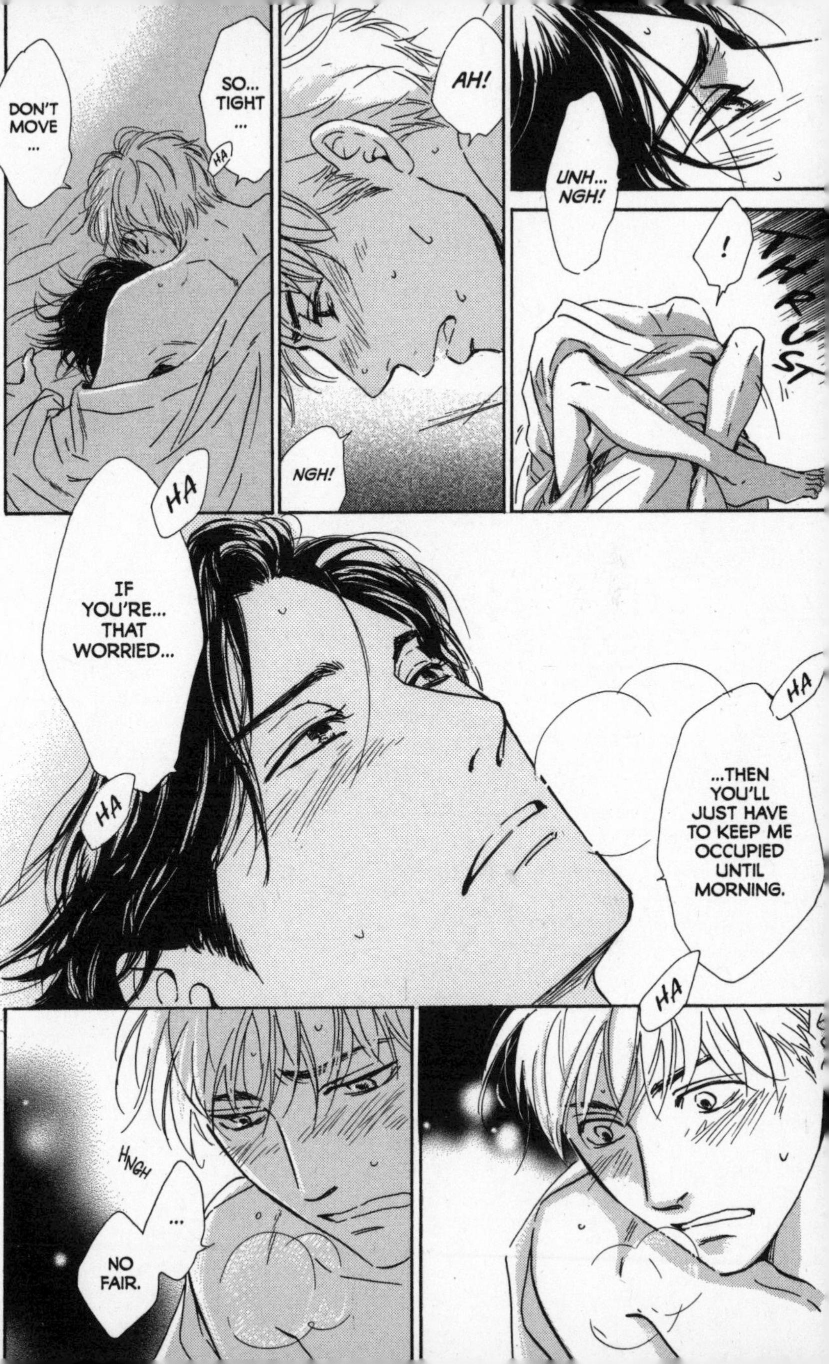
UNH... NGH!
!
THRUST
AH!
NGH!
SO... TIGHT ...
HA
DON'T MOVE ...
HA
IF YOU'RE... THAT WORRIED...
HA
HA
...THEN YOU'LL JUST HAVE TO KEEP ME OCCUPIED UNTIL MORNING.
HA
HNGH
... NO FAIR.

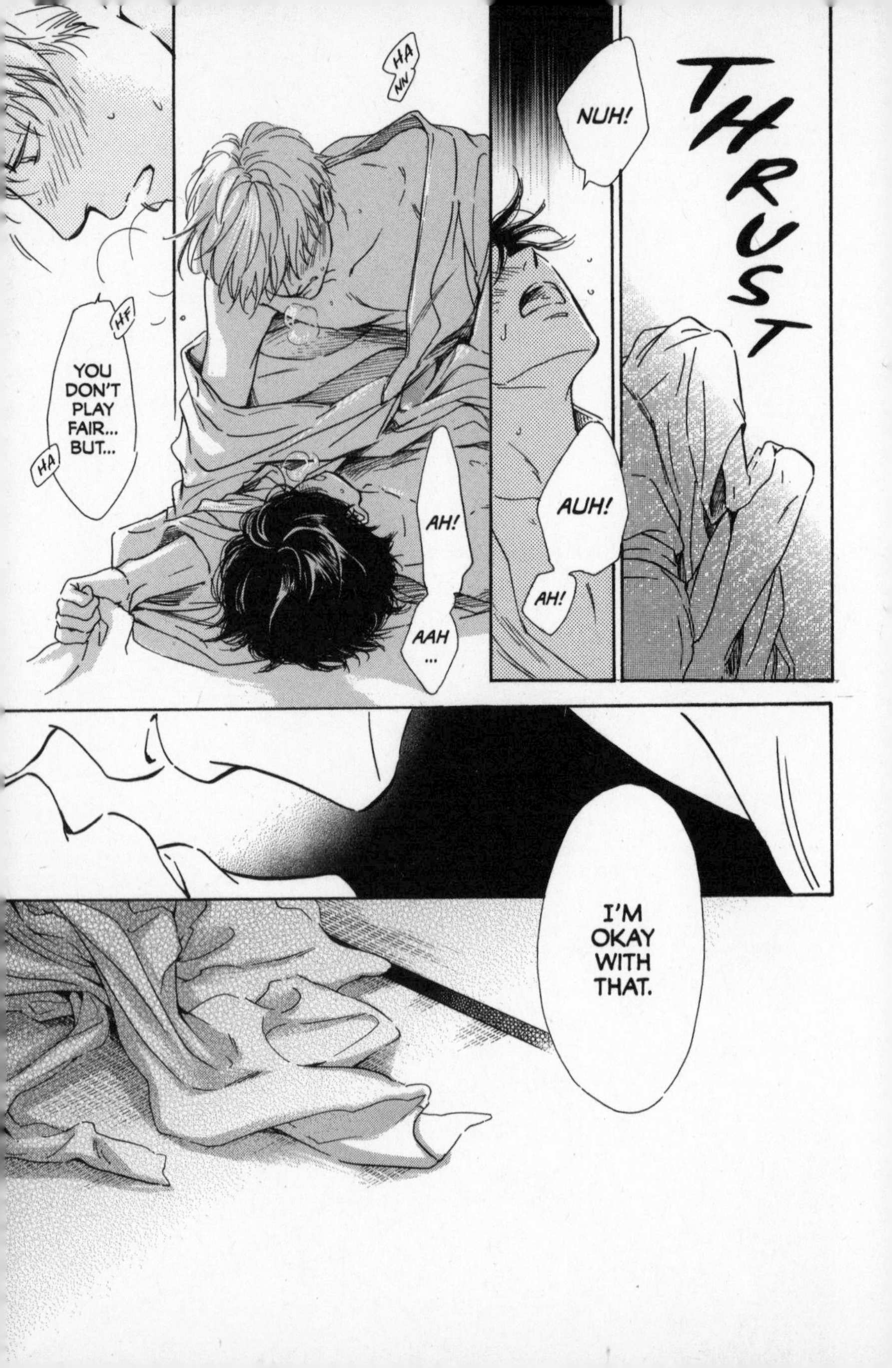
THRUST
NUH!
AUH!
AH!
HA NN
AH!
AAH ...
HF
YOU DON'T PLAY FAIR... BUT...
HA
I'M OKAY WITH THAT.

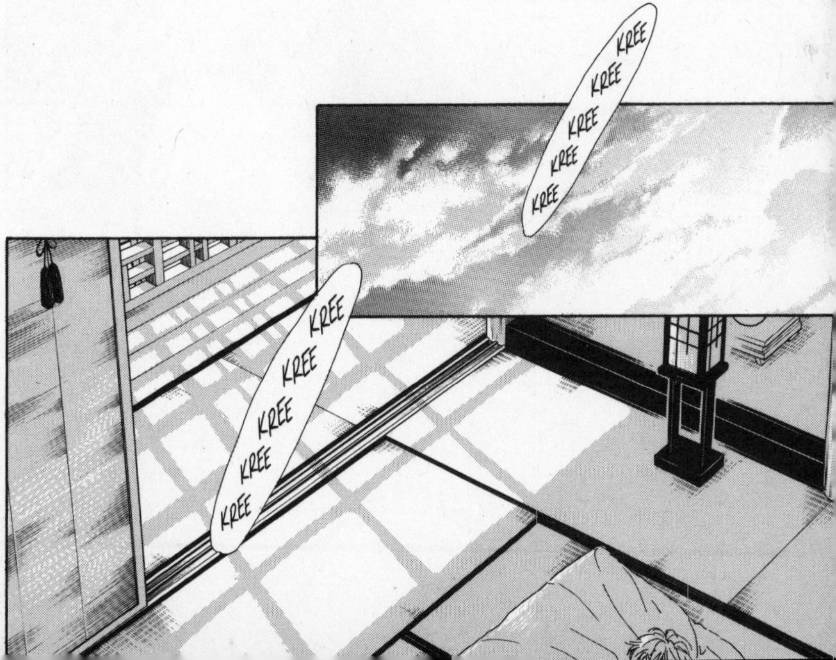
KREE KREE KREE KREE KREE
KREE KREE KREE KREE KREE

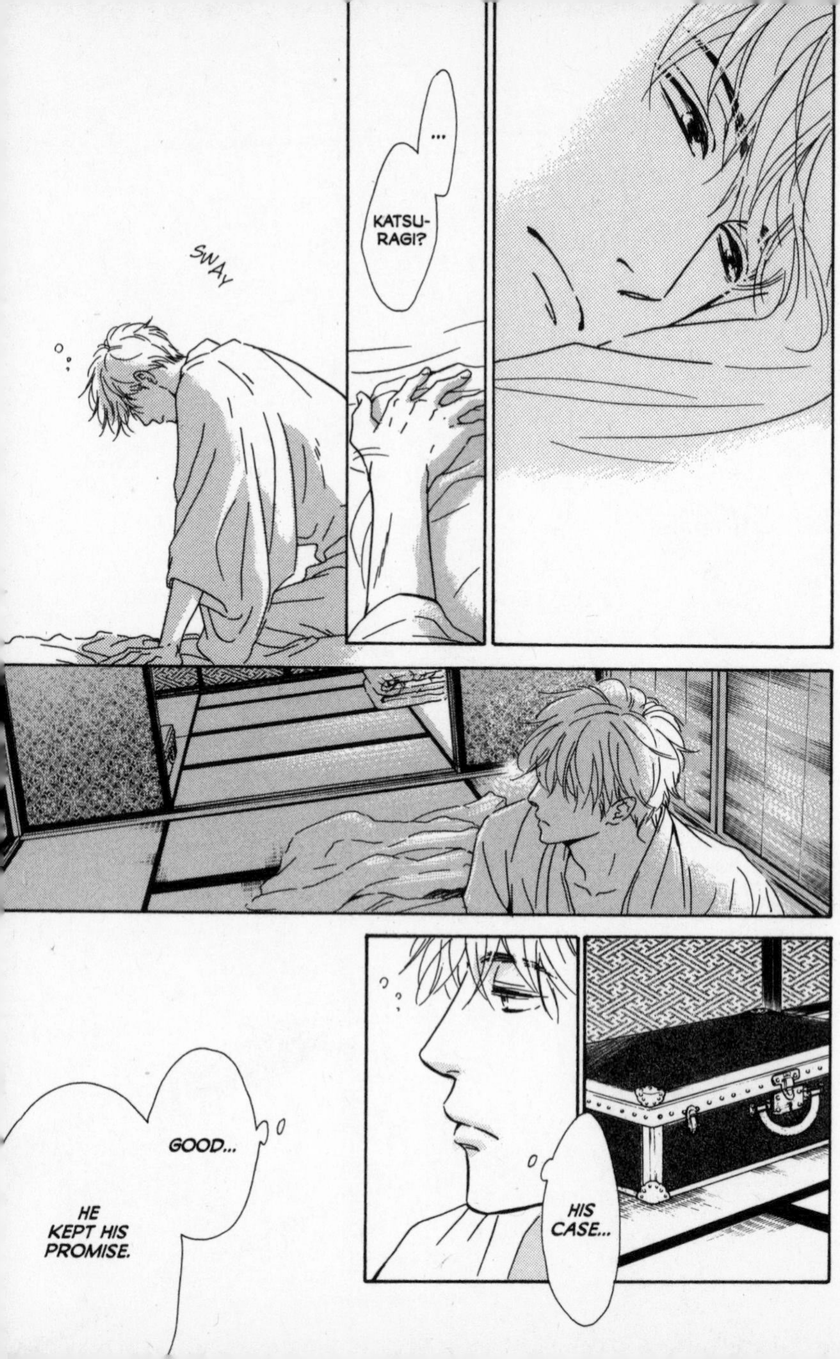

...
KATSU-RAGI?
SWAY
HIS CASE...
GOOD...
HE KEPT HIS PROMISE.

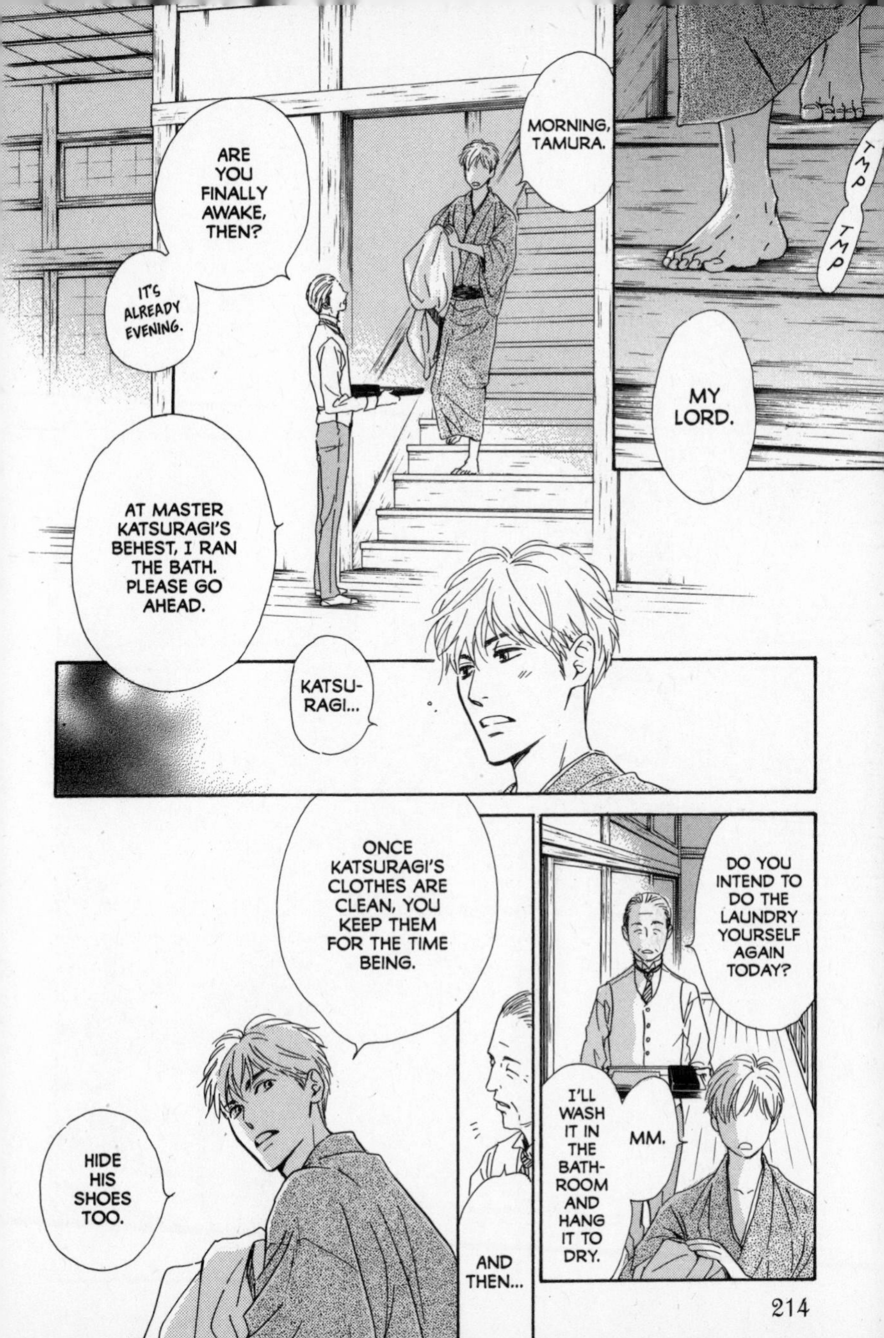
TMP TMP
MY LORD.
MORNING, TAMURA.
ARE YOU FINALLY AWAKE, THEN?
IT'S ALREADY EVENING.
AT MASTER KATSURAGI'S BEHEST, I RAN THE BATH. PLEASE GO AHEAD.
KATSU-RAGI...
DO YOU INTEND TO DO THE LAUNDRY YOURSELF AGAIN TODAY?
MM.
I'LL WASH IT IN THE BATH-ROOM AND HANG IT TO DRY.
AND THEN...
ONCE KATSURAGI'S CLOTHES ARE CLEAN, YOU KEEP THEM FOR THE TIME BEING.
HIDE HIS SHOES TOO.

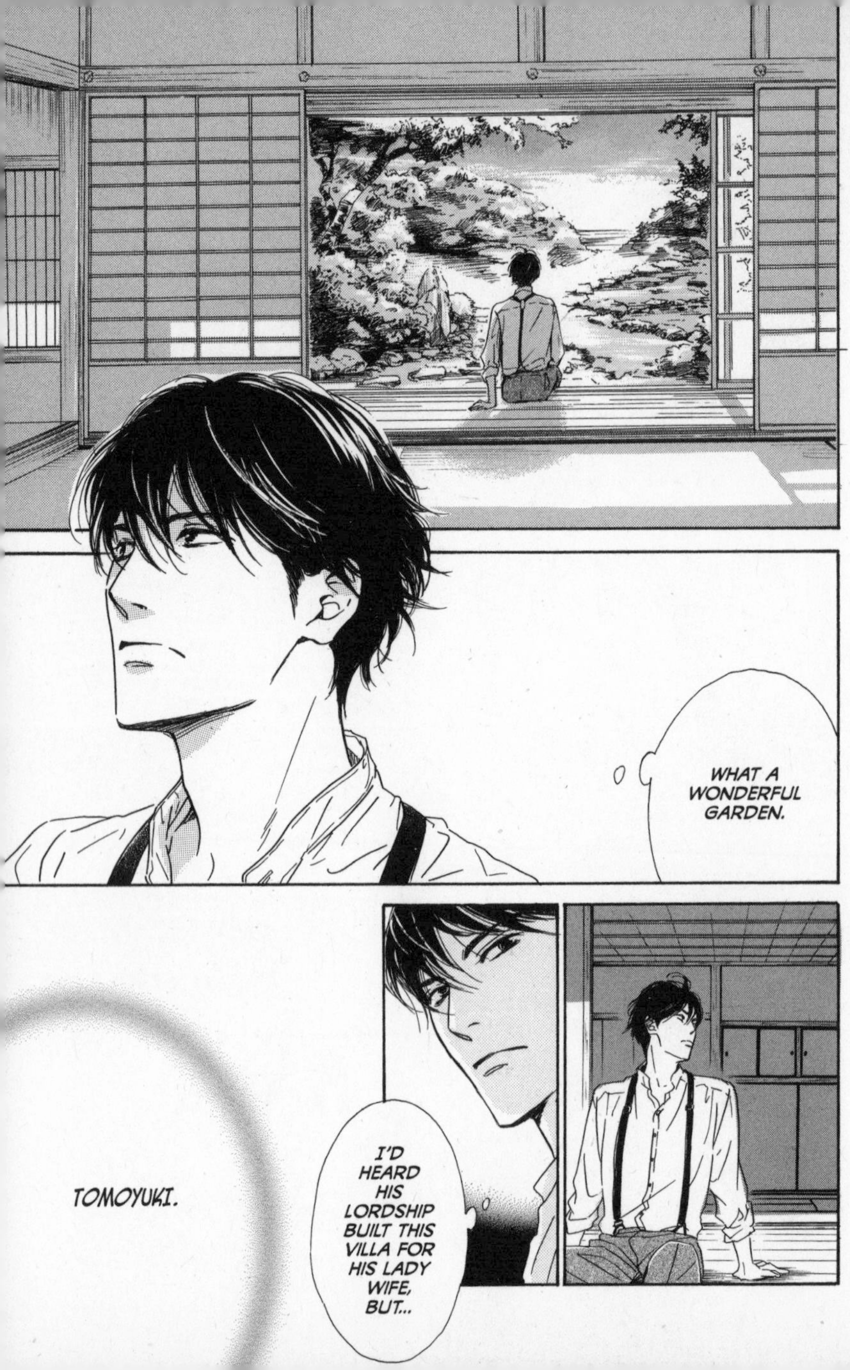
WHAT A WONDERFUL GARDEN.
I'D HEARD HIS LORDSHIP BUILT THIS VILLA FOR HIS LADY WIFE, BUT...
TOMOYUKI.

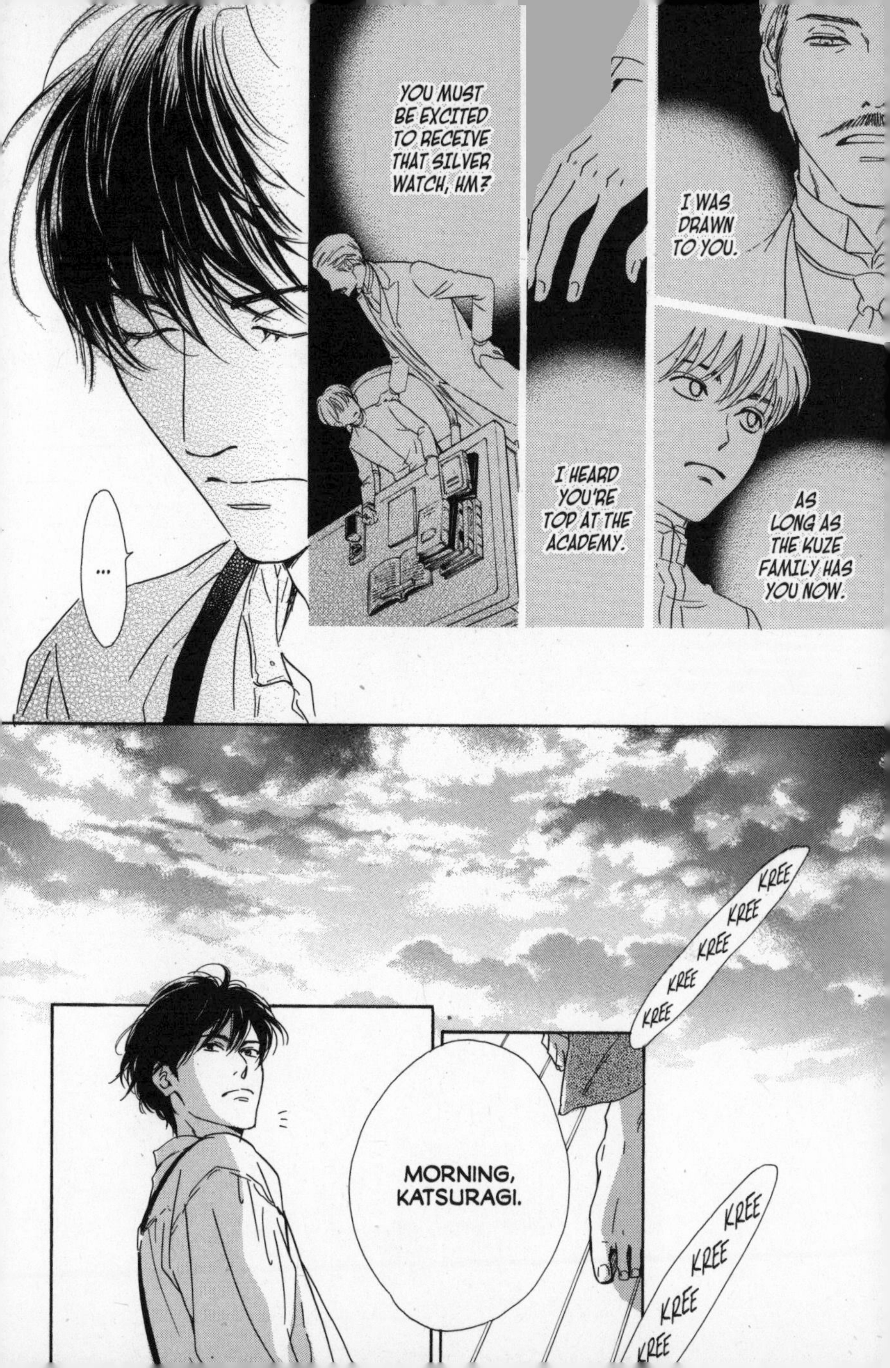

I WAS DRAWN TO YOU.
AS LONG AS THE KUZE FAMILY HAS YOU NOW.
I HEARD YOU'RE TOP AT THE ACADEMY.
YOU MUST BE EXCITED TO RECEIVE THAT SILVER WATCH, HM?
...
KREE KREE KREE KREE KREE KREE
MORNING, KATSURAGI.
KREE KREE KREE KREE KREE

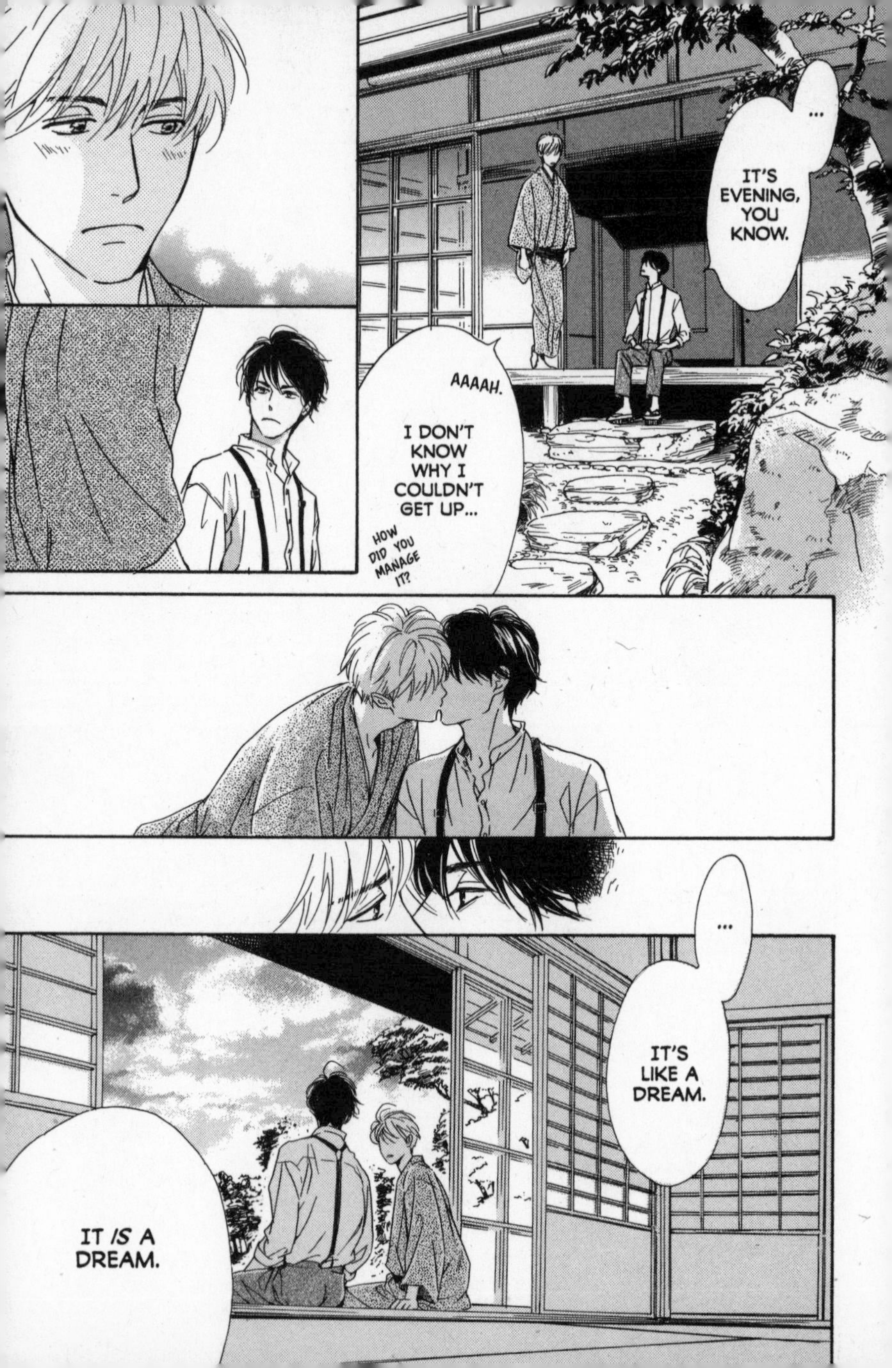
... IT'S EVENING, YOU KNOW.
AAAAH. I DON'T KNOW WHY I COULDN'T GET UP...
HOW DID YOU MANAGE IT?
... IT'S LIKE A DREAM.
IT *IS* A DREAM.

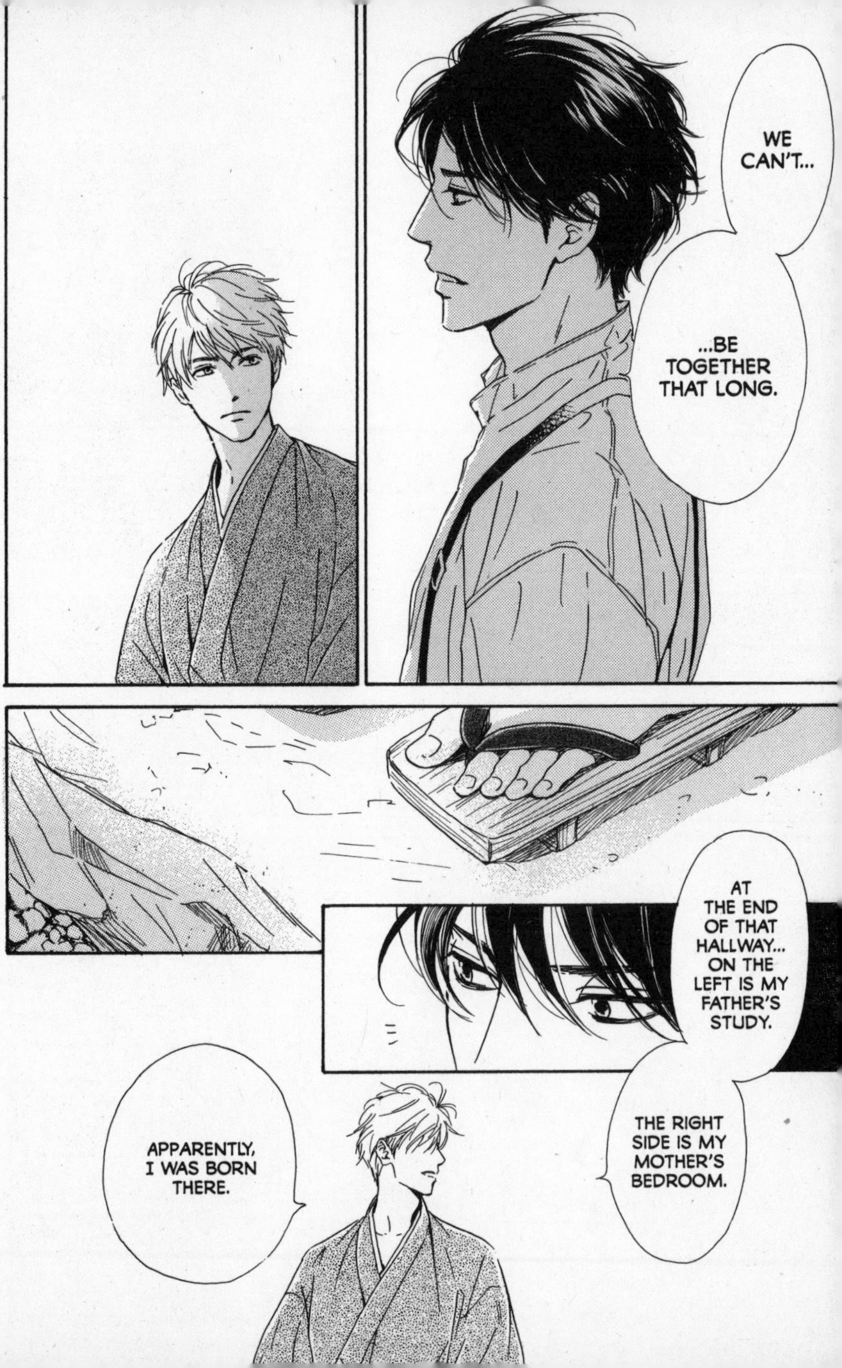
WE CAN'T...
...BE TOGETHER THAT LONG.
AT THE END OF THAT HALLWAY... ON THE LEFT IS MY FATHER'S STUDY.
THE RIGHT SIDE IS MY MOTHER'S BEDROOM.
APPARENTLY, I WAS BORN THERE.

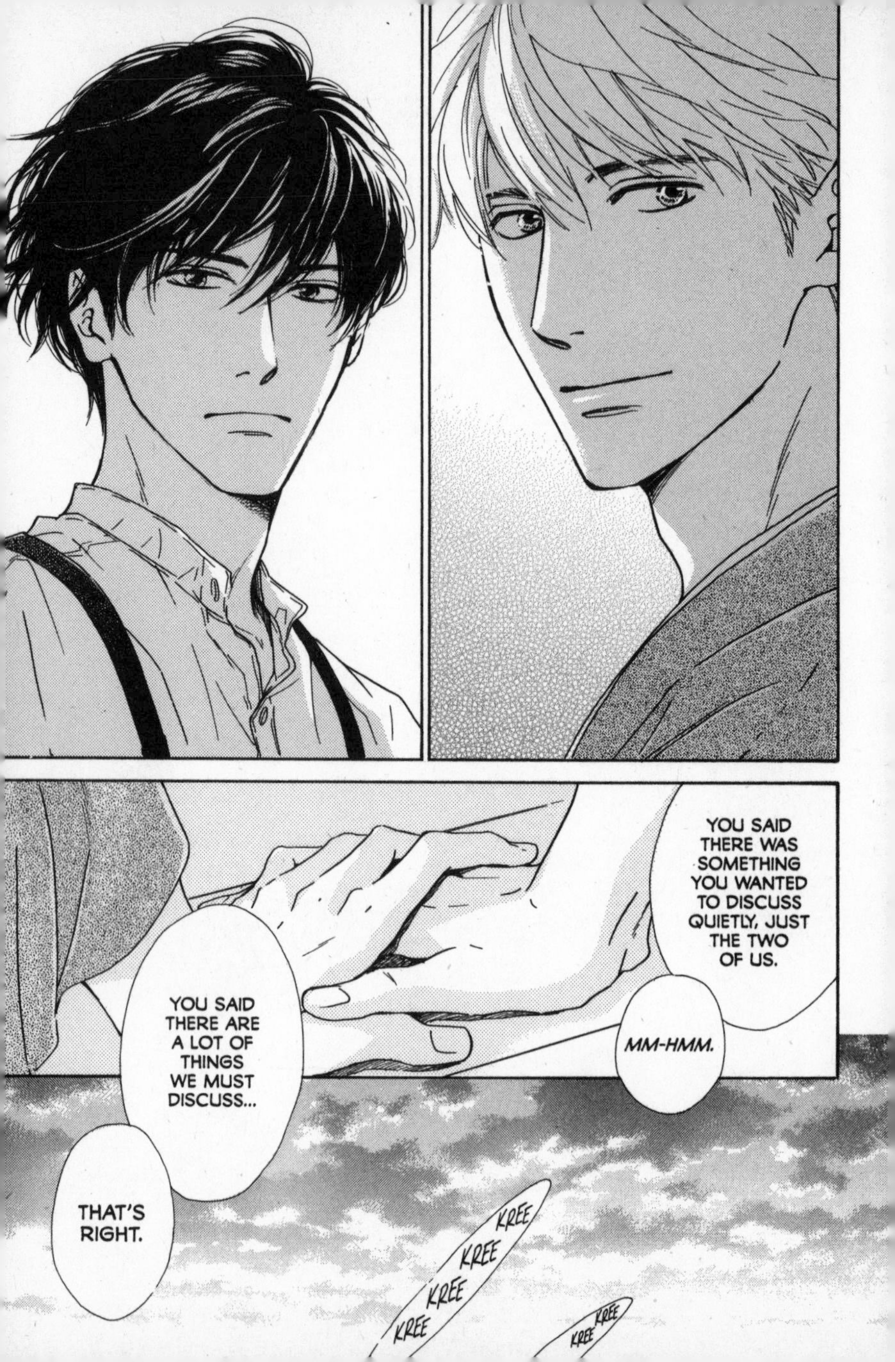

YOU SAID THERE WAS SOMETHING YOU WANTED TO DISCUSS QUIETLY, JUST THE TWO OF US.
MM-HMM.
YOU SAID THERE ARE A LOT OF THINGS WE MUST DISCUSS...
THAT'S RIGHT.
KREE KREE KREE KREE
KREE KREE

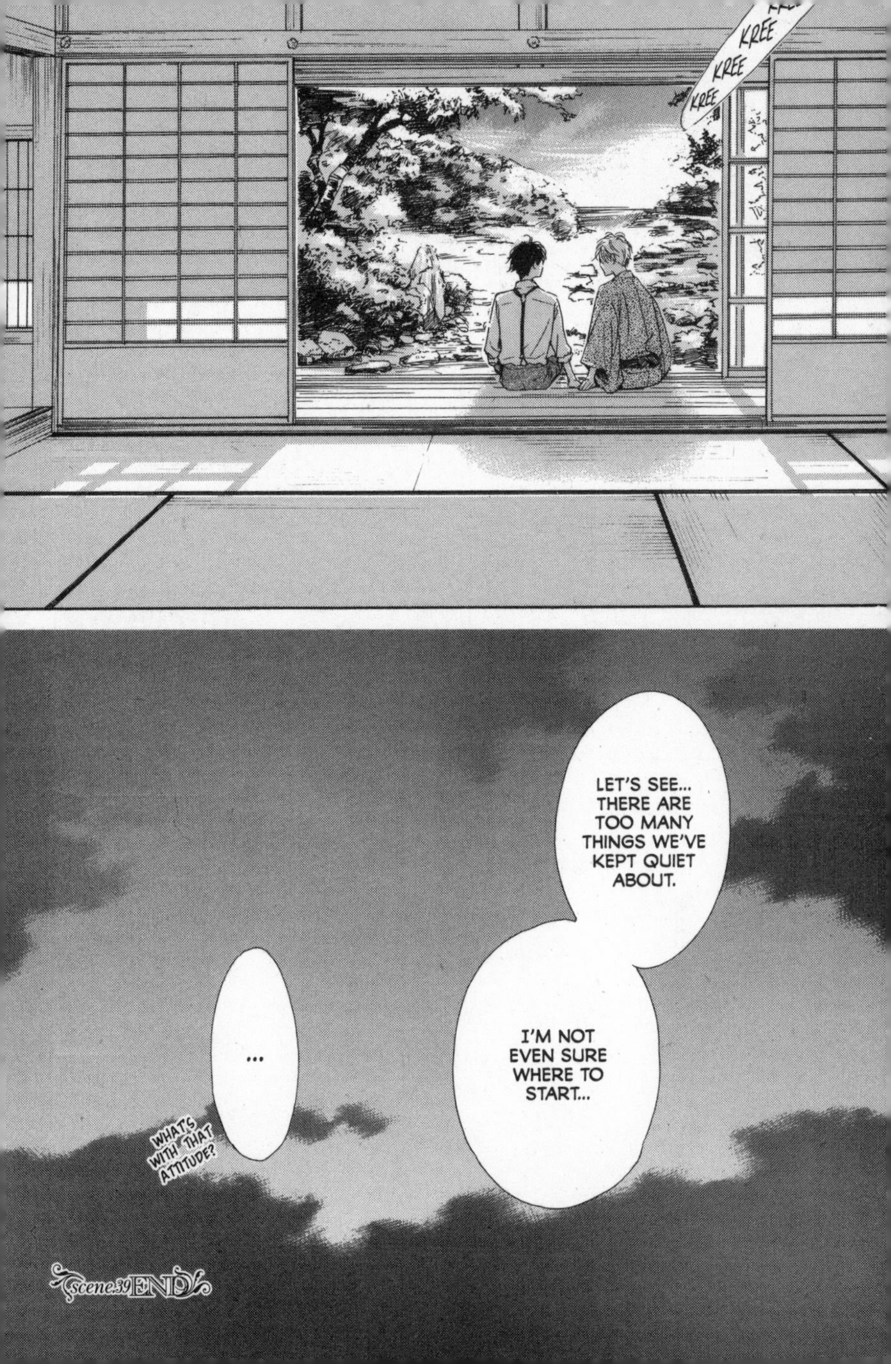
KREE KREE KREE
LET'S SEE... THERE ARE TOO MANY THINGS WE'VE KEPT QUIET ABOUT.
I'M NOT EVEN SURE WHERE TO START...
...
WHATS WITH THAT ATTITUDE?
scene.39 END

憂鬱な朝

Blue Morning

VOLUME SEVEN! I CAN'T BELIEVE IT. THAT THE STORY WOULD GO ON THIS LONG... WELL, IT'S ALL THANKS TO YOU PICKING UP AND READING THESE BOOKS (AND MY LOVELY EDITOR FOR JOINING ME AS WE INCH FORWARD). THANK YOU AS ALWAYS! FOR THE ILLUSTRATION HERE, I WAS ACTUALLY GOING TO DRAW A TWO-PAGE SPREAD WITH AKIHITO, AMAMIYA, AND THE KATSURAGI BROTHERS ON THE RIGHT SIDE, AND KATSURAGI AND THE ISHIZAKIS ON THE LEFT—THE SORT OF ILLUSTRATION THAT WAS LIKELY TO PLEASE NO ONE (AND THAT I COULD PROBABLY ONLY GET THE OKAY FOR AT THE END OF THE COMIC)—BUT THEN I ENDED UP HAVING MY HANDS WAY TOO FULL WITH JUST DOING THE STORY ITSELF, SO I'M SENDING THIS OUT WITH THE USUAL PAIR...

BY THE WAY, IF ALL GOES ACCORDING TO PLAN, WE'LL FINISH IN VOLUME EIGHT, BUT ALREADY, I HAVEN'T MANAGED TO GET TO SCENES I HAD PLANNED. THE BEGINNING OF THE NEXT VOLUME WAS ACTUALLY SUPPOSED TO BE THE END OF THIS ONE... AND SO WE CONTINUE...

IT DOESN'T LOOK TOO GOOD IF I CAN'T SAY FOR SURE "THE STORY ENDS IN THE NEXT VOLUME!" SO I'M GOING TO DO WHAT I CAN, AT ANY RATE. I'D LIKE TO FINISH DRAWING AKIHITO, KATSURAGI, AND EVERYONE CONNECTED WITH THE KUZE HOUSE, SO I WOULD BE VERY DELIGHTED IF YOU COULD JOIN ME IN THE NEXT VOLUME.

THANK YOU SO MUCH FOR READING ALL THE WAY TO THE END! ♥ ♥

AND A BIG THANK-YOU TO ASAKURA, YOKO, NAKAMURA, AND CHIAKI FOR ALL THEIR HELP!
SEE YOU NEXT TIME TOO!

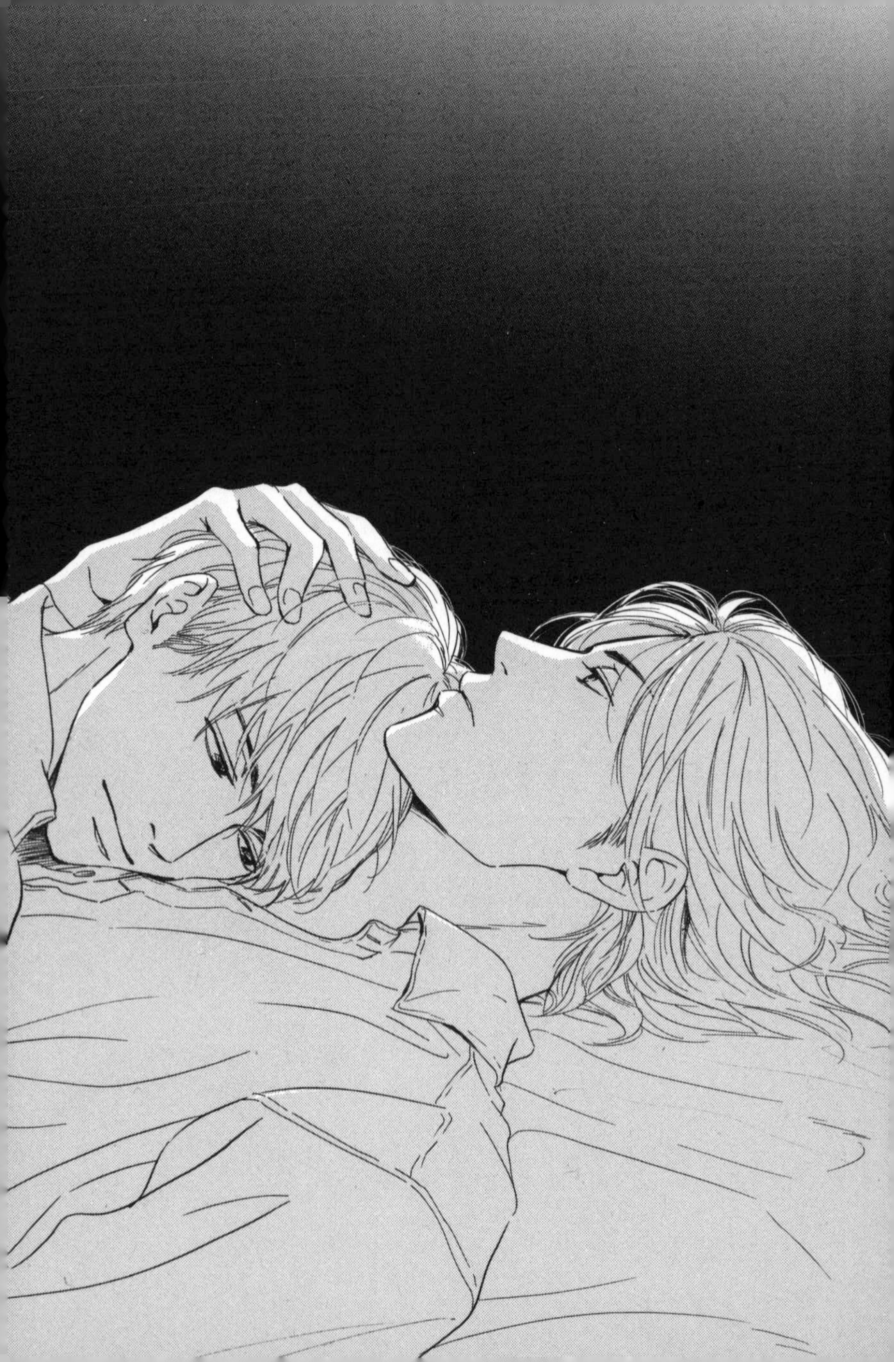

> **That feeling when, finally, you made it this far. But also that you're still not done.**

About the Author

Shoko Hidaka's works have been published in English, French, and German. Her previously published English-language releases include *Restart* and *Not Enough Time*. Born on March 31st in Tokyo, she's an Aries with blood type A.

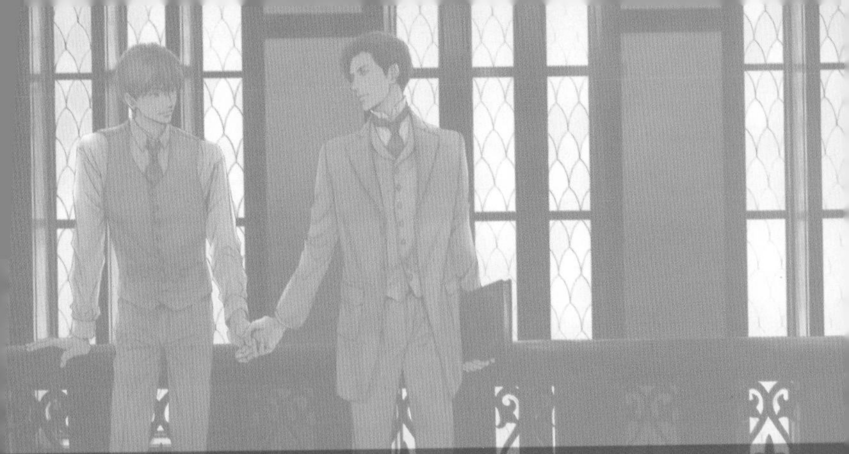

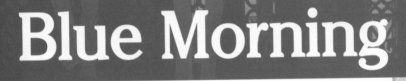

Blue Morning

Story and Art by Shoko Hidaka

volume 7

CONTENTS

SUBLIME

SuBLime Manga Edition

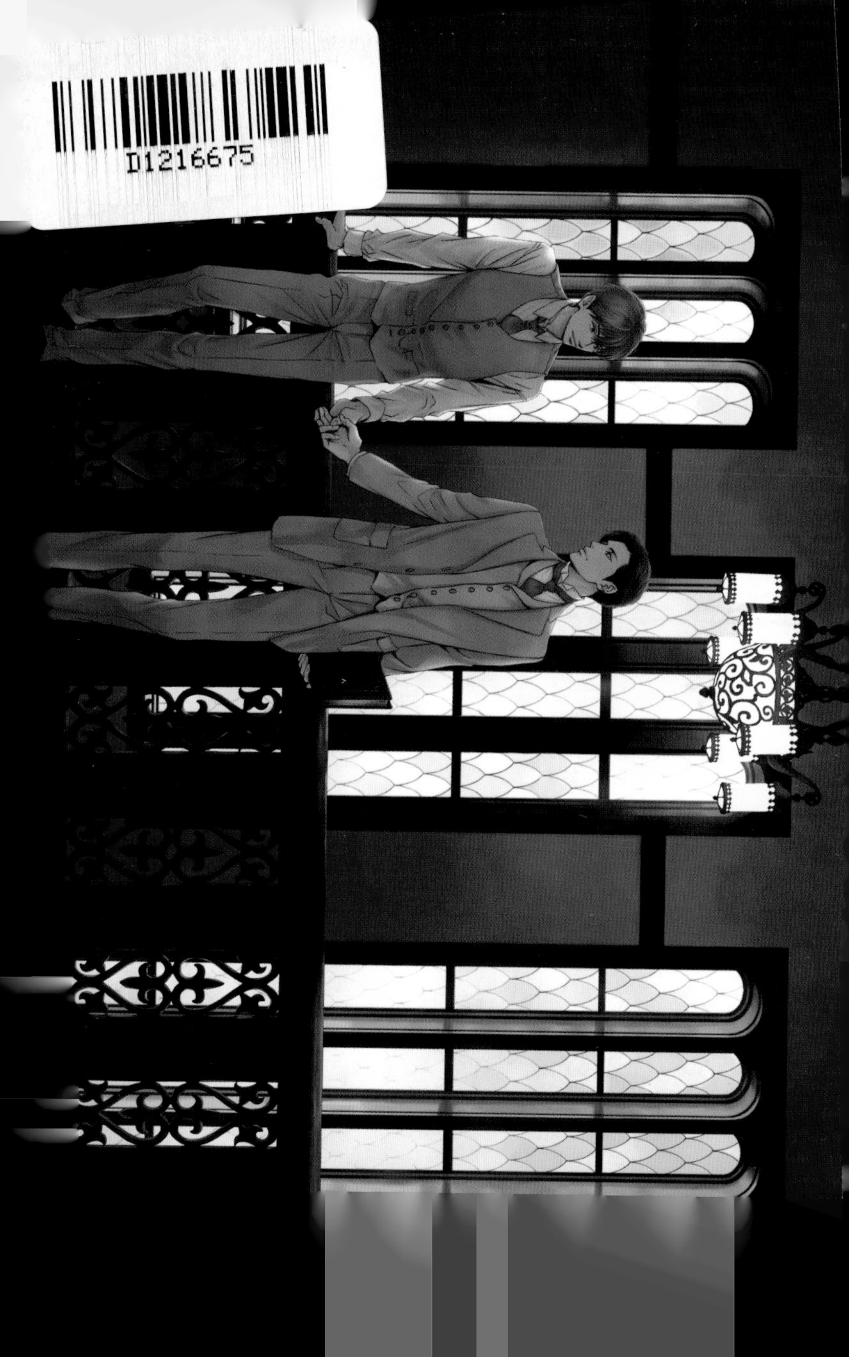